Information Technology and Global Governance

Series Editor

Derrick L. Cogburn
School of International Service
Kogod School of Business
American University
Washington, D.C., USA

Aims of the Series

Information Technology and Global Governance focuses on the complex interrelationships between the social, political, and economic processes of global governance that occur at national, regional, and international levels. These processes are influenced by the rapid and ongoing developments in information and communication technologies, as well as new and innovative organizational practices. At the same time, they affect numerous areas, create new opportunities and mechanisms for participation in global governance processes, and influence how governance is studied. Books in this series examine these relationships and influences.

More information about this series at
http://www.springer.com/series/14855

Derrick L. Cogburn

Transnational Advocacy Networks in the Information Society

Partners or Pawns?

Derrick L. Cogburn
School of International Service
Kogod School of Business
American University, Washington
District of Columbia, USA

Information Technology and Global Governance
ISBN 978-1-137-49263-0 (hardcover)   ISBN 978-1-137-48361-4   (eBook)
ISBN 978-1-349-69687-1 (softcover)
DOI 10.1057/978-1-137-48361-4

Library of Congress Control Number: 2016960579

Cover image: © vaver anton / Alamy Stock Vector

Printed on acid-free paper

This Palgrave Macmillan imprint is published by Springer Nature
The registered company is Nature America Inc. New York
The registered company address is 1 New York Plaza, New York, NY 10004, U.S.A.

*To Sharon, Roscoe, Courtney, Kimberly, Noemí, and Sean Manuel,
the rest of my Arcadia family, and Arroyo families,
and to those civil society advocates struggling to make a difference
around the world.*

PREFACE

With the convening in Geneva of the first phase of the United Nations World Summit on the Information Society (WSIS) in December 2003, the processes of global governance through international conferences was transformed, as was the role of transnational advocacy networks in the process. Historically, governments have dominated the official "conference diplomacy" surrounding these World Summits. However, reflecting the UN General Assembly resolution authorizing WSIS, transnational civil society and private sector organizations were invited to participate as official *partners* in a multistakeholder dialog at the summit alongside the more traditional participants—governments and international organizations. Civil society activists quickly mobilized to take advantage of this historic opportunity. Some of these networks are still active today.

It soon became clear, however, that the structure of participation in WSIS would carefully limit the participation of non-state actors, particularly global civil society, which faced several deficiencies relative to governments and private sector stakeholders. Civil society has a very large number of diverse participants, an extremely heterogeneous set of policy preferences, and few financial and transnational institutional resources on which to draw. In contrast, governments, including those of developing countries, have long established diplomatic infrastructure on which to draw. Private sector participants not only have more financial resources at their disposal, they also have substantial institutional resources, such as the International Chamber of Commerce, which they have used as a secretariat to organize Business Action to Support the Information Society (BASIS).

With these limitations, transnational civil society may have been destined to participate in WSIS more as *pawns* rather than as true *partners*.

As the analysis in this book shows, important lessons for transnational advocacy networks and broader multistakeholder global governance emerged out of the WSIS processes and its follow-on structures: the UN Global Alliance on ICT and Development (GAID) and the Internet Governance Forum (IGF). This book explores the participation of global civil society actors, struggling to make an impact on a dizzying plethora of substantive policy issues in the complex processes leading up to and following the two phases of WSIS. We undertake this analysis in order to better understand the limits and potential of multistakeholder global governance. In this book, we develop a conceptual framework for analyzing these multiple and complex processes, drawn from a voluminous literature on global governance and international cooperation, conference diplomacy, epistemic communities, and transnational advocacy networks. We trace these processes back to the founding of the United Nations and initial attempts to involve ordinary citizens into the work of this multilateral, state-centric body, up to the WSIS, and beyond. We benefit from the use of the voluminous amount of digital, text-based data now available to the social science analyst, along with computational text analysis approaches. Of course, we also benefit from decades of participant observation in nearly all the processes described in this book. In the end, we find mixed results. On the one hand, some of these global governance processes used transnational civil society participants as little more than pawns, claiming to have a much-vaunted *multistakeholder* process, almost as if it were a new religion. However, on the other hand, some of the transnational advocacy networks that emerged out of these processes have been extremely effective, and, although not without their own problems, have formed deep relationships with relevant epistemic communities, overcome their reticence to working with governments and the private sector, used information technology effectively, and developed rich, robust structures and processes of their own to enable them to have a lasting impact on global policy processes related to the information society.

Rock Hall, MD, USA   Derrick L. Cogburn
                                                            25 June 2016

Acknowledgments

While a book like this is ultimately a very solitary process, I would like to thank so many people and organizations for their invaluable contributions. And, since it has taken me so long to complete the manuscript, there are undoubtedly people who will be omitted. To assist my memory, I will proceed chronologically as best I can in these acknowledgments. I would like to begin by thanking my friends, colleagues, mentors, and faculty in the Department of Political Science at Howard University in Washington, D.C., where I did my graduate training. Here, I would also like to thank the W.K. Kellogg Foundation, which provided a graduate fellowship to me through their support for the Ralph J. Bunche Center for International Affairs. It was at Howard that I became involved, interested in the political economy of international telecommunications, and gained many of the insights that would fuel the remainder of my career. In particular, I would like to thank my doctoral colleagues Clarence Lusane, Daryl Harris, and Karin Stanford, along with my mentors at Howard, the late Ronald Walters, Joseph P. McCormick II, Hilbourne Watson, Richard Seltzer, and John Cotman.

Also in Washington, D.C., I would like to thank the United States Congressional Research Service (CRS), especially the Foreign Affairs and National Defense Division; Europe, Africa, and Middle East Section where I served as a research analyst and graduate fellow. Conducting research on telecommunications policy, information technology, and international affairs there helped to sharpen my analysis, as did my last semester of doctoral classes at Georgetown University.

At the Center for Strategic and International Studies (CSIS), I would like to thank Ambassador Diana Lady Dougan and my colleagues at the Global Information Infrastructure Commission, especially, Dr. Ernest J. Wilson, G. Russel Pipe, Joe Young, the late Jim Johnson, Carol Charles, Lara Furar, and Mark Dessauer. Ambassador Dougan and the GII provided an incredibly rich environment for me to learn, grow, and contribute to many of the global processes described in this book, including connecting me to global corporate leaders, the International Telecommunication Union, the World Trade Organization, the World Bank, and some amazing policy analysts around the world.

Based in part on my experiences serving on the official Howard University delegation to observe the historic elections in South Africa in 1994, I was able to return to South Africa for field research on both telecommunications restructuring in South Africa and civil society and global policy advocacy emanating from this critically important country. I would like to thank my colleagues at the University of the Western Cape, and in Pretoria at the Council for Scientific and Industrial Research in South Africa (CSIR). At CSIR, I am deeply thankful for, and indebted to, Ben Fouche, Rasigan Maharaj, Koffi Kouakou, and Naadia Davis, who all helped me to launch the Center for Information Society Development in Africa (CISDA) and to participate in so many of the activities described in this book. Also in South Africa, I would like to thank my colleagues at the University of the Witwatersrand, Graduate School of Public and Development Management (now Graduate School of Government), especially Luci Abrahams, Allison Gillwald, and Charlie Lewis. In the South African government, I would like to thank Andile Ncaba and His Excellency Jay Naidoo for their leadership in and my access to the telecommunications restructuring processes there, as well as the G8/Developing World Information Society and Development (ISAD) Conference. And in the South African civil society, I thank Peter Benjamin and Anriette Esterhysen, and Koos Bekker in the South African private sector.

On the broader African continent, I would like to thank my friends and colleagues in Ethiopia at the United Nations Economic Commission for Africa (ECA), including K.Y. Amoako, Nancy Hafkin, Karima Bounemra, and Makane Faye, and in Egypt, my colleagues at the Regional Information Technology Software Engineering Center (RITSEC) and the Information and Decision Support Center (IDSC) and now in the Ministry of Information and Communication Technologies, Hisham El

Sherif, Sherif Hashem, and Tarek Kamel (the latter now with the Internet Corporation for Assigned Names and Numbers—ICANN). At my first full-time academic home, I would like to thank my colleagues at the University of Michigan, School of Information, especially Dan Atkins, Olivia Frost, Gary Olson, Judy Olson, Tom Finholt, Jeff Mackie-Mason, and Margaret Hedstrom. Also at Michigan I would like to thank my colleagues at the Center for Afro-American and African Studies (CAAS), which is now the Department of Afro-American and African Studies, especially James Jackson, Brent Chrite, and Elizabeth James; in the Department of Communication Studies, Michael Traugott and W. Russell Newman, and across campus Michael Kennedy. Of course, it was at Michigan that I started the Center for Research on Collaboratories and Technology Enhanced Learning Communities (COTELCO), and I would like to thank all of the faculty investigators, doctoral fellows, graduate research associates, and undergraduate research assistants who have worked in COTELCO, especially Kevin Hill, Jessica Goger, Lingling Zhang, Peter Keller-Transburg, K. Michel Nguessan, Soo-yeon Hwang, Jacob Moskol, Clark Ross, and F. Kaluke Mawila. I would also like to thank my colleagues in the Center for Research on Electronic Work (CREW), which also provided me with such camaraderie and stimulating research ideas and opportunities, especially our research on the Science of Collaboratories (SOC), supported by the United States National Science Foundation (NSF).

My insights into the phenomena in this book were strengthened tremendously at Syracuse University, and I would like to thank my colleagues at the School of Information, especially the late Ray Von Dran, Milton Mueller, Lee McKnight, Ruth Small, Marilyn Arnone, and Martha Garcia Murillo, and at the Internet Governance Project, John Mathiason, Brenden Keurbis, and Hans Klein (at the Georgia Institute of Technology) and our work supported by the Ford Foundation. At the Syracuse University Maxwell School of Public Affairs, I would like to thank Margaret "Peg" Herman, Bruce Dayton, and Hans Peter Schmitz, especially for our work together on transnational civil society as agents of change, supported by the NSF. Also at Syracuse, I would like to thank Gina Lee Glauser, Mark Glauser, and Patricia Stith, especially for our work on STEM graduate education supported by the NSF.

At American University, my current academic home, I would like to thank my friends and colleagues in the School of International Service, Nanette Levinson, for her longstanding collaboration and support, Dean

Emeritus Louis Goodman, Amitav Acharya, and Dean Jim Goldgeier; and in the School of Communication, Laura DeNardis (with whom I am co-directing our new Internet Governance Lab IGL, along with Nanette Levinson) and Filippo Trevisan. In addition to our continuing work with COTELCO, I would like to thank all of my colleagues involved with helping me to launch and manage the Institute on Disability and Public Policy (IDPP), especially Maya Aguilar, along with Clyde White, Jennifer Ellis, Marilyn Arnone, Robert Guerra, and our senior research associate Erin Spaniol. In particular, I would like to thank Asvatha Babu, a new research associate, who has contributed substantially to this manuscript, through literature searches, background research, and editorial assistance. Thank you Ash!

My colleagues at the Global Internet Governance Academic Network (GigaNet), Internet Governance Caucus (IGC), and working within the Internet Corporation for Assigned Names and Numbers (ICANN), the IGF, the Global Alliance on ICT and Development (GAID), the ITU, the United Nations Educational, Scientific, and Cultural Organization (UNESCO), are far too numerous to name, but I would like to especially thank Victoria Knight, Patricia Benoit-Guyot, Fernando Lagraña, Lee Tuthill, Serge Kapto, Markus Kummer, and Changetai Massango.

Over the course of my career, I have been blessed with tremendous external support for my research program, and I would like to thank The Nippon Foundation, W.K. Kellogg Foundation, Ford Foundation, Markle Foundation, the NSF, United States Department of Education, J.P. Morgan Chase, Microsoft Corporation and Microsoft Research, Cisco Systems, and Hewlett Packard for the generous support of my research over the years.

Finally, and I think we all know, the last shall be first. I would like to thank my family. Without the deep and sustained love and support of my immediate and extended family, my life would be incomplete and I could not have accomplished a fraction of what I describe in this book or that I have achieved in my life. I especially thank my late mother, Sharon M. Cogburn, my late father, Roscoe C. Cogburn, my "little" sister Courtney Dawn Cogburn and my "big" sister Kimberly Goffinet (and their loving families), my better half and beloved wife Noemí Enchautegui-de-Jesús, my progeny and pride and joy, Sean Manuel Cogburn-Enchautegui, my mother-in-law Carmen, my brothers-in-law Samuel and Manuel (and their loving families).

The insights in this book have been aided by many of you, with great thanks, but the mistakes are of course my own.

CONTENTS

LIST OF ACRONYMS

3WCDRR	3rd World Conference on Disaster Risk Reduction (Sendai, Japan)
A2K	Access to Knowledge
ABT	WTO Agreement on Basic Telecommunications
AISI	African Information Society Initiative
APC	Association for Progressive Communications
APEC	Asia Pacific Economic Cooperation
ARPA	Advanced Research Projects Agency
B2B	Business-to-Business Electronic Commerce
B2G	Business-to-Government Electronic Commerce
BAAP	Buenos Aires Action Plan of ITU
BASIS	Business Action to Support the Information Society
BDT	Telecommunications Development Bureau of the ITU
BRICS	Brazil, Russia, India, China, and South Africa – Alliance
C&T	Content and Themes of the WSIS Civil Society
ccTLD	Country Code Top-Level Domain
CISDA	Center for Information Society Development in Africa
CONGO	Conference of NGOs in Consultative Relationship with the United Nations
COSP	Conference of States Parties to the UN CRPD
CRIS	Communication Rights in the Information Society
CRPD	United Nations Convention on the Rights of Persons with Disabilities
CSB	Civil Society Bureau – of WSIS

UNCSD	United Nations Commission on Sustainable Development
CSIR	South African Council for Scientific and Industrial Research
CSP	Civil Society Plenary—of WSIS
DACST	South African Department of Arts, Culture, Science and Technology
DARPA	Defense Advanced Research Projects Agency
DC	Dynamic Coalition—within IGF
DCCG	Dynamic Coalition Coordinating Group
DESA	United Nations Department of Economic and Social Affairs
DIAUD	Disability Inclusion and Accessible Urban Development
DNS	Domain Name System
DoC	United States Department of Commerce
DOC	South African Department of Communications
DOT	Force Digital Opportunities Task Force of G8
DSPD	Division of Social Policy and Development
DTI	South African Department of Trade and Industry
EC	European Commission
ECA	United Nations Economic Commission for Africa
ECOSOC	United Nations Economic and Social Council
ENUM	Electronic Number Mapping System
EU	European Union
G3ICT	Global Initiative for Inclusive Information and Communication Technologies
G7/8	Group of 7/8 Highly Industrialized Nations
GAC	Governmental Advisory Council of ICANN
GAID	Global Alliance for Information and Communication Technology for Development
GATT	General Agreement on Tariffs and Trade (precursor to WTO)
GBDe	Global Business Dialog on Electronic Commerce
GDDI	Global Digital Divide Initiative of WEF
GEC	Global Electronic Commerce
GEO	Geostationary Earth Orbiting satellite
GigaNet	Global Internet Governance Academic Network
GII	Global Information Infrastructure
GIIC	Global Information Infrastructure Commission
GIS	Global Information Society
GKP	Global Knowledge Partnership

GMPCS	Global Mobile Personal Communications by Satellite
GTLD	Global/Generic Top-Level Domain
HLPF	High-Level Political Forum of the SDGs
HLWG	High-Level Working Group on ICTs of ECA, developed AISI
IANA	Internet Assigned Numbers Authority
IBRD	International Bank for Reconstruction and Development (World Bank)
ICA	International Communication Association
ICANN	Internet Corporation for Assigned Names and Numbers
ICC	International Chamber of Commerce
ICT	Information and Communication Technologies
ICG	IANA Stewardship Transition Coordination Group
ICT4D	Information and Communication Technologies for Development
IDN	Internationalized Domain Names
IDSC	Egyptian Information and Decision Support Center
IETF	Internet Engineering Task Force
IGC	Civil Society Internet Governance Caucus
IGF	Internet Governance Forum
IGP	Internet Governance Project of Syracuse University/ Georgia Tech
ILO	International Labor Organization
IMF	International Monetary Fund
IoT	Internet of Things
IP	Internet Protocol
IPR	Intellectual Property Rights
IPv4	Internet Protocol version 4
IPv6	Internet Protocol version 6
ISAD	Information Society and Development Conference
ISO	International Standardization Organization
ISOC	Internet Society
IST	Information Society Technologies Conferences of the EC
ITR	International Telecommunication Regime
ITU	International Telecommunication Union (United Nations specialized agency)
LEO	Low Earth Orbiting satellite
MAG	Multistakeholder Advisory Group of IGF
MDGs	Millennium Development Goals

MEO	Mid-Earth Orbiting satellite
MGoS	Major Groups and Other Stakeholders
MIT	Massachusetts Institute of Technology
MPCIC	Multi-Purpose Community Information Center
NAFTA	North American Free Trade Agreement
NAM	Non-Aligned Movement
NASA	United States National Aeronautics and Space Administration
NCUC	Non-Commercial Users Constituency
NGBT	Negotiating Group on Basic Telecommunication in WTO
NGOs	Non-Governmental Organizations
NIH	United States National Institutes of Health
NSA	United States National Security Agency
NSF	United States National Science Foundation
NTIA	United States National Telecommunications and Information Administration
NWICO	New World Information and Communication Order
OECD	Organization for Economic Cooperation and Development
PIT	Public Information Terminals
POTS	Plain Old Telecommunications Service
PTO	Public Telecommunications Operator
PTT	Post, Telegraph and Telephone (government telecom operating agencies)
RIR	Regional Internet Registry
RITSEC	Egyptian Regional Information Technology Software Engineering Center
SADC	Southern African Development Community
SAMOS	South African Multiple Option Settlement system
SARB	South African Reserve Bank
SARS	South African Revenue Service
SCRPD	Secretariat for the Convention on the Rights of Persons with Disabilities
SDGs	Sustainable Development Goals (2030 Sustainable Development Agenda)
SME	Small and Medium-Sized Enterprises
SMMEs	Small, Medium and Micro-Sized Enterprises
TAN	Transnational Advocacy Network
TCP/IP	Transmission Control Protocol/Internet Protocol
TRIMS	Trade Related Investment Measures in WTO

TRIPS	Trade Related Aspects of Intellectual Property in WTO
UCLA	University of California Los Angeles
UNA	United Nations Association
UNCED	United Nations Conference on Environment and Development – Earth Summit
UNCITRAL	United Nations Conference on International Trade Law
UNCTAD	United Nations Conference on Trade and Development
UNEP	United Nations Environment Program
UNESCO	United Nations Educational, Scientific and Cultural Organization
UNFCC	United Nations Framework Convention on Climate Change
UNGA	United Nations General Assembly
UNICTTF	United Nations Information and Communication Technologies Task Force
USF	Universal Service Fund
USG	United States Government
VOIP	Voice Over Internet Protocol
VSAT	Very Small Aperture Terminal Satellite
W3C	World Wide Web Consortium
WBG	World Bank Group
WCIT	World Conference on International Telecommunication of ITU
WEF	World Economic Forum
WFUNA	World Federation of United Nations Associations
WGIG	Working Group on Internet Governance
WIPO	World Intellectual Property Organization
WITSA	World Information Technology Services Alliance
WSIS	United Nations World Summit on the Information Society
WTDC	World Telecommunications Development Conference
WTDC	World Telecommunications Development Conference of ITU
WTO	World Trade Organization
WWW	World Wide Web

Timeline of Key Information Society and GII Regime Transformation Events

1865   International Telecommunication Union (ITU) founded as International Telegraph Union

1876   Alexander Graham Bell credited with inventing the telephone (March)

1878   Circuit-switched telephone network developed

1945   United Nations (UN) created

1946   United Nations Associations (UNA) created

1948   Conference of NGOs (CoNGO) in Consultative Status with the UN created

1961   Leonard Kleinrock at MIT publishes the first paper on packet switching theory (July)

1962   J.C.R. Licklider of MIT writes memos describing a "Galactic Network" (August)

1965   Lawrence Roberts and Thomas Merrill used a low-speed telephone line to create the first WAN

1966   Roberts left MIT to head computer science at ARPA, developed a plan for ARPANET

1968   BBN and Frank Heart won ARPA RFQ to develop packet switches called IMPs

1969   NMC at UCLA and Stanford Research institute become the first two nodes on ARPANET

1969   UC Santa Barbara and University of Utah become the second and third nodes on ARPANET

1970   US Congressman Al Gore promotes high-speed telecommunications as engine of growth

1971   ARPA changes its name to Defense Advanced Research Projects Agency (DARPA)

1972   Electronic mail software introduced by Ray Tomlinson at BBN (Bolt Beranek and Newman)

1973   TCP/IP Development begins with Robert Kahn and Vinton Cerf

1974   Vint Cerf and Robert Kahn publish "A Protocol for Packet Network Interconnection"

1980   Defense Community adopts TCP/IP as a standard

1980   *Many Voices, One World*, MacBride Commission report published by UNESCO

1980   New World Information and Communication Order (NWICO) gains momentum

1982   *The Missing Link*, Maitland Commission Report published by the ITU

1983   ARPANET transitioned from NCP to TCP/IP and MILNET splits off

1983   DNS System invented by Paul Mockapertris

1984   The USA leaves UNESCO (followed by the UK and Singapore)

1986   First meeting of the Internet Engineering Task Force (IETF)

1989   Tim Berners Lee invents the World Wide Web (WWW)

1991   First INET Conference held in Copenhagen and launch of the Internet Society (ISOC)

1992   Earth Summit in Rio de Janeiro Convened and Agenda 21 adopted

1994   Global Information Infrastructure (GII) speech by US Vice-President Al Gore to WTDC

1994   *Europe and the Global Information Society*, Bangemann report to the European Council

1995   World Trade Organization (WTO) created in Geneva (January)

1995   Global Information Infrastructure (GII) Principles launched by the USA (February)

1995   Global Information Infrastructure Commission (GIIC) launched by CSIS (February)

1995   Term "Digital Divide" Coined by Larry Irving in the NTIA *Falling Through the Net* report

1995   WTO Financial Services Agreement (July)

1995   WTO Agreement on Movement of Natural Persons (July)

1995   ITU World Telecom (October)

1996	African Information Society Initiative (AISI) adopted by all African countries at UNECA
1996	Information Society and Development (ISAD) Conference convened in South Africa (May)
1996	WTO, IMF, World Bank MOU on Global Electronic Commerce (November)
1997	WTO Agreement on Basic Telecommunications (February)
1997	WTO Agreement on IT Products (March)
1997	Global Knowledge for Development Conference (June)
1997	The USA issues unilateral challenge to the International System of Accounting Rates
1998	WTO E-Commerce Work Program (May)
1998	Internet Corporation for Assigned Names and Numbers (ICANN) formed (September)
1998	OECD E-Commerce Ministerial Conference (October)
1999	WTO Seattle Ministerial Meeting
1999	Washington, DC Meeting of the IMF and World Bank on E-Commerce
2000	World Economic Forum (WEF) Meeting on E-Commerce in Davos, Switzerland
2000	Digital Opportunities Task Force (DOT Force) launched by the G8
2001	Global Digital Divide Initiative (GDDI) launched by the World Economic Forum
2001	UN ICT Task Force launched by UN DESA
2003	UN World Summit on the Information Society (WSIS) Geneva held in Switzerland
2004	Working Group on Internet Governance (WGIG) launches report
2005	UN World Summit on the Information Society (WSIS) Tunis held in Tunisia
2005	Global Alliance on ICT and Development (GAID) formed at the end of WSIS Tunis
2005	Internet Governance Forum (IGF) formed at the end of WSIS, Tunis
2006	UN Convention on the Rights of Persons with Disabilities (CRPD) adopted
2010	GAID shuttered
2010	IGF renewed and given a new five-year mandate

2011   *World Disability Report*, published by World Bank/WHO indicated over 1 billion PWDs

2013   Snowden revelations begin; *The Guardian* newspaper reveals existence of classified NSA leaks

2013   President Dilma Rousseff accuses the USA of violating International Law in UNGA speech

2013   European Commission says the USA has "lost the trust" of the global community, urges action

2014   NetMundial convened in Sao Paulo, Brazil

2014   NTIA issues guidelines and conditions under which it will relinquish core IANA functions

2014   IANA Stewardship Transition Coordination Group (IGC) formed

2015   Post-2015 Sustainable Development Goals (SDGs) adopted by UNGA

2015   IGF given a new ten-year mandate at the UNGA WSIS+10 review

2016   IANA Transition Committee report completed (Marrakech) and submitted to NTIA

Author's Note

Derrick L. Cogburn is an expert on global governance, transnational NGOs, information and communication technologies, and the use of ICTs for socioeconomic development. His research and teaching interests include multistakeholder global governance Internet governance accessible cyberinfrastructure and cyberlearning, global, national, and regional disability policy, geographically distributed collaboration in knowledge work, global virtual teams and organizations, transnational policy networks, and epistemic communities. He is the editor of the Palgrave Macmillan book series on Information Technology and Global Governance. He is Associate Professor of International Communication and International Development at the American University School of International Service. He also Executive Director of the Institute on Disability and Public Policy (IDPP) at American University, a project funded by the Nippon Foundation of Japan and emerging from the Center for Research on Collaboratories and Technology Enhanced Learning Communities (COTELCO), an award-winning social science research collaboratory investigating the social and technical factors that influence geographically distributed collaborative knowledge work, particularly between developed and developing countries. COTELCO is an affiliated center of the Burton Blatt Institute, Centers of Innovation on Disability, where Cogburn serves on the Leadership Council. He has served as principal investigator/project director on more than $7 million in externally funded research, and a total of almost $16 million overall (including co-principal investigator/ investigator awards), including substantial funding from the Nippon Foundation, NSF, US Department of Education, W.K. Kellogg Foundation,

Cisco Systems, Microsoft, Microsoft Research, Hewlett-Packard, and J.P. Morgan Chase. Previously, Cogburn was on the faculty at the School of Information Studies at Syracuse University and the School of Information at the University of Michigan. He has served as Visiting Professor at the University of Malaya in Kuala Lumpur, working with the International Institute on Public Policy and Management, and as a Visiting Professor in the Department of Political Science at Ateneo de Manila University, and as a Visiting Professor in the Faculty of Creative Multimedia at Multimedia University in Cyberjaya, Malaysia. In addition, Cogburn has served as an adjunct professor at the International School of Information Management at the University of Mysore in southern India and as adjunct professor at the Graduate School of Public and Development Management at the University of the Witwatersrand in Johannesburg, South Africa.

He has published over 50 peer-reviewed articles and conference proceedings, three edited books, seven book chapters, 21 working papers and public scholarship, and has delivered over 68 invited lectures and conference presentations nationally and 37 internationally.

Cogburn is the past president of the Information Technology and Politics section of the American Political Science Association (APSA) as well as past president of the International Communication section of the International Studies Association (ISA). He is also a principal and member of the Scientific Committee of the Internet Governance Project (IGP) founding board member and former Vice Chair of the Global Internet Governance Academic Network (GigaNet), and served as a faculty member of the Syracuse University Africa Initiative.

From 1995 to 2000 Cogburn helped to establish and build the Global Information Infrastructure Commission (GIIC), serving as Africa Regional Director, and from 1998 to 2000 served as Executive Director of GIIC Africa. He serves or has served in high-level appointed international positions with the UN Global Alliance for ICT and Development (GAID), the World Bank, the ITU, United Nations Conference on Trade and Development (UNCTAD), and the United Nations Economic Commission for Africa (ECA). He also served on the Committee of Visitors for the NSF, Office of Cyberinfrastructure, and was appointed to the High-Level Multistakeholder Committee to oversee NETMundial: A Global Multistakeholder Meeting on the Future of Internet Governance.

Cogburn received his PhD in political science (International Relations, Political Economy, and Comparative Politics) from Howard University in 1996, where he was a W.K. Kellogg doctoral fellow at the Ralph J. Bunche

International Affairs Center. He also received his MA in political science (Comparative Politics Africa, Political Economy) from Howard University in 1994, and his BA in history (Ancient Near Eastern and Africa)/political science (International Relations) from the University of Oklahoma in 1992.

LIST OF FIGURES

LIST OF TABLES

Transnational Advocacy Networks in the Global Information Society: Partners or Pawns?

CHAPTER 1

Multistakeholderism and Contestation in the Global Governance of the Information Society

INTRODUCTION

Since the founding of the United Nations (UN) in 1945, the question of how to enable effective participation for individual citizens in its multiple and complex deliberative processes has presented scholars and practitioners with a persistent problem. Various solutions to this problem have been explored by a wide range of actors, from the United Nations Associations (UNAs) in 1946, to the Conference of nongovernmental organizations (NGOs) in Consultative Relationship with the United Nations (CoNGO) founded in 1948, to the "Major Groups" framework emerging from the 2000 *Millennium Summit*, to the innovative multistakeholder processes of the WSIS in 2003 and 2005, and its successors the *Global Alliance for ICTs and Development* (GAID) and the *IGF*, to the more expansive "Major Groups and Other Stakeholders" (MGoS) approach taken in the High-Level Political Forum (HLPF) of the 2030 *Sustainable Development Agenda* and the General Assembly of Partners (GAP) and the sixteen Partner Constituency Groups (PCGs) of Habitat III. Each of these approaches has had some success in involving private citizens in the work of the UN, and each has also had its shortcomings. Moreover, no approach has been applied consistently across the UN system to facilitate multistakeholder involvement.

© The Author(s) 2017
D.L. Cogburn, *Transnational Advocacy Networks in the Information Society*, Information Technology and Global Governance,
DOI 10.1057/978-1-137-48361-4_1

So, when the movement toward multiple stakeholders joining state actors in these global deliberations gained momentum, the civil society groups—ostensibly "representing" these private citizens—were given a "seat at the table": an opening, an opportunity. However, how does an incredibly diverse, heterogeneously rich, fractious, and resource-challenged civil society organize itself to participate effectively in these processes, to take advantage of that opening, that opportunity?

This book explores this broad question, especially as it relates to civil society participation in the evolution of the multistakeholder processes related to the Information Society, with a particular focus on their involvement in the restructuring of global telecommunications and the intense engagement over the past several decades in what is now known as global Internet governance. The emergence of the network society (Castells 1996, 1997, 1998), better known as the Information Society, includes an increased focus on the application of information and communication technologies (ICTs) to every area of human life, including work and employment, education, healthcare, recreation, scientific research, entertainment, cultural heritage preservation, and socialization. It also includes the ubiquitous social media networks and the Internet of Things (IOTs) continuously capturing data about our every move and fueling smart cities. The emergence of the Information Society has sparked an interest in telecommunications and information policy from a wide variety of sectors. New actors, who never saw themselves previously playing a role in international telecommunications and information policy formulation, are being drawn into the process. Medical doctors and nurses now interested in telemedicine, teachers interested in distance learning and edutainment, and artists, musicians, writers, and actors interested in digital distribution of creative content see themselves joining human rights activists, engineers, and intellectual property lawyers in the arenas related to global telecommunications and information policy. These policy actors are bringing with them new policy preferences, are interested in a better understanding of these global governance processes, and are looking for mechanisms through which to engage.

The UNAs have worked since 1946 to organize private citizens with an interest in the UN, to raise awareness about the UN, to keep those citizens informed about how the UN operates, and to involve them in its activities. There are now over 120 UNAs globally, organized under the

World Federation of United Nations Associations (WFUNA), with secretariat offices located in New York and Geneva.

Another mechanism for the involvement of private citizens in the work of the UN is CoNGO. Founded in 1948, CoNGO had two types of organizational memberships, with its "Full" members having consultative status with the UN Economic and Social Council (ECOSOC), which effectively operates as a "vetting" mechanism for NGOs that allows some UN member states to "veto" certain NGOs with which they may disagree and its "Associate" members having affiliation with a UN program or agency. CoNGO now has over 500 members, and offices in New York, Geneva, and Vienna. The vision of CoNGO is "to be the primary support and platform for a civil society represented by a global community of informed, empowered and committed NGOs that fully participate with the UN in decision-making and programs leading to a better world, a world of economic and social justice," and its mission is to "[f]acilitate through various means the development of a dynamic and informed world-wide NGO community able to influence policies and actions at all levels of the United Nations" (found on the Internet at: http://www.ngocongo.org/who-we-are/vision-mission-and-objectives).

Many new opportunities for civil society involvement in these processes stimulated a plethora of institutional mechanisms for participating in UN processes. Some of these processes, such as the UN Commission on Sustainable Development (CSD), used the Major Groups Framework, which emerged from Agenda 21 and the Earth Summit, wherein any member of the nine organized "Major Groups"—namely (1) women; (2) children and youth; (3) indigenous peoples; (4) NGOs; (5) workers and trade unions; (6) farmers; (7) scientific and technical community; (8) business and industry, and (9) local authorities—was given access to the UN meeting. This access meant they could register and attend the conference, and in some cases be able to speak on the floor, co-sponsor and propose conference events, and avail themselves to other benefits. As the participant of a Major Group, the person or organization could get access to the conference venue, the materials provided to the participants, they could sit in on official meetings, review the conference documents, and submit recommendations to be considered in the process.

Unfortunately, simply "participating" in these processes is not enough. The bigger question is whether or not civil society can participate "effectively" in these processes. Do they understand the issues on the table, the composition and structure of a conference delegation, the role of a Permanent Mission, and how international organizations and their secretariats can influence the process and the results? Are these civil society stakeholders organized in a way that allows them to influence the outcomes of these processes? Can they do so in a way that enables broad, diverse participation from around the world in their own internal processes? These opportunities place a heavy responsibility on shoulders of civil society. Collectively, we look at this as an understanding of "Conference Diplomacy", described by Kaufmann in 1968 as he brilliantly illuminated the multiple and complex processes of the UN, and how state actors get things done within the context of an international conference. However, Kauffman focused on state delegations, and in a new multistakeholder environment, getting things done in "Multistakeholder Conference Diplomacy" is quite different, and critically important. More importantly for this book, understanding the specific role transnational civil society networks play within a multistakeholder process, still dominated by state actors and multilateral (and bilateral) diplomacy, is paramount.

This challenge is enhanced when one considers the tremendously diverse policy preferences found within global civil society, and the heterogeneous nature of their organizational structures. And, of course, when one considers the differential financial resources among those actors involved in the process (with the global private sector having tremendous institutional and financial resources to engage in these processes).

While the levels of civil society participation in some of the UN processes discussed in this book have been very high, there are not enough financial resources within the global civil society community to get enough people to all the meetings related to their varied interests. This paucity in resources, coupled with the tremendous diversity of participation, sets up a power dynamic that allows those organizations based in New York, Geneva, Vienna, and Washington, D.C. to be disproportionately influential in these processes, relative to other civil society organizations. There are some very clear exceptions—and the Association for Progressive Communications (APC) is a leading example. But, in general, this dynamic is pervasive.

One mechanism that has altered this dynamic and promoted the active involvement of civil society has been through the use of ICTs. Perhaps even more impressive is when civil society organizations use ICTs to create networks of civil society advocates that span the globe, enabling them to participate in a broader range of UN activities. Following the landmark work of Margaret Keck and Kathryn Sikkink (1998), we call these institutions Transnational Advocacy Networks (TANs), and follow their fairly strict seminal definition of what comprises a TAN. We also integrate into our understanding of TANS, insights from Sidney Tarrow's (2005) arguments about New Transnational Activism, and Manuel Castells' (2012) ideas about social movements in the Internet age.

However, in this book we focus not on those movements of civil society actors that are protesting "outside" the system, but instead on the attempts of transnational civil society networks to participate effectively "within" the processes of the UN system (of course, many of these actors have also continued to work outside the system, including leading and participating in protests of and to the official conference processes). In doing so, this book asks whether the TANs active in the global information society (GIS) are influential *partners* in these global governance processes, or merely symbolic tokens—or *pawns?*

As a domain of interest, this book focuses broadly on the Information Society. While a somewhat imperfect and confusing concept—and some would prefer to use the terms "Network Society" or "Knowledge Society" and others still the "Information Community"—the idea of an Information Society has a relatively long history. It is grounded in ideas about a "postindustrial" society (also conceived of as "post-Fordist" or "postmodern"), where ICTs are embedded deeply within systems of production and distribution, and are transforming nearly every aspect of society. Many writers have highlighted this transformation in different ways, including Toffler (1970), Bell (1976), Benniger (1986), Crawford (1983), and Castells (2004). Each of these writers has highlighted different aspects of the Information Society, but all focus on the underlying transformation in society being driven in large part by the application of ICTs. This book does not attempt to be an exhaustive history of these international organizations and movements, or of the role they have played in the GIS. Instead, this book focuses of how and important category of civil society participants use geographically distributed TANS to participate in these processes.

Many international organizations also saw a critical role for themselves in this process. The ITU, which had been in existence for over 100 years saw itself as playing an absolutely key role in these processes, and that interest would raise its head over and over again, even as we get into the specific discussion of the WSIS and global Internet governance. Another key international organization is the vying for a leadership role is UNESCO.

At the heart of the Information Society lie telecommunication networks, and the international reach and network externalities engendered by them. In 1980, a UNESCO publication entitled *Many Voices, One World* (known by many as the MacBride report), articulated a vision of a New World Information and Communications Order (NWICO). The International Commission for the Study of Communication Problems, chaired by Sean MacBride, examined the fundamental imbalances in media ownership, content and representations between the Global South and the rest of the world.

In 1982, the Maitland Commission report titled *The Missing Link* highlighted the role ICTs could play in socioeconomic development and saw this as the key element that had been missing for so many years in our understanding of development.

In May 1994, US Vice-President Al Gore gave a speech to the first ITU World Telecommunication Development Conference (WTDC) in Buenos Aires, Argentina, that outlined the idea of a Global Information Infrastructure (GII), which "will allow us to share information, to connect, and to communicate as a global community....It will help educate our children and allow us to exchange ideas within a community and among nations. It will be a means by which families and friends will transcend the barriers of time and distance. It will make possible a global information marketplace, where consumers can buy or sell products" (ITU 1994).

This landmark speech was followed by Gore's speech in September later that year to the ITU Plenipotentiary Conference, and subsequently by the GII: Agenda for Cooperation (1995) by Ronald Brown, US Secretary of Commerce and Larry Irving, Administrator, US National Telecommunication and Information Administration.

In May 1994, shortly after Vice-President Gore's speech in Buenos Aires, a High-Level Group on the Information Society, led by Martin Bangemann, published a report entitled *Europe in the Global Information*

Society. The Bangemann report, as it is known, outlined a European strategy for harnessing the potential of an information society.

Also at this time, some regional initiatives for an information society were gaining traction, most notably, and somewhat surprisingly, the African Information Society Initiative (AISI). The AISI, convened by the ECA was a forward-looking strategic framework that articulated a continent-wide vision for the Information Society in Africa in 1996. (Full disclosure, the author served on the high-level ECA panel to develop the AISI and convened the Information Society and Development conference where it was launched.).

Manuel Castells—in his landmark three-volume set on the Rise of the Network Society—recognized that there were certain steps and preconditions for a country to be able to capitalize on the advantages provided by an Information Society and highlighted the concept of the space of flows (a similar concept had also been introduced by Saskia Sassen).

The desire to focus on global electronic commerce (GEC) helped to stimulate this process even further, as another international organization, the World Trade Organization (WTO), picked up the challenge of addressing both the global trade in telecommunications and GEC. The principles of a GIS oriented toward GEC are quite different from the progressive Information Society principles in a world envisioned by NWICO. The WTO was the global leading edge of the spear toward the liberalization and privatization of telecommunications, and used the idea of an information society as the rationale and justification for this aggressive push. Its strategy was both the Agreement on Basic Telecommunications (ABT) and the working group in Electronic Commerce. This twin strategy wrestled some of the key elements of telecommunications out of the hands of the ITU and pushed the idea of the Washington Consensus that liberalizing and privatizing telecommunications was the fastest way to enable GEC, which would be the "killer app" to fuel the development of the GIS. Of course, this vision was to be led by the private sector, and organizations like the GIIC helped to popularize this idea. (More full disclosure, the author was one of the founding members of the secretariat for the GIIC, and later led its first spin-off organization, GIIC Africa). The GIIC also wanted to keep these initiatives outside the multilateral system—especially the

ITU—and to have a clear role for the private sector and other non-state actors in the process.

In 2001, the UN went a step further in recognizing the importance it placed on ICTs by creating the UN ICT Task Force in November 2001. The UN ICT Task Force followed the Global Digital Divide Initiative (GDDI) of the World Economic Forum (WEF) and the Digital Opportunities Task Force (DOT Force) of the Group of Eight Industrialized Nations (G8). The UN ICT Task Force and these preceding initiatives were designed to "close the digital divide" that had been identified in 1995 by Larry Irving and the US NTIA of the Department of Commerce in its *Falling Through the Net* report. With its home in the UN, the UN ICT Task Force was seen as both a broader global initiative with substantial participation by developing countries, and as a broad multistakeholder initiative. There was substantial private sector participation in the UN ICT Task Force, including Cisco Systems, Hewlett-Packard, IBM, Nokia, SAP, Siemens, and Sun Microsystems, along with global NGO participation, from the APC and others.

Into this environment for telecommunications restructuring and the desire for the development of an Information Society came a "new kid on the block." The Internet Corporation for Assigned Names and Numbers (ICANN) was created in 1998 to privatize and internationalize the international domain name system, which made the Internet possible, and was an innovative experiment in global multistakeholder governance. The structure of ICANN allowed for multistakeholder participation in Internet governance (as defined within the narrow context of ICANN). It had a role for governments through their participation in the Governmental Advisory Committee (GAC). It had a role for the technical community through the Protocol Supporting Organization (PSO), within which the Internet Engineering Task Force (IETF), World Wide Web Consortium (W3C), Telecommunication Standardization Sector of the ITU (ITU-T) and European Telecommunications Standards Institute (ETSI), participated. It had a role for commercial and private domain holders in the Domain Names Supporting Organization (DNSO).

Prior to the creation of ICANN, the Internet Society (ISOC) had been created in 1992 to promote leadership in Internet-related standards around the world. Located in Reston, Virginia, USA, with major offices in Geneva, Switzerland, ISOC was formed officially by Vint Cerf and Bob Kahn, known collectively as the "Fathers of the Internet." Cerf and Khan both wanted to ensure that the standards development process for the Internet was open and to "provide leadership in Internet-related standards, education, access, and policy." The Mission Statement of the ISOC is "[t]o promote the open development, evolution and use of the Internet for the benefit of all people throughout the world" (found on the Internet at: http://www.internetsociety.org/who-we-are/mission). It now has a membership base of more than 140 organizations and more than 80,000 individual members, who form chapters related to geographic location or special interest. There are now more than 110 chapters around the world.

Prior to the creation of ICANN, the Domain Name System (DNS), the heart of the global Internet, invented in 1983 was administered by one person, Dr. Jon Postel, under contract to the US Department of Commerce and its National Telecommunications and Information Administration (NTIA). As much of the world began to realize the importance of the Internet to their commerce, education, national security, and the entire society, there was the desire to move the governance of this mechanism away from this sole governmental oversight role played by the USA into a much broader international governance structure that would have a role for governments but also recognize the critical role played by the technical community, Internet users, domain name holders, academia, and other actors. While not without substantial controversy, ICANN has played this role since its inception. However, many people felt that the creation of ICANN did not go far enough in privatizing and internationalizing Internet governance. Some critics even wanted the UN to play a much more important role—with some encouragement of this view coming from the ITU and UNESCO. Although previously proposed by the ITU, in 2001 the UN General Assembly authorized the creation of WSIS, and it invited NGOs, civil society, and the private sector to "contribute, and actively participate in, the intergovernmental preparatory process of the Summit and the Summit itself" along with all relevant UN bodies and other international and regional organizations (A/Res/53/183, Para. 5).

It asked the ITU to organize a WSIS in 2003 in Geneva, followed by a second part of the summit in 2005 in Tunis, Tunisia. For many analysts, this opportunity for multistakeholder participation signaled a fundamental shift in the power relations between state and non-state actors. Unfortunately, in practice, the effective participation of civil society and other non-state actors in WSIS lagged behind this lofty rhetoric.

Among others there was more skepticism. While the agenda for WSIS was very broad and addressed a wide range of "information society" issues, many analysts saw WSIS as a strategic opportunity to open up Internet governance to a broader global community, and pry it away from the "dominance" of the USA. This perspective clearly escalated the geopolitics related to WSIS.

Nonetheless, the first phase of the WSIS did engage with a broad range of issues, and stimulated the creation of numerous global civil society networks, through both top-down and bottom-up processes. Internet governance (as expected) remained the elephant in the room. During this first phase, many participants kept calling for broader global and private processes to govern the Internet, and the USA—led by Ambassador David Gross and NTIA senior staffer Fiona Alexander—remained steadfast in its refusal to budge on issues it saw as key to the development of a global, free, and open Internet.

The end of the first phase of WSIS in 2003 (frequently referred to as WSIS Geneva) saw the adoption of a *Declaration of Principles* and a *Plan of Action*, both reflecting a written representation of the multistakeholder consensus generated during the long preparation processes of the Summit. However, the end of the Geneva WSIS also saw a series of unresolved issues related to (1) information and communication for development, particularly the financing for development; and (2) global Internet governance, specifically how to continue the multistakeholder political momentum generated from WSIS for fundamental changes to the international regime for global Internet governance outside the narrow confines of the now entrenched *ancien regime* of the ICANN. To address at least one of these shortcomings, a Working Group on Internet Governance (WGIG) was created, and tasked, inter alia, with coming up with an acceptable consensus definition of Internet governance that could be used in the second phase of the Summit and to lay the ground for negotiations at the second phase of WSIS. The ultimate WGIG definition of Internet governance—"Internet governance is the development and application by Governments, the private sector and civil society, in their respective roles, of shared principles, norms, rules, decision-making procedures, and programmes that shape the evolution and use of the Internet" (WGIG 2005)—resembled very closely the textbook definition by Krasner (1982) of an International Regime in the second phase of WSIS in 2005 (held in Tunis, Tunisia).

On 18 November 2005 at the conclusion of WSIS Tunis, the Summit introduced the *Tunis Agenda* (and its focus on "Enhanced Cooperation") (WSIS-05/TUNIS/DOC/6(Rev.1)-E). The Tunis Agenda addressed the two key issues of the second phase of WSIS, namely financing for ICTs for development and Internet governance. These two major issues, both of tremendous importance to civil society and the Global South, were addressed as an official outcome of WSIS, when the UN created two potentially innovative multistakeholder institutions: the IGF to address the former and the GAID to address the latter.

Of these two, the IGF has been the more successful. Both organizations were given initial five-year mandates, but the GAID was eventually closed, while the IGF was given an additional five years, and in December 2015 at the WSIS+10 review by the United Nations General Assembly (UNGA), the IGF mandate was extended for another ten years. In addition, like WSIS itself, the IGF spawned a number of its own TANs. Partially as a function of its own structure, with a Multistakeholder Advisory Group (MAG), appointed by the UN Secretary-General serving as its primary governance body, and a system of Dynamic Coalitions (DCs, which were required to be multistakeholder) establishing the intellectual content of its annual meetings, the IGF has become one of the most innovative multistakeholder global governance mechanisms, and perhaps the most successful outcome of the WSIS process. The IGF also spawned another influential organization, the Global Internet Governance Academic Network (GigaNet). GigaNet serves as an interdisciplinary global network of academics, all studying Internet governance from a wide variety of perspectives (More full disclosure, the author was one of the founding members and officers of GigaNet, serving as its inaugural Communications Chair, and subsequently as Vice Chair). While engaging in too much "advocacy" from some perspectives, GigaNet has enabled a constant source of intellectual ideas to be funneled into the IGF processes over its entire lifespan and has served in some ways as an epistemic community for the IGF and broader Internet governance debates.

However, the IGF is not without its own shortcomings. Yes, the IGF has been extended for at least another ten years. But, the fact that this extension appears to be under the stronger leadership of UN staffers within the Department of Economic and Social Affairs (DESA) may prove to be highly problematic to the hard-won credibility of this multistakeholder institution.

These are some of the broad issues explored in this book. It examines the role of TANs in enabling effective participation for individual citizens in the deliberative processes of global governance broadly speaking, and for Internet governance in particular. Contextualized around the international conference setting of the UN-sponsored WSIS in 2003 and 2005, and its follow-on mechanisms IGF and GAID, this book sees epistemic communities and ICTs as critical to the effectiveness of critical to the effectiveness of multistakeholder global governance.

The UN General Assembly resolution authorizing the World Summit on the Information Society made WSIS an explicitly multistakeholder process. Civil society and private sector organizations were invited to participate as official partners in a multistakeholder dialog at the Summit alongside the more traditional governments and international organizations. This active participation, and the structure of civil society participation in WSIS (both top-down and bottom-up processes, and the enabling factors along with inhibiting factors) helped to strengthen some of the existing transnational civil society networks active in these spaces, and enabled the creation of a plethora of new TANs. Some of these networks have had more longevity than others, and some have been far more effective at policy advocacy than others. Why?

This book provides an answer and asks whether TANs active in the GIS are influential partners in these global governance processes or merely symbolic tokens—or pawns. It explores the factors that enabled some networks—such as the Internet Governance Caucus (IGC)—to persist and thrive, while others failed. It also sees linkages with epistemic communities—such as the GigaNet and the use of ICTs as critical to the effectiveness of some networks.

TRANSNATIONAL CIVIL SOCIETY: PARTNERS OR PAWNS?

While this introduction and background have illustrated a tremendous increase in the opportunities for civil society participation in global processes, and has highlighted the important role of TANs in facilitating this participation, it has not addressed the broader impact of their involvement. It is beneficial to the UN, and to many of the powerful national and private sector participants in WSIS and the various post-WSIS institutions for them to be seen as "multistakeholder." However, assessing the degree to which these non-state actors are *partners* in the global governance of these domains, or if they are being used as *pawns* is an open question. Are these transnational civil society networks having a substantive impact on the policy and decision-making within these global governance processes, or are they being used to lend legitimacy to these processes? Is the involvement of civil society on the *inside* of these processes, neutering the ability for them to protest on the *outside* of these processes?

Purpose

The purpose of this book is to explore the participation of global civil society actors in the processes leading up to and following the two phases of WSIS, and its follow-on institutions, the IGF and GAID, in order to better understand the limits and potential of multistakeholder global governance for the information society.

The book asks three broad primary questions:

(1) What theoretical frameworks help us to best understand the institutional history and evolution of WSIS, IGF, and GAID and why?

(2) What were the stated objectives of WSIS, IGF, and GAID and what were the similarities and differences among multistakeholder perspectives on the degree to which they accomplished them?

(3) In what ways did WSIS, IGF, and GAID use ICTs to facilitate multistakeholder participation in the global governance of the information society?

Taking a mixed-methods research approach, the book combines substantial qualitative and quantitative data into a comparative case study of WSIS, GAID, and IGF. The author was a participant observer in most of these policy processes, including participant observation at both WSIS summits and most of their preparatory processes, and nearly all follow-on meetings of both the GAID and IGF. The resulting data set includes an 85-item panel survey of all participants in both phases of WSIS, interviews, focus groups, email archives, participant lists, official and unofficial documents, including materials from the global stocktaking and evaluation processes of the IGF and a formal evaluation of GAID conducted by students at the Maxwell School at Syracuse

University under contract to the GAID secretariat. These data are analyzed through the innovative use of computer-assisted, mixed-methods data analysis tools, including advanced keyword and content analysis and social network analysis.

Key findings include the continued importance and resilience of international regime theory as a conceptual framework with TANs being critical for civil society involvement; surprising multistakeholder support for the reauthorization of IGF with far less consensus on the future of GAID; a substantial and sustained attempt by IGF to use ICTs to enhance remote participation, with limited attempts by the GAID. The book concludes by discussing what the existence and continuation of IGF and GAID mean for the literature on TANs and global multistakeholder governance, especially what they mean for power dynamics in conference diplomacy. It argues that the IGF represents a new form of international institution, which through its unique nature as a nonbinding multistakeholder forum for Internet governance has contributed to the "convergence of expectations" predicted by international regime theory as the foundation for an emergent global governance mechanism, while the GAID represents less of a step in this direction.

STRUCTURE OF THE BOOK

We conclude Part 1 by presenting the conceptual framework for the study. In Chap. 2 we focus on contending perspectives of global governance and highlight the continuing explanatory power of International Regime Theory, highlighting its contributions to our understanding of global governance. The chapter also contrasts international regime theory with other explanatory approaches. We then propose a critical reformulation of international regime theory to take into consideration the important role of transnational networks of non-state actors, especially in this historic era of globalization and an information society. Also in Chap. 2, we also explain the concept of Conference Diplomacy and its evolution into our current conception of Multistakeholder Conference Diplomacy. Here, we highlight the contribution civil society organizations are theorized to make to a global governance process. Finally, we discuss the concept of TANs and describe the role they might play in international regime formation and multistakeholder conference diplomacy, particularly as a vehicle for transmitting knowledge and for stimulating a convergence of ideas related to norms, principles, and values of a particular issue area in international affairs. This chapter ends with a brief discussion of the data available for this study, and the multiple methodologies employed to understand these issues. Here, we review the voluminous qualitative and quantitative, primary and secondary data available for this study. For primary data, we have conducted multistakeholder surveys in both the first and second phases of WSIS, as well as interviews and focus groups with some of the members of various TANs, and participant observation at nearly all the events discussed in the book. In terms of secondary data, we find a treasure trove of text-based data available for analysis, contained in websites for each of the conferences, preparatory meetings, summits, and fora. These websites often include participant lists, policy recommendations/submissions. We also have access to numerous public email archives of these groups. Methodologies used to analyze this data include traditional descriptive and predictive statistical modeling, but also social network analysis, along with inductive and deductive text mining techniques.

The remainder of the book is structured largely chronologically to explore the broad questions under review in the study. Part 2 of the book focuses on Global Regime Restructuring. It looks at the broad contestation of ideas and policy interests in global telecommunications and broader communications, to the emergence of electronic commerce as a key driver of the GII, to the specific issues related to Internet governance, and then to the broader Information Society.

Chapter 3 takes us back to the global contestation of the NWICO, where some of the more influential civil society actors in the information society got their start. This chapter also illustrates how the ideological battles being fought in NWICO were continued into the broader restructuring of the international telecommunications regime (ITR), leading to what the chapter calls the Global Information Society (GIS) versus GEC debate. This framing of the debate highlights the differences between the principles and values required to facilitate the development of GEC (which were perceived to be more corporate driven) and those principles and values of a GIS (which were perceived to be more open and "people" driven).

In Chap. 4, we focus on the people, networks, and issues giving rise to the fundamental changes to the ways in which the Internet was to be governed, and what it means to "govern" the Internet. We talk about the creation of the ISOC by the two "Fathers of the Internet"—Vint Cerf and Bob Kahn—to provide a stimulus toward informed policy- and standard-setting for the Internet. We then talk about the landmark creation of the ICANN as an innovative multistakeholder institution, designed to address the growing calls for the internationalization and privatization of the oversight and maintenance of the key technical functions related to the stability and functioning of the Internet.

Part 3 of the book focuses on understanding the catalytic role played by the WSIS in stimulating the creation of numerous TANs that participated in its processes, as well as the various post-WSIS institutions. Chapter 5 organizes this analysis by focusing on WSIS itself, and the contestation between the top-down Civil Society Bureau (CSB) and the purported bottom-up Civil Society Plenary (CSP). It also looks at all the 30 thematic and regional civil society caucuses and working groups and the various organizational structures that emerged to enable civil society participation in WSIS. Most of these networks have faded away, but the IGC remains an active force in the global governance processes for the Internet.

Chapter 6 examines the first of the two major post-WSIS institutions, which is the UN GAID. GAID was designed as an innovative mechanism to enable private sector leadership, and multistakeholder involvement in addressing the plethora of follow-up issues emerging from the Tunis WSIS. Chaired by Intel CEO Craig Barrett, and holding its first meeting in Silicon Valley, the GAID came out of the gate as a distinctly different UN institution. It was clearly designed to encourage the private sector to become more involved in the global development agenda, and it spawned some interesting initiatives, the most successful of which was the Global Initiative for Inclusive Information and Communication Technologies (G3ICT). However, GAID barely made it through its first five-year mandate, and it has subsequently disappeared. This chapter examines what went right with GAID, and what went horribly wrong.

Next, Chap. 7 focuses on the other major post-WSIS institution, the IGF, and what it got right. Established simultaneously with GAID, the IGF took a different approach from the beginning. It did not attempt to privilege one stakeholder (i.e. the private sector) over another, but developed interesting governance and management mechanisms and policies. The combination of its MAG and the plethora of DCs, which were required to be multistakeholder, and which led to the submission of substantive sessions for its yearly meetings, has helped to stabilize the IGF. Further, its ability to handle very thorny issues, and weather the rocky shoals of the Snowden revelations and other highly sensitive matters has instilled within the IGF a level of legitimacy, perhaps beyond any other multistakeholder global governance body. Its initial five-year mandate was renewed for five years, and as a testament to its widely perceived value, in December 2015, the UN General Assembly, in its review of the IGF extended it for another ten years. However, the IGF is not without its detractors, and its self-inflicted wounds. The key arguments against the IGF are that it is a "talk shop" and that it does not really accomplish anything in that it has no formal output, or conference declaration. Moreover, some argue that it even though it is called the "Internet Governance" Forum, it does not really engage in any actual "Internet governance" functions. While this latter argument has a great deal of technical merit, and the former argument is also functionally accurate (unlike most UN conferences, there are no formal outcome documents from IGF), they both ignore the broader contributions the IGF can make to international regime formation for the Internet. The IGF was seen as a "New Hope" for multistakeholder Internet governance and has also been a catalyst for the formation and concomitant longevity of the GigaNet. GigaNet, formed just ahead of the IGF at a pre-conference meeting of the International Communication Association (ICA), used the occasion of the first IGF in Athens, to convene its first GigaNet Symposium. GigaNet has held an annual symposium at every subsequent IGF, and is now preparing for the 11th GigaNet Annual Symposium at IGF 11 in Guadalajara, Mexico, during the 11th IGF.

While, like WSIS itself, the IGF has spawned a number of transnational networks, working through its DC structure, Chap. 8 focuses on the degree to which the Civil Society IGC has evolved out of its WSIS origins, and has played an important role at the leading Transnational Advocacy Network in Internet governance. We look at the wide variety of policy preferences within the IGC, how they have evolved, how they are aligned with the DC structure of the IGF, and how it has structured itself to have a high level of policy legitimacy and relevance, including the close integration with GigaNet, which we see as playing the role of an epistemic community for the IGC. However, the IGC is not without substantial challenges, and challengers. This chapter also looks at the internal struggles of the IGC, some of which have led to defections from key civil society activists into new bodies like the Best Bits Coalition.

The book concludes in Part 4, where we look at the fundamental transformation currently under way in global Internet governance, and tries to present a summary of our arguments related to the future of TANs and their role in the multistakeholder global governance of the information society. Chapter 9 turns to the events that sent a shockwave through the global Internet governance ecosystem, collectively referred to as the "Snowden revelations" and their aftermath. That chapter starts with an overview of the extensive Internet surveillance program of the US National Security Agency (NSA), which was revealed by former NSA contractor Edward Snowden, who through his leaked documents was able to also show the level of corporate compliance with the NSA. As the extent of this electronic surveillance continued to be revealed, confirming what many had believed was occurring for many years, anger increased around the world. This anger was directed primarily at the USA, and the "caretaker" role it had been in since the Internet was developed in the labs of the US Defense Advanced Research Projects Agency (DARPA). As more and more revelations unfolded, the simmer became a slow boil, and then erupted into an explosion with Brazilian President Dilma Rouseff using her speech at the UN General Assembly to claim the USA had "violated international law." Most of the major organizations involved in the technical governance of the Internet met in Montevideo to issue a statement that a new set of principles and values and governance mechanisms (a new "international regime") needed to be developed to make Internet governance more global and independent. This was followed by Brazil hosting the *NetMundial*—the Global Multistakeholder Meeting on the Future of Internet Governance from 23 to 24 April 2014 in São Paulo, Brazil. NetMundial was highly influential for a number of reasons. It mobilized the global multistakeholder community to reimagine what the Internet governance ecosystem could look like and to formally submit recommendations for new principles and values for this global community. Also, since it was driving to a specific conclusion and conference outcome, NetMundial demonstrated what a multistakeholder meeting might look like as an alternative to the IGF, with governments standing in line for their five minutes to speak, just like civil society, academia, the business community, and the technical community. Ultimately, it was the proposition by the European

Union that the USA had lost the trust of the global community in its role as caretaker of the Internet, and its assertion that the USA needed to "do something to regain the trust of the world" that was the final straw. On 14 March 2014, the NTIA of the Department of Commerce issued a set of guidelines to the global Internet community. These guidelines outlined the conditions under which the US government would turn over one of the core Internet governance responsibilities known collectively as the Internet Assigned Numbers Authority (IANA) functions to a new global multistakeholder body, and the requirements of that body. For many in the global Internet community, especially those in the Global South, and in much of civil society, this was the "holy grail," and like that ancient relic, something they thought they would never see. However, it was then incumbent upon the international community to meet those requirements, and the IANA Transition Committee was formed. After two years of deliberations, the committee has finally delivered a plan, with a global consensus, that meets the conditions set forth by the NTIA. That plan now awaits final action by the US Congress and the Obama Administration.

Chapter 10 closes the book with a discussion of what we have learned about multistakeholder participation in global governance for the Information society broadly, and for the Internet in particular. It discusses the critical role of TANs as a model for multistakeholder partnerships that can avoid making civil society simply pawns in this process. The chapter explores the factors that enabled some networks to persist and thrive, while others failed, and sees linkages with epistemic communities and the use of ICTs as critical to network effectiveness. We see how these networks enable civil society to harness its enormous intellectual resources, institutional resources, and energy to enable sustained engagement in multiple global policy processes.

We conclude the chapter and the book by summarizing what we have found, make specific recommendations for civil society and the UN to harness the potential of TANs as a model for multistakeholder global governance, especially through the use of what we call "Policy Collaboratories," and lay out an agenda for future research.

CHAPTER 2

Contending Perspectives on Multistakeholder Global Governance: Theory, Conceptual Framework, Data, and Methods

INTRODUCTION

In the preceding chapter, we took a whirlwind tour through the major developments in the emergence of the information society, and the evolution of efforts to involve civil society and non-state actors in the processes of decision-making for this complex, critical, and multi-layered domain of global governance. This chapter takes a similar tour in reviewing the relevant literature on contending perspectives of global governance and cooperation, and lays the conceptual foundation for how we understand these processes, and how they will be explored throughout this book.

In particular, we focus on the explanatory power we find in international regime theory and highlight the contributions it has made to our understanding of global governance. Here, we propose a critical reformulation of regime theory, which takes into consideration the important role of transnational networks of non-state actors, especially in this historic era of globalization and an information society. In addition, we explain the concept of "conference diplomacy," and describe its evolution into our current conception of *Multistakeholder Conference Diplomacy*. In doing so, we highlight the contribution civil society organizations are theorized to contribute to a global governance process. Finally, we discuss the concept of Transnational Advocacy Networks (TANs) and describe the role they might play in international regime formation and multistakeholder conference diplomacy, particularly as a vehicle for stimulating a convergence of

© The Author(s) 2017
D.L. Cogburn, *Transnational Advocacy Networks in the Information Society*, Information Technology and Global Governance,
DOI 10.1057/978-1-137-48361-4_2

ideas related to principles, norms, and values of a particular issue area in international affairs.

This chapter ends with a brief discussion of the diverse forms of data available for this study, and the multiple methodologies employed to understand these issues. Here, we highlight the voluminous qualitative and quantitative, primary and secondary data available for this study. For primary data, we include the 85-item multistakeholder panel survey of participants in both the first and second phases of WSIS, as well as interviews and focus groups with some of the members of various transnational advocacy networks, and participant observation at both summits and their preparatory processes, follow-on meetings of both the GAID and IGF, and nearly all the events discussed in the book. In terms of secondary data, we find a treasure trove of text-based data available for analysis, contained in websites for each of the conferences, preparatory meetings, and summits. These websites often include participant lists, policy recommendations/submissions. We also have access to numerous official and unofficial documents, including materials from the global stocktaking and evaluation processes of the IGF and a formal evaluation of GAID. We also have access to numerous public email archives of these groups.

Methodologies used to analyze this data include not only traditional descriptive and predictive statistical modeling, but also social network analysis, along with inductive and deductive text-mining techniques.

CONFRONTING THE ANARCHY PROBLEMATIQUE

Global Governance and International Cooperation

Our approach to global governance starts from an assumption of what is called the "Anarchy Problematique." The anarchy problematique is based on the reality that the international system is *national* in scope and consists of a set of anarchic nation-states possessing *de jure* sovereignty and equality, with a *de facto* imbalance in the distribution of power (represented by economic, political, technological, and informational resources). Within the Westphalian nation-state system, countries have nearly absolute control over their national population and geography.

Within this anarchic world-system, a sovereign nation-state can reasonably expect that other states and international organizations will not interfere in its internal affairs. However, this anarchic system of nation-states frequently confronts these transnational policy issues raising significant conflict between the global and the local. The problem is that many of the policy issues currently facing the world are *transnational* in scope, meaning that they go beyond the level of any individual nation-state. So, in a world comprised of sovereign and equal nation-states, and without a global govern*ment*, are we able to achieve any level of global govern*ance* of issues that are transnational in scope?

For example, as conceptualized by many scholars, the Information Society includes a range of ICTs policy issues including: (1) customs and taxation; (2) electronic payments; (3) uniform commercial code and dispute resolution; (4) intellectual property protection; (5) privacy and data protection; (6) security and encryption; (7) awareness building and trust; (8) technical standardization; (9) content development; (10) universal service; (11) labor and social impact; (12) human rights; (13) public and private partnerships; (14) infrastructure development and financing; (15) content development; and (16) many of the issues encapsulated by the politically charged term "Internet governance."

Since the 1960s, international relations scholars have studied problems surrounding the *anarchy problematique* and the evolution of global cooperation and global governance in the absence of a global government and tried to understand the underlying mechanisms that facilitate international cooperation and collaboration in global policy processes (Gourevitch 1978; Krasner 1983b; Keohane 1984; Axelrod 1985; Keohane and Nye 1989).

Achieving levels of coordination, cooperation and decision-making within this anarchic environment, especially on issues that are transnational in scope and importance, is one of the primary challenges of global governance in a globalizing world. *De jure* sovereignty means that no one state actor in the world-system can legally "force" any other state actor into action against its will, though various forms of power are frequently used to accomplish just this goal, weakening *de facto* sovereignty.

Several contributing factors have been identified, including economic power and military might (Keohane 1984; Keohane and Nye 1989), agenda setting (Schattschneider 1964; McCombs and Shaw 1972; Kingdon 1984), and most recently global policy or issue networks (Keck and Sikkink 1998; Slaughter 2001; Haufler 2001; Rischard 2002).

As Evans (2000) argues in this extended quote, the USA and its foreign policy elite provide some of the primary challenges to the development of global governance institutions.

The task of global governance is particularly difficult because it is opposed by a powerful current of elite ideology in the country that is economically, politically, and militarily hegemonic in the 'new world order' – the United States. This stream of elite ideology is both profoundly distrustful of any kind of public governance institutions and deeply apprehensive of anything that might reduce the absolute sovereignty of the United States itself. This creates a real dilemma for the more cosmopolitan, internationalist segments of the elite (everyone from Robert Rubin and the "Davos crowd" of transnational managers to traditional financial elites within the Republican party). They would like to have global governance which enforces those rules most central to profitability (like intellectual property rights) without having to worry about issues which relate to well-being, like labor standards. Yet, a narrow definition of what kind of governance these institutions must deliver risks ending up with no global governance institutions at all. A narrow definition puts progressives and a broad range of populists firmly into the opposing camp. Many ordinary citizens will always see their jobs and culture threatened by internationalist strategies. If progressive groups of the internationalist sort that are the focus of this discussion also come to define global governance institutions as unredeemably narrow, it is hard to see how the project is left with an untenably narrow political base. (Evans 2000, p. 238)

International Regime Theory

For more than three decades, international relations scholars have grappled with the question of the "anarchy problematique" and the evolution of cooperation at national, regional and global levels (see, *inter alia*, Keohane and Nye 1977; Krasner 1983b; Keohane 1984; Axelrod 1984). These theorists have attempted to understand how global governance and cooperation can occur in a world-system of "sovereign and equal" national states, and in the absence of a global government to make and enforce rules. International Regime theory has been one of the most resilient mental models for addressing this problem, and has been formulated from a wide variety of epistemological and scholarly traditions.

In 1983, a special issue of the journal *International Organization* attempted to build a consensus around the theoretical and applied approaches to International Regime theory. Here, Krasner (1983b) and his colleagues defined regimes as "sets of implicit or explicit principles, norms, rules and decision-making procedures around which actors' expectations converge in a given area of international relations." *Principles* are seen as beliefs of fact, causation, or rectitude; *Norms* are seen as standards of behavior defined in terms of rights and obligations; *Rules* are specific prescriptions or proscriptions for action; and *Decision-Making Procedures* are the prevailing practices for making and implementing collective choice (Krasner 1983b). More directly, international regimes are the "rules of the game" for a specific issue area within the world-system and the collective enforcement mechanisms for those rules.

There are three dominant schools in international regime theory: (1) liberal/neo-liberal; (2) realist/neo-realists and Marxist/neo-Marxist; (3) and what might be called (3) post-modernist. In the liberal/neo-liberal school, there is a focus on the importance of functions. Theorists working in this school, focus on the impact that international regimes have in the creation of peace and in reducing transaction costs. These scholars argue that while regime actors to have self-interests, they are able to see the possibility of creating a global environment, where the majority of good can be created for the majority of actors through cooperation. In this approach, no single actor would get the exact regime that it wants, but that through interdependent cooperation it can achieve enough of its aims, while allowing other actors to achieve a sufficient amount of their aims. This approach is designed to create an international regime based on peace and stability.

Those theorists working within the realist/neo-realist and Marxist/neo-Marxist schools tend to focus on the importance of power in the formation and maintenance of international regimes. These global power dynamics can take the form of hegemonic states against weaker ones, or of a global power-wielding corporate elite against the unorganized global working class.

Finally, there is a school of regime theory that might be considered post-modernist. Theorists working in this tradition focus on the formation of cognitive frameworks and the ability to set global agendas through the use of media and other tools. These scholars see the regime formation dynamics as based on what forces can influence the acceptable forms of problem definition and solution. These forces form the "epistemic community" for that particular issue area in international affairs, and creates its "accepted" belief system.

In a slight modification of the classic definition of international regimes posited by Krasner (1983b), international regimes are represented by the convergence of multistakeholder (e.g., governments, private sector, and civil society) expectations around the principles, values, norms, rules and decision-making procedures in a specific area, or interrelated areas, of international affairs such as telecommunications (Cowhey 1990).

Rittberger (1995) argues that international regime theory has maintained exceptional stability and integrative capabilities within the discipline of international relations, and includes insights from international political economy, comparative politics, and other areas in world affairs. Subsequently, several scholars have improved upon the approach. For example, Hasenclever et al. (2000) enhanced its explanatory power by integrating the diverse strands of international regime theory. Each of these strands has articulated and defended a distinct view on the origins, stability, and consequences of international regimes. As a result, over the last several decades, scholars have documented the emergence and efficacy of international regimes in a variety of issue areas including: shipping, air transport, post, atomic energy and weapons, environmental issues, the global "commons" (e.g., the high seas and outer space), diamonds and telecommunications.

However, there are some compelling problems with the use of international regime theory that are addressed in its use for this study including: (1) its overreliance on the state as the primary unit of analysis; (2) a focus on establishing agreements rather than on compliance with them; (3) insufficient attention to the role of agenda setting; (4) an inadequate understanding of the mechanisms through which knowledge and information influence the emergence and maintenance of regimes; and finally (5) insufficient attention to the global power dynamics that are at play in contemporary regime formation processes.

Multistakeholder Global Governance

States are clearly the central players in regime formation. Getting governments in both developed and developing countries involved in any particular international issue area is a critically important step in regime formation (Shiffman 2003). However, many regime theorists have approached the state as a unitary actor, often ignoring subnational fractures and domestic contestation to the policy preferences articulated by the state as it participates in international conferences in the "name" of its citizens. Additionally, the heavy focus on state actors ignores the increasingly important role played by non-state actors, namely the private sector and the international civil society sector.

As such, the state-centric approach often misses many of the most interesting political and economic dynamics occurring during these policy processes at national, regional, and global levels. In contrast, some contemporary regime theorists argue for the active inclusion of non-state and transnational actors (corporations, NGOs, policy and issue networks) in regime analyses (Haufler 2001). Mayer et al. (1995) argue that, "if international non-governmental organizations interacting in an issue area agree upon principles, norms, rules, and decision-making procedures in order to regulate their interactions, one can speak of transnational regimes" (p. 404).

Some scholars are exploring the potential impact of this increasing civil society involvement in these global policy formulation processes. Lipschutz (1996) argues that global governance will be changed fundamentally through the involvement of an emerging global civil society.

While increasing calls for "multistakeholder" global governance are opening the doors to many of these international conferences for elite actors from civil society organizations and developing countries as *partners* in a global development process (WEF 2012), some evidence suggests that they continue to be *pawns* in these processes rather than true partners (Maclean, et al. 2002; Cogburn 2004a, c). Engaging effectively in these global governance processes is difficult for most governments (especially for developing countries), and even the most seasoned private sector actors. It is even more challenging, however, for civil society organizations and developing countries working with limited financial and institutional resources.

Finding effective means to integrate developing countries and civil society organizations into a system of multistakeholder global governance for the information society is proving to be a major challenge. Developing country and civil society stakeholders participating in these "multistakeholder" processes have frequently formed themselves into transnational social movements (Smith et al. 1997), or what Keck and Sikkink (1998) call "transnational advocacy networks," and what Peter Evans (2000) collectively calls "transnational networks." Evans (2000) believed that the increased penetration of ICTs around the world would lay the foundation for resurgence of global organizing via transnational networks. Further, he believed that these transnational networks could serve as counterweights to the existing corporate-dominated globalization processes, what he calls a "counter-hegemonic" globalization or "globalization from below" (Evans 2000).

These transnational networks, says Evans, may even provide a model of "new ways of uniting the world's workers" (Evans 2000).

Evans argues that, "It is too soon to say what the long run effects of these transnational efforts will be, but it is certainly time to pay more attention to them. Trying to think more systematically about what can be accomplished by 'acting globally' and how it might be most effectively accomplished should be a priority (Evans 2000)."

These new actors and their diverse interests are eroding the convergence that once existed within the ITR and are changing the character of global ICT policy negotiations. Each of these transnational advocacy networks may hold differing visions about the continued growth and evolution of cyberinfrastructure, creating additional tension in the development of an information society (Cogburn 2002, 2003a, 2004). Even when developing countries and civil society organizations are allowed to participate, they frequently have limited impact on the outcome of the conference (Global Contract 2003; MacLean 2003; Cogburn in-press). Frustration with these processes has even led to drastic actions by developing countries in some fora, such as the walkout from the WTO Ministerial Meeting in Cancun (*The Economist* 2003). Neither developed- nor developing-country interests are well served by this continued imbalance in the world-system (Sachs 1999; Soros 1998, 2002).

TRANSNATIONAL ADVOCACY NETWORKS

Numerous scholars have attempted to understand how civil society actors are engaging with these global governance processes, working in what some scholars refer to as "policy-actor networks" (Slaughter 2001; Bockman and Eyal 2002) and others call "transnational advocacy networks" (Kirk and Sikkink 1998; Betsill and Bulkeley 2004). These networks are a key source of integrating non-state knowledge, expertise, and innovation into the international decision-making process. The knowledge and expertise of these non-state actors is seen as even more critical because of the frequent turnover of personnel from nation-states participating in the global governance process.

Of the ideas for the involvement of global civil society in global policy processes, one of the most resilient has been the concept of Transnational Advocacy Networks (TANS) which emerged out of the seminal work of Keck and Sikkink (1998). A TAN is defined as "networks of activists, distinguishable largely by the centrality of principled ideas or values in motivating their formation" (Kick and Sikkink 1998). Some analysts of transnational advocacy networks argue that such organizational structures have three defining characteristics: (1) the centrality of values or principled ideas; (2) the belief that individuals can make a difference; (3) the creative use of information; and (4) the employment by nongovernmental actors of sophisticated political strategies in targeting their campaigns (Keck and Sikkink 1998, p. 2).

WORLD SUMMITS, INTERNATIONAL CONFERENCES, AND GLOBAL GOVERNANCE

Global governance for ICTs is being driven by an interrelated set of formal and informal, public and private international conferences, convened by a range of institutions. International conferences can serve as a primary location for the contestation of the principles, values, and norms of an emerging international regime. For example, in ICT, contestation for ideas involves an interrelated set of ICT policy processes that revolve around a complex set of formal and informal institutions, including such diverse public and private organizations as the ITU, WTO, World Intellectual Property Organization (WIPO), Organization for Economic Cooperation and Development (OECD), and nongovernmental organizations like World Economic Forum (WEF), GIIC, Global Business Dialogue on Electronic Commerce (GBDe, and the ICANN.

Each of these organizations is involved with various international conferences, which have become the primary locations for the vigorous contestation of principles, values, norms, rules, and decision-making procedures that are the core of any international regime. At these international conferences, policy-actors attempt to represent the interests of their various constituencies bringing to bear their knowledge and expertise on final conference outcomes (e.g., declarations, agreements, and statements). Collectively, these conference outcomes are facilitating the emergence of a new regime for the global governance of ICTs.

Levy et al. (1995) argue that international organizations are "arenas for conference diplomacy," seeing these organizations and the international conferences they organize as mechanisms for the pursuit of common goals and as players in the creation and operation of international regimes.

However, within this domain, World Summits and other United Nations global conferences are still unique (Schechter 2001, 2005). Not only does the convening power of the United Nations encourage some of the best and brightest minds around the world to participate in the conference activities and preparatory processes, but it can also produce outcomes that are—in theory—binding internationally on its nation-state participants. As such, United Nations World Summits and international conferences are preceded by heavily drawn out negotiation processes.

From Conference Diplomacy to Multistakeholder Conference Diplomacy

When the ideas related to United Nations conference diplomacy first emerged (Kaufmann 1968; Schechter 2001, 2005), they were clearly focused on nation-states. These early ideas were basically designed to help prepare new international civil servants to work effectively on behalf of their national capital when serving on a delegation to an international conference (Kaufmann 1989) and to help scholars understand their importance (Schechter 2001, 2005). Kauffman was interested in questions such as the following: How would they get an initiative adopted at the international conference? What might cause their proposal to be accepted or rejected by other delegations? How is a delegation composed? What is a permanent mission? What effect can the conference president have? What are the rules of the conference? What is the impact of the secretariat? Schechter wanted to help us understand the role of these conferences in international order, and how that role was being changed by information technology.

However, an ongoing series of events has pushed for the more active involvement of non-state actors in the processes of the United Nations conferences and events. Going back to "Agenda 21" and the Earth Summit in 1992, the UN created the "Major Groups" Framework as a vehicle for the active engagement of organized groups of: (1) women; (2) children and youth; (3) farmers; (4) indigenous peoples; (5) NGOs; (6) trade unions; (7) local authorities; (8) science and technology; and (9) business and industry (UNGA 47/191 and UNGA 66/288). Although there are problems with this approach to involvement of non-state actors, including the fact that substantial groups—such as the more than one billion persons with disabilities—are left out of the process, many UN conferences and events have used this major groups framework, especially those related to environment and sustainable development, including the CSD, United Nations Environment Program (UNEP), and (United Nations Framework Convention on Climate Change (UNFCCC). Nonetheless, several subsequent UN conferences have reified this approach, including the newly created HLPF to oversee the 2030 Sustainable Development Agenda.

However, there were also important steps taken to further broaden out and enhance participation of non-state actors in UN conferences and events, especially with the creation of the UN WSIS and its explicit multistakeholder approach. This multistakeholder approach is seen as critical, in part, because of the tremendous knowledge base and institutional memory held constant within civil society.

Knowledge and Ideas in International Conferences

However, if international conferences are the location where contestation occurs and hopefully consensus emerges, how exactly is this consensus generated? One of the major deficiencies in the use of regime theory, and the one on which we place the greatest emphasis in this project, is the insufficient accounting of the mechanisms through which knowledge and information influence the erosion, establishment, and maintenance of regimes. Previous research has shown that epistemic communities can work to promote the convergence of knowledge and interpretive schemas (Haas 1980, 1990; Adler 1992). While the earliest definition of an "epistemic community" comes from Foucault (1973), a more appropriate definition comes later from Haas et al. (1977). They argue that an epistemic community is, "a network of individuals and groups who are able to influence the future by virtue of their shared specialized knowledge of certain crucial phenomena." Individuals belonging to an epistemic community often "seek to use their knowledge as a way of organizing cognition collectively" (Haas et al. 1977, p. 38).

As these transnational policy-actor networks engage in the conference diplomacy that characterizes these international conferences, they often seek to mobilize knowledge and information to support their policy objectives. As Haas (1992, p. 4) suggests, "Epistemic communities are one possible provider of this sort of information and advice. As demands for such information arise, networks or communities of specialists capable of producing and providing the information emerge and proliferate. The members of a prevailing community become strong actors at the national and transnational level as decision makers solicit their information and delegate responsibility to them."

Knowledge is critical to regime formation. It helps to create the foundation for international cooperation by, "illuminating complex interconnections that were not previously understood. Knowledge not only enhances the prospects for convergent state behavior, it also transcends 'prevailing lines of ideological cleavage'" (Haas 1980, pp. 367–368). While, Dimitrov (2003) argues that only consensual scientific knowledge, or information around which there is a sufficient consensus from scientists, scholars, and experts, has an impact on policy formulation, we see that where there is the collective acceptance of a "schema of interpretation" (supported by empirical data and theoretical explanations to provide support for alternatives), policy-makers pay attention (Haas et al. 1977; Shiffman 2003).

Epistemic communities are usually, but not always, directed at policy processes. Edwards (2001) has argued forcefully that elements of the open source software movement resemble epistemic communities, and have similar dynamics. He also argues that this community will soon get involved in policy processes moving them into a full-fledged epistemic community (Edwards 2001, p. 10).

These epistemic communities contribute to global governance through their direct and indirect influence of the dense transnational networks of policy-makers and issue stakeholders. For example, Adler (1992) argues that an epistemic community comprised of scholars from Harvard, MIT, and the RAND Corporation developed and promulgated the intellectual concept of "arms control" which served as the basis for the US negotiating position with the USSR that led to the signing of the 1972 ABM treaty.

Frequently, these epistemic communities are closely linked with what some scholars call "policy-actor networks" (Slaughter 2001; Bockman and Eyal 2002) and others call "transnational advocacy networks" (Kirk and Sikkink 1998; Betsill and Bulkeley 2004). These networks are a key source of integrating knowledge and bringing new ideas from epistemic communities into the international decision-making process.

Another way in which knowledge and information influence the regime formation process is through the ability to define terms, positions, and alternatives. This ability to define matters greatly in public policy processes (Kingdon 2002). As early as 1964, EE Schattschneider argued that "the definition of the alternatives is the supreme instrument of power" (Shattschneider 1964, p. 68). McCombs and Shaw (1972) introduced the term "agenda setting" into the political science and communications literature with their landmark study, of Chapel Hill, North Carolina. They preceded a range of studies mostly confirming the agenda-setting hypothesis. However, while this body of literature has grown, few scholarly studies have examined the effect of agenda setting in international relations (for two notable exceptions, see Keohane and Nye 1998; Soroka 2003). This study analyzes Phase I of WSIS as an agenda-setting moment, but also looks at the overall process of agenda setting within the summit.

As these policy-actors engage in the conference diplomacy that characterizes these international conferences, they often seek to mobilize knowledge and information to support their policy objectives. As Haas (1992, p. 4) suggests, "Epistemic communities are one possible provider of this sort of information and advice. As demand for such information arise, networks or communities of specialists capable of producing and providing the information emerge and proliferate. The members of a prevailing community become strong actors at the national and transnational level as decision makers solicit their information and delegates responsibility to them."

REFORMATION OF INTERNATIONAL REGIME THEORY: ALTERNATIVES AND POWER DYNAMICS

While international regime theory provides a very useful theoretical framework to help us understand this period of rapid transformation, there are some problems with its use (Strange 1982). In some cases, those that have used regime theory have approached the state as a unitary actor, and ignored domestic contestation to the regime formation processes.

Also, in most cases, there is a very heavy focus on state actors, at national, regional, and global levels. This focus ignores the increasingly important role played by non-state actors, at each of these levels, particularly by global non-governmental organizations representing the interest of the private sector. Also, there are often insufficient linkages between the processes of global economic restructuring and its influence on domestic actors and political-economic processes. Finally, there is often insufficient attention paid to the factors that affect "state autonomy," or the ability of the state to exercise *de facto* sovereignty.

In this study, we have primarily adopted the Krasner (1983b) approach to international regimes. This causes us to look at the issues of regime transformation, and the emergence of consensus in four critical areas: (1) principles and values; (2) norms; (3) rules; and (4) enforcement mechanisms. However, in our use of regime theory, we will also have an important focus on the impact of non-state actors in the regime formation process.

Out of this work on international regime theory, one of the broadest and most interesting conceptual mechanisms identified by these scholars has been the role of international regimes in the global governance of specific issue areas within international affairs (Gourevitch 1978a and b; Krasner 1983b) such as telecommunications (Cowhey 1990), the environment (Breitmeier et al. 2006), and ICTs (Cogburn 2003a). International conferences play a critical role, particularly those international conferences that bring together policy-actors from multiple sectors and involve them in formal and informal negotiations. These international conferences provide a location for contestation and convergence around the specific policy preferences that will shape the principles, values, norms, and rules of the emerging cyberinfrastructure regime (Cogburn 2004a). In a slight modification of the classic definition of international regimes posited by Krasner (1983b), international regimes here are represented by the convergence of multistakeholder (e.g., governments, private sector, and civil society) expectations around the principles, values, norms, rules and decision-making procedures in a specific area, or interrelated areas, of international affairs.

Of the multiple and complex institutional processes shaping the emergence of a new international regime to provide global governance for ICTs (Krasner 1983a, 1991; Cowhey 1990; Cogburn 2003a; Braman

2004), international conferences play a critical role, particularly those international conferences that bring together policy-actors from multiple sectors and involve them in formal and informal negotiations. These international conferences provide a location for contestation and convergence around the specific policy preferences that will shape the principles, values, norms, and rules of the emerging cyberinfrastructure regime (Cogburn 2004a).

However, it is clear that within these multistakeholder global policy processes such some actors are more "powerful" than others. Through various mechanisms, these powerful actors are able to secure more of their objectives and achieve higher levels of satisfaction in the process than are their less powerful counterparts. There have been numerous complaints from many sectors that developing countries and civil society organizations have not been able to successfully secure their specific policy objectives within the WSIS processes (Global Contract; Klein forthcoming; O'Sichorou 2004).

An obvious factor potentially influencing the level of power in an international conference is the socio-economic status of the country. However, are there more subtle factors affecting the perceived power of actors in these international ICT policy conferences? For example, within the study of international regimes, several scholars have highlighted the contributions to global governance made by various types of transnational networks (Evans 2000) characterized variously as transnational advocacy networks (Keck and Sikkink 1998); global policy networks (Slaughter 2001), global issue networks (Rischard 2002); policy-actor networks (Bockman and Eyal 2002), and epistemic communities (Haas et al. 1977; Haas 1980, 1990; Adler and Haas 1992; Adler 1992; Drake and Kalypso 1992). Perhaps some of these factors may have a significant impact on the ability of a policy-actor to influence the specific policy processes of an international ICT policy conference such as WSIS.

Finally, much of regime theory has ignored the importance of global power dynamics in regime formation processes. These issues include the impact of the size and diversity of delegations participating in these global policy processes, the personal relationships and networks (both public and private) as well as the financial, technological, and epistemic resources that the more powerful actors are able to bring to the table. Krasner (1991) attempts to deal with the limitations of regime theory arguing that the interests and relative power capabilities of the actors in each case can explain variations in outcomes of regime formation. Krasner (along with Keohane and others) points to the role that power can play in these international conference negotiations, including determining who may participate, determining what the rules are, and threatening to retaliate against other players in order to get their way. Our approach to international regime theory will take each of these criticisms into consideration. A stable and strong regime promotes the development of "agreements," rules, treaties, and cooperation in the particular area of international relations. We will include an analysis of these agreements in our study, but simply generating these agreements is insufficient for the existence of a regime. Some measure of compliance with these agreements must be developed to contribute to strengthening regime analysis (Checkel 2001; Recchia 2002). In the theoretical model for this study, we address this deficiency by including a component of "post-conference follow-up" to gauge compliance with the emerging regime.

CONCEPTUAL FRAMEWORK FOR THE BOOK

Drawing from the literature above, the conceptual framework for this book has primarily adopted the Krasner (1983) approach to international regimes. This causes us to look at the issues of regime transformation, and the emergence of consensus in four critical areas: (1) principles and values; (2) norms; (3) rules; and (4) enforcement mechanisms. However, we also have a focus on the epistemic community, and on the role of global non-state actors in the formation of these regime components.

We see transnational advocacy networks (TANS) as key vehicles for international regime formation. They have the potential to capitalize on enhanced opportunities provided for civil society engagement in global decision-making processes and to engage in multistakeholder conference diplomacy to help facilitate a convergence of ideas and expectations related to the principles, norms, and values related to the GIS. The hypothesized factors affecting the effectiveness of these transnational advocacy networks include use of information and communication technologies to help facilitate communication and collaboration, high levels of collaboration readiness (including high levels of various types of trust within the network), alignment between leadership preferences and emergent leadership structures, formalized structures for decision-making and mechanisms for the regular turnover in leadership, and strong linkages with functional epistemic communities.

The analysis of regime formation processes that include transnational networks of both state and non-state actors has been neglected in the literature. By synthesizing the results of this literature review, we are able to develop a theoretical framework that promotes a more complete analysis of international regimes and allows us to capture more of the actual regime formation dynamics. Based on the preceding literature the following theoretical model, presented as Figure 2.1, provides an illustration of these concepts. The actual model tested in the quantitative analysis of this study is a simplified version of this larger theoretical model (the multiple regression models attempt to predict perceived policy power based on membership in a policy network, while controlling for demographic variables and other covariates, and while exploring the moderating impact of linkages with epistemic communities).

DEFINITIONS

Epistemic Communities

Epistemic communities are networks of individuals and groups of multiple disciplines possessing expert specialized knowledge of certain crucial phenomena, who work in knowledge-oriented "invisible communities" that share a primary commitment to a common epistemic causal model and a common set of political values and work to influence public policy through active advocacy for those political values (formulated from Haas et al. 1977; Holzner and Marx 1979; Haas 1980, 1990). In the data set, this variable (EPIS_MEM) is measured by asking the respondent: "to what extent do you agree or disagree that you work in concert with other experts in your field to disseminate your ideas to the global ICT policy community?" The options are a five-point scale (where 1 = strongly disagree and 2 = strongly agree).

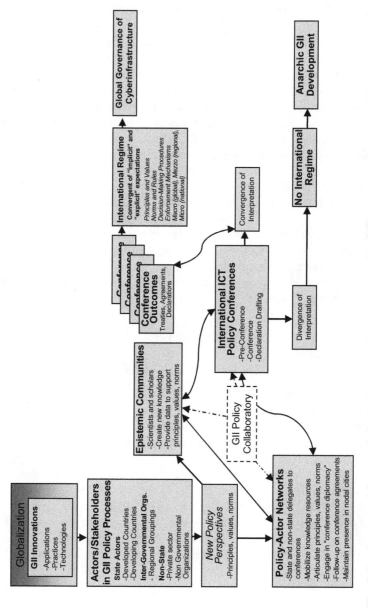

Fig. 2.1 Conceptual framework for TAN involvement in multistakeholder global governance

Policy-actors

Policy-actors are delegates to international conferences and international organizations exercising leadership through their representation of a state (both developed and developing countries), the private sector enterprise, and non-governmental organizations. All of the participants in the study are considered to be "policy-actors."

Transnational Policy-actor Networks

Policy-actor networks are dense transnational networks of policy-makers and non-state issue stakeholders (drawn from Bockman and Eyal 2002; Slaughter 2001) interacting as delegates at elite international conferences where they mobilize knowledge resources in an attempt to bring about convergence of interpretive schemas (principles and values) among various actors in the process through international "conference diplomacy" (Levy et al. 1995). In the data set, this variable (GPN_MEM) is measured by first giving the respondent the following definition of a Global Policy Network: "a Global Policy Network is ...." Then the respondent is asked, "based on the preceding definition, are you currently a member of a 'Global Policy Network' for information and communications technologies?" There was a binary response option (where 1 = no and 2 = yes).

International Policy Conferences

International policy conferences are international meetings that come in a variety of flavors based on the degree of formality (formal x informal), resource commitment (optional x mandatory), and type of final agreement (binding x non-binding). At the formal end of the spectrum, there are international conferences that formulate formal rules, adopt treaties and agreements. Slightly less formal are those international conferences that create non-binding principles and values, and promote the formation of international norms. These conferences are mostly organized by formal intergovernmental organizations (e.g., ITU or WTO). However, highly influential non-state actors are now organizing many important international conferences (e.g., GIIC, GBDe, and the World Economic Forum—WEF).

International ICT Policy Conference

An international ICT policy Conference is one that addresses the multiple social and technical policy issues around the development and use of information and communications technologies. WSIS is an example of an international ICT policy conference.

Conference Outcomes

At the close of an international conference, there are identifiable conference outcomes. These outcomes represent the "convergence of interpretation" that the policy-actor networks sought to achieve. These conference outcomes can be formal (treaties, agreements), semiformal (conference declarations), or informal (chair's conclusions or conference summary). Some conferences have a combination of these outcomes. Divergent interpretations are almost never included in the conference outcomes—with the rare occasion of publishing dissenting conclusions or stakeholder conclusions. Within the WSIS process, there were two primary conference outcomes to be considered in this study: (1) the *WSIS Declaration of Principles*; and (2) the *WSIS Action Plan*.

International (or Global) Regime

The most simple, consensus definition of an international regime, is "sets of implicit or explicit principles, norms, rules and decision-making procedures around which actors' expectations converge in a given areas of international relations" (Krasner 1983b). International conferences such as WSIS can help to create an international regime through their role in facilitating the convergence of interpretation of policy-actors about these issue areas. However, our definition of international regimes goes further, to include the convergence of expectations among multistakeholder (e.g., governments, private sector, and civil society) expectations around the principles, values, norms, rules and decision-making procedures in a specific area, or interrelated areas, of international affairs. We so appreciate the role of non-state actors that there is a preference to refer to these as global regimes, rather than international regimes.

Perceived Policy Power

Within an international conference, policy power is generally seen as the ability for a given policy-actor to achieve its stated or unstated objectives. However, we are interested also in perceptions of self-efficacy within this environment. As such, our definition of "perceived policy power" is the degree to which a policy-actor feels that their ideas are influential within the process (IDEAINFL), and to which their organization was successful in getting specific language into the policy process (ORGSUCC), and to which they feel they have sufficient knowledge and information to influence the process (SUFINFO) and to which they believe they have influenced to two conference outcome documents, the WSIS Declaration of Principles (DP_IMPAC) and WSIS Action Plan (AP_IMPAC). Each of these variables is measured on a five-point scale (where 1 = lowest and 2 = highest). A detailed description of how "perceived policy power" (POLPOWER) is used as a dependent variable in this study is given below under the methodology section.

DELIMITATIONS

While the larger *Pawns to Partners* initiative will include the analysis of ten clusters of major global ICT policy processes (including WTO, ICANN, WIPO, etc.), this study will focus only on WSIS. Of specific interest are the major variables of policy-actor networks, epistemic communities, and perceived policy power (all as defined above). We will also explore the role of potentially important intervening variables (e.g. age, education, income, experience, trust, and policy focus). While other variables are present in these processes, they will not be studied at this time.

DATA AND METHODS

There is an interesting corollary to studying transnational advocacy networks in the GIS; they produce a voluminous amount of qualitative digital data. This project employed a concurrent mixed-method design. Each chapter in the book benefits from these diverse data sources and uses a slightly different methodology, with some overlap from chapter to chapter. Here, we highlight the voluminous qualitative and quantitative, primary and secondary data available for this study. For those readers not interested in the details of the data collection, you may want to skip ahead to Chap. 3.

OVERVIEW OF MIXED-METHODOLOGY FOR THIS BOOK

This study is part of a larger research program called, *"From Pawns to Partners: Policy Collaboratories and Their Impact on the Global Governance of Cyberspace."* From *Pawns to Partners* is a longitudinal mixed-method study of the role of ICTs in the global governance of ICTs. The concurrent mixed-method design for this study has been chosen in order to allow us to develop a deeper understanding of the multiple and complex processes of global cyberinfrastructure governance by facilitating the convergence of broad numeric trends from quantitative approaches with the in-depth detail of qualitative techniques. This approach will also allow us to explore the views and perceptions of participants in these global information policy processes from both developed and developing countries. This phase in the study continues the analysis of this rather large and rich data set. Four primary data collection methods were used in the study: (1) a survey of global ICT policy leaders; (2) participant observation; (3) interviews; and (4) computer-assisted content analysis of archival research.

Sites/Participants

The site for much of this study was the United Nations-sponsored and ITU-organized WSIS, along with its formal and informal preparatory processes, and the meetings of its follow-up mechanisms—the GAID and the IGF. WSIS was scheduled in two phases (Geneva 2003; Tunis 2005) and has been purposefully selected for study as an exemplar of the multistakeholder international conference important to the global governance of cyberinfrastructure described above. The broad participants of the study, especially of our international survey of ICT policy leaders, were the registered delegates to the WSIS and its preparatory processes from four sectors: (1) governments (both developed and developing); (2) private sector; (3) civil society; and (4) intergovernmental organizations. These delegates were engaged in discussions and negotiations about the fundamental principles, values, norms, rules, decision-making, enforcement, and awareness-raising mechanisms for many of the socio-technical and politico-economic aspects of the development of a GIS.

For primary quantitative data, we include the 85-item multistakeholder panel survey of participants in both the first and second phases of WSIS, as well as interviews and focus groups with some of the members of various transnational advocacy networks, and participant observation at both summits and their preparatory processes, follow-on meetings of both the GAID and IGF, and nearly all the events discussed in the book. In terms of secondary data, we find a treasure trove of text-based data available for analysis, contained in websites for each of the conferences, preparatory meetings, and summits. These websites often include participant lists, policy recommendations/submissions. We also have access to numerous official and unofficial documents, including materials from the global stocktaking and evaluation processes of the IGF and a formal evaluation of GAID. We also have access to numerous public email archives of these groups. To capitalize on all this quantitative and qualitative data, the study employed a mixed-method data analysis tool called the Provalis ProSuite (http://provalisresearch.com/). This tool, which includes three modules: (1) QDA Miner—a CAQDAS package; (2) WordStat—a text-mining package; and (3) SimStat—a statistical analysis package, allowed us to combine all the data from the study.

Survey Research

A survey of global ICT policy leaders was conducted by the principal investigator from 24 November 2003 to 29 January 2004 using a commercially available web-based survey tool (www.surveymonkey.com). The survey was pilot tested in person by a convenience sample of delegates during Prepcom 3 in September, 2003. Numerous modifications to the survey were made based on the pilot test and observation of the participants completing the survey. A sampling frame was developed from the published lists of participants to the three WSIS Preparatory Committee meetings (Prepcom 1, Prepcom, 2, Prepcom, 3, Prepcom 3a) in Geneva and the ad hoc Content and Themes Meeting (Paris). From this initial sampling frame ($N = 3190$), those delegates with missing email addresses ($n = 751$) were removed, yielding a smaller frame

(N = 2439). In the first automated attempt to create the mailing list, all duplicate addresses were removed (n = 414), with the computer randomly selecting which of the duplicates would be kept. Also, several of these addresses were structurally invalid (n = 16). It was possible to repair some of these addresses (n = 8) based on obvious typographical errors, such as transposed characters and add them to the frame. Several more (n = 5) were additional duplicates, one was structurally invalid, and two were incomprehensible. The remaining structurally invalid email address was fixed and added, resulting in a smaller (N = 2018) but cleaner sampling frame.

The final survey was sent out to this frame on Monday, 24 November 2003, in English (with a brief statement in Spanish and French on the importance of linguistic diversity and an apology for the English-only survey). However, a substantial number of addresses in the frame were invalid (n = 331) and were returned. A database was created that included data for those delegates that were sent the invitation, and those that never received the invitation (based on invalid email addresses and returned mail) which yielded our final actual sampling frame (N = 1687). This data set allowed us to calculate an accurate response rate, as well as allowing us to analyze the specific characteristics of the non-responders. The database was cleaned extensively by the principal investigator, one doctoral and one master's student. One recurring problem noted in the data cleaning that yielded the bounced back email invitations was transposed characters. If we had caught these problems early enough, some of them could have been addressed. For example, we could have included these corrected addresses in the reminder email sent out (on 16 December 2003). However, since the data were only cleaned in February when the survey was already closed, we decided against sending a third reminder.

Of those ICT policy leaders contacted, a substantial number (n = 322) responded, resulting in an acceptable response rate (19 %) for a web-based elite survey (Sproull 1986; Kittleson 1995; Nucifora 2002; Fricker and Schonlau 2002; Drizin 2003; Alvarez et al. 2003). The overwhelming majority of these respondents (n = 313; 97 %) agreed to participate in the survey, with a very small number (n = 9) of "purposeful non-responders," meaning those who took time to go to the website and answered "No" to the question on the consent form regarding participation in the survey. One reminder invitation was sent out to the non-responders on Monday, 16 December 2003. Finally, the study sample was compared to the final frame and was found to be closely correlated on key demographic variables (e.g., region, organizational type, and gender) giving us a high level of confidence in the survey data.

The survey contained a total of 83 questions (both open-ended and closed-ended), including three important nested components based on skip logic/conditional questions. The average respondent was asked 58 questions. The average civil society respondent was asked 65 questions. In addition to individual demographic measures (age, gender, education, training, income, region, race/ethnicity, and language) and organizational characteristics (organizational size and type), the survey included a range of important measures such as, existing levels of trust, experience with ICT tools, levels of satisfaction and success in the WSIS process, experience with ICT policy processes, participation in policy networks, and use and identification of epistemic resources.

Participant Observation

The principal investigator of the project traveled to Geneva from September 9 to 29, 2003 and again from 10 November 2003 to 14 November 2003 to attend the Third Preparatory Commission (Prepcom 3) for WSIS and the Resumed Prepcom 3a as a registered civil society delegate, accredited under International Possibilities Unlimited (IPU), a partner organization to the study. IPU is an international nongovernmental organization in consultative status with the ECOSOC. He also attended the actual Summit from December 7 to 14 with a team of four doctoral and graduate student researchers from the University of Michigan, registered with ORBICOM, the UNESCO International Network of Chairs and Associates in Communication.

As a registered delegation for Prepcom 3, Prepcom 3a, and the Summit, we were allowed complete access to the conference site, all plenary sessions, public meetings, civil society and business bureau meetings, the cybercafe, and limited participation in the private working group meetings (observers were limited to the first five minutes). For the purposes of the study, it was important to engage in observation of the so-called "Frontstage" or the formal public activities, as well as those informal and private activities that occur "Backstage" (Goffman 1959). Frontstage observations were made of the plenary meetings of the Prepcom, as well as the plenary meetings of the civil society and the Civil Society Bureau meetings. Backstage observations included the coffee shops, meals, and cybercafe. Notes from these observations were included in a database for qualitative analysis.

Interviews

During Prepcom 3 and subsequently, 21 delegates representing each sector (government, civil society, and private sector) participated in informal interviews. These interviews were loosely based on the draft interview protocol developed for use at the WSIS conference in December and were designed to generate information about the character of civil society participation in the WSIS preparatory processes, including the substantive issues and debates on policy alternatives. Notes from these interviews were also included in the database for qualitative analysis.

Archival Research (Content Analysis)

As a registered delegation, the principal investigator was allowed access to all of the official documents of Prepcom 3, Prepcom 3a, and the Summit, as well as all of the documents made available to delegates by other delegates and interested parties. Numerous documents were collected and added to the database for qualitative analysis. Most important among these documents were the initial and subsequent drafts of the *WSIS Declaration of Principles, WSIS Plan of Action,* and *WSIS Rules and Procedures.* In addition, the entire archive of the civil society public plenary (5 MB) and bureau (1 MB) as well as numerous public documents were added to the database for qualitative analysis. The initial database covered a ten-month period from 13 March 2003 to 13 December 2003, and at this point only focused on content in English (other languages such as Spanish and French will be analyzed in subsequent publications). The initial cleaning (removal of images and file transfer encoding) and organization of the data yielded 38 text files, 148 free nodes, and 116 tree nodes. Appendix A presents the initial axial coding schema used in the content analysis. In the presentation of data from these public archives, all identifying information has been removed (although active participants in these processes may certainly recognize themselves).

In addition to these WSIS archival resources, the post-WSIS processes have yielded just as much publicly available digital data, if not more. We are able to access the websites, email archives, meeting notes, chat logs, recordings, meeting transcripts and more from each of the meetings under review in this study.

PART 2

Global Regime Restructuring: Telecom, Internet Governance and the Information Society

CHAPTER 3

From NWICO to Global eCommerce: Telecommunications Restructuring and the GII

INTRODUCTION

As we discussed in Chap. 2, for more than three decades, international relations scholars have grappled with the question of the "anarchy problematique" and the evolution of cooperation at national, regional, and global levels (see, inter alia, Keohane and Nye 1977; Krasner 1983b; Keohane 1984; Axelrod 1984). These theorists have attempted to understand how global governance and cooperation can occur in a world system of "sovereign and equal" national states, and in the absence of global government to make and enforce rules. International regime theory has been one of the most resilient mental models for addressing this problem, and has been formulated from a wide variety of epistemological and scholarly traditions.

In 1983, a special issue of the journal *International Organization* attempted to build a consensus around the theoretical and applied approaches to the international regime theory. Here, Krasner (1983) and his colleagues defined regimes as "sets of implicit or explicit principles, norms, rules and decision-making procedures around which actors' expectations converge in a given area of international relations." *Principles* are seen as beliefs of fact, causation, or rectitude; *Norms* are seen as standards of behavior defined in terms of rights and obligations; *Rules* are specific prescriptions or proscriptions for action, and *Decision-Making Procedures*

© The Author(s) 2017
D.L. Cogburn, *Transnational Advocacy Networks in the Information Society*, Information Technology and Global Governance,
DOI 10.1057/978-1-137-48361-4_3

are the prevailing practices for making and implementing collective choice (Krasner 1983). More directly, international regimes are the "rules of the game" for a specific issue area within the world system and the collective enforcement mechanisms for those rules.

Further, Rittberger (1995) argues that international regime theory, while once thought to be a "passing fad," has maintained exceptional stability and integrative capabilities within the discipline of international relations, and included the insights from international political economy, security experts, comparative politics, and other areas in world affairs. He asserts that regime theory has become an increasingly important intellectual tool in European scholarly circles, especially in Germany and Scandinavia, and attempts in his work to "enhance integration and communication" among scholars of international regimes (Rittberger 1995).

Over these several decades, scholars around the world have documented the emergence and efficacy of international regimes in a wide variety of issue areas within the world system, including (1) international shipping; (2) international air transport; (3) international post; (4) international atomic energy and weapons; (5) international environmental issues; (6) global "commons" (e.g., the high seas and outer space); and even (7) commodities (e.g., diamonds). However, one of the oldest and most successful international regimes has been the International Telecommunications Regime (ITR) (Cowhey 1990).

Based on ITU and an epistemological community that supported the concepts of the preferred natural monopoly for telecommunications, and the "clubby" and "cartelized" relationships between ministries and officials of monopoly Post, Telegraph, and Telephone entities (PTTs), ITU officials (many of whom are former PTT officials), and a limited number of upstream suppliers to the PTT in the national capitals, the ITR was highly successful (Cowhey 1990; Freiden 1996). So successful was this regime that it emerged before international regime theory was in vogue and has been largely unchallenged until recent times.

However, it is this regime that is now facing tremendous transformative pressures as the historical processes of globalization and an Information Age continue to unfold. A wide range of social, political, economic, cultural, and technological factors are challenging the ITR and pressing for the emergence of a new regime. This new regime is based on the Internet, which uses global wireless and wired telecommunications networks as its backbone infrastructure. The ISOC, the ITU, and many others see the Internet as an information infrastructure that is the prototype of the much-vaunted Global Information Infrastructure (GII) (Jipguep 1995).

So, in this book, we see the successor to the ITR as the GII regime. We also see two possible variants of this regime emerging, one focused on an open, collaborative, development-oriented GIS, or one that focuses mostly on securing the technical and policy requirements for GEC and commercial uses of the Internet. Later we will characterize this as the GII/GIS versus the GII/GEC debate.

What are the emerging "principles, values, and norms" of this new regime, and what stakeholder interests are best represented by them? What will be the rules of this new regime, and in what international body will they be based? Who wins and who loses from this emerging regime? And what can be done to influence the direction of this regime to ensure the development of a more just and equitable GIS? These are the research questions that this chapter seeks to address.

Over the past decade tensions between diverse multistakeholder interests as well as a series of social, political, and economic factors has seriously eroded the ITR and a new regime for the governance of cyber infrastructure is emerging (Cogburn 2002, 2003a, 2004a, b; Braman 2004). Existing literature on global governance generates two rival approaches to explain this regime emergence. One explanation, which is realist and neo-realist in orientation, focuses on the role of power and national interests. Another approach, which is constructivist in orientation, focuses on the role of knowledge and ideas in reducing transaction costs and facilitating cooperation. In previous research, I leaned toward the constructivist side in developing a theoretical model for the global governance of cyber infrastructure in which international policy conferences play a critical role in regime formation by serving as the primary strategic location in which networks of policy-actors (Bockman and Eyal 2002) meet and organize their networks (Keck and Sikkink 1998), mobilize knowledge resources from epistemic communities (Haas 1990), and practice "conference diplomacy" (Young and Osherenko 1993) as they attempt to contest the convergence of principles, values, and norms of the emerging regime (Cogburn 2002, 2003). With some notable exceptions, the role of these international conferences has been underexamined in the scholarly literature (Dunn 1996; Weilemann 2000).

In analyzing the emerging cyber infrastructure regime, scholars have found two competing foci—maximizing social welfare and maximizing economic goals—and that policy-actors from developing countries have been far less effective participants in these processes than have those from developed countries (Cogburn 2003, 2004; Ó Siochrú 2004). In addition, there has been little empirical work done on the role of ICTs in facilitating the linkages between these various components, and the limitations facing developing countries and civil society organizations within these processes (MacLean et al. 2002; Markle 2002; Cogburn 2002, 2003; MacLean 2003). Keck and Sikkink (1998) have done an outstanding job of analyzing the causes, structure, growth, functioning, and efficacy of transnational advocacy networks. In addition, they have contributed to our understanding of the "boomerang effect," which is the strategy of some local NGOs, when direct access to their own state apparatus is blocked, to seek out international allies, through which they hope to pressure their own governments (Keck and Sikkink 1998, p. 12). This is a strategy used frequently in human rights domains. However, while they recognize the importance of "information politics" to network functioning, they have not systematically analyzed the strategic uses of collaborative ICTs within these networks.

Encouraging and facilitating higher levels of competence, participation, and ownership of these elite decision-making processes by developing countries and civil society organizations, requires us to develop a better understanding of the multiplicity of factors that currently limit their effective participation, and to suggest potential solutions that may address these limitations. Moreover, the inclusion of multiple stakeholders must go beyond simple calls for "increased participation and capacity development" and lead to far more than symbolic representation in conferences and meetings. These are major challenges confronting the global policymaking community in general, and particularly for those decision-makers involved in the formulation of the ICT policies, which lie at the heart of cyber infrastructure.

This historical period of ongoing globalization and development of the information society and information economy, all highly contested terms, is contributing to a transformation of the underlying structures of the global economy. Each sector of society is being affected by these changes, from global and multinational corporations, developed and developing countries, international organizations, nongovernmental and community based organizations, and other non-state actors. As with any major transformation, it is likely that there will be "winners" and "losers" in this restructuring, one that is likely to go beyond simply North–South divisions that may not line up neatly with the previously developed and developing country perspectives.

There are a number of responses to this transformation, including international conferences (and declarations), agreements, projects, and national, regional and global collaboration. This transformation is putting stress on existing mechanisms of global governance.

BIRTH (AND DEATH) OF THE NEW WORLD INFORMATION AND COMMUNICATION ORDER

In 1980, the UNESCO published *Many Voices, One World* also known as the MacBride Commission Report, named after the commission's Nobel Prize winning chair, Sean MacBride. The MacBride Commission Report is subtitled "Towards a new more just and more efficient world information and communication order," and lays the foundation for the NWICO. *Many Voices, One World* became known as one of its most controversial documents. This report followed more than a decade of scholarly and civil society debate focused on the substantial differential in power between so-called developed and developing countries in the ownership of the means of information and communication production and distribution, and called for action to address this imbalance.

The scholarly contributions on which NWICO was based date back to the mid-1960s and included analyses of the differential coverage of developed country events relative to coverage of events in the developing countries. This imbalance in coverage, argued these scholars, leads to a distorted view of events and the perceived importance of the developed versus the developing world (Schramm 1964) and that developing countries were being left out of ownership and decision-making processes for international communications infrastructure, even those that were set up ostensibly to benefit them (Schiller 1969).

These issues became part of the broader geopolitical debates in the Cold War, and were included in the agenda of the Nonaligned Movement (NAM), which is a group of mostly developing countries that are not formally aligned with or against any major power. UNESCO became a central location for these debates within the United Nations (UN). In addition to the lack of representation of developing countries in media content, NWICO included a focus on emerging technologies, and the dual uses of new ICTs for military as well as commercial purposes (these issues will emerge again several times in this book, including in Chap. 8 when we discuss the Snowden revelations of the extent of corporate compliance with surveillance of Internet users by the United States NSA). It highlighted the imbalance in location of technologies such as mainframe computers and data centers, and the strategic and military implications of access to satellites and broadcasting capabilities.

NWICO stimulated the imagination of progressive media rights activists around the world, and served as a catalyst for transnational civil society activists right up to the WSIS and beyond (especially as we will see in Chap. 5, the CRIS Campaign). It also led in 1984, to the USA under President Ronald Regan, withdrawing from UNESCO, citing the "politicization" of UNESCO in "virtually every subject it deals with" and that it "has exhibited hostility toward the basic institutions of a free society, especially a free market and a free press" (*NY Times*, 30 December 1983). Shortly thereafter, the UK and Singapore followed the USA in withdrawal from UNESCO. Some of the concerns expressed by the USA included explicit references to the attempt to set up a "New World Information Order," but also "the 'collectivist' trends in [UNESCO], which...promotes 'group rights' at the expense of individual human rights,...and the attention given to the so-called New International Economic Order, in which wealthy countries are supposed to transfer resources to the poorer ones" (*NY Times*, 30 December 1983). The USA remained outside of UNESCO until 2003, when, under President George W. Bush, it rejoined the international organization, stating that "as a symbol of our commitment to human dignity, the United States will return to UNESCO. This organization has been reformed and America will participate fully in its mission to advance human rights and tolerance and learning" (State Department, http://www.state.gov/p/io/unesco/usunesco/). The UK rejoined in 1997.

GLOBALIZATION, THE INFORMATION ECONOMY AND THE RISE OF E-COMMERCE

While these global debates about a NWICO were continuing, a new set of developments were occurring—deeper understanding of globalization and the emergence of an information economy and the critical importance of GEC.

While there has been a tremendous amount written about globalization and the information economy, there is still little consensus on the fundamental meaning of these two concepts, which are among the most contested of recent times. "Globalization" means very different things to different people.

The popular perception of globalization is simply that people, societies and nations are bound increasingly together, and there is a particular focus on how closely bound together are international markets. While this perception of interconnectedness is an important aspect of globalization, the actual processes go much further. McGrew (1992) asserts that globalization is

> the multiplicity of linkages and interconnections that transcend the nation-states (and by implication societies) which make up the modern world system. It defines a process through which events, decisions, and activities in one part of the world can come to have significant consequences for individuals and communities in quite distant parts of the globe. (McGrew 1992)

One of the foremost thinkers about globalization and its processes has been Anthony Giddens. He considers globalization to be one of the most "visible consequences of modernity," and asserts that "globalization concerns the intersection of presence and absence, the interlacing of social events and social relations 'at a distance' with local contextualities" (Giddens 1991). Giddens also argues that "larger and larger numbers of people live in circumstances in which disembedded institutions, linking local practices with globalized social relations, organize major aspects of [their] day-to-day life" (Giddens 1991).

With this expanded and more precise definition, we see that globalization is not just about the deepening of financial markets, but includes a whole range of social, political, economic, and cultural phenomena. We refer to these areas as the "spheres" of globalization. One of the reasons that the Information Economy offers such promise to Africa is that each of these "spheres" of globalization is supported by the application of electronic commerce. Also, through strategic planning, the opportunity exists for key geographic areas in Africa to exploit information and communications technologies to become "spaces" of globalization.

Fundamental Transformation in the Global Economy

The information economy is based on a fundamental transformation of the underlying structure of the global political economy. Many analysts are now arguing that this change is so definitive that it warrants the label of a techno-economic paradigm shift. This shift reflects changes in science, technology, the organization of business and production, learning, and entertainment. Aspects of this transformation include: (1) the nature of the manufacturing company; (2) the changing nature of business dynamics; (3) major changes in the research and development (R&D) activities of firms; (4) demand articulation in technological development; (5) technology fusion; and (6) institutional inertia. These changes are affecting nearly all sectors of the world system, including intergovernmental organizations, the private sector, regional organizations, national states, and nongovernmental organizations.

This period of change engenders a potential restructuring of power relations and the development of new forms of inequality in the world. It is possible that inequality in the information economy could go beyond a division between the so-called developed and developing countries to exacerbate intra-country divisions. Specifically, divisions could sharpen between those individuals possessing the knowledge, skills, and abilities to contribute to the global information economy (wherever they may happen to be located) and those who do not possess such skills.

Toward a Definition of the Information Economy

In defining the information economy, the author acknowledges the existence of a rich academic and popular debate on the subject. A key component of this debate is the impact of globalization on the formation of a "knowledge economy" in general, and the emergence of an "information economy" in particular. One characteristic of this current period of globalization is the emergence of a new techno-economic paradigm, which some analysts call innovation-mediated production. Within this framework, knowledge is increasingly embedded within the production process itself. One major issue that contrasts the knowledge economy from the industrial economy is that in many cases, the barriers to entry are much lower. In the new economy, information and knowledge become the most important factors of production. This mode of production characterizes the overall "knowledge economy," within which the "information economy" is playing an increasingly important role.

The author argues that the terms "information economy" and "knowledge economy" are very closely related and can be used synonymously in most cases. However, for the purposes of this chapter, the author argues that the term "information economy" refers to a specific component of the emerging knowledge economy wherein the production of information goods and services dominates wealth and job creation (Shapiro and Varian 1999; Varian 2000; Tapscott 1996, 1998, 1999; Quah 2000; Kahin and Brynjolfsson 2000).

Perhaps the most important development within the information economy is the economic explosion caused by GEC (e-commerce). E-commerce is the production, distribution, marketing, sale, or delivery of goods and services by electronic means. This includes the integrated use of information and communications technologies (e.g., the GII) as the medium through which goods and services of economic value are researched, designed, produced, advertised, catalogued, inventoried, purchased, distributed, accounts settled, follow-up support provided, and management information systems implemented.

Already, e-commerce is facilitating a process of disintermediation, where traditional intermediary functions are being replaced by new products and intelligent agents. However, many new markets are being developed for information goods, and to cope with such a dramatic increase in the availability of information, new information mediaries (infomediaries) are emerging. Whole new industries are emerging and new markets (and new types of markets) are being developed. Also, an unprecedented amount of information is being collected on individual consumers, allowing new and closer relationships to be forged between business and their customers, while at the same time creating new concerns about privacy in the online world.

The global information economy could be characterized as disciplinarian. Its interdependent nature ensures that "bad" decisions are punished immediately, and "good" decisions are rewarded with the same speed. With such a global, interdependent, knowledge-based economy, it is critical that appropriate mechanisms be developed at a global level to "govern" the global information economy – a global information economy regime.

Global and Regional Responses to the Information Revolution

First ITU World Telecommunications Development Conference (1994)
In response to these numerous challenges, countries and international organizations around the world have moved toward collective and individual efforts to harness resources, ideas and strategies. One of the earliest activities was the First WTDC, hosted by the Telecommunications Development Bureau of the ITU (BDT). Held in Buenos Aires, Argentina, the WTDC addressed the issue that was raised decades earlier in the Maitland Commission Report,

chaired by Sir Donald Maitland. Known popularly as the "Missing Link" report, the Maitland Commission Report argued that there was a conclusive link between telecommunications penetration and socioeconomic development. The WTDC reassessed this argument and ended with the same conclusions, adding that the gap between developing and developed countries had grown, not diminished, since the Missing Link. The conference attempted to harness the resources necessary to address this widening gap.

Group of Seven (G7) and the Information Society (February, 1995)
Following this landmark meeting, ministers from the leading industrialized countries in the world gathered in Brussels, Belgium for the First Information Society Ministerial Meeting. These ministers were attempting to understand how they could work together to harness the increasing potential of information and communications technologies to address the increasing challenges facing their individual countries. Emerging from the G7 (actually the G8 with the inclusion of Russia at the meeting) Information Society ministerial meeting, was a series of Eleven Information Society pilot projects, that were designed to identify "best practices" and "lessons learned" from collaborative efforts among the G8 members. Several of these projects (namely the Government Online and the Global Marketplace for SMEs) actively encouraged participation from developing country members. Results from these pilot projects were analyzed continuously, and the European Commission (EC) established the Information Society Projects Office (ISPO) to further disseminate the lessons coming from the pilot projects.

However, one major challenge for the meeting was that, as a G8 meeting, there was almost no participation from developing countries. The primary exception was that South African Deputy President Thabo Mbeki, was invited to speak "on behalf of the developing world." In his address, he argued that the participants at the meeting could not build a GIS with only the eight participants sitting around the table, but that they had to involve a wide cross section of the developing world. He offered South Africa as the host of such an initiative, and this challenge ultimately led to the G7/Developing World ISAD conference, which will be discussed below.

Global Information Infrastructure Commission (February 1995)
While the G8 governments were meeting to develop their collaborative strategies for confronting the information society and exploring ways to involve the developing world, another important meeting was occurring in Brussels.

A group of Chief Executive Officers from some of the leading information and communications companies in the world met to further challenge the G8 governments. As they launched their new organization, the GIIC, they argued that while Deputy President Mbeki was right in arguing for more developing country involvement in building the information society, it had to go even further. The GIIC members argued that governments alone would be unable to build the information society, and that private sector leadership was critical in partnership with the public sector if a truly "global" information society would be built. Their fifty members pledged to work for the next three years to help to promote the important role of the private sector in building the GII and to engage with public sector actors to help spread that message.

United Nations Economic Commission for Africa (1995/1996)
During the G7 ministerial meeting, Thabo Mbeki's remarks were well received. However, it took considerably longer for the G8 members to actually agree on a way to engage with the developing countries (in fact the agreement to participate in the ISAD conference only happened at their meeting in Nova Scotia.) In the meantime, Africa did not wait for this potential blessing. In April 1995, the ECA, hosted what has become known as a landmark meeting called the Telematics for African Development Symposium. The ECA is the largest UN presence in Africa. Headquartered in Addis Ababa, Ethiopia, it is one of three major regional organizations designed to facilitate regional socioeconomic development in all 53 African countries (the other two being the Organization for African Unity, also located in Addis Ababa, and the African Development Bank, located in Côte D'Ivoire). This Telematics for African Development Symposium brought together numerous African experts in the use of information and communications technologies for development.

One result of the conference was a resolution for the Council of Ministers entitled "Building Africa's Information Highway" that called for an African response to the challenges of the information society. This resolution was adopted, and the Council created a High-Level Working Group (HLWG) on information and communications technologies. Working mostly virtually (meeting physically only twice, once in Cairo and again in Addis Ababa), the HLWG developed a high-level response for Africa called the AISI. The AISI was adopted by the Council of Ministers in May 1996 and was endorsed by the African Ministers of Communications meeting in Abidjan, Cote d'Ivoire to finalize the drafting of the *African Green Paper on Telecommunications*. One key component of the AISI is its focus on National Information and

Communications Infrastructure (NICI) planning in each African country. AISI was given its public launch at in South Africa at a luncheon hosted by the GIIC at the ISAD conference.

Information Society and Development Conference (May 1996)
As the result of Thabo Mbeki's challenge to the G8, the ISAD conference was hosted in South Africa in May 1996. As planned, a wide cross section of developing countries participated in the ISAD conference, and challenged significantly the process of regime formation being led by the highly industrialized countries. Key issues placed on the global agenda were the following: (1) multipurpose community information centers; (2) universal access; and (3) employment issues. Major plans to host a follow-up conference (ISAD II, proposed by the Arab Republic of Egypt) never materialized.

ITU Universal Right to Communicate
Moving in the same direction, Dr. Pekka Tarjanne, Secretary-General of the ITU, proposed that another principle be added to the UN Universal Declaration of Human Rights, this being the Universal Right to Communicate. Several other organizations have now taken up this cry and are moving toward trying to include this principle on the larger global agenda. This addition elevates universal access from a luxury to a recognized basic human right.

Partnership for ICTs in Africa
The AISI is grounded in the assumption that effective socioeconomic development requires partnerships between many partners, including (1) international development agencies; (2) donor agencies; (3) private sector actors; and (4) nongovernmental actors.

Global Knowledge for Development (June 1997)
In the vacuum left by the non-starting ISAD II, the World Bank initiated a similar conference to fill the void, but with a fairly different character. The Global Knowledge for Development conference was held in June 1997 in Toronto, Canada, and organized by the World Bank and the government of Canada. The developed country orientation of this new conference was quite apparent. South African Minister of Communications Jay Naidoo, took the podium at one point and argued that "this conference is not the ISAD follow-up, that conference is yet to take place." Unfortunately, that conference has still not taken place (a second Global Knowledge conference was held in February 2000 in Malaysia, but there were significant

confrontations between the developing and developed country contingents and international organizations.)

Second ITU World Telecommunications Development Conference (1998)
The tiny island of Malta played hosted to the second ITU WTDC in 1998 attempting to assess the progress on the Buenos Aires Action Plan and to produce the program of work for the BDT for the next four years. Key issues gaining prominence at this conference was the addition to the agenda of a focus on women's access to information and communications technologies. The conference ended with the adoption of the Valetta Action Plan, hoping to consolidate the progress toward the development of an information society.

OECD Global Electronic Commerce Ministerial Meeting (1998)
In 1998, another distinctive shift began to happen in the movement toward an information society. While commercial issues have always been important, the increasing importance of Electronic Commerce (e-commerce) and a global information economy began to dominate discussions of an information society. In 1998, the OECD, which represents the 27 most industrialized countries of the world, hosted a ministerial level conference on GEC. A few developing countries were invited to participate in the event (including Minister Naidoo of South Africa), but many complained that their interests were clearly not important to the overall OECD agenda.

European Commission Information Society Technologies Conference (1998)
As an attempt to counter the perceived continued US dominance in information and communications technologies, the EC launched a new series of conferences for its members and strategic partners. These Information Society Technologies (IST) conferences started in 1998 in Vienna and were designed for focus on stimulating cooperative research through the Fifth Framework Initiative for collaborative research.

Africa TELECOM (May 1998)
The ITU is primarily a politically oriented intergovernmental organization. Its meetings are mostly intergovernmental negotiations on standards and agreements. However, it also has an alternative format for meeting called its TELECOM conferences. These conferences are able to raise issues and try to promote consensus in a less politically charged and threatening environment. World TELECOM is the centerpiece event, and it

occurs every four years in Geneva, Switzerland. Given its quarter-annual format, it is often referred to as the "Olympics of telecommunications." After the World event, the conferences move around the world to the three major regions (Asia TELECOM, Africa TELECOM, and Americas TELECOM). In May 1998, South Africa hosted the Africa TELECOM event and brought considerable attention to the perspectives of Africa in the movement toward an information society. Also during the Africa TELECOM, the GIIC launched its first regional organization called GIIC Africa. GIIC Africa, with its motto of "Africanizing the GIS with Private and Public Sector Cooperation," is designed to bring together 50 African private sector leaders to create additional momentum toward building the GII/GIS in Africa. Further, a grouping of African ministers of communications used the conference to issue its *African Connection* agenda, designed to further develop consensus among the African public sector on the importance of information and communications technologies to development.

GLOBAL GOVERNANCE OF THE INFORMATION ECONOMY AND SOCIETY

A transformation of such historic proportions is engendering substantial change in the mechanisms of governance as well. In this section, we have primarily adopted the Krasner (1983) approach to international regimes, which causes us to look at the issues of regime transformation, and the emergence of consensus in four critical areas: (1) principles and values; (2) norms; (3) rules; and (4) enforcement mechanisms. However, we also have a focus on the epistemic community, and on the role of global non-state actors in the formation of these regime components. This section of the book asks four research questions:

Research Question 1: To what degree is the ITR eroding, and by what factors is it being eroded?

Research Question 2: What evidence exists that a new regime for information and communications policy is emerging, and what are its principles, values, rules, and enforcement mechanisms?

Research Question 3: What are some of the more important regional, subregional, and national responses to this transition?

Research Question 4: What are the implications of this regime transformation for developing countries, and what can be done to influence the direction of the emerging regime so that it might be more just and equitable for a wider grouping of the world's citizens?

The methodology adopted in this portion of the study is qualitative in nature and uses a theory-driven case study approach. Multiple qualitative data collection techniques were employed, including (1) participant observation; (2) observer observation; (3) in-depth interviews; and (4) content analysis of primary and secondary sources. Data collection was focused primarily on developing a thick-narrative case study of the impact of regime transformation on an emerging economy. The case selected for analysis was the Republic of South Africa. South Africa was chosen for a number of reasons, including (1) in 1996 it implemented a fairly wide-ranging restructuring of its telecommunications sector (see, inter alia, Cogburn 1998b); (2) it was a founding member of the WTO; (3) it plays a strong political and economic leadership role in the African region, and within the broader developing country context, including the BRICS alliance; (4) it participated in, and made an acceptable offer to the WTO Agreement on Basic Telecommunications; (5) it has developed a unified telecommunications and broadcasting independent regulatory body; (6) it is currently in the process of a Green/White Paper preparation to develop an electronic commerce policy; and finally (7) there has been significant activity from non-state actors in South Africa, at both the national, regional, and global levels.

TECHNOLOGY AND EROSION OF THE EXISTING REGIME

Are there social, political, economic, cultural, and technological factors that are challenging the ITR, and if so what are they? The answer to this question is, simply put, yes. Let us look at examples, of each of these factors eroding the ITR.

Social Factors

Emerging out of all of the multiple information society conferences and initiatives discussed above, is a recognition of the many applications that are possible in the emergence of an information and knowledge society (Castells 1996; Mansell and When 1998). Table 3.1 below, illustrates the wide range of applications that have been identified for use in a Global Knowledge and Information Society.

This focus on applications moves us beyond the original "club" of the telecommunications regime, to include teachers, nurses, and small businesses, to name but a few new stakeholders. It is this broad stakeholder grouping that makes the social pressures for this new regime so strong.

Political Factors

Further, this move to focus on applications and to include more societal actors means that more political actors now see a more valuable stake in this emerging regime. While under the ITR, there were clear "stovepipe" relationships between the ITU and national ministries of communications, the emerging regime is going to broaden out the stakeholders. Ministries of health, finance, education, trade and industry, and others, are increasingly clamoring for an increased role in defining their needs for GII and the development of a GIS.

As example, take the G8 ISAD conference discussed above. In South Africa, the planning for this important global event started with the Ministry of Foreign Affairs (MOF). Subsequently, as more people became aware of the potential of an information society, the Department of Arts, Culture, Science and Technology (DACST) stepped in to play the lead organizing role. However, as the time for the actual conference approached, the Department of Communications (DOC) wrestled control of the activities away from DACST and held center stage during the actual conference (much to the chagrin of DACST and its political leaders).

Unlike the telecommunications ministries, which are fairly narrowly focused, and were previously conceived to have a narrow group of stakeholders, these ministries are more broadly focused and have a broad group of stakeholders.

In addition to these national political factors, transformation of the international accounting rate mechanism, and the unilateral declaration by the USA that it will pay only a limited amount for telecommunications settlement payments have also accelerated the transformation of the telecommunications system into a new international regime.

Economic Factors

The development of a global information economy fuels the need for corporations to explore the "global option," and engage in geographically disarticulated research, production, distribution, and management. Also, the increased focus on the global trade in services as opposed to the global

Table 3.1 An applications driven Global Information Society

General application	Specific examples	Epistemic support
Education, research and training	Distance education Collaboratories Asynchronous training	WTDC G8 conference
Digital libraries	Library of Congress UMDL IPL JSTOR	WTDC G8 conference
Electronic museums and galleries	Louvre	WTDC G8 conference
Environment management	GIS applications	WTDC G8 conference
Emergency management	EMS	WTDC G8 conference
SMMEs, employment creation and e-commerce	PEOPLink African crafts market	WTDC G8 conference
Maritime information	Early warning systems	WTDC G8 conference
Electronic government services	E-passports Sharing and reuse of records	WTDC G8 conference
Debt management and financial services	Debt management systems Electronic bill payment	WTDC G8 conference
Tourism	Hotel and package booking Promotion and data mining	WTDC G8 conference
Health care	Telemedicine Health education and information	WTDC G8 conference
Legislation and legal services	Parliament information systems Legal database access	WTDC G8 conference
Transportation of people and goods	Transportation system management	WTDC G8 conference
Business development and trade efficiency	Trade promotion B2B e-commerce	WTDC G8 conference
Universal access	Community information centers Public Internet terminals	WTDC G8 conference
National systems of innovation	Collaboratories Geographically distributed research teams	WTDC G8 conference
Entertainment and leisure	Online gaming Adult-oriented material	WTDC G8 conference

trade in goods—especially for knowledge-oriented services and products is also eroding the existing international regime.

Cultural Factors

Many people are worried about globalization and the information society leading only to the erosion of national cultures, and the "Americanization" (also called the "McDonaldization") of the rest of the world (see Barber 199x). The emergence of a GII and GIS means that there are now tools and mechanisms to promote the preservation of local cultures, and to project them globally (e.g., www.si.umich.edu/chico).

Technological Factors

There are numerous technological factors that contributed to this process, and technological innovation continues to develop. However, one of the biggest technological breakthroughs was being able to send voice over the Internet, called Voice over Internet Protocol (VOIP). As we have discussed earlier, and will discuss again later, telecommunications companies were able to maintain their perceived "natural monopoly" on telecommunications because they required circuit-switched communication networks to make voice communications possible over distance ("tele" communications). These circuits had to be dedicated to one conversation, and had to be kept open during the entire time for that one call. When the Internet was introduced, one major innovation was the use of "packet-switching" (more about this issue in Chap. 4). This meant that each message was broken up into individual packets and sent along the network through various channels, and reassembled at the user's computer. This was a much more efficient use of the network. VOIP calls were initially of inferior quality than circuit-switched communications, but were much, much cheaper. However, over time, the quality increased tremendously, while the cost remained low. Once voice communication could be sent in this same way using VOIP, it represented a major and fundamental existential threat to traditional telecommunications providers, and they responded vociferously. VOIP communications was banned in many countries around the world, as the monopolized POTS (Plain Old Telephone System) and national PTT (Post, Telegraph, and Telephone operators) used their national monopoly power to try to exclude these new technologies.

Other innovative technologies that also accelerated these processes included Very Small Aperture Terminal (VSAT) satellites, which provided telecommunications and Internet connectivity that bypassed local telecom operators, and "Call-Back" systems where people in one country were able to place a very short call to an international number, and have that number call them back at very low international rates.

This discussion has helped to highlight the social, economic, political, and technological factors eroding the existing ITR. Now, we will examine the follow-up question: "Is there evidence that a new regime is beginning to emerge in the transformation of the International Telecommunications Regime, and what are its principles, values, and norms?"

The Emerging GII/GIS Regime and Its Principles, Values, and Norms

Our theoretical framework would suggest that evidence of an emergent regime would come initially from the development of global consensus on the principles, values, and norms around a particular issue area of international affairs. In this case, we are looking for this consensus in the fundamental issues of information infrastructure development and an information society.

As discussed above, one area of emerging consensus is that the information society should be "applications driven." Meaning, that as we look at the other areas of more technical issues, the point of putting in hardware, increasing bandwidth and telecommunications services, is to provide the information infrastructure for applications.

Another area of harmonization is that there should be universal access to high-bandwidth connectivity, services and the applications described above. How to achieve this objective is still the subject of much debate, but that universal access is a target has generated a high degree of global consensus. One driver of this consensus is the high level of focus on the potential of GEC (e-commerce) to meet the employment creation demands and economic development objectives of the developing countries (we will explore the implications of this focus in later chapters).

Perhaps the most controversial principle seeking consensus, but seen as most important by many actors, is the liberalization and privatization of telecommunications markets and reciprocal market access for both products and services. In order to promote harmonization around these important principles, a number of high-level meetings have been held (some of these meetings were discussed above).

The Buenos Aires Action Plan (BAAP) that emerged out of the First WTDC highlighted these points. These points were then taken up at a higher level of consensus in the meeting of Ministers of the Group of Seven Highly Industrialized Economies (G7).

What emerged from the G7 Ministerial Meeting was the so-called Brussels Principles for the information society. Table 3.2 below presents these eight high-level principles.

At this meeting of industrialized country leaders, the only major representative of the developing world was Thabo Mbeki, then Deputy President of the Republic of South Africa (now president). In his keynote address, Mbeki argued that there was no way that a "Global" information society could be built with the eight countries sitting around the table at the meeting (at the time Russia was a "visiting" member of the G7, became a full member of the G8, and has now been expelled.) He urged the G7 to consider an initiative that would involve a cross section of the developing world. His challenge was accepted, and after substantial political maneuvering, the G7 countries met, for the first time, in South Africa, along with a cross section of the developing world (see Cogburn 1997).

One unstated objective of that meeting was an attempt on the part of the developed countries to further the emerging consensus, embodied in the "Brussels Principles," within the key leadership in the developing world. However, this objective met with substantial resistance, when the developing countries (led by South Africa) refused to simply "endorse" the Brussels Principles as stated. After significant, behind-the-scenes activity and near crises, a modified statement was accepted, known as the "ISAD Principles." They included the Brussels Principles, but added several items of particular interest to the developing countries. In some cases these ISAD principles were not

Table 3.2 G7 Brussels principles	Promoting dynamic competition
	Encouraging private investment
	Defining an adaptable regulatory framework
	Providing open access to networks
	While
	Ensuring universal provision of an access to services
	Promoting equality of opportunity to the citizen
	Promoting diversity of content, and
	Recognizing the necessity of worldwide cooperation

new, but simply further clarified (or qualified) aspects of the Brussels Principles to be more "just and equitable." See Table 3.3 for the ISAD Principles.

Hopefully, this discussion serves to illustrate the point of the multiple processes that have occurred during the interregnum between the demise of the ITR and the emergence of a new GII and GIS regime. There is another interesting story to be told about what happened to the momentum generated by this ISAD conference and its declarations, but that full story is beyond the scope of this study. For the moment, this brief account will have to suffice.

At the close of the ISAD conference, the head of the Egyptian delegation took the floor during the ministerial meeting and urged for a follow-up conference, and pledged Egypt as the host for the conference. This position was completely uncaucused within the developing world delegates. Nonetheless, it was accepted by the ministers and it was agreed that Egypt would host the follow-up conference the subsequent year. This conference never occurred. Even with substantial urging from the EC, the UN ECA and other regional and global bodies, no further ISAD activities have been held.

In the vacuum created by the failed ISAD movement, a new initiative led – not by the developing world, as the ISAD processes were – but by the World Bank emerged. This new initiative, called the Global Knowledge for Development conference, was launched in June 1997 in Toronto, Canada. At the inaugural meeting, then South African Minister of Telecommunications Jay Naidoo took the microphone in one session and emphatically stated that "this is not ISAD, the ISAD follow-up meeting is still to come." But alas, it was not.

Table 3.3 ISAD principles for the information society	Universal service
	Clear regulatory framework
	Employment creation
	Global cooperation and competitiveness
	Diversity of applications and content
	Diversity of language and culture
	Cooperation in technology
	Private investment and competition
	Protection of intellectual property rights
	Privacy and data security
	Narrowing the infrastructure gap
	Cooperation in research and technological development

To summarize, Table 3.4 below presents a comparison of the "old" ITR and the "emerging" GII/GIS regime. Table 3.5 that follows presents a brief chronology of these major regime transformation events.

So we can clearly see the contours of principles, values, and norms emerging for a new information infrastructure regime. However, this transition to a new regime will not be completely smooth. Already, there has been significant contestation to the emergent regime. There has been a contest between the USA and the EC over privacy concerns, especially related to global e-commerce. Here, we see a fundamental clash of principles and values. The European perspective is based on a cherished belief that individuals have the right to own information about themselves and should give authorization for any information to be collected, stored, or disseminated. In contrast, the dominant US perspective is that companies have the right to collect information on their citizens, in order to be able to provide them with better and more targeted advertising and services.

Significant opposition is emerging to globalization and the global process of developing regime principles, norms, and rules by elite bodies, behind closed doors, regardless of whether those doors are in Seattle, Washington DC, or Davos. There was significant hesitation by developing countries to make offers to the WTO Agreement on Basic Telecommunications (e.g., in the end, only five African countries—including South Africa—actually made accepted offers, thus joining the agreement.) Further, even South Africa has refused to join the WTO Information Technology Agreement, which will lower tariffs on imports of mostly all information technology products to near zero.

Table 3.4 Comparison between ITR and the emerging GII/GIS regime

International telecommunications regime	Emerging GII/GIS regime
Limited competition: natural monopoly for telecommunications	High competition: liberalization and privatization for telecommunications
Single issue: telecommunications	Multiple issue: telecoms, broadcasting, health, education, SMMEs, debt management
Single ministry: telecoms, PTT	Multiple ministries: broadcasting, education, health, trade and industry, finance
Single industry: telecoms and equipment suppliers	Multiple industries: content providers, ASPs, ISPs, e-commerce
Limited stakeholders: telecoms, employees, and experts	Multiple stakeholders: nurses, educators, small business owners
Epistemic community: narrow	Epistemic community: wide

Table 3.5 Brief chronology of regime transformation

WTO born (January 1995)	WTO agreement on IT products
G7 ministerial meeting	(March 1997)
GII principles (February 1995)	Global Knowledge for Development
GIIC formed (February 1995)	(June 1997)
WTO financial services agreement	USA issues unilateral challenge to the
(July 1995)	international system of accounting rates at ITU
WTO Agreement on movement	(1997)
of natural persons (July 1995)	WTO E-commerce work program
ITU telecom (October 1995)	(September 1998)
ISAD (May 1996)	OECD E-commerce ministerial conference
AISI adopted (May 1996)	(October 1998)
WTO, IMF World Bank MOU	WTO Seattle ministerial meeting (1999)
(November 1996)	Washington, DC meeting of the IMF and World
WTO agreement on basic telecoms	Bank (1999)
(February 1997)	World Economic Forum meeting in Davos
	(2000)

RULES AND ENFORCEMENT OF A NEW GII/GIS REGIME

If we now agree that the old regime is being transformed, and a new regime is emerging, complete with its own set of principles, values, and norms, then what are the rules of this newly emerging regime and what international body will enforce these rules?

To answer the second question first, there is little doubt that the centerpiece organization will be the WTO. However, unlike the ITR that was based primarily on a single intergovernmental organization, the ITU, the emerging regime will rely on a host of governmental and nongovernmental organizations to enforce its rules.

Thus, in addition to the WTO, the ten most important organizations for the "governance" of this emerging regime will be the following: (1) World Intellectual Property Organization (WIPO); (2) OECD; (3) ICANN; (4) GIIC/Global Business Dialogue (GBD); (5) Group of 8 Industrialized Countries (G8); (6) World Economic Forum (WEF); (7) World Bank Group; (8) EC; (9) ITU; and (10) Bilateral aid agencies. Table 3.6 illustrates these organizations, their organizational type, and the primary regime function.

To illustrate this point, take the example of South Africa, as it attempts to develop its new e-commerce policy. What are the ongoing processes of global regime formation within the international system that have an

Table 3.6   GII/GIS regime enforcement organizations

Organization	Organization type	Regime component(s)
WTO	Intergovernmental (Global)	Principles, values, norms, rules, **enforcement**
WIPO	Intergovernmental (Global)	Principles, values, norms, rules, **enforcement**
OECD	Intergovernmental (Regional)	Principles, values, norms
ICANN	Global Non-governmental	Principles, values, norms, rules, **enforcement**
GIIC/GBD	Global Non-governmental	Principles, values, norms
G8	Intergovernmental	Principles, values, norms
WEF	Global Non-governmental	Principles, values, norms
World Bank group	Intergovernmental (Global)	Principles, values, norms, rules, **enforcement**
EC	Intergovernmental (Regional)	Principles, values, norms
ITU	Intergovernmental (Global)	Principles, values, norms
Bilateral aid agencies	Governmental	

impact on South Africa's ability to harness the digital economy? What has been South Africa's recent involvement (1995–2000) in these ongoing processes of international regime formation?

INTERNATIONAL REGIME THEORY AND THE DIGITAL ECONOMY

The transition to a global information-oriented economy has created new challenges for global governance and regulation of these processes. The borderless nature of this global economy raises fundamental questions about how we might be able to achieve higher levels of harmony and reduced transaction costs as electronic commerce continues to develop. These fundamentally global processes are illustrative of a quandary facing international relations theorists around the world: when dealing with issues that are transnational in scope, how do we achieve significant levels of global governance in the absence of a global government? This dilemma, often referred to by scholars as the "anarchy problematique," has confronted numerous issue areas from diamonds to telecommunications to the high seas. One solution to this dilemma comes in the form of international regime theory, where we try to look at the emergence of norms, principles, and values around a particular issue area and mechanisms to enforce them.

Globally, there are a number of primary norms, principles, and values that are emerging around electronic commerce and the information economy (Cogburn 2001). Some of these include (1) telecommunications and information infrastructure—the importance of liberalization, privatization, and a pro-competitive environment; (2) customs/taxation—the Internet and e-commerce should continue to be a "tax-free" zone; (3) electronic payments—multiple options should continue to emerge (both inside and outside money) that are interoperable and allow for anonymous, pseudonymous, and traceable methods; (4) commercial code—a common global commercial code should emerge to provide for the global rule of law and protection for contracts and private property; (5) intellectual property protection—IPR regulation needs to be revised to reflect the realities of the digital economy, while still providing an incentive for the production of information goods; (6) domain names are an important and contested commercial asset, and famous marks should be protected while not allowing them to abuse smaller enterprises, and ICANN is the legitimate body charged with the responsibility to deal with domain name issues; (7) personal data should be protected, while at the same time allowing for legitimate corporate uses of data profiling and targeted advertising; (8) security and encryption is an important national and personal security concern that has to be balanced with personal privacy concerns; (9) awareness/trust is a limiting factor for the growth of e-commerce; (10) trust—might be enhanced with the widespread use of authentication and digital signatures; (11) technical standards should be technology-neutral and industry-driven to the fullest extent possible; (12) local content should be promoted and protected, if e-commerce is going to reach its full potential; (13) labor and society will be affected by the move toward a digital economy and we should work to minimize the negative impact, while harnessing the potential; (14) universal service/access or lack thereof, as characterized by the "digital divide," is one of the most potentially limiting factors for global e-commerce; and finally (15) human resources and capacity require immediate global attention.

One of the most successful international regimes in history was the ITR (Cowhey 1990). This regime was based primarily on a specialized agency of the UN, the ITU. However, due to various social, political, economic, and technological factors, this regime is being eroded and new regimes are emerging, the broadest of which might be called the GII/GIS regime and its critically important subset which is the GEC regime (Cogburn 2001).

Unlike the highly successful ITR, which was based primarily on one intergovernmental organization, the norms, principles, and values of the emergent information regime are being promoted, debated, contested, and will ultimately be enforced by a range of global organizations, both intergovernmental and nongovernmental. At the center of this regime's enforcement structure is the WTO, supported by the ITU and various specialized international and regional organizations, such as the WIPO, the OECD, International Labor Organization (ILO), International Organization for Standardization (ISO), the ICANN, UNESCO, United Nations Conference on Trade and Development (UNCTAD) and the World Bank. In addition, several national governments and regional governmental groupings have taken important steps toward influencing the emerging regime, such as the G8, EC, Government of the United States of America (USG), and the Asia-Pacific Economic Cooperation (APEC). Each of these organizations will play a specific and important role in providing governance to the international regime for GEC and the information society.

The Importance of Policy Issues

While technical issues are critical to the development of electronic commerce and the digital economy, they are far from decisive. A number of other legal and regulatory hurdles have to be addressed. Jonathan Coppel of the OECD argues that:

> Despite the phenomenal growth in the Internet for commercial purposes there are a number of legal and technical obstacles, which could hinder the full potential of e-commerce from being reaped....And the absence of commercial codes and legal recognition covering areas such as the acceptance of electronic signatures and documents, contract enforcement and greater certainty vis-à-vis liability for damages that may arise as a result of electronic transactions, will limit the take-up of e-commerce, particularly in the B2B sphere. These concerns are magnified when trading across borders.... For example, the virtual environment of electronic markets makes it more difficult to determine who the contracting parties are, where an electronic commerce operator is established and whether that operator is complying with all relevant legal obligations and regulatory regimes (OECD 2000, p. 13).

Further concerns are raised about electronic transactions across borders, for example, the difficulty of verifying electronic signatures and documents. We will now explore these issues within the context of a specific country, the case of one of the leading countries in the developing world, the Republic of South Africa.

PROGRESS TOWARD AND E-COMMERCE REGIME IN SOUTH AFRICA

While global e-commerce is being driven in many ways by the leadership of the private sector, there are very important information policy issues that will facilitate its optimal growth, both within South Africa and around the world. One challenging paradox of e-commerce is that while its scope is clearly global, national regulation continues to provide the legal and regulatory basis for its operation.

The South African government took these responsibilities very seriously, and the DOC launched an important national Green/White paper process on electronic commerce that was designed to lead to specific national policy in 2001. The process of developing and conducting this process was consultative and tried to include the voices of as many relevant stakeholders as possible. This section will briefly examine the policy perspectives that are emerging in South Africa's movement toward an e-commerce regime. Our primary data source for this section is the national Green Paper on Electronic Commerce, the background papers commissioned by the DOC, the papers of the working groups, other published government documents, academic literature, and news accounts.

Of significant interest for our analysis, is the fact that the Green Paper makes constant reference to the need to harmonize its emerging national e-commerce regime with the growing global consensus and in line with its extant commitments to the WTO. "In embarking on a national policy development initiative on e-commerce it is imperative that SA take cognizance of its WTO commitments, firstly, to ensure that such policy is compatible with the relevant WTO rules and regulations, and secondly, to determine the impact of e-commerce on those commitments" (RSA Green Paper on Electronic Commerce, p. 48). The WTO has worked to review the impact of e-commerce on its structure and planning. At its last ministerial meeting, held in Seattle, Washington, the USA and other developed countries, wanted to explore the possibilities of a more comprehensive involvement for the WTO in e-commerce issues. "In the Seattle Ministerial Conference, South Africa, together with the Southern African Development Community (SADC), supported the extension of the moratorium until the next Ministerial Conference when it would be reviewed" (RSA Green Paper, p. 49). The current policy perspective recognizes that "any regulatory regime that South Africa adopts must be consistent and compatible with international frameworks" (RSA Green Paper, p. 18).

General Principles on Electronic Commerce Consensus on general principles around issues of international import are a key indicator of the emergence of a new regime. In terms of the e-commerce policy formulation process, South Africa's approach is based on eight key principles, which are: (1) quality of life; (2) international benchmarking; (3) consultative process; (4) flexibility; (5) technology neutrality; (6) supporting private sector-led and technology-based solutions and initiatives; (7) establishing and supporting public–private partnerships, and supporting small, medium and micro-sized enterprises (SMMEs) (RSA Green Paper, p. 18).

In terms of the substantive principles, South Africa believes the following: (1) the recognition that there is a need for legislation to support the national implementation of e-commerce transactions, within a framework of international standards; (2) that commercial transactions should be able to be effected through both paper and electronic means, without creating uncertainty about the latter; (3) promoting a framework that increases the efficiency of South African commercial transactions, without being overly cumbersome; (4) the framework should be technology neutral; (5) to develop a uniform commercial framework that conforms to international standards; (6) that South Africa should build on the work of others and not reinvent the wheel; and that (7) South Africa should strive to maintain its sovereignty and independence, and meet its strategic national socioeconomic development objectives. (RSA Green Paper, pp. 25–28).

Telecommunications and Information Infrastructure Without increased access to information and communications infrastructure, e-commerce will not be able to meet its full potential (RSA Green Paper, p. 85). Since the restructuring of the telecommunications sector in South Africa in 1996, there have been a number of information infrastructure initiatives in the country (Cogburn 1998). The DOC has been at the forefront of this effort, particularly with its *Info.Com 2025* Strategy, Public Information Terminals, Public Key Infrastructure Pilot, and numerous other e-commerce and e-government initiatives. As these infrastructure initiatives unfold, the strategy should be to develop an infrastructure that is capable of handling a wide variety of applications and services. From the South African policy perspective, "the challenge confronting South Africa is to create an ideal market structure for e-commerce that will stimulate and modernise network development and infrastructure; accelerate universal access; support affordable access; encourage investment and innovation" (RSA Green Paper, p. 82). There is a realization in the Green Paper that the infrastructure for e-commerce will consist of a range of networks, including "backbone networks, end-user equipment and access services."

The success of e-commerce will depend on the available of speedy access infrastructure, high quality of service within the backbone networks, and affordable prices. Access will not only be through fixed networks (terrestrial, wireline, and cable TV) but also through wireless networks (cellular, satellite, and digital broadcast spectrum) (RSA Green Paper, p. 83).

Perhaps one of the most important emerging regime principles is the importance of liberalization, privatization and a pro-competitive environment for telecommunications and information infrastructure. South Africa is proudly a founding member of the WTO, and has been working actively to promote the multilateral trading system (Address by Minister of Finance, Trevor Manuel, as chairman of the Board of Governors, IMF).

At the moment, Telkom, the commercialized Public Telecommunications Operator (PTO) has a monopoly on the provision of basic fixed telephony services. While the government chose to adopt a strategic equity partnership (between SBC and Telkom Malaysia) for Telkom, the Green Paper recognizes that "Telkom's efforts alone are not sufficient to achieve all of the infrastructure needs for e-commerce [in South Africa]" (RSA Green Paper, p. 85). As such, South Africa submitted an accepted offer in the WTO's Agreement on Basic Telecommunications, and is now bound by the terms of that agreement to liberalize and privatize its telecommunications sector by 2002 (WTO Agreement on Basic Telecommunications). However, at present, South Africa has not yet signed the WTO Information Technology Agreement (ITA), which would bring tariffs on a wide range of information and communications technologies down to zero.

Universal Service/Access As stated above, there is a significant recognition that all of the potential benefits of GEC for South Africa will not be realized without sufficient attention to increased access to information and communications technologies for a wider portion of South African society. Often characterized as the "digital divide," this disparity of access both within countries and between them is one of the most potentially limiting factors for global e-commerce.

In order to combat the digital divide and try to meet its universal service goals, the DOC has promoted a number of public access initiatives such as the development of Multipurpose Community Information Centers (MPCICs), the Universal Service Agency (USA), and Public Information Terminals (PITs) to help provide access for larger numbers of its citizens to the benefits and opportunities of GEC.

Customs/Taxation South Africa recognizes that the transition to a digital economy engenders new ways of doing business, and new products and services. Many of these products and services are presenting tremendous challenges to the taxation regimes of governments around the world. "There is a legitimate concern by certain governments that the development of the Internet may have the effect of shrinking the tax base and hence reducing fiscal revenue" (RSA Green Paper, p. 36). In addition, South Africa recognizes that there are significant difficulties in defining jurisdiction in electronic commerce and to administer and enforce any kind of taxation scheme.

The South African Revenue Service (SARS) believes that the global consensus that is emerging around taxation principles, being led by the OECD, does not conflict with its views. The important basic principles of this emerging regime are: (1) neutrality; (2) efficiency; (3) certainty and simplicity; and (4) flexibility. Of particular interest is there is apparently no opposition in the South African approach to the idea of "no need for a special new tax such as a "flat rate" or a "bit" tax, and that the Internet and e-commerce should continue to be a "tax-free" zone. (RSA Green Paper, p. 37).

However, South Africa wants to promote the idea of "indirect taxes," being at the place of consumption. "Indirect taxes should apply where consumption taxes place, and an international consensus should be sought on the identification of the place of consumption. Consensus is important to avoid double taxation or unintentional non-taxation" (RSA Green Paper, p. 40).

There is concern in South Africa that the development of electronic money that is "unaccounted," and "network" or "outside" money, will lead to additional challenges in terms of tax monitoring, collection, and enforcement. However, it believes that there is significant cultural conservatism that will limit the impact of these new forms of money. In order to promote compliance, South Africa believes that it should require that certain information should be a part of South African e-commerce.

The following information should be furnished on any commercial website owned by a South African resident, company, close corporation or trust: trading name of the business; the physical as well as the postal address for the business; and e-mail address; telephone or other contact information and statutory registration number in respect of companies; close corporations and trusts (RSA Green Paper, p. 44).

The emerging tax perspective recognizes that there are additional complications that reduce storage and transmission costs, and that storing information overseas is becoming easier and cheaper. As a result, South Africa believes that there is the need for a "greater degree of international cooperation in revenue collection than currently exists" (RSA Green Paper, p. 45). It appears that South Africa supports the role of the OECD, as a leader for this aspect of the regime, especially with its Model Tax conventions.

Electronic Payments The emerging policy perspective in South Africa is that multiple options should continue to emerge (both inside and outside money) that are interoperable and could allow for anonymous, pseudonymous, and traceable methods. There is particular concern about the "threat of cybercash" and the impact of unaccounted money on the South African economy (both in the form of network-based money and stored value cards.) Both of these methods have the potential to exchange value without identifying the user and without linking to specific bank accounts (RSA Green Paper, p. 99). South Africa sees this as a "make-or-break" issue for electronic commerce in South Africa.

Another major challenge for South Africa, given its history of racial oppression and segregation, is the ability for the "unbanked" to have access to electronic payment systems.

South Africa has a well-developed financial system, and the South African Reserve Bank (SARB) has taken the lead on these e-payment issues.

In 1998, it developed the South African Multiple Option Settlement (SAMOS) system that allows real-time settlement between banks. The SARB has also published a position paper on e-money in April 1999. The Reserve Bank is pushing hard for the principle that "only banks would be allowed to issue electronic money," although there is the recognition that "the issuance of electronic money may fall outside the definition of [the] 'business of a bank', as defined in the Banks Act 94 of 1990" (RSA Green Paper, p. 102). The goal is to protect users, who the Reserve Bank feels may find themselves "unprotected," in the event that the issuers of electronic money remain unregulated. The Reserve Bank feels strongly that "primary and intermediary issuers of electronic value will therefore be subject to regulation and supervision by the South African Reserve Bank" (RSA Green Paper, p. 102).

Global Commercial Code South Africa recognizes that GEC is posing a challenge to its national legal systems that support commercial transactions. The current legal framework in South Africa, like in most countries, was developed for an era of paper-based commerce, and thus contains words such as: "document," "writing," "signature," "original," "copy," "stamp," "seal," "register," "file," "deliver," and so on (RSA Green Paper, p. 28). The South African Law Commission found that the Computer Evidence Act 57 of 1983 was insufficient to address the admissibility of "computer evidence" in civil proceedings, and this will have to be addressed in an emerging e-commerce regime.

Also important is the ability to determine the attribution of electronic documents. Given the existing law in South Africa, this issue has to be addressed.

However, in terms of the doctrine of "estoppel" in South African law, a purported originator who never sent nor authorized a communication to be sent, may nevertheless be held bound in law if his negligent conduct, whether by action or commission, induced a reasonable belief of authenticity in the mind of the addressee, which caused the latter to act thereon to his/her peril (RSA Green Paper, p. 32).

Additionally, it is important to ascertain the time and place of an e-commerce contract, in order to determine whether or not South African courts have "jurisdiction to adjudicate a dispute involving both local and foreign nationals and, if so, which country's laws our courts would apply" (RSA Green Paper, p. 32). How to effect a signature in cyberspace is another important issue for the South African policy environment. A framework for understanding electronic signatures (and the more specific subset "digital signatures") must be put in place, and a common global commercial code should emerge to provide for the global rule of law and protection for contracts and private property.

As the leading regime component in this area, South Africa strongly supports the United Nations Conference on International Trade Law (UNCITRAL) and its Model Law on Electronic Commerce.

Intellectual Property Protection The South African policy approach recognizes that the transition to a digital economy presents new challenges for intellectual property protection. Digital goods can be copied and distributed around the world with relative ease, putting additional pressure on the system of intellectual property protection in South Africa and countries around the world. Intellectual property regulation needs to be revised to reflect the realities of the digital economy, while still providing an incentive for the production of information goods, and thus balancing the needs of the individual with the needs of society.

"South African intellectual property law is not fully equipped to deal with the implications of the Internet, convergence, multimedia, digital technology and hence ecommerce. The advent of the Internet has changed the underlying assumptions of the original copyright laws entailed in the Copyrights Act 98 of 1978" (RSA Green Paper, p. 57). South Africa has already made an attempt to comply with the WTO's Agreement on the Trade-Related Aspects of Intellectual Property (TRIPS) by amending its Intellectual Property Laws Amendment Act (Act 38 of 1997).

In order to try to help move forward in the development of a global e-commerce regime, the WIPO has developed its "digital agenda" to guide its work in this area over the course of the next two years. The South African Department of Trade and Industry (DTI) convened a consultative meeting in South Africa to discuss South Africa's accession to these WIPO treaties and processes. "The majority of stakeholders cautioned that before acceding to them, South Africa should analyse the benefits which accrue to small and medium enterprises" (RSA Green Paper, p. 60).

Domain Names Currently, there are no direct linkages between domain names and trademark holders. This area, perhaps better than any other, highlights the significant contradictions that are at play in the development of GEC, in an environment of national-based legislation. As the South African Green Paper argues: "trademarks are territorial in nature, i.e. their registration applies to a particular country or jurisdiction. There is a general discrepancy between the national scope of trademark and the international nature of electronic commerce, particularly since e-commerce is borderless and instantaneous in nature" (RSA Green Paper, p. 63).

South Africa recognizes that domain names are an important and contested commercial asset, and famous marks should be protected while not allowing them to abuse by smaller enterprises. There is some concern that ICANN has not yet achieve complete legitimacy as the body charged with the responsibility to deal with domain name issues. South Africa is questioning whether or not it should support these structures, as well as structures such as African Network Information Center (AFRINIC), which has been formed to try to better represent the interests of Africa within ICANN (RSA Green Paper, p. 97).

South Africa does, however, support the role of WIPO in its dispute resolution activities. It also supports the idea that in an information economy, the so-called Country Code Top Level Domains (ccTLDs) should be managed by national governments as a national asset (RSA Green Paper, p. 94). The South African DOC has proposed the creation of an independent Domain Name Authority (DNA) to represent all relevant stakeholders (private sector, public sector, and civil society) and to manage the domain name issues for South Africa.

Personal Data and Consumer Protection In order to enhance trust in the digital economy, South Africa recognizes that personal data should be protected. The challenge is to what degree the South African policy perspective will allow for legitimate corporate use of data mining and profiling, targeted advertising, and the use of other Customer Relationship Management (CRM) tools. As fundamental principles, South Africa believes that consumers should be protected against the following dangers:

- Unsolicited goods and communication;
- Illegal or harmful goods, services and content (e.g., pornographic material)
- Dangers resulting from the ease and convenience of buying online;
- Insufficient information about goods or about their supplier since, the buyer is not in a position to physically examine the goods offered;
- The abundantly accessible nature of a website
- The dangers of invasion of privacy

- The risk of being deprived of protection through the unfamiliar, inadequate or conflicting law of a foreign country being applicable to the contract; and finally
- Cyber fraud (RSA Green Paper, p. 75).

South Africa also recognizes that when moving into electronic commerce, suppliers also face new dangers, especially in exposing themselves to new liabilities. The South African policy process would like to ensure that South African digital enterprises are an attractive competitor in the cyber world. The DOC sees this as "an opportunity [for South African businesses] to establish a reputation for sound e-commercial practices, not only locally or within the SADC but also worldwide" (RSA Green Paper, p. 78).

Of particular importance to South Africa is the impact that its privacy and consumer protection policies may have on its relationships with its trading partners, especially the European Union which has a very stringent privacy policy and consumer protection perspective. There is a recommendation in the Green Paper that "a combined government and industry database be set up to enable South African businesses to establish practices in any EU member-country from which they may acquire personal data, for example, to establish profiles of their customers in that country" (RSA Green Paper, p. 80).

Security, Encryption and Trust South Africa believes that "security measures used in conventional commerce may not be adequate to provide trust in the electronic economy" (RSA Green Paper, p. 66). At the same time, it is important that national and personal security concerns are balanced with personal privacy concerns. Four key elements are seen as crucial to ensuring that transactions in the digital economy can take place securely. These elements are: (1) authentication; (2) confidentiality; (3) integrity; and (4) -repudiation. From South Africa's perspective, achieving this level of security for the digital economy "requires active partnership between government and the private sector" (RSA Green Paper, p. 66).

These technologies are seen as critical to promoting trust in the digital economy, among both consumers and producers. It appears that South Africa is comfortable with the leading role being played by the OECD in promoting a regime consensus in this area.

Awareness In South Africa, as in many other parts of the world, low levels of awareness about the potential benefits and opportunities in electronic commerce, is a limiting factor for its growth. South Africa is developing a strategy to promote these opportunities, both to consumers and among the SMME sector.

Central to this issue is educating the wider population about the opportunities and potential threats of e-commerce. Coupled with that is the need to popularize or publicize an e-commerce policy process so as to invite participation. The creation of awareness and other related initiatives by government and its partners from the academic and business sectors to promote technological development should be done in an integrated approach. We need to build a new e-community that can take effective advantage of the e-commerce opportunities (RSA Green Paper, p. 112).

Within the South African public, private and civil society sectors, there are many bodies working to promote this level of awareness. Within the government, the DOC is playing a leading role. Numerous private sector enterprises and bodies such as the Electronic Commerce Association of South Africa (ECASA) and the African Connection are also contributing in this area. In the civil society, the University of the Witwatersrand's Learning, Information, Networks, and Knowledge (LINK) Center is engaged in promoting an enhanced intellectual understanding of these issues, and the ISOC of South Africa is building technical and user awareness.

Technical Standards The emerging South African perspective on technical standards is that they are of critical importance to the development and proper functioning of the Internet and GEC. "Standards are rules, and serve as a basis for comparison and a form of order. The major objective for standardization is to achieve interoperability between networks and services and ensure compatibility" (RSA Green Paper, p. 91).

"Standards are needed for long-term commercial success of the Internet since they can allow products, services and applications from different firms to work hand in hand. Standards encourage competition and reduce stress or uncertainty in the market place" (RSA Green Paper, p. 91). However, there is also a recognition that "standards can also be employed as de facto non-tariff trade barriers to "lockout' non-indigenous business from a particular national market" (RSA Green Paper, p. 92).

Furthermore, there are also tremendous challenges developing standards in "an environment in which technology is developing rapidly [and] may be counterproductive at this stage of e-commerce." (RSA Green Paper, p. 92). There is the recognition that these standards should be technology neutral and industry driven to the fullest extent possible.

South Africa supports the international organizations playing the leading role in developing this component of the global e-commerce regime, especially the role of the ISO and the ITU (RSA Green Paper, p. 92).

Local Content There are numerous possibilities for promoting local content in the digital economy. In South Africa, there is a growing recognition that perhaps the primary source of this local content will be the growth and development of the SMMEs sector. Small, medium and micro-sized enterprises will be looked to increasingly to create employment opportunities for South Africa.

Several international organizations, both governmental and nongovernmental, including the UNCTAD, the WIPO, the International Chambers of Commerce (ICC), and others are working to promote the impact of both developing countries and SMMEs on the digital economy.

Labor and Society As South Africa moves toward a digital economy, it is important to work to minimize the negative impact of e-commerce, while harnessing its potential. It is clear that both of these aspects are real possibilities in South Africa. On the one hand, new growth and new types of employment are indeed possible, while on the other hand, "many workers could become displaced, temporarily or permanently as a result of this transformation" (RSA Green Paper, p. 112). The e-Commerce Green Paper also identifies the need for further employment related research, which would "evaluate the nature and number of jobs that could be created by e-commerce" as well as those jobs that would be "lost or displaced" through this new approach to conducting business in an information economy and society (RSA Green Paper, p. 112). It also identifies a new breed of e-commerce firm called "the infomediary" which is aligned to take full advantage of the Internet. (RSA Green Paper, p. 112).

Globally, many of the high-technology workers who have sought fame and fortune in the digital economy are now becoming highly disillusioned (Lessard and Baldwin 2000). Recently, high-technology workers at one of the most widely known e-commerce companies, Amazon.com, have attempted to unionize in the Washington Area Technology Workers (WashTech), a union structure within the Communications Workers of America (CWA).

Currently, the ILO is reasserting itself as an important player in the international regime formation process for e-commerce, with a focus on understanding the impact on labor issues.

Human Resources and Capacity While the shortage of human resources with the requisite skills in information and communications technologies requires immediate global attention, this situation is particularly problematic in South Africa. In South Africa, the Human Science Research Council (HSRC) states that "there is a chronic shortage of highly skilled human resources in various segments of the market. The scarcity of technical expertise and skills, in the country is further exacerbated by the 'brain drain'" (RSA Green Paper, p. 111).

South Africa further recognizes that human development must occur on at least five different levels: (1) skills and human resources; (2) digital literacy; (3) digital skills for all South Africans; (4) skills for business; and (3) skills for the future (RSA Green Paper, p. 111). Distance education and virtual campuses are seen as important elements of this strategy and should be supported and developed in South Africa.

CONTESTING AND SHAPING THE EMERGING REGIME

As we can see from this case study of South Africa, this newly emerging regime will be wide ranging, and have a tremendous impact on nearly every area of how we "live, work, and play," as the evolving mantra goes. If this is so, it means that this regime involves perhaps the most important set of principles, norms, and values that we have seen in an international regime. What can be done to influence the direction of the emerging regime so that it might be more just and equitable for a wider grouping of the world's citizens?

The spatially disarticulated nature of the global economy and its systems for R&D, production, testing, distribution, and management is challenging the models of global governance. These are the issues that are leading the revolution in the ITR, and that will influence the emergence of the new GII/GIS regime. In this case, the international regime of norms, principles, values, and enforcement mechanisms for this new economy are being developed as various societal actors around the world attempt to influence this process. Further, as this new regime is being developed, many societal actors are assessing and reassessing their roles and strategies.

Most likely, this new GII/GIS regime will be based upon the WTO, the Geneva-based successor organization to the General Agreement on Tariffs and Trade. Global market access and a liberalized, rule-based, multilateral trading environment for tangible goods and intangible services are some of the key principles that already define this new economic order. These challenges require strategic responses from both state and non-state actors to include participation and partnerships from all relevant societal actors (public, private, and voluntary sector entities). The senior public, private and civil society leadership in Africa and other developing regions must find ways to strengthen their voices in the high-level processes of regime formation if the rules of the new economy are to adequately reflect some of their interests.

Central to the development of an information society is the underlying infrastructure on which various information society applications depend. While we currently refer to this collectively as the Internet, previously, the idea of a GII, on which the relevant data and applications travel, had a great deal of salience. The GII is based fundamentally on global telecommunications networks. These networks have been successfully "governed" for over a century by the convergence of principles, values, and norms facilitated by an ITR (Drake 1989; Cowhey 1990; Zacher and Sutton 1996; Freiden 1996).

The potential of cyber infrastructure for socioeconomic development is overwhelming, as illustrated by a wide range of new and innovative Internet-based applications (e.g., distributed scientific collaboratories, distance-independent learning, and global electronic transactions.) These applications have created a new class of stakeholders from developing countries and civil society organizations who frequently represent interests and are engaging in the arcane processes of governing global cyber infrastructure.

The global governance of cyber infrastructure involves an interrelated set of ICT policy processes that revolve around a complex set of formal and informal institutions, including such diverse public and private organizations as the including such diverse organizations as the ITU, WTO, WIPO, OECD, and nongovernmental organizations like WEF, GIIC, GBDe, and the ICANN.

Each of these organizations is involved with various international conferences, which have become the primary locations for the vigorous contestation of principles, values, norms, rules, and decision-making procedures that are the core of any international regime. At these international conferences, policy-actors attempt to represent the interests of their various constituencies bringing to bear their knowledge and expertise on final conference outcomes (e.g., declarations, agreements, and statements). Collectively, these conference outcomes are facilitating the emergence of a new regime for the global governance of cyber infrastructure.

CHAPTER 4

ISOC, ICANN, and Experiments in Multistakeholder Global Internet Governance

INTRODUCTION

In the last chapter, we sketched the developments in the erosion of the ITR and the emergence of a new international regime, which we called the GII regime. We highlighted the contested nature of the collection of principles and values of this emerging regime from a vision of a GII designed to support an open and sharing GIS, contrasted with one designed to support the needs of GEC. We even posed the question "Did eCommerce Kill the 'Net'?" because of the stark differences in these two approaches. This chapter explores more deeply the almost parallel developments that were occurring in the global governance of the highly technical and politically sensitive policy issues related to the global governance of the Internet and the World Wide Web.

BIRTH OF THE INTERNET AND INTERNET GOVERNANCE

The history of the development of the Internet and the World Wide Web has been well documented. Perhaps the most definitive consensus account of this history was published by the ISOC, and written by the founders of the Internet themselves (including Vinton Cerf, Robert Kahn, and Jon

© The Author(s) 2017
D.L. Cogburn, *Transnational Advocacy Networks in the Information Society*, Information Technology and Global Governance,
DOI 10.1057/978-1-137-48361-4_4

Postel). However, for the purposes of this book, especially our subsequent discussions and institutional analysis, we will highlight some of the key moments and actors in this history, without going into too much technical detail.

Early History of the Internet Predecessors

Working at the Massachusetts Institute of Technology (MIT), Leonard Kleinrock published in July 1961 what is known as "the first paper on packet switching theory" (Leiner et al. 2009). The concept of packet switching, where information is broken up into small "packets," sent along the network through different routes, and reassembled at its ultimate destination, would later become a critical element of the Internet and a key differentiation between the traditional circuit-switched telephone networks.

In August 1962, J.C.R. Licklider working at MIT began writing a series of memos that discussed the possibilities of a "Galactic Network" that would connect computers globally to share information between interested parties. In October 1962, Licklider became head of computer science research at the Advanced Research Projects Agency (ARPA), taking his global networking concepts with him, and influencing the agency and subsequent leaders of computer science research at ARPA of the advantages of packet switching over circuit switching. In 1965, Roberts in Massachusetts worked with Thomas Merrill in California to use low-speed telecommunication networks to connect two computers creating the first wide area network (WAN) and highlighted the problems of circuit-switched networks for computer networking, confirming the need for packet switching (Leiner et al. 2009).

Subsequently, in late 1966, Roberts left MIT for ARPA to head the computer science research program and developed a plan for the ARPANET, which he published in 1967. The ISOC reports that networking research at three separate groups, MIT (1961–1967), RAND (1962–1965), and in the UK at NPL (1964–1967) had all occurred in parallel without any of the researchers knowing about the other (Leiner, et al. 2009).

In December 1968, a research group at Bold Beranek and Newman (BBN) led by Frank Heart won an ARPA RFQ to develop the packet switches called Interface Message Processors (IMPs). The University of California at Los Angeles (UCLA) became the first node on ARPANET in 1969, as its Network Measurement Center was the recipient of the first IMP installed by BBN. This was followed in the same year by the Stanford Research Institute (SRI), which became the second node. Later the same year, the University of California Santa Barbara and the University of Utah became the third and fourth nodes on ARPANET. Throughout the early 1970s, ARPANET continued to grow, adding new computers around the country, and "network users finally could begin to develop applications" (Leiner, et al. 2009).

Founding Father(s) of the Internet

In the 1970s, US Congressman Albert Gore began promoting the idea that high-speed telecommunications could contribute to social and economic growth, and later that ordinary Americans should be given access to the emerging network (Kahn and Cerf 1974). And while some criticized Gore and accused him of claiming to have "invented" the Internet, Gore never made such a claim, and is noted by Internet pioneers Robert Kahn and Vint Cerf as being "the first elected official to grasp the potential of computer communications to have a broader impact than just improving the conduct of science and scholarship. Though easily forgotten, now, at the time this was an unproven and controversial concept" (Kahn and Cerf 1974). They also argued that "there is no question in our minds that while serving as Senator, Gore's initiatives had a significant and beneficial effect on the still-evolving Internet" (Kahn and Cerf 1974).

In 1971, ARPA changed its name to DARPA. At the International Computer Communication Conference in 1972, Robert Kahn organized the first large-scale public demonstration of ARPANET. In this same year, the first "Killer App" for the network was developed—Electronic Mail.

Building upon a foundation of related and previous work, Kahn and Cerf began work in 1973 on the fundamental protocols of the Internet, known eventually as the Transmission Control Protocol/Internet Protocol (TCP/IP), publishing a landmark paper on their TCP work in 1974, and subsequently breaking off the IP focused on addressing and packet forwarding to form TCP/IP. This period is generally seen as the "birth of the Internet." On 1 January 1983, ARPANET was switched from its previous Network Control Protocol (NCP) over to TCP/IP. This transition also allowed a separate MILNET to be split off from ARPANET.

By 1985, a plethora of network options began to emerge, mostly as closed scientific and academic communities. These included, MFENet for Department of Energy researchers working on Magnetic Fusion Energy and HEPNet for DoE High-Energy Physicists, SPAn for NASA Space Physicists, CSNET for computer science researchers funded by the US NSF, USENET from AT&T, and BITNET to link academic mainframe computers. However, in 1984, JANET the British academic network and in 1985 NSFNET the US NSF both declared their intentions to serve the "entire higher education community, regardless of discipline." Indeed, a condition for a US university to receive NSF funding for an Internet connection was that "the connection must be made available to ALL qualified users on campus" (Leiner, et al. 2009). When NSFNET adopted TCP/IP, it laid the groundwork for the Internet we have today. In 1988, NSF commissioned a report titled "Towards a National Research Network," produced by a National Research Council committee, chaired by Kleinrock (Leiner, et al. 2009). This report was highly influential on then US Senator Al Gore. Working in CERN, the particle accelerator in Geneva, Sir Tim Berners Lee, a British computer scientist invented the World Wide Web in 1989.

The Internet Society (ISOC)

To provide a bit of global context to these historical developments, in 1992, the Earth Summit was held in Rio de Janeiro, Brazil and Agenda 21 for sustainable development was adopted. This was the same year, following the first INET conference in Copenhagen, that Cerf and Kahn launched The ISOC as a membership-based organization designed "to promote the open development, evolution, and use of the Internet for the benefit of all people throughout the world" (ISOC). A subsequent 1994 National Research Council report commissioned by NSF and entitled "Realizing the Information Future: The Internet and Beyond" revealed the blueprint for the evolution of the Internet as "Information Superhighway" that continues to influence the development of the Internet today. Following the strategy in this report, in 1995, the NSF effectively privatized the Internet by defunding the NSFNET backbone.

GROWTH OF THE INTERNET: IN SIZE, SCOPE, AND IMPORTANCE

Since these historic developments, the global use of the Internet has grown faster than almost anyone could have imagined. In 1995, there were an estimated 16 million global users of the Internet, up from the very small handful over the preceding two decades. However, by 2013, the estimated number of Internet users has grown to 2.7 billion users worldwide (found on the Internet on 16 September 2013 at: http://www.

internetworldstats.com/emarketing.htm). In addition to this continued growth of the Internet itself, there has been a concomitant growth in the use of the World Wide Web and numerous applications and services that run on top of this infrastructure.

These developments have fundamentally changed the lives of individuals, governments, international and regional organizations, businesses, and civil society organizations. They have affected nearly every area of human existence, including education, employment, entertainment, recreation, and cultural preservation, simultaneously affecting national security and broad socioeconomic growth. The applications areas using the Internet and World Wide Web include electronic commerce, telemedicine, distance learning, virtual organizations, and teams. It is hard to think of some area modern society that has not been touched by the Internet.

Since its inception in 1982, the stability and functionality of the Internet has been amazing. Consider the profound developments, which we now take as commonplace. Nearly every day, students, faculty, researchers, government officials, and business leaders send and receive between 144 billion and 294 billion e-mails. About 1.9 billion e-mail users (Radicati Group, Mashable) access shared files and data repositories, engage in video and voice-based teleconferences, use web-conferencing tools for virtual meetings and sharing screens, culminating in more than 27,000 petabytes (PG) of IP traffic per month, with 597 PB being on mobile devices, which are experiencing phenomenal growth in traffic.

This almost instantaneous global communication seems almost futuristic. Most people may not know exactly how the Internet works; they just know it works.

Understanding Internet Governance

While the stability of the Internet has been very strong, the fact that it "just works" is no accident. In fact, the Internet is an extremely complex global technical infrastructure that requires enormous global coordination between a multitude of entities such as governments, private sector, regional organizations, and several voluntary associations.

The essential governance functions of the Internet focus on managing the root zone file which matches the specific IP addresses (e.g., 147.9.1.186) of each device connected to the Internet with the domain names (e.g., American.edu) used to find them as well as coordinating the process of allocating those domain names in the first place and managing the maintenance and development of the underlying technical standards for IP and TCP, which enable data to be transmitted through the system.

The efficient conduct of these technical and policy processes determines the stability, security, and robustness of the Internet as we know it today. In addition, some of the more policy-oriented processes, such as authorizing new global top-level domain names (gTLDs), the processes of managing the use of Country Code Top Level Domains (ccTLDS), and implementing Internationalized Domain Names (IDNs) have been highly politicized.

Within this environment, multiple stakeholders who have been involved for years are now contesting for power within these governance processes and creating new institutions to enhance the global governance of the Internet.

Providing global governance for the Internet that ensures stability, reliability, and growth for this critical international resource presents numerous conceptual and empirical challenges. This process is complicated further by deepening globalization, economic integration, financial crises, transnational security threats, and growing networks of non-state actors (both malignant and benign), all of which contribute to complicating the study of global governance. Within this environment, understanding global Internet governance is particularly challenging, as it traverses disciplinary boundaries from political science, economics, sociology, and communications to computer science and information studies. In fact, in many ways governing the Internet poses a classic and fundamental global governance challenge. We have an issue area that is transitional in scope, critical to the social, political, and economic development of the planet, with no centrally governed institution existing to manage it fully, and with much of the resources required for its proper functioning lying in private, not government, hands.

Even with this complexity, Internet governance has been a relatively stable international regime. From the founding of the Internet in US military research and development labs, to the technical management of TCP/IP via contracts with the US Department of Commerce, to the grand global experiment in privatization and internationalization of Internet governance through the creation of the ICANN—a registered US not-for-profit corporation headquartered in Marina del Rey, California—the stability of the global Internet has been sponsored by the US government and backed by US private sector interests at the core and a wide variety of private and governmental actors on the periphery. Substantial cracks in the stability of this international regime started to appear in 2003 with the convening of the UN WSIS as developing country interest and others started to use this "multistakeholder" environment to articulate a range of divergent policy preferences. We will discuss WSIS in great detail in the next part of this book. In this part, we want to discuss the global governance environment for ICTs leading up to WSIS, what regime theorists would call the *ancient regime.*

This cacophony of voices, which at one point seemed to fuel speculation about alternative Internet governance arrangements, perhaps through the UN and especially the International Telecommunications Union, was eventually shunted into a new global post-WSIS multistakeholder body called the IGF. For seven years, relative calm and stability returned to the US-dominated international Internet governance regime, as the IGF established itself as an innovative vehicle for multistakeholder Internet governance discussion and debate, while the technical processes of Internet governance actually occurred elsewhere in ICANN and a host of other organizations, such as the Regional Internet Registries (RIRs), the Internet Engineering Task Force (IETF), and others. However, in June 2013 as the damaging revelations began to trickle from the Snowden NSA leaks about the extent of US global surveillance of the Internet and the deep complicity of the US private sector, shockwaves began to be felt within the primary Internet governance institutions. In October 2013, most of the leaders of the organizations responsible for the global coordination of the technical infrastructure of the Internet signed and issued the Montevideo Statement on the Future of Internet Cooperation in which the goal of globalizing the ICANN and IANA functions into a true global, multistakeholder environment would be accelerated. During her speech to the United Nations General Assembly, President Dilma Rousseff of Brazil called the surveillance a breach of international law and issued an invitation to an unprecedented summit to be held in Brazil in early 2014 to address these issues. In an unexpected turn of events, all the heads of the major Internet governance organizations responsible for coordination of the Internet technical infrastructure agreed to attend the summit. In addition, a flurry of national and regional conferences, have been organized to address these issues as well. These issues dominated the most recent Eighth IGF, held in Bali. It appears that the revelations by Edward Snowden have helped to shine a spotlight on widespread government use of techniques for surveillance and contributed to the potential for a radical restructuring of Internet governance that was not achieved in previous attempts by certain governments, or international organizations such as the ITU.

As we discuss the functional logic of Internet governance, the chapter presents an overview of the technical nature of the Internet (and related software and technology like the World Wide Web and applications that run on top of it like social media). The goal of this overview is to help the reader to understand the subsequent dynamics of Internet governance. Our technical definition of the Internet, focusing on the IP Suite (TCP/IP), enables us to carefully specify what institutions and individuals are involved in the norm creation and decision-making processes that allow the Internet to operate as a "network of networks." Even this narrow focus is difficult, as we get pulled between the highly technical and specific aspects of coordinating the software and hardware protocols and standards, and the broader policy-oriented aspects of managing the scarce resources related to the Internet. For context, this section also provides an overview of the history of the Internet and background to the current system of Internet governance. It also explores the relationship between Internet governance and the broader concepts of the global governance of cyberspace, social media, and the Information Society.

In answering the remaining research questions, this chapter highlights the social, political, economic, and technological pressures leading to the erosion of previous global governance systems for international telecommunications and the emergence of new institutions to govern the Internet, including the ICANN. It includes a discussion of the fundamental contestation among international organizations and major stakeholders for dominance in the contemporary governance of the Internet, including the substantial conflicts occurring at the UN WSIS and most recently at the World Conference on International Telecommunication (WCIT). We also examine the post-WSIS creation of two new multistakeholder follow-up institutions, the GAID and the IGF. The IGF, with its MAG and Dynamic Coalitions, represents an entirely new mechanism for global governance. However, the IGF has major limitations. Participants in the IGF represent themselves, not their countries or organizations; it is nonbinding and has no decision-making capabilities, and the range of issues addressed by the IGF are incredibly broad, far beyond the narrow technical issues many analysts include as part of Internet governance. These limitations are so great that some scholars will not include the IGF as an Internet governance mechanism. They favor the strict technical Internet governance provided by the aggregation of ICANN, IETF, and the Regional Internet Registries (RIRs).

Understanding that there is no "one stop shop" for Internet governance, the paper ends with a discussion of the implications of these findings and recommendations for the global governance of the Internet.

A critical usage of international regime theory forms the conceptual foundation for this chapter. Early in its development, regime theory identified the convergence of expectations of actors in a given area of international affairs as an imperative to international regime formation and thus, global governance for the specified sector (Krasner 1983b). Nonetheless, most scholars working in this area do not pay sufficient attention to the mechanisms that might facilitate that convergence. As a contribution to a better understanding of this convergence, the conceptual framework used in this chapter focuses on international conferences, and conference diplomacy, as the primary location for the negotiation of the norms, principles, and values around which intentional regimes may be built (Cogburn 2003a). As these international conferences become more multistakeholder oriented, it is critical that we have a better understanding of how the actors that have been historically excluded from these formal processes—namely civil society and the private sector—are able to organize themselves for effective participation in global governance. More specifically, we are interested in how these multistakeholder actors use transnational networks to participate in the international regime formation processes and the role they play in facilitating the convergence of expectations required for the emergence of an international regime?

International conferences serve as focal points for contestation in regime formation; they nurture global networks of recognized policy experts, and policy actors interact at these global by participating in "conference diplomacy." Engaging effectively in these international conferences requires active participation in all five stages of conference diplomacy: (1) pre-conference activities; (2) conference; (3) drafting processes; (4) post-conference follow-up; and (5) active presence in global nodal cities. But how do entities that are relatively weaker, in terms of fiscal and organizational resources, participate effectively in these processes? Previous research suggests two components are key: (1) transnational policy networks; and (2) subject matter knowledge and expertise. Also, organized epistemic communities wield tremendous influence in information policy formulation at national, regional, and global levels. They wield this influence primarily through their acquired knowledge and expertise (Haas 1992; Cowhey 1993, 1990). Transnational policy- actor networks, comprised of elite policy experts, serve as powerful knowledge networks (Clark 1998; Creech and Willard 2001). Keck and Sikkink (1998) suggested that a Transnational Advocacy Network (TAN) might hold substantial potential for influencing the principles, values, and norms of the emerging international regime.

When considering the role of knowledge in the policy process, we draw upon Krasner who argued that "in a highly complex world, where *goals are often ill-defined* and many links are possible, *consensual knowledge* can greatly facilitate agreement on the development of an international regime (Krasner 1983, p. 20, emphasis added). He continues, saying that "without consensus, knowledge can have little impact on regime development in a world of sovereign states" (Krasner 1983, p. 20), and that "it must be widely accepted by policy makers" (Krasner 1983, p. 20).

The conferences critical to Internet governance have evolved tremendously over the past several decades, led largely by adoption by the UN General Assembly of resolution (A/Res/53/183, Para. 5) authorizing the creation of the WSIS. This resolution required the WSIS to be a multistakeholder conference.

Within the first phase of WSIS, Internet governance issues took on a prominent role, giving rise to the Civil Society Internet Governance Caucus, Working Group on Internet Governance (WGIG), and ultimately a broad-based challenge to the existing Internet governance regime dominated by the ICANN and a host of highly technical meetings (including the IETF and the World Wide Web Consortium).

More recently, the evidence of substantial US surveillance revealed by the Edward Snowden revelations has stimulated a whole new set of meetings. Since there is no single central global governance body for the Internet that plays the role of, say, the WTO for trade, these international conferences become even more important. This is especially true, as they have become the key location for contestation around the principles, norms and values, and actual practices of governing the Internet.

As these international conferences become more multistakeholder oriented, it is critical that we have a better understanding of how the actors that have been historically excluded from these formal processes—

namely civil society and the private sector—are able to organize themselves to participate in global governance processes. More specifically, we are interested in how these multistakeholder actors use Transnational Advocacy Networks to participate in the international regime formation processes for Internet governance and the role they play in facilitating the convergence of expectations required for the emergence of an international regime.

This critical usage of international regime theory, focused on the multistakeholder interaction at international conferences related to Internet governance, will be informed further by the *Why Govern?* approach developed by Acharya (2013). This approach focuses on the empirical analysis of the strategic, functional and normative logics of global governance, while also emphasizing the domestic and regional dynamics driving global governance and the differential resources of those actors participating in these processes. It also requires us to explore the tensions and relationships between and among these variables.

RESEARCH QUESTIONS AND METHODOLOGY

Based on this conceptual framework, we ask six interrelated research questions in this chapter:

1. What *functional* factors drive the processes of global Internet governance?
2. What *strategic* factors influence the processes of global Internet governance?
3. What *normative* factors drive the processes of global Internet governance?
4. In what ways does *domestic politics* influence the processes of global Internet governance?
5. How does *regionalism* affect the processes of Internet governance?
6. What are the relationships, tensions, and complementarities between these variables?

To answer these questions, we focus primarily on unobtrusive techniques to gather data. Data for the chapter are drawn from a variety of qualitative sources, and include both primary and secondary data. Nonintrusive data collection techniques include downloading data from websites related to the IGF and its multiple regional variants (e.g., EuroDIG, Africa IGF, etc.), the WSIS and its regional and preparatory meetings, the ICANN and its regular meetings, the Business Action to Support the Information Society (BASIS), the Civil Society Internet Governance Caucus (IGC), the GigaNet, BestBits, and several other civil society networks related to the Brazilian meeting on Internet governance, including 1Net. We also collected data from the websites and open archives of the IETF. Primary data collection also took place through analysis of publicly available e-mail archives and participant observation at these various meetings. All these textual data were analyzed using computer-assisted qualitative data analysis software (QDA Miner and WordStat).

THE GLOBAL GOVERNANCE OF CYBERSPACE

One area of international affairs that is yielding to innovative practices in global governance is in the information society, cyberspace, and more specifically global Internet governance. With its explicit focus on multistakeholder participation, the UN WSIS helped to spawn a number of conceptually interesting institutions and mechanisms for participation among all sectors, and between developed and developing countries. In this chapter, we ask six overarching research questions. In this section, we will use primary and secondary empirical data to answer these questions.

FUNCTIONAL FACTORS INFLUENCING GLOBAL INTERNET GOVERNANCE

There are a number of functional factors influencing the development of Internet governance. The underlying nature of coordinating the dissemination of IP addresses and domain names is the primary problem facing Internet governance. This coordination cannot be accomplished through unilateral national action. Initially, the USA and its private sector actors played this role, but as the users of the Internet increased, and the demand for privatization (getting Internet governance out of the hands of government control) and internationalization (spreading Internet governance to a host of international actors) increased, this unilateral role became untenable. The nature of the Internet is such that unilateral national action is not possible to sustain the robust functioning of the global Internet, even for a country as powerful as the USA. Further, the technical nature of the Internet requires expertise beyond that contained in most national government delegations.

In this section, we will explore the underlying coordination and control problems of Internet governance, where a constant eye is needed for maintaining the stability and security of this critical global resource. Global coordination in Internet governance is not an option. The fragmentation and regionalization that presents a constant danger to the Internet would be devastating to the viability of this resource. Contrast the value of being able to turn on your computer and send an email message to anyone on the planet that has an email address and an Internet connection, with the scenario of having that message only to be sent to persons within a regional or national networking arrangement. Some countries threaten this regional fragmentation constantly, especially those opposed to what they see as the continued "US domination" of the Internet. These calls have increased in the wake of the Snowden revelations of widespread US surveillance of Internet communications.

Defining the Internet

While many of us are deeply familiar with what we know of as "the Internet," most people do not understand what the Internet is exactly. In order to help advance the debate, we will focus on very carefully defined aspects of what may be more broadly referred to as cyberspace and social media. Cyberspace itself is a term that emerged in the 1980s in science fiction, and in popular culture in the 1990s. The term "information society" has a very broad connotation. It includes all of the online spaces, including the Internet, World Wide Web, and specific applications using these specific systems. There is an even broader conception known as the Information Society, which includes the broad social systems and ways in which societies around the world are being reshaped by the uses of ICT. Social media is one category of ICT that is included in these broad approaches. In this chapter, while we will make frequent references to these broader constructions, our focus will be on the specific aspects of Internet governance.

There are three functional areas to global Internet governance: (1) technical standardization; (2) resource allocation and assignment; and (3) policymaking (Internet Governance Project 2004).

Technical standardization refers to the processes of decision-making about the core protocols and applications that make the Internet work. These technical standards include the Transmission Control Protocol/IP, the overall DNS, the migration from IP Version 4 (IPv4) to IP Version (IPv6), and standards like ENUM/E.164.

Resource allocation and administration focuses on how the critical and scarce resources that enable the Internet to function are allocated and administered. These scarce resources include the actual domain names, including the expansion of global or generic top-level domains (GTLDs), the IP addresses themselves, regional registries, and handling dispute resolution around these issues.

The policymaking function of Internet governance focuses on the formulation of specific policies for the Internet, as well as monitoring and enforcement of those policies and dispute resolution processes. Some of the policy issues related to these issues include customs and taxation issues; electronic payments; privacy and data protection; freedom of expression; security and encryption; authentication and digital signatures; knowledge, ideas, and intellectual property; human rights; content creation and protection; labor and social impact; infrastructure development and financing, and universal service access and the "right to communicate."

To begin discussion on these functional Internet governance issues, let us return to our example about the domain name for American University (American.edu, or more properly formed in hypertext markup language, http://american.edu/). This is of course a very recognizable address for the university, and one that is used in most marketing materials and in other ways for the university, its various schools and colleges, sports teams, and other units. Under the current system of Internet governance, this domain name is unique. No other entity in the world can use the domain name American.edu. There are a variety of mechanisms to ensure that, and to dispute resolution processes in the event that some violation occurs.

However, what technically enables that reality is how the DNS works. First, intimately linked to that domain name is the IP address of American. edu. This IP address happens to be 147.9.3.21 (notice the four "blocks" of numbers in this IP address, and we will return to the importance of that shortly). If you type this IP address into your browser for the World Wide Web (e.g., Safari, Firefox, or Google Chrome), the American University website will magically appear. Most people are not familiar with IP addresses, and instead rely on the far more recognizable and easy-to-remember domain name. Of course, we have to remember telephone numbers all the time, and in some ways an IP address is like a telephone number, which in its complete form (i.e., country code, area code, number) is also a unique resource that no other entity in the world can have. Domain names make it easier for people to remember the web address of a particular site and for organizations to brand their presence on the Internet. But how does this process work?

The DNS (also called the Domain Name Space) is a structured set of instructions for allocating each of those four blocks in the IP address, which collectively moves the user from network to network and location to location around the world from the computer where the request is first made (where you enter the domain name into your e-mail client or web browser) to ultimately, the computer where the files you wish to receive are located. This process happens almost instantly as the domain name gets resolved, by first matching it to the unique IP address associated with the requested domain name, and then resolving each block of the IP address, with each block getting you closer and closer to the actual computer storing the files you are requesting.

This process is related to a broader model called the Open Systems Interconnection (OSI) model, which identifies different layers for information and communication networks moving at the most fundamental physical level based on hardware and the physical network infrastructure up through transport layers, which are more software- and protocol-driven, ultimately to the presentation and application layers, which is what most users are able to see. The OSI model corresponds to the TCP/IP model.

This brief discussion about the OSI model and TCP/IP model should help to illustrate the range of thorny, and potentially intractable, policy issues being debated in Internet governance circles. These issues range from whether or not there should be an expansion of global top-level domains (the original GTLDs were .org, .com, .gov, .net, .edu), which are the appropriate entities to manage country code top level domains (e.g., .us, or e.g., .uk, .za).

- Privacy and data protection issues, along with security and encryption issues, dominate the news, especially after the Snowden revelations.
- Freedom of expression and human rights issues on the Internet are other hot-button policy issues, along with labor and social protection.
- Authentication and digital signatures, intellectual property rights, content creation and protection, and
- Access issues, such as infrastructure development and financing and universal service access are all included. While these are all policy issues, they will be discussed in more detail in our section focused on normative factors affecting Internet governance.

Finally, one of the most pressing functional problems facing the world in Internet governance is that there is a shortage of IP addresses. As more and more users around the world begin to use the Internet, and as the new "Internet of Things" begins to emerge with companies and individuals needing multiple IP addresses for their refrigerators, thermostats, lights, doors, cars, bicycles, and so on, there is a global shortage of IP addresses. The four-block model described above (IPv4) has a finite number of possible unique numbers, and we are quickly approaching the use of all those possibilities.

Fortunately, the technical Internet governance community has already come up with a solution to this problem; it just requires global coordination and cooperation to implement. The solution is to transition away from the use of IP Version 4, to the newer IP Version 6 (IPv6). IPv6 has a number of advantages, in terms of security and functionality, but perhaps its most important immediate aspect is that, because of its structure, it has far greater capacity to generate unique IP addresses.

STRATEGIC FACTORS INFLUENCING GLOBAL INTERNET GOVERNANCE

Transformation of the International Telecommunication Regime

As we begin to discuss the strategic factors influencing the transformation of the current Internet governance regime, it is important first to understand the ITR, upon which the Internet governance regime is built.

The international telecommunication regime is based upon the ITU, a specialized agency of the United Nations. Scholars have described the ITR as being characterized by "multiple 'Cs'" including consensus, collaboration, consultation, culture, clubiness, consortia/cartels, and collusion. This international regime was strongly supported by national level institutions. The regime was focused on a single, albeit complicated, issue: *Single Issue* (telecommunications); it focused on a *Single Ministry* at the national level (Ministry of Posts, Telegraph and Telecommunications) and on a single industry (in most countries, a monopoly PTT operator) more generally. Some of the principles and values on which the ITR was based include the shared understanding that telecommunications was a *natural monopoly*, and as such the nation-state had a responsibility to monopolize the provision of telecommunications infrastructure within a state-owned ministry of telecommunications, both to provide infrastructure and promote national security. These principles and values were promoted through a variety of mechanisms, including international conferences such at the ITU World Telecommunications conference and its regional variants (TELECOM), and the WTDC. This regime generally had limited stakeholders, because it was a complex, highly technical environment that required enormous expertise in order to understand and participate in any international meetings/conferences related to telecommunications. This expertise was limited to a very narrow group of experts, and "epistemic communities" to support international telecommunications.

This once powerful international regime was substantially eroded by a series of technological, economic, political, and social factors. For example, some of the technological factors eroding the ITR included the rapid technological development in information and communications technologies, including Very Small Aperture Terminal satellites (VSATs); Voice Over IP (VOIP); call-back systems, and Global Mobile Personal Communications by Satellite (GMPCS) systems. Some of the economic factors included a focus on creating the infrastructure GEC and the need for what was being called the GII. Political factors included the World Trade Organization's (WTO) Negotiating Group on Basic Telecommunications (NGBT) and subsequently, the ABT; the restructuring of Intelsat and international accounting rates, and the overall global trend toward liberalization and privatization, referred to collectively as the *Washington Consensus*. Finally, there was the societal demand for access to "Information

Society" applications, such as telemedicine, distance learning, and video-on-demand. The diverse nature of the potential of the Internet and information society created a diverse group of stakeholders, most of who had never been involved in international negotiations or conferences in the past (e.g., nurses, teachers, doctors etc.). There were also numerous, and competing "epistemic communities" able to weigh in on these varied issues (e.g., groups of nurses, teachers, and doctors).

Collectively, these pressures coalesced to demand universal access to low-cost, high-bandwidth Internet connectivity, access to Internet-based services and applications, and the ICT and information infrastructure to support business and small, medium and micro-sized enterprises (SMMEs) to develop goods and services for the information society.

These changes fundamentally altered the logic for the ITR. While the international telecommunication regime was a highly technical issue area (dominated by experts) and based on one ministry, the newly emerging "Global Information Infrastructure" Regime (Cogburn 2003), largely because of the range of application areas, was based on multiple ministries. For example, telemedicine required the ministries of health to become interested and involved; distance education required similarly for departments of education. Environmental applications required ministries of environment to get involved, and trade and electronic commerce applications required ministries of trade and industry to get involved. The private sector, also was extremely interested in many of these issue areas, as well as civil society and other non-state actors. This erosion of the old international telecommunication regime has tremendous implications for Internet governance, the development of an information society, broader cyber infrastructure, and other issue areas that rely on telecommunications and the rapid movement of information. Further, the ITU has been losing some of its centrality in governing telecommunications to the WTO and its focus on the global trade in services (especially Type II trade in services, which includes virtual teams and organizations). For several years, I have argued that there is the need to understand this period as an "interregnum"—the period when one international regime is being eroded, and a new regime is not yet in place. An interregnum is frequently a period of tremendous contestation over the principles, norms, and values of the emerging regime. In this case, the emerging regime could take two distinct directions: one that is more open and focused on the development of an inclusive information society, and another that is narrower and focused on creating the environment to support electronic commerce and global corporate interests.

Several international conferences and organizations were supporting the development of principles, values, and norms related to this emerging regime. For example, the G7 articulated the "Brussels Principles for the Information Society" (found on the Internet on 30 September 2013 http://www.itu.int/osg/spu/wsis-themes/access/backgroundpaper/ IS%20Principles.pdf). These principles included a focus on: (1) promoting dynamic competition; (2) encouraging private investment; (3) defining an adaptable regulatory framework; and (4) providing open access to networks; *while* (5) ensuring universal provision of an access to services; (6) promoting equality of opportunity to the citizen; (7) promoting diversity of content; and (8) recognizing the necessity of worldwide cooperation. These Brussels Principles tried to balance the corporate interests (the first four) with citizen interests (the second four). This balancing act between corporate/national security and citizen interests continues in the current Internet governance regime and will be addressed in the section on normative factors.

A subsequent conference called the ISAD conference organized in 1996 in South Africa by the G7 and a cross section of the developing countries, articulated a set of principles called the "ISAD Principles." The ISAD Principles promoted 12 principles including (1) universal service; (2) clear regulatory framework; (3) employment creation; (4) global cooperation and competitiveness; (5) diversity of applications and content; (6) diversity of language and culture; (7) cooperation in technology; (8) private investment and competition; (9) protection of intellectual property rights; (10) privacy and data security; (11) narrowing the infrastructure gap; and (12) cooperation in research and technological development.

This shift toward this new set of principles and values was illustrated in a number of ways in 1995. One important way was the 1995 TELECOM conference in Geneva, organized by the ITU, which saw a substantial and prominent presence of computer companies for the first time. Similarly, non-state actors representing all the interests of the different application areas described above participated in TELECOM in record numbers. Global e-Commerce was seen as a prominent driver of these changes, and new organizations like the GIIC were created at the CSIS to address these global issues.

The WTO, not the ITU, was seen as the leader of this newly emerging international regime. It had taken on global trade in services, electronic commerce, and telecommunications liberalization and privatization, all principles and values critical to the emergence of this new regime.

During this period, many new epistemic communities began to organize and/or attempt to mobilize and influence this regime formation process. In my previous work (Cogburn 2003), I have focused on the role of international and regional conferences in regime formation because of their role in facilitating a convergence of expectations in the principles, values, and norms of the emerging regime. There is a multiplicity of complex processes that enable this process: some formal, others informal; some public, and others very private. There is also a multiplicity of policy actors involved in these processes: governments (including OECD, G8, APEC); international organizations (e.g., WTO, ITU, WIIPO, UNESCO, UNCITRAL, ICANN); private sector (e.g., GIIC, GBDe, ICC); experts and epistemic communities, including telecommunications experts, Internet experts, trade experts, private sector, and public sector interest groups, international lawyers (e.g., IETF, WC3, NANOG), and finally other private and civil society groupings and individuals (e.g., WEF, WSF).

EMERGENCE AND TRANSFORMATION OF THE INTERNET GOVERNANCE REGIME

As the transformation of the ITR was underway, a somewhat concomitant process was occurring in the Internet and applications that would run on top of these international communication networks. Within each component of the conceptual framework employed in this study, great power dynamics, especially involving the USA, have been exceptionally influential. US influence extends into the multistakeholder conference environment, where US NGOs and academics have also wielded tremendous influence within the civil society networks involved in Internet governance. The middle powers have also played an important role; sometimes siding with the USA, but at other times serving as a major alternative (especially Canada in regards to information policy and privacy).

International conferences, such as the UN WSIS and the IGF continue to play a critical role in the processes of global governance. They frequently provide concrete opportunities for formal and informal negotiations around the principles, norms, values, and decision-making procedures around which convergence is required in order for an international regime to emerge in a particular domain of international affairs (Krasner 1982). Historically, governments have dominated the official "conference diplomacy" surrounding these World Summits and their preparatory processes (Kaufmann 1988; Gelman 2000). However, when the UN General Assembly authorized WSIS in 2001 it sparked a fundamental change in what has been called multistakeholder participation in global governance processes (A/Res/53/183, Para. 5). The UNGA invited NGOs, civil society, and the private sector "to contribute, and actively participate in, the intergovernmental preparatory process of the Summit and the Summit itself" along with all relevant UN bodies and other international and regional organizations (A/Res/53/183, Para. 5).

For many analysts, this opportunity for multistakeholder participation signaled a fundamental shift in the power relations between state and non-state actors. For example, in the private sector a networked called BASIS (Business Action to Support the Information Society) was formed to provide a vehicle for global private sector organizations including the international chamber of commerce, the GIIC, and the WITSA to participate in and influence the WSIS. Regional groupings were formed for Africa and Latin America, including regional preparatory meetings. Transnational civil society organizations were able to participate formally in the WSIS processes.

While the Internet is seen as beginning a research network with eventual transition into a corporate and educational network, its actual origins are the US ARPA and subsequently DARPA as a means for secure military communication. The most recent *Global Trends 2030: Alternative Worlds* report, published by the National Intelligence Council, argues indirectly that the impact and governance of the Internet and new technologies will be one of the decisive "mega-trends" that will be "game-changing" and affect the structure of the coming world order (December 2012).

As we discussed above, the Internet's TCP/IP was designed to enable electronic messages to be broken apart from the sending machine and routed around network failure and reassembled on the receiver's machine—all in the event of a nuclear attack or other military disaster. So from the very beginning, the Internet was of strategic military importance, initially to the USA and subsequently to the rest of the world. The strategic importance of the Internet was amplified tremendously when in 1993 the NSF, which had by then taken control of the management of the Internet, began to allow its use for commercial purposes and to facilitate integration between the previously government funded NSF Net and the commercial networks. This combined military-economic nexus ratcheted up the strategic importance of this global communication network.

The formative background of the Internet as a US-funded military and scientific asset, and subsequently as a commercial resource, has given the USA a particularly powerful interest in determining the governance of the Internet and a certain perceived legitimacy. However, as the rhetoric about the development of an Information Society and a knowledge-based economy continued to develop in the mid-1990s, more and more countries around the world were encouraged to embrace the Internet as a vehicle to fuel their economic growth and for socioeconomic development. Initiatives such as the Bangemann Commission Report in 1993 articulated a strategic framework for developing the Information Society within the European Union. In the USA, the initiatives stimulated by the US Vice President Al Gore about the development of an "Information Superhighway" did the same (1992). Similar initiatives were promoted by the ITU, especially for the developing world through, for example, its WTDC and TELECOM (World TELECOM, Africa TELECOM, Asia TELECOM, Americas TELECOM) events.

These efforts corresponded with the broad global developments around the so-called Washington Consensus to promote the liberalization and privatization of telecommunications, and subsequently the focus on promoting the use of ICTs to support the Global Trade in Services coming out of the WTO and the emerging focus on GEC within the WTO, ITU, and others. These developments were fueled in many ways by the negotiations around the ABT within the WTO. Many of these initiatives also had an implicit socioeconomic development goal, to reduce poverty, provide enhanced educational opportunities, and close the so-called digital divide.

Also, numerous regional strategies were developing to address these issues, such as the AISI, organized by the UNECA in 1996, and the subsequent ISAD Conference organized in South Africa (1996) as a partnership between the G7 and a cross section of the developing world.

The combination of these issues led to the increasing calls for the privatization and globalization of Internet governance. The privatization calls argued that the Internet was becoming too powerful a tool to be in the hands of only one government, and that there needed to be private, nongovernmental control of this critical communication network. The globalization calls echoed this sentiment, with the argument that the Internet was important to the social and economic development of countries around the world and as a result should no longer be dominated by US institutions. These calls led to the eventual creation of the ICANN, which would take over the functions previously performed by the IANA.

On 18 September 1998, the ICANN was founded. It was established as a not-for profit corporation, headquartered initially in Marina del Rey, California (ICANN now has offices in Los Angeles, Istanbul, Singapore, Beijing, Brussels, Montevideo, and Washington, DC).

While it was a step toward privatization and internationalization of Internet governance, and a major global experiment in multistakeholder Internet governance, it did not go far enough to satisfy most critics. This structure for ICANN was indeed a step removed from US governmental control, but still clearly controlled at arm's length by the operating contracts with the US Department of Commerce. A Memorandum of Understanding (MoU) with the US Department of Commerce initially established the parameters for how ICANN would operate.

Although ICANN came into existence out of its own global transformation, in conjunction with the technical experts at the IETF and W3C, it now clearly represents the center of the existing, or *ancien regime*. Contesting with ICANN for institutional dominance in any newly emerging regime for Internet governance is the ITU (organizer of the WSIS and the World Conference on International Telecommunications).

The current challenge to the power of ICANN began in earnest with the convening of the first phase of the WSIS. With its focus on multistakeholder involvement, active leadership from the ITU, eager to play a more important role in this new environment (and to further justify its continued existence), WSIS became a perfect vehicle to again raise concerns about the limited nature of the privatization and internationalization of Internet governance. This was coupled by the continued rise in importance of GEC and other application areas favored by the USA and global private sector.

Within the WSIS processes, the public position of the USA has consistently focused on the need to maintain the stability and efficient functioning of the Internet and to maintain its global scope. However, its more "backstage" interests have consistently included national security interests.

In addition, the USA has consistently promoted an "Internet Freedom" that gained tremendous traction under the leadership of Secretary of State Hillary Clinton. However, one major contradiction is that even as the USA professes to justify its continued dominance of the Internet to help promote it as a tool to enhance freedom throughout the world (through the use of the Internet, social media), it simultaneously has been using these very same networks for worldwide surveillance. The extent of the Snowden revelations has already been enormous, and everything has not yet been released.

During the first phase of WSIS, it became clear that while progress was being made on many of the difficult issues of broad information society development, there were going to be thorny and probably intractable issues related to Internet governance. As a pre-emptive move, a suggestion was made in 2003 to set up the Working Group on Internet Governance (WGIG). The WGIG was set up toward the end of the first phase of the WSIS and given the mandate to (1) develop an agreed-upon working definition of Internet governance; (2) identify the public policy issues that are relevant to Internet governance; and (3) develop a common understanding of the respective roles and responsibilities of governments, existing international organizations, and other forums, as well as the private sector and civil society from both developing and developed countries (WGIG 2003).

The WGIG consisted of members from diverse stakeholders, including from developed and developing countries and the private sector, and worked during the period between the first phase of WSIS held in Geneva (2003) until the second phase held in Tunis (2005). On one interesting note, after tremendous effort, the WGIG finally came up with a definition many international relations scholars, drawing on Krasner (1983), could have produced over an afternoon coffee. The WGIG definition of Internet governance is as follows: "Internet governance is the development and application by governments, the private sector and civil society, in their respective roles, of shared principles, norms, rules, decision-making procedures, and programmes that shape the evolution and use of the Internet" (WGIG Report 2005).

In 2005, at the end of the second phase of the WSIS in Tunis, two major issues were left unresolved: (1) ICTs for development; and (2) global Internet governance. As a result, the UN created two new and potentially innovative multistakeholder solutions to address these issues, the GAID (http://un-gaid.org/), and the IGF (http://intgovforum.org/). Both institutions were given five-year mandates, have undergone official evaluation, and the participation of transnational civil society networks has continued into the two institutional offspring of WSIS.

The Internet Governance Forum (IGF) is a very interesting global governance model (Cogburn 2008, 2010; Levinson and Derrick 2011). The IGF is multistakeholder in nature. It is open to all organizations that participated in the WSIS processes, and has subsequently accredited even more participants. It is a nonbinding arena. The IGF is focused on discussions and does not produce outcome documents, statements, declaration, or any of the normal results of international organizations. In theory, participants are registered to the IGF in their personal capacity, not in an organizational one. The agenda is developed by an innovative new creation called the MAG. The MAG reviews proposals from a new innovative creation called Dynamic Coalitions (DCs). Proposals from DCs have to include participants from government, the private sector, and civil society. The more diverse the better, and priority seems to be given to proposals that represent diversity in terms of region, sector, gender, race and ethnicity, and a number of other factors. In addition, the IGF is the location for yet another new creation, the GigaNet, which is the leading association of interdisciplinary scholars studying Internet governance in the world (full disclosure: the author was a founding member of the GigaNet steering committee, and served as its inaugural Communications Chair, and subsequently as Vice Chair).

Beginning in Greece, from 30 October to 2 November 2006, there have been eight IGF Annual Meetings (the most recent meeting was held in October 2013 in Bali, Indonesia).

There have also been regional and national IGFs created, which now exist in every region of the world. Regional IGFs are found in Africa, Arab, Asia-Pacific, Central Africa, Commonwealth, East Africa, European, Pacific, and West Africa, and national IGFs in Bangladesh, Benin, Canada, Côte d'Ivoire, Germany, Ghana, Italy, Japan, Kenya, Malta, New Zealand, Nigeria, Russia, the Gambia, Togo, Tunisia, Uganda, Ukraine, UK, and USA. There are also four "youth"-oriented IGF events.

Numerous policy issues have been addressed at these regional and global IGF meetings, and they will be addressed in the next section on normative factors influencing Internet governance.

NORMATIVE FACTORS INFLUENCING GLOBAL
INTERNET GOVERNANCE

Our brief discussion above about the OSI model and TCP/IP model should help to illustrate the range of thorny, and potentially intractable, policy issues being debated in Internet governance circles. Ideas and norms play a key role in the global governance of the Internet.

In particular, one international norm toward multistakeholder participation in global governance is widely accepted in Internet governance. The UN General Assembly resolution authorizing the WSIS created an equal opportunity for civil society organizations (and businesses) to have a seat at the table during the summit and its preparatory processes. This multistakeholder governance has continued into the two post-WSIS institutions: the GAID and the Internet Governance Forum (IGF). These new institutions may be seen in some quarters as having more legitimacy because of their representation; but they are in some ways reinventing inequality of limiting the ability for some actors to participate more fully. The elite nature of these conferences processes, and the lack of remote participation, reinforces certain characteristics of the participation (large NGOs, based in western Europe, speaking in English).

The information society agenda taken up by WSIS was substantively huge. It was dealing with the reality that a number of major innovations have been occurring in the use of the Internet—sometimes referred to as the GII at the time. These innovations fueled new entrants into the normative policy space represented by WSIS. ICT applications such as telemedicine, distance learning, remote scientific collaboration, and many others helped to fuel these policy perspectives. From a broad global policy perspective, these innovations were aided in some ways by the increases in the Global Trade in Services facilitated by the WTO.

These new applications helped to create a new set of stakeholders in what is now known as Internet governance. Far from the traditional disciplines involved in telecommunications policy, such as engineering, computer science, economics, and law, many of these new entrants were nurses, medical doctors, teachers, community activists and other entrepreneurs. The inclusion of all these new actors put tremendous pressure on the nascent structures of global civil society to represent these voices.

In addition to these new entrants to the Internet governance arena, these new application areas stimulated renewed interest in these issues from developing countries. In 1995, the ECA launched the AISI. In 1996, South Africa hosted the ISAD Conference in South Africa. The ITU convened the WTDC, promoting the benefits to developing countries of electronic commerce and other Internet-enabled applications for socioeconomic development. As more developing countries and civil society actors became aware of and involved in these issues, it also became clear that the existing global governance processes were not working well for developing countries and civil society organizations (MacLean, Souter, Deane, Lilley 2002; Cogburn 2003). This reality was not just in the information society domain, but also in the broader global governance arena. One study indicated that civil society and developing countries participate in ICT policy processes with little influence (Global Contract 2003).

Broad frustration with this overall lack of influence is one of the main factors leading to the developing country walkout at the WTO meeting in Cancun in 2003. Several leading scholars and philanthropists argued that the continued imbalance in the world system did not serve the interests of the developed or the developing world (Sachs 1999; Soros 2000, 2002). The UN Task Force on ICTs and other bodies have tried to address these issues.

In the meantime, there were a number of top-down and bottom-up structures that formed within the WSIS processes to facilitate civil society participation in WSIS. Some of these structures included the infamous Civil Society Bureau (CSB), the CSP, which was an e-mail mailing list, and a host of Thematic Caucuses and Working Groups.

One of these Thematic Caucuses was the Civil Society Internet Governance Caucus (IGC). The IGC is primarily organized around an e-mail listserv (governance@lists.cpsr.org), the archives of which may be found at: http://lists.cpsr.org/lists/info/governance, hosted by the Computer Professionals for Social Responsibility (CPSR). It has 464 subscribers (which includes a number of people, about ten who are registered with more than one e-mail address). The IGC was formed out of the preparatory processes for the UNWSIS—more about that below—and while it does have limited opportunities per year when some of its members can meet face-to-face (normally —two to three times per year) there has never been a time when the majority of "members" were collocated. This e-mail-based organizational structure mimics the larger civil society organized for WSIS and reported on in Cogburn 2005a).

Members of the IGC are individuals acting in their own personal capacity, who come together voluntarily (many of them do belong to the same organizations, such as the APC, the IGP, Information Technology for Change (IT4Change), and the Communication Rights in the Information Society (CRIS) Campaign, more about the impact of these organizations is discussed below). There is no salary or funding associated with being a member, participant, or leader in the Internet Governance Caucus (at least directly). While a constitution was eventually developed, the original organizational structure was very loose, and the two "co-coordinator" structure remains in place.

One critical consideration is the increased pressure to include participants beyond the governmental sector in decision-making processes. This multistakeholderism, as it is called, is a lofty goal. However, it is tremendously challenging both theoretically and practically to understand how to do this effectively. How can civil society and private sector actors sit at global governance tables alongside government officials? In practice, however, the effective participation of civil society and other non-state actors lagged substantially behind this lofty rhetoric. However, the active participation of civil society along with the active involvement of developing country blocs, helped to facilitate some important policy debates. Using the language of the time, in earlier work, Cogburn (2003) saw the WSIS period as an "interregnum" between the existing International Telecommunication Regime and an emerging Information Infrastructure Regime. This was essentially a debate that would determine the character of the emerging Internet governance regime. It was seen as the difference between a GII regime based on citizen-centric principles of openness, universal provision of services, accessibility, equality and opportunity, diversity of content, employment creation, and global cooperation and sharing of resources—which I called the Information Society (GIS) regime and one that was based on corporate/national security principles of promoting dynamic competition, encouraging private investment, protection of intellectual property rights, and limited regulatory oversight, which I called the GEC regime. I saw this normative debate as one leading to a GII/GIS regime, or a GII/GEC regime (Cogburn 2003). It was clear at the time which side was winning, and in many ways it is still clear.

Other normative policy issues included in the debate range from whether or not there should be an expansion of global top level domains (gTLDs), since the original gTLDS (.org, .com, .gov, .net, edu) were deemed to be insufficient to meet global demand.

Another issue was who would be the appropriate entity to manage country code top-level domains, or ccTLDS (e.g., .us, or .uk, .za). Developing countries argued strongly that the ccTLDs should be seen as a national resource and controlled not by the country, and not by a private sector entity, as was the case in South Africa and several other countries.

Some of the policy debates were around the introduction of new Internationalized Domain Names (IDNs). Arabic-speaking countries, among others, were arguing that the Internet should not be limited to the use of Latin characters, and that freedom and equity of expression for non-Latin-based countries required the development of these IDNs.

In all these areas, civil society policy preferences have been fairly clearly siding with the GII/GIS-oriented Internet governance principles. Developing countries have been more mixed, with greater heterogeneity in their policy preferences.

Some of the key policy issues of interest to the IGC are (1) network neutrality; (2) a development agenda for Internet governance; (3) Internet rights and principles; (4) enhanced cooperation; and (5) transparency and inclusive participation in Internet governance.

DOMESTIC POLITICAL FACTORS INFLUENCING GLOBAL INTERNET GOVERNANCE

Interestingly, there are a number of domestic political factors that influence global Internet governance. This is true especially in the USA, but also in other countries around the world. First, within the current Internet governance regime, government influence is wielded directly through the GAC. The establishment and functioning of the GAC has been somewhat contentious within the Internet governance space, because the goal of privatization of Internet governance and the establishment of ICANN placed governments in an "advisory" role. Governments do not usually see themselves in an advisory role, and they increasingly sought to expand their capabilities.

One example of how domestic politics influenced Internet governance processes via the GAC was the debate around approval of the .xxx domain. In 2005, the ICANN board voted to approve a new gTLD for adult content (.xxx). The US representatives on the GAC responded by arguing that such a move would create a "global red light district" (Cogburn et al. 2005). This argument was driven by the organized and sustained protests of the Family Research Council (FRC), which argued that such a move would increase access to adult content among children, making it easier for them to find. Similarly, there have been the discussions, though not yet substantiated, that the USA has used its influence to remove certain countries from the root directory during certain times of military conflict.

Other domestic political factors influencing Internet governance include hate speech, and of course the recent privacy revelations.

In other cases, it is the domestic political considerations that drive certain state actors to make decisions in a certain way, or engage in the negotiations in a certain way. For example, US-based corporate lobbyists have worked to influence US negotiating positions as they argue for a pro-competitive environment, and driven by their needs for electronic commerce and global business. Additionally, new communication tools and social media are influencing how these domestic civil society groups are engaging on the world state. So, how the "local" civil society engages with the "global" civil society is critical.

REGIONAL FACTORS INFLUENCING GLOBAL INTERNET GOVERNANCE

Regionalism is another area that is having a tremendous impact on the processes of Internet governance. From the tremendous power being wielded by China in these processes (including vetoing within ECOSOC some of the NGOs applying for accreditation to these various conferences) to the perception of developing country blocs siding with an enhanced role for the ITU, to strategic groupings of authoritarian countries getting together to articulate certain policy perspectives at these various conferences, regional factors are clearly influencing Internet governance.

As discussed above, the developing country policy perspective has been less coherent and more diverse than that of the global civil society. There are frequently differences within Africa, and differences between Africa, Latin America and the Caribbean (LAC), and Asia. The BRIC countries (Brazil, Russia, India, and China) have certainly been influential in this space, but frequently do not have harmonized positions. Brazil and India have consistently argued for a more open Internet governance regime that supports the needs of developing countries better, while China has frequently taken its own path.

China certainly plays a critically important role in these debates, most frequently arguing against any focus on human rights, access to information, privacy, and security. China has also frequently used its role on the ECOSOC to veto applications to WSIS and other Internet governance-related conferences from civil society organizations it deems overtly hostile to its interests. China has also been accused of having engaging in a variety of activities that may fall under the heading of cyber espionage and perhaps even cyber warfare. It has been accused of using the Internet to steal corporate intellectual property, while simultaneously using a wide variety of techniques to monitor its domestic population and crackdown on dissent. A number of high-profile companies pulled out of China as a result, but for many companies, the lure of such an enormous market makes such a move difficult or impossible.

South Africa, along with several other African countries throughout the continent, building on the organizing mechanisms of the ECA and the African Union, has been surprisingly organized and active in Internet governance debates.

The USA has frequently acted in concert with western Europe, but there have been some instances where this alliance has fractured, some very high profile. The leading issue fragmenting the US alliance has frequently been around privacy, security, and data protection. The European Union data protection regime is much stronger and based on a different philosophical approach than that of the USA.

COMPARATIVE ANALYSIS OF FACTORS INFLUENCING GLOBAL INTERNET GOVERNANCE

Our conceptual framework has allowed us to explore five different dimensions and approaches to understanding Internet governance, and each aspect has proven to be helpful in illuminating these global governance processes. However, we will now turn to a comparative analysis of the relationships, tensions, and complementarities between these variables.

The logic of each of these factors has clearly helped us to articulate the contemporary landscape for Internet governance. At this point, it is difficult to determine if one grouping of factors has been more influential than others.

What is clear is that, as with other areas of global governance, there is tremendous fragmentation in the Internet governance space as well. The sheer number of venues and annual international conferences is overwhelming. Most of these are multistakeholder and open to all accredited organizations. Others are more elite and invitation-only (sometimes, both combined, such as the most recent IGF meeting in Bali, which had the usual open and transparent multistakeholder registration process, but simultaneously on the opening day of the forum, held a "high-level" meeting in the same venue that was invitation-only).

This multiplicity of venues is a tremendous problem for democratic and legitimate global governance, primarily because it is a tremendous problem for civil society and many developing country participants. The cost of trying to attend all of these meetings in person, all over the world, and within all the key regions, is unbelievable. So without a huge budget, and lots of time, participants have to begin to "pick and choose" where they will go, and hope that they have made the right choices to try to wield the influence they would like. Also, one of the problems with the regional IGFs for example, is that they tend to have very limited influence on the global IGF, and there seems overall to be fairly limited engagement between the multiple conferences (except for those "elite" individuals that are well funded, and in most cases are specifically employed to follow these processes). So, these regional arrangements certainly do not replace the global arrangements, but it is difficult to see the degree to which they supplement them as well. One possibility is that the regional meetings, help to build the knowledge base, networks, and confidence of regional actors and new civil society entrants, who might then be more likely to engage actively at the global level.

The upcoming Global Multistakeholder Meeting on the Future of Internet Governance in Sao Paulo, Brazil, which was initiated by President Rouseff in the aftermath of the Snowden revelations should be interesting. The 2013 Bali meeting, which, because of the recent Snowden revelations, had the potential to be a disaster, was in fact very productive. By some accounts, including from Ambassador David Gross, who led the US delegations to almost all of the WSIS and post-WISIS meetings and has attended every Internet Governance Forum, this IGF was perhaps one of the best ever (Microsoft, Bali IGF Debrief, 2013).

However, it is very likely that the Brazil meeting will be far more contentious, as it is explicitly trying to chart a new course for global Internet governance that reduces US dominance, and it does not have the limitations placed on it by the UN that the IGF does.

Discussion

What are the implications of these findings? What do they mean for developing countries, for civil society organizations, and for various types of societies? What do these developments mean for how we understand Internet governance in a post-Snowden surveillance environment, and for global governance broadly speaking?

First, we will turn to assessing the outcomes. There is a tremendous amount of activity related to Internet governance. Much of this activity, some of the more narrowly focused analysts would not consider to be Internet governance at all (they would include in this assessment, or more accurately exclude, the Internet Governance Forum as well). So, from this very narrow, technical perspective, the Internet governance regime is working exceptionally well. Anyone with Internet access around the world is able to send and receive messages, access their desired websites and files, from both mobile and fixed devices. Overall, infrastructure is getting better, bandwidth becoming broader and more readily available, and costs are going down. Success of the regime, right?

Clearly, while many observers and some developing country and civil society participants would agree with this statement, the vast majority would probably argue that it is insufficient. A stability of the Internet governance regime that is supported by nondemocratic practices, where civil society is less influential even though it is well represented throughout all of these formal and informal structures (with a similar critique from developing countries) is not a success.

The meeting in Brazil is being attended by the head of every major Internet governance organization on the planet, as well as experts and multistakeholder representatives from around the world. There is the potential for this meeting to put in place a process that fundamentally alters the trajectory of Internet governance, away from the US-dominated model to one that is more democratic, transparent, and has more perceived legitimacy.

However, any emerging alternative to the existing Internet governance regime will have to address the "legitimacy-effectiveness" trade off. From the perspective of the USA and its private sector (who as they say, did build and pay for the development of the Internet), any new arrangements must not alter the stability and effectiveness of the existing Internet.

So any new Internet governance regime has to go beyond the simple "involvement" of multistakeholder actors, to developing ways for them to have a greater impact on the emerging norms, principles, values, decision-making procedures, and enforcement mechanisms and the concomitant feeling of "ownership" of the regime that would probably engender. And what role would the emerging powers of China and India play at this critical time? From my analysis of civil society debate of these issues, there is clearly what one might call a "strong developing world civil society/developing country progressive block" emerging in Internet governance. Led largely by the Indian civil society, and supported by key and respected activists from Africa and Latin America, something is definitely happening.

PART 3

Transnational Advocacy Networks in the WSIS "Revolution" and Post-WSIS Institutions

CHAPTER 5

World Summit on the Information Society: Catalyst for Transnational Advocacy and a Milestone for Multistakeholder Global Governance

INTRODUCTION

In previous chapters we have mentioned the United Nations WSIS. However, in this chapter, we will present a detailed case study of the history and evolution of WSIS. It highlights the historical steps taken to include civil society and non-state actors in the official summit preparatory processes and the summit itself. For many analysts, this opportunity for multistakeholder participation signaled a fundamental shift in the power relations between state and non-state actors. In practice, however, the effective participation of civil society and other non-state actors lagged substantially behind this lofty rhetoric. This chapter sets the stage for subsequent chapters by highlighting the key policy issues left unresolved by WSIS—Internet governance and ICT and development—which presaged the two institutions created by the UN to address them: the Internet Governance Forum (IGF) and the GAID. Both institutions were given five-year mandates, have undergone official evaluation, and have generated voluminous digital data.

© The Author(s) 2017   129
D.L. Cogburn, *Transnational Advocacy Networks in the Information Society*, Information Technology and Global Governance,
DOI 10.1057/978-1-137-48361-4_5

BACKGROUND

The GII is the core socio-technical foundation on which the information society is being built. Today, it includes the Internet, the World Wide Web, and all the ICT applications that address so many of society's needs and wants in an information society.

Bringing the information society into existence requires four interrelated foci, which are (1) information infrastructure development; (2) building a legal and regulatory infrastructure; (3) content creation, and (4) human capacity development. Each of these areas requires substantial international cooperation, financing, and the development of consensus on the principles, values, norms, rules, and decision-making procedures for the information society across public, private, and civil society sectors. Each of these areas is embedded in a framework of ICT policies. These policy issues range from the arcane technical issues of Internet domain names, privacy, security, intellectual property, and even further to the socially oriented issues of human rights, culturally sensitive content creation, and the empowerment of youth, women, and indigenous peoples. Each of these issue areas has a complex set of institutional processes through which issues get presented, framed, refined, debated, and eventually recommended as specific policy options (Kingdon 2003).

Frequently, this consensus building, as well as intense contestation, occurs within specific ICT policy processes at national, regional, and international levels. Some of these policy formulation processes are driven by highly structured formal international organizations, such as the ITU, WTO, World Intellectual Property Organization (WIPO), and other United Nations agencies such as UNESCO and the United Nations Development Program (UNDP). Other highly influential policy processes, although sometimes less visible, are driven by quasi-autonomous and independent international private sector organizations wielding tremendous influence on global ICT policy. These organizations include the ICANN, International Chamber of Commerce (ICC), GIIC, GBDe, and the World Economic Forum (WEF). Collectively, these multiple and competing institutional processes contribute to the global governance of the GII and potentially to the information society as a whole.

Within these policy processes, international conferences play an important role as locations of contestation and consensus for the principles, values, norms, and sometimes rules and decision-making procedures—the international regime—among the participating stakeholders

(Cogburn 2004a, b, c). Most of these conferences are organized by one of the formal or informal organizations listed above. In many of the previous international conferences addressing issues of information and communication policy, developing countries and civil society organizations have been unable to wield sufficient influence to engender policy outcomes that meet their socioeconomic and development goals (Cogburn 2003a; MacLean 2003). Negotiating within these complex processes to achieve specific policy objectives is a daunting task, even for the most seasoned governments and private sector organizations. However, it is perhaps even more challenging for the international civil society organizations that are participating increasingly in these global multistakeholder governance processes.

In December 2003, the United Nations sponsored the WSIS as an attempt to provide a forum to begin to address, in a comprehensive manner, the multiple and challenging policy issues confronting the world community in the development of an information society. Organized by the ITU, WSIS is a unique example of the international ICT conferences described above, and brilliantly illustrates these global governance processes at work. For example, WSIS is distinctive in that it was organized as a world summit with two discrete phases. Phase I was held in Geneva in December 2003, with Phase II of the summit scheduled for Tunis in November 2005. The organizers were adamant in saying that WSIS was "one summit with two parts" and not two summits. Second, WSIS was attempting to address perhaps a wider range of ICT policy issues than any previous international conference of this magnitude. Finally, the WSIS process represented an explicit, though flawed, attempt at global multistakeholder governance, with the active recruitment and attempted involvement of thousands of civil society and private sector actors on a relatively co-equal basis with the governmental and intergovernmental actors that normally inhabit these formal intergovernmental processes.

So the transnational civil society was invited to participate in WSIS, but what is "civil society?" Ostensibly a simple question, defining and recognizing civil society is actually quite complex. Nonetheless, the civil society participants in WSIS have loosely defined themselves as "organisations — including movements, networks and other entities—which are autonomous from the State, are not intergovernmental or do not represent the private sector, and which in principle, are non-profit-making, act locally, nationally and internationally, in defence and promotion of social, economic and cultural interests and for mutual benefit" (WSIS CS 2003).

Further, the APC and the CRIS Campaign suggest the following components of a definition:

It includes representatives from "professional" and grassroots NGOs, the trade union movement, community media activists, mainstream and traditional media interest groups, parliamentarians and local government officials, the scientific and academic community, educators, librarians, volunteers, the disability movement, youth activists, indigenous peoples, "think-tanks," philanthropic institutions, gender advocates and human and communication rights advocates. (APC/CRIS 2003, p. 9)

Regardless of the definition used, the civil society sector represents a tremendous diversity of voices and perspectives that are critical to development of a GIS. This diversity could matter greatly in the ICT policy formulation process, bringing new ideas and energy to bear on old, seemingly intractable problems.

The active and theoretically co-equal involvement of the international civil society in these global governance process was a major step forward. Their involvement was an explicit recognition, at least on the part of the organizers and most of the participants, that civil society brings to these processes a diverse array of subject matter expertise in many of the policy areas addressed by the summit, as well as the energy and resources (along with the private sector) to continue developing the many applications and projects which give rise to the information society. To engage in the policy processes in which they are experts (such as human rights, privacy, open source software, and Internet governance), many of these civil society actors participate actively in what some scholars call "transnational advocacy networks" (Keck and Sikkink 1998) and form deliberate linkages with what other scholars call knowledge networks or "epistemic communities" (Haas 1992). The diversity of expertise and perspectives represented by the transnational civil society participating in WSIS is critical to the development of the information society.

However, there are serious challenges affecting the participation of civil society in global multistakeholder governance processes such as WSIS. For example, these organizations vary tremendously in size, strength, experience, organizational capacity, ICT policy issue area, and focus. Perhaps one of the biggest hurdles is that the members of these organizations are geographically distributed and can have a presence in both developed and developing countries. Finding ways to knit these geographically distributed and diverse organizational strands into a coherent and representative international civil society tapestry that functions as an effective transnational advocacy network drawing on the best epistemic communities from around the world and engaging effectively in the highly complex WSIS institutional processes is a significant challenge. Newly emerging organizational models, such as the policy collaboratory, may offer solutions to these challenges of geographically distributed knowledge work between developed and developing countries (Cogburn 2003). However, such solutions require an interdisciplinary approach and draw on insights and lessons that range from sociology and communication studies, to political science, and computer-supported cooperative work.

PURPOSE AND RESEARCH QUESTIONS

The purpose of this chapter is to explore the creation and role of the United Nations WSIS and to assess the degree to which transnational civil society actors were able to use this summit to organize their work, and to assess their use of computer-mediated communication (CMC) tools. Based on a critical usage of international regime theory, this study asks six specific research questions related to the WSIS civil society: (1) What are the characteristics of the WSIS policy formulation processes that affect civil society? (2) What is the structure and nature of civil society participation in WSIS? (3) What are the CMC capabilities within civil society as they relate to the WSIS processes? (4) What are the levels of "collaboration readiness" within civil society, including levels of cognitive and affective trust? (5) To what degree do global policy networks exist within civil society and what is their relationship with epistemic communities? (6) How successful and satisfied is civil society with their efforts in WSIS? Each of these questions is answered with empirical data collected specifically for this project.

This study is embedded within a larger research program called "From Pawns to Partners: Policy Collaboratories and Their Impact on the Global Governance of the Information Society." With some notable exceptions (Keck and Sikkink 1998; O'Brien et al. 2000; CTO 2003; Cogburn 2003; MacLean 2003), most of the literature exploring the specific factors limiting the influence of developing countries and civil society organizations in these international ICT processes is largely theoretical and anecdotal. What does exist, points to several potential social, political, technological, and economic variables that may contribute to this ineffectiveness. The conceptual framework presented in Chap. 2, draws on Cogburn (2004) and develops a theoretical model which posits a reexamination of the role played by international conferences in the governance of cyber infrastructure. This chapter begins to empirically test that theoretical model through a mixed-method analysis of the international civil society participation in WSIS and points to some of the potential uses of CMC tools to alter the existing imbalances.

THE EMERGENCE OF WSIS

What is the United Nations WSIS? What are the characteristics of its policy formulation processes, and what are the implications of WSIS for civil society? We know that United Nations-sponsored world conferences are major affairs addressing issues as diverse as human rights, racism, gender, and the environment (Schechter 2001). Under UN auspices, a "summit" is an international conference that meets at the highest level of officials, including heads of state, CEOs from the private sector, and executive directors and presidents from civil society. A "world summit" is an even more special designation, reserved for those global conferences that attempt to bring together as much of the leadership of humanity as possible to forge a common vision for a particular international issue area. Previous world summits have included the World Summit on Sustainable Development, World Conference Against Racism, and the World Peace Summit, and the World Summit for Social Development. The most recent of these world summits is the WSIS.

Officially, WSIS emerged as a result of Resolution 73 of the 1998 Plenipotentiary Meeting of the ITU held in Minneapolis (ITU 1998). As the governing body of the ITU, this resolution at the "plenipot" instructed the Secretary-General of the ITU to "place the question of holding a world summit on the information society on the agenda of the United Nations Administrative Committee on Coordination [now called the United Nations System Chief Executive Board—CEB], with a view to meeting the necessary conditions for holding such a summit before the next plenipotentiary conference" (ITU 1998). After agreement from the CEB, the UN decided that Secretary-General Kofi Annan would provide the high patronage for the summit, with organizational responsibility resting with the ITU (UNGA 15/183).

Unofficially, there has been a long line of international and regional meetings outlining and laying the groundwork for most of the issues being addressed by the WSIS process. Some of the earliest meetings held in the 1970s and 1980s addressed the global imbalances of information creation and dissemination. The movement around these issues became known as the NWICO. The NWICO movement galvanized activists around the world in response to a UNESCO report entitled, *Many Voices, One World* (UNESCO 1980). In some ways the CRIS Campaign, one of the leading organizations involved in the WSIS civil society which argues for a broader "communication society" over a narrower "information society," is the intellectual descendent of the NWICO (Ó Siochrú 2004).

Subsequent to NWICO, there were the ITU World Telecommunications Development Conferences starting in Buenos Aires, Argentina, in 1994, with subsequent conferences in Valetta, Malta (1998), and Istanbul, Turkey (2002); the G7 Ministerial Meeting on the Information Society, held in Brussels, Belgium in 1995; and the G7/Developing World ISAD Conference held in Johannesburg, South Africa, in 1996 (Cogburn 1996). For various reasons, the ISAD agenda lost momentum and GIS issues moved to other international fora such as the Global Knowledge Conferences held in Toronto in 1997 and Kuala Lumpur in 2000 (Cogburn 2004).

As illustrated by the following paragraph from the *UN General Assembly Resolution 56/183* authorizing WSIS, organizers of the summit had the explicit goal of forging an international consensus among the major actors regarding the principles, values, norms, rules, and decision-making procedures—the international regime—of the GIS in order that it might benefit the majority of the world's citizens.

> *Convinced* of the need, at the highest levels, to marshal the global consensus and commitment required to promote the urgently needed access of all countries to information, knowledge and communication technologies for development so as to reap the full benefits of the information and communication technologies revolution, and to address the whole range of relevant issues related to the information society, through the development of a common vision and understanding of the information society and the adoption of a declaration and plan of action for implementation by Governments, international institutions and all sectors of civil society. (UNGAe 15/183)

Another unique aspect of WSIS is that, from the beginning, it was authorized as one summit, to occur in two phases (UNGA 2003). Phase one was authorized for Geneva, 10–14 December 2003, and phase two was authorized in Tunisia, 16–18 November 2005. Background interviews suggest that even these early decisions, both to hold the summit in two phases, and to hold the second phase in Tunisia, were highly politically charged decisions.

WSIS was promoted as a major step forward in global multistakeholder governance, especially in the processes of formulating global ICT policy. UN General Assembly Resolution 56/183 recommended that the multiple planning processes for the summit take place in an open and transparent manner:

> *Recommends* that the preparations for the Summit take place through an open-ended intergovernmental preparatory committee, which would define the agenda of the Summit, finalize both the draft declaration and the draft plan of action, and decide on the modalities of the participation of other stakeholders in the summit. (UNGA 15/183 2003)

In addition to the government representatives, from both developed and developing countries, paragraph five of this resolution "encourages other intergovernmental organizations, including international and regional institutions, non-governmental organizations, civil society and the private sector to contribute to, and actively participate in, the intergovernmental preparatory process of the Summit and the Summit itself" (UNGA 15/83 2003).

The ability to define terms, positions, and alternatives in public policy matters (Kingdon 2003). As early as 1964, Schattschneider argued "the definition of the alternatives is the supreme instrument of power" (Shattschneider 1964, p. 68). The theoretical model adopted in this study suggests that we should find in an international conference such as WSIS, clear agenda-setting processes at work, with much of the most important work of defining the agenda and alternatives happening long before the actual summit.

In the case of WSIS, this is exactly what we find. For example, starting in May 2002, we find that the agenda-setting phase for WSIS has been an elaborate, elongated, and complex preparatory process. For example, three full Preparatory Committee meetings (Prepcoms) were held, an intersessional meeting (held between Prepcom 2 and Prepcom 3), and five regional meetings (Africa, Pan European, Asia-Pacific, Latin America and Caribbean, and western Asia). With the failure of Prepcom 3 to reach a consensus on the primary documents, the *WSIS Declaration of Principles* and the *WSIS Plan of Action* (which was its primary objective), an additional intersessional meeting was scheduled for 10–14 November 2003 (called the Resumed Prepcom 3a). Finally, a High-Level Resumed Prepcom 3a was held on the weekend immediately preceding WSIS itself.

During each of these meetings, especially the formal Prepcom meetings, numerous important meetings and events are held concurrently. Delegates have to decide which of these multiple event/meetings they will attend, and how they will disperse their delegation members. For example, in order to help guide civil society delegates through the myriad of overlapping activities during Prepcom 3, the civil society sector produced a multicolored chart highlighting this bewildering cacophony of events (shown in Fig. 5.1).

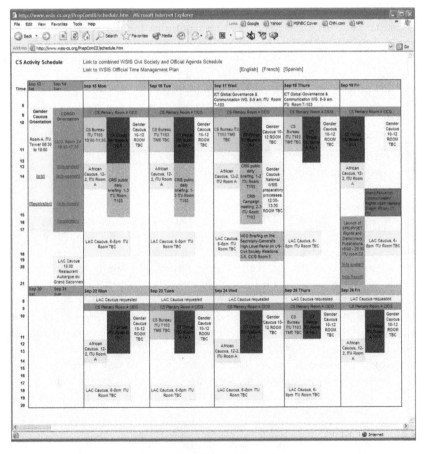

Fig. 5.1   Screenshot of Civil Society schedule during Prepcom-3

This chart of overlapping events, which highlights just those events being organized by civil society, helps to illustrate how much the structure of these international conferences benefits those countries and organizations that are organized in advance of the summit, can afford to bring larger delegations, or are actively engaged in the transnational policy-actor networks that can enhance their presence.

While some would argue that this multiplicity of preparatory processes provides additional strategic locations for continued multistakeholder intervention, from another perspective, they in fact provide multiple avenues of continued exclusion. In some ways, these extended preparatory processes are an illusion and provide only symbolic multistakeholder participation. For example, formal participation in the summit was open to any civil society organization that wanted to take the time to go through the accreditation process and to register their delegation. This open registration (in contrast to the numerous invitation-only international conferences such as WEF, GBDe, GIIC, and others), along with the formal United Nations pronouncement about multistakeholder participation in WSIS and allowing all delegates "full" access to the summit—and not just perfunctory access which is normal for these types of conferences—provided the appearance that this was a fully multistakeholder process.

However, the reality was significantly different. Government delegates still received preferential treatment within the formal processes, and only elite "insiders" were able to participate in other more informal WSIS planning events (such as the weekend retreat on Lake Geneva during the weekend in between the two weeks of Prepcom 3).

Numerous examples of this preferential treatment for governments and insiders can be found both during the preparatory processes and at the summit itself. During the prepcoms, government delegates were issued with name badges containing gold-colored bars. If a delegate did not have one of these golden name badges, they were excluded from sitting in certain sections, entering certain rooms, and were asked to leave certain meetings as described below. The exceptions to this rule were those civil society members (and private sector) who were actually registered on governmental delegations. This led to some joking (and perhaps some envy) within civil society about the digital divide between those sector members possessing "Gold Cards" and those who did not.

For example, the Prepcoms were all held in the Centre of International Conferences Geneva (CICG). The CICG is a massive conference center with large plenary rooms, observation sections, numerous break-out rooms, office spaces, pigeon holes, cafeterias, and a cyber cafe. Here, civil society was given much higher access to the entire venue than at most previous international summits. However, the "devil is in the details" so to speak.

Yes, civil society was allowed to enter and sit in the plenary rooms, meaning that civil society had high levels of access to the governmental delegates and summit organizers. However, civil society was only allowed to speak during the first five minutes of each plenary session (through the voice of their single chosen representative for that time slot). The same procedure applied to the private sector delegations. During this five-minute period, this lone civil society delegate had to address all of the paragraphs (of the draft *WSIS Declaration of Principles* and the *WSIS Action Plan*) that were to be discussed and negotiated during that specific plenary meeting (usually a —three- to four-hour period during a morning, afternoon, or evening session). After these brief interventions, the "real" discussions started, as each individual government could (and most did) take the floor multiple times to comment on each paragraph, sentence, and word of the text being negotiated.

Also, in order to deal with the most contentious issues that arose during the negotiations around the two draft texts, seven separate working groups were established, and headed by a governmental representative. These working groups then met in break-out rooms to negotiate and debate the specific issues relevant to that working group. Initially, civil society was invited to these working group meetings as active participants. However, almost as soon as these working groups were established and the issues became contentious, the civil society and business delegates were asked to leave (by the government delegates). A subsequent practice that emerged, after the outrage of the civil society and private sector delegates, was that they could each address the meeting for five minutes and then leave.

In addition, government delegations were given priority in reserving rooms, and could "bump" civil society from a reserved room if necessary. Also, a civil society division of the WSIS secretariat was established to facilitate civil society participation in the summit and the preparatory processes. However, there seemed to be little recognition within the secretariat about the tremendous diversity among the civil society, and the kinds of requests that would be made and support needed.

During the summit, which was held in the expansive Geneva Palexpo, many of these same practices continued, with civil society delegates having full access to the ICT4D platform, civil society office space, and to the Agora. Civil society was also allowed access to the plenary rooms, though civil society access was limited and controlled by so-called over-passes that had to be handed out every day. The allocation of these "over-passes" proved to be a highly contentious issue within civil society, and is discussed in a subsequent section. Civil society delegates were also seated in the third tier of seats in the plenary room with governments closest to the podium, followed by the private sector, and then finally civil society.

While some participants see these multiple preparatory meetings as engaging participants in the decision-making process, they are in fact debilitating to many of the participants, especially those from developing countries and most civil society organizations. These multiple processes are confusing and require delegates to be in many difference places simul-taneously. This is a particularly intractable problem for small delegations (in all sectors), and forces them to make some critical choices about which events they will and will not attend. Further, these preparatory processes are incredibly expensive, both to organize and to attend. Frequently they are held in some of the most expensive cities in the world and often for very long periods of time. For example, in WSIS, all three of the formal Prepcoms were held in Geneva (ranging from five to ten days) with a key meeting on content and themes of the summit held in Paris. Table 5.1 illustrates the increase in civil society e-mail traffic.

According to our international survey, Prepcom 3 was seen as the most important of these preparatory processes among civil society respondents, while the summit itself was seen as the most important among the entire

Table 5.1   Increase in civil society plenary e-mail traffic with WSIS events

Month	Archive file size	Txt file size	Pages	WSIS events
October 2003 (28 October)	1 MB	1.1 MB	542	Resumed Prepcom 3a 10–14 November (Geneva)
September 2003	9 MB	1.9 MB	897	Prepcom 3 September 2003 (Geneva)
August 2003	491 MB	411 KB	185	(Traditional European holiday months)
July 2003	2 MB	2 MB	913	Intersessional Meeting July 2003 (Paris)
June 2003	600 KB	120 KB	58	
May 2003	110 KB	142 KB	70	
April 2003	10 KB	32 KB	15	Second High Level Summit Organizing Committee (HLSOC) April 2003 (Paris)
March 2003	248 B	2 KB	1	Prepcom 2 February 2003 (Geneva)

sample. This indicates important recognition on the part of civil society delegates that these preparatory processes are more important to achieving one's policy objectives relative to the actual summit itself. Prepcom 3 was also where most of the substantial work began on developing the alternative civil society benchmark document, which was entitled, "*Shaping Information Societies for Human Needs: Civil Society Declaration to the World Summit on the Information Society.*"

One intriguing question that emerges from this analysis, but is beyond the scope of this book, is did this level of partnership and participation stifle—or co-opt—what is normally a robust external program of civil society activity, which frequently evolves into external protests? Also, while there were numerous external side events, these were so dwarfed by the size of the summit (as well as being raided by the police and other logistical and technological challenges) that they were relatively ineffective.

WSIS Participants and Multistakeholder Structures

What is the structure and nature of the WSIS participation, particularly the civil society participation. For a deeper look at the WSIS participants, we turn to our survey results. The majority of respondents were male (70 %, $n = 180$). The modal education level was a master's degree (48.3 %, $n = 125$), with a majority (64.1 %, $n = 164$) describing themselves as either "Upper Middle" or "High" income in their own countries. The modal age was 48, the mean 43.61, and the range 19–68. Western Europe represented the largest geographic region within the study sample (28 %, n = 72), followed by Africa (24.1 %, $n = 62$). Most of the respondents (68.2 %, $n = 174$) did not speak English as their primary language. The overwhelming majority of the participants accessed the Internet/World Wide Web from "Office or work" (76.2 %, $n = 141$). No one reported having no access or that their primary access was via cell phone or PDA, and only a negligible number (1.1 %, $n = 2$) reported having their primary access from a "Cyber Café or other public access" terminal. As one might expect from these findings, this means that the vast majority (84.2 %, $n = 154$) reported having "Broadband (e.g., LAN/ISDN/DSL/Cable Modem)" access to the Internet/World Wide Web. Finally, a large majority of respondents (72.7 %, n = 113) reported either "Agreeing" or "Strongly Agreeing" that they "currently have sufficient technical support for information and communication technologies within [their] organization."

Governments, both developed and developing countries, participate in United Nations conferences and events through their official intergovernmental structures. Governments will have a permanent representative at the United Nations, who will lead a mission, representing the head of state or government. In some cases, the head of state or government may come to the UN conference, such as to the General Assembly, or to a World Summit such as WSIS.

The private sector participates in United Nations conferences and events in at least two ways. Individual corporations may have specific policy staff, who are responsible for following certain areas of international policy related to the business interests of that specific company. However, most businesses also participate in private sector associations to organize their engagement with national and international policy processes. In the case of WSIS, businesses participated in associations such as the World Information Technology Services Alliance (WITSA), the GIIC, and the eventually all these efforts came together within the Business Action to Support the Information Society (BASIS). Table 5.2 illustrates the preparatory processes, their dates, cities, and participants by the three key sectors. It shows that the number of private sector participants tends to be numerically smaller, but they are highly organized and have substantial policy impact.

So, while governments have the intergovernmental infrastructure of the United Nations and businesses have their financial and organizational resources, it is the civil society that has perhaps the most heterogeneous policy perspectives and simultaneously, the least financial and institutional resources.

Nonetheless, the international civil society sector involved in WSIS was quite active at each stage of the various preparatory processes as illustrated by Table 5.2. The sector was particularly active following Prepcom 2 as it developed and prepared to introduce into the process a civil society statement on the Content and Themes for the summit. During each of the prepcoms, civil society participation substantially outnumbered that of business delegates.

The civil society sector is organized as a complex structure, with multiple self-constituting caucuses and other moving parts. For example, there are distributed working groups on Content & Themes (C&T), a CSP, 19 different Thematic Caucuses and Working Groups, and various ad hoc drafting committees. Table 5.3 highlights these different structures.

The diverse interests represented by the international civil society sector is tremendous, including the following: education, academia and research; science and technology; media; creators and promoters of culture; cities

Table 5.2 Civil Society participation in WSIS Preparatory Committee events other sectors

Name	City	Length	Government	Civil Society	Business
			Participation by sector		
Prepcom 1	Geneva	5	607	233	34
Prepcom 2	Geneva	10	901	394	60
Prepcom 3	Geneva	10	878	537	68
WSIS	Geneva	2	4,590	3,310	514

Table 5.3 Overview of Civil Society structures

Structure	Components
Civil society plenary	CSP is open to everyone and is the main body of civil society for discussion and general decision-making
Civil society bureau	CCSB functions as an interlinkage between the CSCT and the intergovernmental bureau for procedural and technical issues
Content & themes	CSCT coordinates the work of the numerous regional and thematic caucuses and working groups. It is the main body for discussion and decisions on content-related issues
Civil society families	CSF represent the various themes and interests of members on the bureau, a total of 20 including regional representation
Thematic caucuses and working groups	TCWG also represent the various thematic interests within the civil society, including cities and local authorities, community media caucus, cultural and linguistic diversity, e-government/e-democracy, education and academia caucus, education and academia LAC, environment and ICTs, human rights, indigenous peoples, global ICT governance, media, gender strategies, patents, copyrights, and trademarks, persons with disabilities, privacy and security, scientific information, trade unions, values and ethics, volunteering and ICTs

and local authorities; trade unions; NGOs; youth; gender; volunteers; indigenous people; networks and coalitions; multistakeholder partnerships; philanthropic institutions; think tanks; and people with disabilities. During Prepcom 2, the CSP authorized the creation of a Civil Society Bureau (CSB), comprised of 20 representatives from diverse Civil Society Families, with the stated function of "facilitating and engaging as much as possible the contribution of the civil society and the elaboration of a common and shared vision of the information society" (ITU 2003). Fig. 5.2 illustrates the overall structure of the Civil Society Sector.

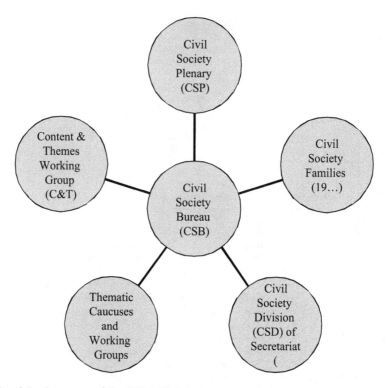

Fig. 5.2 Structure of the WSIS Civil Society sector (CSS)

Based on the subsample of civil society delegates from the survey (n = 74, 28 %), we learn more about the characteristics of the members of the WSIS civil society. The majority of civil society delegates were male (64 %, n = 45). The modal education level was a master's degree, with a slight majority (52 %, n = 36) reporting to be of either low or middle income in their own countries. Western Europe represented the largest geographic region within the sample (32 %, n = 23), followed by Africa (27 %, n = 19). Most of the respondents (58 %, n = 41) did not speak English as their primary language. Most were directors or managers within their organization and "education and academia" was the most frequently cited organizational theme.

Within the various structures of civil society, the CSB is perhaps the most controversial. The controversy is based primarily on the top-down way in which the CSB was constituted, and the ongoing concern that it lacks transparency and legitimacy. Many active participants within the civil society sector feel as if the CSB was imposed by the conference organizers as a way to limit the effectiveness of the organic, bottom-up organizing processes that emerged after the earlier prepcoms. These concerns were amplified because the organizers allowed the CSB to make important political and economic decisions for the sector (such as allocating office space, determining fellowships for prepcom events, and allocating entry badges—overpasses—into the WSIS plenary sessions). The following e-mail excerpt indicates the level of frustration with CSB. These e-mail excerpts are presented in their original form and set in block quotations within the text. The only exception is the removal of names, organizations, and other readily identifiable information. As such, all grammatical and spelling errors are from the original (these errors are mostly due to a wide diversity of native language speakers, all trying to communicate using English as a common written language).

> Let me only add that the civil society bureau has been highly controversial since its proposal at Prepcom2. Apparently, this situation is not improving, specially since some of the CSB members seem to speak for themselves, without any mandate....Although there were disagreement on this constitution for the reason stated above, the two only volunteers were "appointed."...Since then, I've seen neither any report nor any request for comments or proposal on any issue raised in the CSB....If it was not thanks to – forwarding some important messages to the plenary, or through – sending some messages addressed by the CSD to the CSB, I would never hear of what's being discussed – and, who knows?, decided – in the CSB.
>   I don't know of other "families". But this absence of legitimacy and representatity, as well as this opacity, speak for themselves. The civil society plenary, which does exist simply because we have commonly created it following consensus and because we are using it, remains the most legitimate instance.

The CSB was set up primarily as an interface with the WSIS secretariat and the corresponding entity for governments called the Government Bureau. However, what became clear is that while the motives of the CSB may have been benign, it engaged in what some organizational theory scholars call "mission creep," and was trying to move further into work on substantive matters of ICT policy. Clarification on these issues was finally provided with the following rationale from a CSB member.

In the recent Paris meeting, nobody in the CS-B questioned the fact, that the CS-B is NOT responsible for content related issues. If content related issues pop up in the CS-B, the CS-B should transfer this issue to the CS-CTG or the relevant caucuses, themes groups etc. The so-called families of the CS-B are representing groups of networks and coordinate the activities of these networks formally. They are NOT content groups, although there is some overlapping (take the "media family" and the "media themes group" as an example. But note also that there is an "CS Internet Governance Caucus" but no "Internet Governance Family"). In the family, the organizations, which are linked to them, keep their own position and have no obligation, to take a common position on an issue (like in the "Trade Union" family, where you can have a unique position on procedural question, but divergent voices on content themes, which is both natural and does not create any problems, because the CS-B is responsible for procedural questions only [sic]. To make it short: A family is NOT a CS negotiating body, the CS negotiating bodies are the content and themes groups and caucuses.

Of these various structures, the component that appears to have the highest degree of power is the Content & Themes Working Group (C&T). From within the civil society sector itself, C&T is seen as "the main body created by the Civil Society Plenary of WSIS at the first Prepcom to bring together the content proposals of civil society organizations participating in the WSIS process" (Ó Siochrú et al. 2003). Following C&T as the second most powerful component in the structure, but in some delegates' minds having the most "legitimacy," is the CSP.

Contrary to this perspective, some delegates have argued that a WSIS civil society "plenary" does not, and could not exist within the WSIS structures, as does one CSB member here.

There does not exist a forum at the WSIS referred to as "Civil Society Plenary," nor was there ever one at any other U.N. sponsored Summit in the past. A "Plenary" signifies a fixed group of members or member states and the actual official definition is: 1. Complete in all respects, unlimited or full: a diplomat with plenary powers, 2. Fully attended by all qualified members: a plenary session of the council. As you can see, Civil Society does not fulfill this definition or its prerequisites. In Paris, we had three (3) mechanisms.

Nonetheless, the transnational civil society used these various structures to organize its work and to engage with the WSIS policy processes. As a result, they were able to produce five significant policy documents and statements, most in three languages, (English, Spanish, and French), and to post them on the web in rich-text, pdf, text, and html formats.

COMMUNICATION CAPABILITIES

What are the CMC capabilities within the WSIS civil society sector and how do they relate to the WSIS policy formulation processes? As we will explore in more detail below, the vast majority of civil society communication within WSIS takes place using e-mail lists, with nearly all of the respondents to our international survey (89 %, $n = 47$) reporting that they communicate with civil society colleagues frequently or very frequently using e-mail lists over the past six months. More advanced communication tools are used far more infrequently, such as blogs (90 %, $n = 43$) either not et al.l or very infrequently, and wiki webs (96 %, $n = 44$) being used even less frequently.

The organization of these civil society structures began with support for their distributed work via CMC tools starting after the Prepcom 2 in February 2003. The first plenary mail list was set up in March, with only one "test" message being transmitted (248 bytes). In April, the traffic picked up slightly (10 KB), with almost immediate calls to use web-based tools to facilitate their geographically distributed work, such as editing, voting, and other aspects of developing proposals and policy papers. For example, this excerpt taken from the third e-mail posted to the newly established e-mail list for the civil society plenary calls for volunteers to provide collaboration tools.

> We need volunteers to help facilitate the technical aspects of this proposal. We are trying to identify a Web-based tool that will assist us in this process (group editing, voting, etc.). We have collected a list of candidate systems. We need volunteers who have Linux system administration experience and also people or organizations who could possibly host a system on their server.

This call was followed up subsequently when talking about proposed working practices that the civil society hoped to have available—an "online collaborative editing tool."

As the CSP prepared for the Paris Intersessional Meeting scheduled for 15–18 July 2003, new calls were made for face-to-face assistance with being the "eyes and ears" at the intersessional meeting for the rest of the CSP. One plenary member volunteered for and called for assistance to coordinate an "NGO Monitoring Group" for the intersessional meeting, reporting back to the entire plenary the work of the meeting. In stating the importance of this function, this CSP member said:

> I believe this reporting is a critical function for us to play, since I am sure some governments are counting on the fact that much fewer NGOs will be able to attend the intersessional in such an expensive city during the height of the tourist season. The only way all our voices can be heard is if groups around the world know what is going on in a timely manner.

While the complexity and diversity of the civil society structures reflects the diversity and nature of civil society itself, organizing the sector for effective participation in an equally complicated global ICT policy process like WSIS becomes particularly difficult. This difficulty is compounded by the more limited financial resources available to civil society delegates, relative to other sectors such as global and multinational corporations organized as the Coordination Committee of Business Interlocutors (CCBI) and coordinated by the ICC.

The WSIS Civil Society Sector has worked diligently to encourage civil society organizations from around the world to participate actively in its processes; however, there is still concern that the wide variety of civil society organizations around the world are not represented within its structures, and that its cliquish nature makes it difficult for newcomers. For example, one CSP member from France argued as much in the following e-mail excerpt.

> Thank you for your warm wishes; I send attached to this e-mail the text of my presentation at the SC-2 plenary on thursday in both english and french. I take the opportunity to stress once more that themes such as these dealt with in my presentation are completely "off the agenda" in the SC meetings and at least not considered as priorities in our debates....When at last does the "civil society" dare tackle this issue of paramount importance ?...At some extent I've got the feeling through the different Prepcoms and meetings that there are mainly Internet lobbyists or instigators and a new breed of "media representatives" in our plenary occupying the floor.

However, many of these apparent liabilities can perhaps be turned into assets through the use of collaboratory tools and practices. Following the Paris Intersessional meeting, additional information regarding the need for civil society to collaborate more effectively, and to mind the needs of geographically distributed knowledge work was produced. The discussions on the list then turned to strategy. One CSP member produced and circulated a very detailed document containing several points of interest to the civil society (CS) sector and its distributed collaboration: (1) transparency; (2) participation; (3) technology; (4) scalability; and (5) diversity/representation. The focus on distributed participants is particularly important for this study. The CSP member suggests the following:

> We should always have in mind the people who are not able to come to Geneva. They depend on us for the latest infos on what is going on, and we depend on (some of) them for their input and ideas in our lobbying work. The "info security" caucus for example consisted at least of two persons not present in Geneva and Paris, but who were actively involved. This principle also should help us think of all the interested people in Geneva who do not belong to the "inner circle" (whatever this is).

This delegate continued by producing a detailed recommendation as to the structure of civil society that would lead to the greatest maximization of its collective resources, arguing even more forcefully for the use of distributed collaboration tools:

> [L]ive-feed of the monitors in the plenary sessions to IRC or elsewhere, with the possibility for real-time comments and analysis via the internet (I imagine something like this : "ONLINE CS PARTICIPANT FROM KOREA: last comment from delegation XYZ is dangerous. It would imply ABC, and they have already tried this at the asian regional conf.")

- have a screen, in a room for CS, which broadcasts comments which could include extracts from email messages, real-time chats, etc.
    - have a video-feed from the sessions broadcast over the internet.

COLLABORATION READINESS WITHIN WSIS CIVIL SOCIETY

What is the level of "collaboration readiness" within the WSIS civil society sector, including the levels of cognitive and affective trust? Working in a distributed environment poses numerous challenges (Olson and Olson 2000), some of which include building trust and common ground (Rocco 1998); coordinating the activities and communications of distributed teams (Kiesler et al. 1984), and discussion control (Kraut et al. 1982). With the inclusion of participants from both developed and developing countries, these problems are further complicated, including managing interinstitutional and cross-national cultural differences (McCroskey 1990) and differential experience with CMC tools (Gersick 1988).

In much of the work done on distributed collaboration in science, one institutional form that has received significant attention is the "collaboratory" (Wulf 1989). Studies of collaboratories have shown that one of the most important indicators of potential success of geographically distributed collaboration within a collaboratory is "collaboration readiness" (Olson and Olson 2000; Olson et al. 2000, 2002). The concept of collaboration readiness has three important dimensions, articulated here as: (1) collaboration *orientation* readiness; (2) collaboration *infrastructure* readiness; and (3) collaboration *technology* readiness. This research question contributes significantly to our knowledge base about distributed collaboration within civil society in anticipation of the future research described below in the final section. Based on preliminary research, the civil society sector has a high degree of collaboration readiness on all three of these dimensions.

Collaboration Orientation *Readiness*

One aspect of this collaboration orientation readiness is the friendliness and openness of the distributed community. For example, when one CSP member commented about how expensive Paris was (the site of the inter-sessional meeting on the WSIS content and themes), another member responded with the following message:

> Just one point I don't agree with you: Paris isn't such an expensive city ! It's (far) less expensive that Geneva and much more funny ! And you can really enjoy this fun because – unlike in Geneva – it's affordable. So please don't worry " you'll be fairly well there [sic]. At least I hope so.

Another humorous aspect of the level of collaboration readiness within the WSIS civil society, can be found in an exchange from a person wanting to have his name and organization added to one of the civil society family mailing lists.

Hi All, talking about Caucuses and Families...[w]hom can I direct myself to if the head of the media-'family' (Mr. ____) doesn't answer my e-mails in which I ask him to include me in this family? Does anybody know about a 'supreme family court' or something like that? Thanks for orientation!

Shortly thereafter, the person responsible for the family in question responded with another humorous email continuing the legal metaphors, as this excerpt indicates:

Dear Plaintiff (_____) --
　　Sorry I haven't answered you. I had a very serious operation at the start of April, and, as soon I was able, I had to go on three out-of-town trips in succession.
　　There is nothing magical or mysterious about joining the media family. When we meet during the intersession in Paris or at Prepcom 3 in Geneva, the meeting times and places will be posted, and you should show up if you are in town.
　　I hope this satisfies any desire you may have for litigation.
　　Best regards,

While our assessment is that there is a high level of collaboration orientation readiness, exhibited by cheerful communication, transparency, openness, and trust, the sector is not without its problems. At one point in June, in the middle of a particularly chatty thread discussing the various lists that were being created to facilitate cooperation, one CSP members sent the following e-mail using all caps as indicated, and signing the name in lower case.

CAN ANYONE TELL ME WHAT THIS FORUM IS ALL ABOUT. YOU CAN'T REALLY BE SENDING US E-MAILS TALKING ABOUT THIS OR THAT LIST WHEN CLEARLY THAT COULD BE DONE PRIVATELY. IF THIS FORUM WAS CREATED FOR THIS KIND OF COMMUNICATION THENPLEASE TAKE US OFF.

This was followed up quickly by another participant who agreed with sentiment of the initial post but did not appreciate the format of the message (in e-mail "netiquette," sending an e-mail message in all upper-case lettering is considered the equivalent of shouting) and thus sent the following message:

> Dear all, I agree with _____ that sometimes it can be unnerving to get a mail that could have better been sent privately on this list. It is equally so when I get mails in uppercase.
> No offense intended

The hostility was diffused expertly and a potential "flame war" averted by one of the list moderators who answered by saying:

> hi _____, It's a good point. Some of these communications don't need to be on the list. On announcement with a request to send information to a private email address should suffice. At the moment, we are simply trying to bring together as much information as we can, about existing WSIS caucuses (regional and thematic) and their work spaces...and to make that information available via a central point.

As the policy processes unfolded, the CSP members began to use their e-mail list to coordinate their work more effectively. For example, when debates emerged regarding the draft civil society input into the Paris Intersessional meeting, one CSP member asserted: "What do you mean by this statement: 'We cannot, of course, expect a consensus document to be perfect for everyone; that is part of the compromise that consensus implies.'" The original author again averted conflict by responding very courteously: "Simply that every organization will still find something they would have liked included or improved." These selected examples illustrate the high level of collaboration orientation readiness, and the possibility of building on this foundation to further develop the collaboration infrastructure and communication technologies within the civil society sector.

Collaboration Infrastructure *Readiness*

Another indicator of potential success in computer-mediated collaboration is the existing of collaboration infrastructure. Following Prepcom 2, several electronic working spaces were established for civil society. Some within civil society called this an "online reorganization" and saw it as part of the overall process of formalizing the structure of the CSP. This online reorganization included the creation of a CS domain, website, and mailing lists. Subsequently, the Content & Themes group set up an online collaboration space called Basic Support for Collaborative Work (BSCW) to help cordinate the drafting of various documents by a wide range of geographically distributed participants.

Another excellent example of collaboration infrastructure readiness within civil society, is that in keeping with the spirit of transparency that is so prevalent within the civil society sector, several of the CSB members make a concerted attempt to use the e-mail lists to keep the rest of the plenary informed of what the Bureau is doing. By the middle of July, after the Paris Intersessional meeting, over 240 persons around the world were members of the Civil Society Plenary list. For example, one CSB member posted an early message in May saying: "This is just to keep you up to date on some Bureau activities. At the bottom is a note sent from the CSD [Civil Society Division of the WSIS Secretariat] to Bureau Members, which has some useful information about the process." Notes of this sort help to bridge the gap between "Bureau" members and the rest of the plenary. They also help build trust among the civil society sector as a whole, and toward specific civil society members as well (such as those frequently posting these messages and thus "exhibiting" the principles of transparency).

Collaboration Technology *Readiness*

Finally, the members of civil society are using collaboration technology and the actual tools with which to pursue distributed collaboration. The civil society sector is already using a range of tools to assist with their distributed collaboration. For example, in addition to their multiple e-mail lists, they are using a web-based portal as a document repository as explained in the following e-mail excerpt.

1) Content & Themes Drafting Portal (***New***): The Content & Themes group is now making use of a Web portal called BSCW for posting contributions, drafts, and released documents. It allows the public to submit comments on content that is posted in the portal.

This BSCW web portal was used as a document repository from May through June of 2003 to assist the Content and Themes working groups in their document drafting. Figure 5.3 is a screenshot illustrating the use of this document repository.

Yet another example of the use of collaboration technologies by civil society is the Internet Relay Chat (IRC) channel for WSIS established by one CSP member who announced it to the plenary in the following e-mail excerpt:

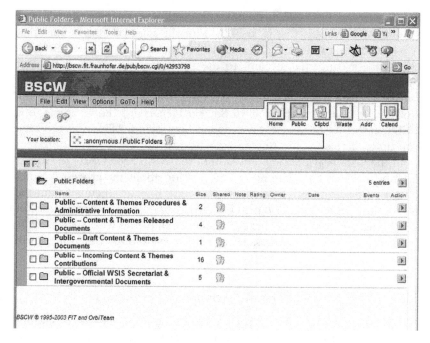

Fig. 5.3   Screenshot of web-based digital repository used by civil society

Just a quick note to let you all know that I have setup a WSIS IRC chat channel. with it, we'll be able to chat in real time both before, during and after the upcoming Prepcom. the details are as follows.

Later, another participant set up a weblog to talk about content and themes issues:

I just set up a blog we can use to inform the CT Group about the advancement of the subcommittee 2 sessions. To read, please go to wsis-cs.blogspot. com To contribute, please send me your name and your email address. I will send you all the instructions.

During Prepcom 3, the use of live video streaming from the conference center, coupled with the up-to-date reporting by civil society members on the ground helped to involve participants more actively in the process as the following two posts illustrate.

And yes, I am checking this webcast from my Tokyo home with cable broadband connection, and at least the audio is very clear. They don't show the speakers from the clear. And no translation is hard for non-English speeches to understand. I feel not too remote...but missing all the great friends to mingle. Now they finished para 40, right?

And also followed by:

Across the sea here, in a very different time zone, Vancouver, BC is also following the sessions – thank you virtual global community for this opportunity!

In addition to these qualitative examples, from our survey we learn even more about the levels of general trust, as well as specific types of trust (i.e., cognitive and affective) within the WSIS civil society sector? There is a high degree of general trust among members of the WSIS civil society, both in general and among the members of civil society. On a binary measure of trust (i.e., most people can be trusted; most people cannot be trusted), a vast majority of civil society (93 %, n = 66) reported high levels of general trust. When we look specifically at two important dimensions of trust—affective and cognitive trust—we also find high levels. For example, a majority of civil society respondents (64 %) either "agree" or "strongly agree" with an index of items measuring cognitive trust within the sector (e.g., members "are reliable and will not make my job more difficult by careless work," rated 1–5, with 5 being "strongly agree"). On an index of items measuring affective trust within the sector (e.g., "We have a sharing relationship; We can freely share our ideas, feelings, and hopes"), the majority of civil society respondents (65 %) chose either "agree' or "strongly agree."

TRANSNATIONAL POLICY NETWORKS AND EPISTEMIC COMMUNITIES

To what degree do global policy networks exist within the WSIS civil society sector and what is their relationship with epistemic communities? Previous research has shown that epistemic communities can work to promote the convergence of knowledge and interpretive schemas within public policy processes (Haas 1980, 1990). While the earliest definition of an "epistemic community" comes from Foucault (1973), a more appropriate definition comes later from Haas et al. (1977). They argue that an epistemic community is, "a network of individuals and groups who are able to influence the future by virtue of their shared specialized knowledge of certain crucial phenomena."

These epistemic communities "seek to use their knowledge as a way of organizing cognition collectively (Haas et al. 1977, p. 38)," and contribute to global governance through their direct and indirect influence of the dense transnational networks of policy-makers and issue stakeholders, what some scholars call "policy-actor networks" (Slaughter 2001; Bockman and Eyal 2002) and others call "transnational advocacy networks" (Kirk and Sikkink 1998; Betsill and Bulkeley 2004). These networks are a key source of integrating knowledge and bringing new ideas into the international decision-making process.

This research question has produced some of the most exciting findings. A majority of civil society delegates (66 %, $n = 31$) agree or strongly agree that they "work in concert with other experts in [their] field to disseminate [their] ideas to the global ICT policy community." Interestingly, when given an explicit definition of a "global policy network" and then asked if they are involved in such a network, a large majority (77 %, $n = 39$) answered yes. This second question was asked as triangulation for the first question on policy networks. The explicit definition provided to respondents was as follows: "A "Global Policy Network" can be defined as an international network of policy actors that could consist of governmental and/or nongovernmental actors. Frequently, the members of such a Global Policy Network will interact as delegates to international conferences where they attempt to work collectively to influence the outcome of the conference."

These findings are very much in line with the earlier work done by Kirk and Sikkink (1998) on transnational advocacy networks.

When asked about their impact on global ICT policy processes, a majority (67 %, $n = 28$) felt that their ideas have been either important or very important in influencing the perspectives of global ICT policy actors and a large majority (79 %, $n = 26$) believe that their global policy network has helped them to influence global ICT policy processes. Finally, nearly all of the respondents that identified themselves with a global policy network (84 %, $n = 26$) believed that their network was "associated with a group of scholars, scientists, or other continuous source of knowledge and information," meaning an epistemic community.

When asked whether or not they worked "to generate specialized knowledge on issues relevant to global ICT policy" within their organization, the vast majority (83 %) responded affirmatively. The most fre-quently cited (34 %, $n = 14$) method for disseminating their specialized knowledge to the global ICT policy community is through "public pre-sentations (e.g., conferences)." Most civil society delegates (89 %, $n = 39$) rely on other civil society organizations for the knowledge and informa-tion necessary to prepare for global ICT policy conferences, as opposed to government, private sector, or international organization resources. However, only a minority of respondents (47 %, $n = 22$) agree or strongly agree that they "have sufficient knowledge and information to be effective in global ICT policy processes." These issues will be explored more fully in future research.

To begin the quantitative analysis for this study, we started by select-ing the two measures from our survey of our key independent variables, namely "Membership in a Global Policy Network" (GPN_MEM) and "Membership in an Epistemic Community (EPIS_MEM). In addition, we identified three other related variables, measuring "Perceived Influence of your Global Policy Network" (GPN_INFL).

As a dependent variable (DV), we created a composite variable called "Perceived Policy Power" (POLPOWER), comprised of five related variables, each measuring a different dimension of potential impact on a ICT policy conference. These four variables each used a five-point scale (1 = lowest; 5 = highest), and are characterized as follows: "Influence of your ideas" (IDEAINFL), "Success of your organization in getting specific language into the conference documents" (ORGSUCC), "Posses sufficient knowledge and information to be successful" (SUFINFO), and finally "Perceived impact on the WSIS Declaration of Principles (DP_INFL) and the WSIS Action Plan (AP_INFL)."

Principal components and factor analysis of these five variables showed that they all loaded onto one factor, which I have labeled "Perceived Policy Power." The composite dependent variable was created as the mean of these five items (IDEAINFLU, ORGSUCC, SUFINFO, DP_INFL, and AP_INFL), the internal reliability of this composite variable was mod-erately high (Cronbach's Alpha = 0.80).

Finally, we identified 12 independent variables (IVs), which are expected to be covariates of possible theoretical importance. These IVs were as fol-lows: "Region born" (REGBORN), AGE, GENDER, TRUST (a binary measure of high or low general trust), "Organizational size" (ORGSIZE), "Organizational type" (ORGTYPE), "Years of ICT policy experience" (ICTYEARS), INCOME, "Highest Level of education completed" (EDUC),

"Level of activity in ICT policy processes" (ICTACTIVE), "Level of focus on ICT policy processes" (ICTFOCUS), and "Economic status of country where you are based" as measured by membership in the OECD.

CHARACTERISTICS OF THE SURVEY SAMPLE

Before we begin our analysis, let us describe the sample. The majority of WSIS delegates were male (70 %, n = 180). The modal education level was a master's degree (48.3 %, n = 125), with a large number of participants holding doctorates (22 %, n = 57). The vast majority of delegates reported being either "high" or "upper middle" income in their own countries (64.1 %, n = 164). Interestingly, this is contrasted by the opposite in exploring a subsample of civil society delegates, where a slight majority (52 %, n = 36) reported to be of either "Low" or "Middle Income" in their own countries. Western Europe represented the largest geographic region within the study sample (28 %, n = 72), followed by Africa (24.1 %, n = 62). Most of the respondents (68.2 %, n = 174) did not speak English as their primary language. Most respondents (84.2 %, n = 154) have a "Broadband (e.g., LAN/ ISDN/DSL/Cable Modem)" connection to the Internet, with most (76.2 %, n = 141) connecting from their "Office or work."

TRANSNATIONAL POLICY-ACTOR NETWORKS IN WSIS

Our first research question asks a basic empirical question: "To what extent are transnational policy-actor networks engaged in the WSIS processes?" Given that the emerging literature on transnational networks theoretically posits their existence and importance, the first task for us is to see if transnational policy-actor networks are actually present within the WSIS processes. Respondents were given the following definition of a Global Policy Network: "A Global Policy Network is...." They were then asked, "Based on the preceding definition, are you currently involved in a "Global Policy Network" "for information and communication technologies?" Their binary responses were coded "1″ for No and "2″ for yes. A majority of respondents (69.1 %, n = 143) said that they were indeed members of a transnational policy network. A large number of respondents (n = 104) continued to give us the name of their transnational network, and several respondents (n = 85) even provided detailed qualitative information about how their transnational policy networks began. Based on this simple descriptive analysis, we find substantial evidence that transnational policy-actor networks do exist within the WSIS process.

Character and Structure of Policy-Actor Networks in WSIS

Next, since we found that transnational policy-actor networks do exist within the WSIS processes, our second research question asks, "what is the character and structure of these transnational policy-actor networks?" We operationalized this question by asking: "which factors significantly predict membership in a policy network? Based on our theoretical model, we would expect to find several factors that would significantly predict membership in a policy network.

To answer this question a binary logistic regression was performed between "Membership in a Global Policy Network (GPN_MEM) as the dependent variable and several demographic and theoretically interesting measures as the independent variables. These variables were: AGE, GENDER, "Organizational Size (ORGSIZE), INCOME, "Highest level of education completed" (EDUC), "Organizational Type" (ORGTYPE), "Years of ICT policy experience" (ICTYEARS), "Level of activity in ICT policy processes" (ICTACTIVE), and "Level of focus on ICT policy processes" (ICTFOCUS), "Country Status" (OECD), and "A dichotomous measure of low or high general trust" (TRUST). The analysis was performed using SPSS Regression, with assistance from SPSS Frequencies to evaluate assumptions for the logistic regression. No variables needed to be transformed (though there is a need to consider removing a possible outlier on ORGSIZE). Table 5.4 displays the statistics from the variables in the logistic regression model.

Three variables are statistically significant in their ability to predict membership in a transnational policy network, these are level of activity in ICT policy (ICTACTIV) B = 0.68, $p < 0.001$; level of focus on ICT policy (ICTFOCUS) B = -1.28, $p < 0.01$; and membership in the OECD (OECD) B = 0.86, $p < 0.01$. Years of experience in ICT policy (ICTYEARS) was marginally significant B = 0.09, $p < 0.06$. Table 5.5 below summarizes the logistic regression model.

Based on the two pseudo R^2 measures, we see that the logistic regression model predicts about 23 % for the Cox and Snell R^2 (or 31 % for the Nagelkerke R^2). The model is statistically significant (X^2 43.9, df 11, $p < 0.001$).

Table 5.4   Summary of variables in the logistic regression model

Variables	B	S.E.	Wald	df	Sig.	Exp (B)
REGBORN	0.010	0.056	0.035	1	0.851	1.010
AGE	-0.012	0.021	0.353	1	0.552	0.988
GENDER	-0.012	0.426	0.325	1	0.569	0.785
TRUST	0.084	0.579	0.021	1	0.884	1.088
ORGSIZE	0.000	0.000	0.490	1	0.484	1.000
ORGTYPE	−0.032	0.126	0.063	1	0.801	0.969
INCOME	0.225	0.264	0.723	1	0.395	1.252
EDUC	0.135	0.170	0.631	1	0.427	1.145
ICTYEARS	0.09			1	0.05?	
ICTACTIV	0.682	0.202	11.457	1	0.001	1.978
ICTFOCUS	−1.277	0.417	9.395	1	0.002	0.279
OECD	0.861	0.414	4.323	1	0.038	2.367

Variable(s) entered on step 1: REGBORN, AGE, GENDER, TRUST, ORGSIZE, ORGTYPE, ICTYEARS, INCOME, EDUC, ICTACTIV, ICTFOCUS, OECD

Table 5.5 Logistic regression model summary

Pseudo R^2	
Cox and Snell R^2	0.23
Nagelkerke R^2	0.31
X^2 43.9, df 11, $p < 0.001$	

Linkages to Epistemic Communities

After identifying these transnational policy-actor networks, and better understanding their character and structure, we wanted to understand the extent to which these networks were linked to specific knowledge producing or epistemic communities. On our survey, we asked respondents who had already indicated their membership in a transnational policy-actor network if their network was "associated with a group of scholars, scientists, or other continuous source of knowledge and information?" A large majority (74.1 %, n = 83) of participants in policy-actor networks reported that their network was linked to an epistemic community. These respondents also provided detailed qualitative information about the epistemic community.

Impact of Transnational Policy-Actor Networks on Perceived Policy Power

Our final question is "What impact do these policy-actor networks and epistemic communities have on perceived policy power within WSIS?"

We operationalize this question by asking "Does membership in a policy network increase perceived policy power, when adjusting for covariants?" A related follow-up question was asked: "What other factors significantly predict perceived policy power?" And finally, the last operational question was asked: "Is perceived policy power moderated by linkages with epistemic communities?"

To address the first operational question "Does membership in a policy network increase perceived policy power, when adjusting for covariants?" a standard multiple regression was performed with Perceived Policy Power (POLPOWER) as the dependent variable, and the following independent variables and covariates: AGE, GENDER, "Organizational Size (ORGSIZE), INCOME, "Highest level of education completed" (EDUC), "Organizational Type" (ORGTYPE), "Years of ICT policy experience" (ICTYEARS), "Level of activity in ICT policy processes" (ICTACTIVE), and "Level of focus on ICT policy processes" (ICTFOCUS), "Country Status" (OECD), "A dichotomous measure of low or high general trust" (TRUST), "Membership in Global Policy Network (GPN_MEM), and EPISMEM. The analysis was performed using SPSS Regression, with assistance from SPSS frequencies to evaluate assumptions for the logistic regression. No variables needed to be transformed. Table 5.6 presents the summary statistics from this regression model.

Table 5.6 Model summary for standard multiple regression

Model	R	R^2	Adj. R^2	S.E.	R^2 change	F change	df1	Df 2	Sig. F change
					Change statistics				
1	0.657(a)	0.432	0.369	0.57714	0.432	6.841	13	116	0.000

Predictors: EPIS_MEM, ORGTYPE, ORGSIZE, TRUST, INCOME, ICTFOCUS, EDUC, GENDER, ICTACTIV, OECD, ICTYEARS, AGE, GPN_MEM

Table 5.7 displays the statistics from the standard multiple regression including, the correlations between the variables, the unstandardized regression coefficients (B) and intercept, the standardized regression coefficients (β), the semipartial correlations (sr2).

Our regression equation is statistically significant and predicts about 43 % of the variance in perceived policy power ($\Delta R^2 = 0.43$, $p < 0.001$). As expected, membership in a policy network was statistically significant, explaining about 29 % of the variance in predicting perceived policy power ($\beta = 0.29$, $p < 0.001$). This regression equation also allows us to answer the second operational question "What other factors significantly predict perceived policy power?" From the analysis of this model, we find six other variables that were also statistically significant in their ability to predict perceived policy power. These variables were, AGE, which is negatively correlated ($\beta = -0.18$, $p < 0.05$), years of ICT policy experience (ICTYEARS) ($\beta = 0.17$, $p < 0.05$), level of activity in ICT policy (ICTACTIVE) ($\beta = 0.21$, $p < 0.05$), economic status of country (OECD) ($\beta = -0.20$, $p < 0.05$), trust (TRUST) ($\beta = -0.19$, $p < 0.05$) and membership in an epistemic community (EPISMEM) ($\beta = 0.23$, $p < 0.01$) Table 5.8 presents a summary of the model and Table 5.9 presents the coefficients from the hierarchial regression.

Table 5.7 Presentation of coefficients for standard multiple regression

	Unstandardized coefficients		Standardized coefficients					
	B	S.E.	B	t	Sig			
AGE	−0.014	0.006	−0.183	−2.272	0.025	−0.080	−0.206	−0.158
GENDER	−0.105	0.122	−0.063	−0.860	0.392	0.000	−0.079	−0.060
TRUST	0.450	0.179	0.185	2.513	0.013	0.219	0.226	0.175
ORGSIZE	0.000	0.000	0.023	0.320	0.749	0.091	0.030	0.022
ORGTYPE	−0.050	0.034	−0.108	−1.469	0.145	−0.179	−0.135	−0.102
ICTYEARS	0.019	0.009	0.173	2.167	0.032	0.272	0.197	0.151
INCOME	0.052	0.072	0.057	0.719	0.474	0.052	0.066	0.050
EDUC	0.054	0.051	0.077	1.068	0.288	0.107	0.098	0.074
ICTACTIV	0.155	0.060	0.207	2.559	0.012	0.401	0.230	0.178
ICTFOCUS	0.153	0.115	0.103	1.350	0.186	0.065	0.122	0.093
OECD	−0.296	0.116	−0.203	−2.538	0.012	−0.121	−0.229	−0.177
GPN_MEM	0.454	0.129	0.290	3.517	0.001	0.356	0.309	0.245
EPIS_MEM	0.218	0.069	0.234	3.154	0.002	0.342	0.280	0.220

Dependent variable: POLPOWER

Table 5.8 Model summary

Model	R	R^2	Adjusted R^2	SE	Change statistics				
					R^2	F	df1	df2	Sig. F
1	0.518	0.268	0.218	0.65229	0.268	5.301	11	158	0.000

Table 5.9 Standard multiple regression coefficients

	Unstandardized coefficients		Standardized coefficients	T	Sig.
	B	SE			
AGE	−1.378E-02	0.006	−0.182	−2.438	0.016
GENDER	−0.148	0.116	−0.090	−1.271	0.205
TRUST	0.416	0.160	0.183	2.596	0.010
ORGSIZE	3.136E.07	0.000	0.036	0.515	0.607
ORGTYPE	−3.558E-02	0.034	0.077	−1.050	0.291
INCOME	−3.208E-02	0.070	−0.034	−0.461	0.646
EDUC	9.100E-02	0.047	0.136	1.942	0.054
ICTACTIV	0.223	0.053	0.323	4.199	0.000
ICTFOCUS	−3.857E-02	0.309	0.025	−0.353	0.725
OECD	−0.164	0.109	−0.110	−1.503	0.135
ICTYEARS	2.384E-02	0.010	0.195	2.495	0.014

Dependent variable: POLPOWER

Finally, to address the last operational question "Is perceived policy power moderated by linkages with epistemic communities?" a hierarchical regression was performed, with "Perceived Policy Power" (POLPOWER) again as the dependent variable, and the same independent variables as the previous standard multiple regression. However, this time an interaction term was created between "Membership in a Policy Network" (GPN_MEM) and EPIS_MEM and also added to the IV list. This term was entered into the hierarchical multiple regression. No statistically significant interaction was determined from the linkage with an epistemic community on predicting perceived policy power.

TRANSNATIONAL POLICY NETWORKS

The implications of these findings are important in many ways. First, regarding our understanding of transnational advocacy networks, it is clear from our analysis that transnational policy-actor networks exist within the

WSIS process. Much more analysis is needed to tease out the qualitative and more of the quantitative details of this story, but there is a significant number of these networks active.

Influential Factors

We have found that three factors are statistically significant in predicting membership in a transnational policy network. These variables are "Level of ICT policy activity (ICTACTIV, .001), "Level of ICT policy focus" (ICTFOCUS, .002), and "Country Status" (OECD, .038). Another variable, "Years of experience in ICT policy" (ICTYEARS, .062), was marginally significant. These findings are not surprising. All three of these variables reflect the degree to which a person is actively involved in global ICT processes, and it makes sense that the same kinds of people would be involved in transnational policy networks. What was interesting is that some factors that we might suspect to be important are not even marginally statistically significant, such as, AGE, ORGTYPE, EDUC, and INCOME.

Perceived Policy Power

Finally, as we consider the concept of perceived policy power, we find that that membership in a transnational policy network (GPN_MEM), significantly predicts perceived policy power, but five other variables in our model are also statistically significant. These variables are AGE, which is negatively correlated, years of ICT policy experience (ICTYEARS), economic status of country (OECD), and membership in an epistemic community (EPIS_MEM). These are all variables that we might suspect would influence policy power in an international conference. We were surprised, however, that there was no statistical interaction between the linkage of a policy network and an epistemic community in predicting perceived policy power.

Impact on Overall Theoretical Model

Overall, this analysis strengthens our theoretical model. We are encouraged to find the existence of transnational policy networks within WSIS, and to better understand what factors may be influencing influence participation in these networks. However, the fact that there was no interaction from linkage with epistemic community suggests that we may need to revisit this part of the model.

SUCCESS, SATISFACTION, AND POLICY IMPACT

Given the analysis above, how successful and satisfied was civil society in the WSIS policy formulation processes? One of the most important measures of "success" in United Nations summits is the degree to which delegations are able to get specific language into the conference documents (Schechter 2001). Interestingly, a slim majority of civil society organizations (54 %, n = 38) felt either successful or very successful at getting specific language into the WSIS policy formulation process. However, when asked about their specific impact on the two major WSIS documents, only a small minority (26 %, n = 11) agreed or strongly agreed that they had a "significant impact on the *WSIS Declaration of Principles*, and an even smaller number (19 %, n = 8) felt that they had a significant impact on the *WSIS Action Plan.*

With such a high level of awareness of the structure and importance of the process, and with the substantial use of CMC tools to mediate the impact of distance and the numerous competing meetings, the civil society sector should have been well positioned to influence the WSIS policy formulation process. From the perspective of civil society, the key policy issues to be included in the *WSIS Declaration of Principles* are encapsulated by an overarching focus on using the GII to create a more people-oriented information society. As an example of the pursuit of policy alternatives within the civil society sector, one plenary member sent the following e-mail to the plenary list:

> A discussion list for people planning alternatives to the World Summit on the Information Society (WSIS) including another summit, countersummit, walk-out, protest, or other strategies to advance communication as a human right and as a public good. To counter corporate hijacking of the WSIS for private interest or Bushwacking of the WSIS in the name of a "war on cyberterrorism."

Table 5.10 presents an overview of the key policy issues and perspectives as presented by the civil society sector. Most of these issues became the centerpiece of the civil society inputs into the Paris Intersessional meeting, and subsequently, the focal point for civil society discontent with the draft *WSIS Declaration of Principles* and the *WSIS Action Plan* (Global Contract Foundation 2003). This led to civil society producing an alternative document at WSIS called the *WSIS Civil Society Benchmark.*

Table 5.10 Primary policy issues of concern to civil society

Broad issue	Specific	Implications
Global governance	Usually refers to Internet governance and specifically ICANN, WIPO	Hotly contested issue, ranging from focus on removing root from US control to democratizing ICANN (with more influence for governments), to establishing a new Intergovernmental organization (IGO) for Internet governance
Open access to knowledge	Global knowledge commons, pen journals and open archives initiatives	
Human rights	UDHR in principle and action and enforcement	
Relaxed property rights	FLOSS	Traditional IPR seen as the industrial control of information
Cultural and linguistic diversity in content		
"Right to communicate"	Communication Rights in the Information Society (CRIS Campaign)—NWICO-oriented	Impact of ICTs on human rights, would be seen as creating a new human right
Education (distance learning and open knowledge)	NRENS as backbone for dissemination of knowledge	
Health		
Local initiatives	Respect for the primacy of local initiatives	
Cyber security	Privacy and information security	
Cyber crime		
Accessibility and disabilities		
Gender	Gender equality and nondiscrimination	
Sustainable democratic development		
Work/employment	Creating genuine sustainable employment and work	
Access to information infrastructure	Some opposition to using GII and "Digital Solidarity" the former as US-centric and the latter as neocolonialist	Would create a new funding instrument (opposed by Germany)
Youth	Empowering youth	

For many of these policy issues, such as global governance, it has been difficult to achieve a consensus within civil society. Control of domain names is an especially contentious area of global ICT governance. Here, one CSP member requested that a critical section on global ICT governance be removed.

I request that the following paragraph be deleted from the Civil Society Priorities Document:

> "To these ends, the current management of Internet names and numbers and other related mechanisms should be re-examined with the full participation of all stakeholders in light of serving public interests and compatibility with human rights standards." It can only serve to support the arguments of governments that wish to gain control over Internet resource allocation, and others hoping to see the ITU or some other inter-governmental organization take control of Internet naming and addressing.

At stake in this part of the policy debate is the governance of the domain name and IP addressing systems for the Internet. This debate is highly polarized, with the perception on the one hand that Internet governance, specifically within ICANN, continues to be dominated by the US government through the Department of Commerce and US corporate interests and that authority for a global resource such as the Internet should be transferred to a truly global, representative forum; and on the other hand, sits the perspective that while the current Internet governance system is not perfect, it should not necessarily be transferred to what may be a less efficient decision-making body, especially one subject to governments that may be hostile to the free flow of interests represented by the Internet. One CSP member articulates the debate succinctly in this e-mail excerpt.

> While ICANN is not the organization we hoped it would be, its policy making processes are quite open to Civil Society (certainly compared to the alternatives.) We can and do have a direct influence (I know, I've done it.) And recent changes to ICANN policy making processes indicate that there will be more opportunities in the future, not less. If we were in a debating hall I would be more than happy to stand up and list problems with ICANN. But this week, all this is besides the point. It's not the issue. We are here reacting to an effort by some governments to take control of Internet naming and addressing. They believe they should have sovereign rights not only to TLDs but to IP address allocation and to control of the root server system (read the working documents and contributions). Other governments want to

see these functions become the responsibility of an "inter-governmental organization." It is quite clear that the organization they are thinking of is the ITU. What's at stake this week is very simple. Will the draft documents support the status quo, ICANN? Or will they support change? By asking for "re-examination" we will support change. Governments like Syria will take us as supporting their efforts. Governments and the ITU will use our words to their advantage. There is no plan C. There is nothing other than the two options. If you want to risk supporting ITU and government control of Internet naming and addressing, leave the paragraph in place.

Many CSP members, especially those active in the ICT Governance Caucus want to ensure that ICANN is not undermined, because they fear the alternative—which would be government control directly, or via the proxy of intergovernmental organizations such as the ITU. This perspective is articulated by a CSP member not participating in the ICT Governance Caucus.

Hi all, It seems that we have a serious point of disagreement in the "Global ICT governance" section of the draft CS document. The sentence at stake in the document is: To these ends, the current management of Internet names and numbers and other related mechanisms should be re-examined with the full participation of all stakeholders in light of serving public interests and compatibility with human rights standards.

Interestingly, beyond the specifics of any given policy issue, there are debates within the civil society as to their role in the world system. While some CSP members argue for a more expansive role for civil society and the private sector "on par with governments," others argue specifically against this.

Dear ___, We should certainly claim more adequate spaces for debate and expression at the WSIS, but I don't believe there's consensus among civil society organizations about requesting a status as "equal partners" with governments. As imperfect as the democratic system is, and although a number of governments in the world are not democratically elected, governments should be answerable to their peoples and assume responsibility for the decisions taken at summits such as this. Many consider that our role as civil society organizations is different (I won't go into detail on the arguments here); but above all would strongly oppose opening the possibility to the private sector, that represents particular interests, to sit as equal partners with governments at a UN Summit.

Impact on Conference Outcomes

In this multistakeholder process, the CS sector plays a critically important role, representing much of the energy and applied innovation of the GIS. Also, as argued above, the civil society has been well organized, there is a high level of collaboration readiness, and the sector has been aided by organizations such as the APC in using CMC tools to attempt to harness the talents and energies of the members of its sector from around the world.

However, by any number of measures, the current WSIS process has not been able to include sufficiently the voices of civil society. For example, during Prepcom 3, the Civil Society delegates were not allowed to participate fully in the Working Groups where key and sometimes contentious issues of the draft *WSIS Declaration of Principles* and the *WSIS Plan of Action* were being discussed (civil society and private sector participation was limited to the first five minutes of the meeting). This led to considerable frustration and to the production of an analysis of civil society participation in the WSIS preparatory process called "From Input to Impact," which argued that more than 60 % of the civil society recommendations to the final declaration had been completely ignored (Global Contract Foundation 2003). Further, the decision to "resume" Prepcom 3 from 10 to 14 November 2003, without providing fellowships for civil society delegates, and even excluding some countries (e.g., Argentina) from receiving fellowships to the actual summit, meant that key elements of the final documents were decided on by a group that was much too small to represent the multiple stakeholders of the GIS.

As a result of these developments, many call WSIS a failure, and there are continued suggestions that the civil society should disengage from the process and refuse to continue being "pawns" in a multistakeholder process that will not fully consider and integrate their perspectives. On the other hand, if civil society can use the WSIS process as a catalyst for stimulating dense, robust networks that can engage more effectively in global governance processes, it will have been a tremendous success.

IMPLICATIONS FOR MULTISTAKEHOLDER GLOBAL GOVERNANCE OF THE INFORMATION SOCIETY

In order to build a truly equitable GIS and to harness the potential of ICTs for socioeconomic development, the active participation of a diverse civil society is critical. This is true, even if that participation is through the innovative and active use of computer-mediated communication tools. Civil society participation is critical not only because of the diversity of perspectives and expertise that they bring to the table, but also because in many countries, these are the very organizations that will play a leading role in implementing the *WSIS Plan of Action*. Without the support and participation of these civil society organizations, the potential of the information and communication society will be severely limited.

From one perspective, the civil society sector can be seen as an example for other participants in this global multistakeholder process. We have shown that with very limited resources, civil society has developed complex organizational structures sufficient to be able to pull together coherent, focused, substantive, and powerful contributions to the WSIS process. We have shown that the WSIS civil society has a very high degree of collaboration readiness, including high levels of cognitive and affective trust. These characteristics are critical to engaging in long-term, substantive, geographically distributed collaborative knowledge work. We have also shown how, although limited primarily to e-mail lists and web-based archives, civil society has been able to use CMC tools to help involve people from around the world in their WSIS policy activities.

However, from another perspective, if civil society is to forge a success out of the WSIS process—regardless of their ultimate impact on specific policy documents—by building the policy-actor networks and linkages to epistemic communities required to engage in sustained transnational advocacy and global governance work, then they are going to have to overcome some major challenges. They are going to have to learn how to capture the full potential of its ostensible membership by better organizing the diverse and geographically distributed civil society participants from around the world.

The WSIS civil society will have to address the twin issues that have continued to be the "elephant(s) in the living room," of these multistakeholder global governance processes. These twin problems are legitimacy and structure. The legitimacy issue has multiple prongs (Hudson 2001). First, there is the question of whom the participants in the WSIS civil society actually represent. The overall number of civil society participants is quite large. Most of them come from Western Europe (32 %), are well educated (modal education level, master's degree), and male (64 %). Africa makes up the second largest percentage of civil society delegates (27 %). However, with some notable exceptions, there are very few African delegates in formal or informal leadership positions within the civil society sector. Even fewer civil society leaders come from Latin America, the Caribbean, Asia, and the Middle East. Even further, when many of the African delegates raise issues of importance to them, such as civil society support for the Digital Solidarity Fund, support for Tunisia as an African host for Phase II of the summit, or increased mechanisms that might facilitate enhanced virtual participation for those not physically able to attend the summit, these suggestions are generally met with lukewarm support, at best.

Furthermore, there are currently several major crises within the structure of civil society. There has been no resolution to numerous issues raised by delegates from around the world about the composition of the CSB, what role it should play vis-à-vis the plenary, how its members were appointed, whom they represent, whether or not the current members of the Bureau are supposed to continue into the second phase of the summit, how individual members of the Bureau get replaced, what happens in the absence of a Civil Society Division (CSD) of the secretariat, and many other unresolved issues. Individual caucuses are having additional problems, such as whether or not any member of the civil society Internet governance caucus will be chosen to participate in the UN Secretary-General's Working Group on Internet Governance; and if so, who will be the "representative," how will they be chosen, and whom will they represent?

There seems to be no urgency to address these issues on the part of the members of the WSIS civil society. Currently, many of the fortunate ones are gearing up for the preparatory processes of the Tunis phase of WSIS. Many of the most fortunate ones are busy planning their travel plans to the seaside resort town of Hammamet, where Prepcom 1 will be held or to the numerous other thematic meetings that make up Phase II of the WSIS preparatory process. This is happening while the sector has not addressed any of the above issues, or prepared a strategy for what to do once those privileged few get to Tunis or the other venues. Perhaps they will solve all of the problems when they get there. Not likely. To date, there have been no widespread systematic efforts to involve remote participants in the meetings, other than continuing the e-mail traffic (though actually, there has been relatively little substantive e-mail traffic on either plenary lists, or the caucuses which we monitor), and competing and uncoordinated offers to host civil society documents on various websites.

Perhaps most important, what happens to all of these issues when there is no funding available to support civil society participation in the process, and little willingness on the part of funding agencies and governments to commit the same level of funding present during the first phase of the summit. Interestingly, the African civil society has been perhaps the most active since leaving the summit in December 2003. They have evolved a number of structures and mechanisms for organizing their regional cooperation, which includes closer involvement with governments, the relevant regional and subregional organizations, and with the private sector.

However, these findings set up one of the more disturbing implications of this study. While the transnational civil society sector members have overcome tremendous obstacles, both internal and external, in their ability to organize themselves in a geographically distributed manner using a wide range of CMC tools (though mostly limited to e-mail lists), and to tap into the creative energies, optimism, and dedication that seems to be almost omnipresent in those participating actively in the civil society sector, they have still had limited impact on the WSIS policy processes. Their efforts to promote a more socially oriented vision for the emerging GIS regime have been largely ineffectual. As a result, the WSIS policy documents represent much more of an "information" society than the possible "communication" society articulated by some scholars (Ó Siochrú 2004); and looks much more like the GEC (GII/GEC) regime than the GIS (GII/GIS) regime described by others (Cogburn 2003).

This reality has caused the conference organizers, participants, and supporters to assess what they learned from participation in Phase I of WSIS as they actively prepare for Phase II in Tunis. For the conference organizers—who are now located primarily within the Tunisian government—they see the added expense and logistical difficulties of trying to involve a very diverse group of civil society voices from around the world. These realities are quite different from the private sector participants who not only fund their own travel and participation in these preparatory and summit events, and often provide financial support for the summit itself. Many of the civil society participants do not have the financial resources to participate on their own, and thus require financial assistance from the organizers or external sources, such as foundations and development agencies. For civil society organizations, several questions emerge, such as "was it worth the effort to participate with so much energy, and still achieve such mediocre results?" Will civil society organizations ever be "equal" partners with governments; and perhaps more importantly, should they? For funding and supporting agencies, questions of whether or not they should continue supporting the travel, accommodation and other expenses for civil society and developing country participants to attend these meetings. Even with that said, there are already over 45 civil society participants registered to attend in the June Prepcom 1 for the Tunis phase.

Another implication of this study is that there is a certain understandable irony in the tension between governments and civil society, particularly with smaller governmental delegations. These small government delegations are often only one or two in number and must cope with complex substantive issues ranging from Internet governance to human rights. They are often unable to spread themselves across the wide varieties of thematic working groups. Even if they were able to attend to all of the themes, they frequently do not have the technical or substantive background on these issues. A great coalition could be formed by civil society organizations with their expertise and these small governments. Examples of this potential can be seen in the strategies employed by some civil society caucus, such as the disability caucus, to work with like-minded government delegations to get their issues heard and included within the government plenary sessions.

However, the finding in this study that the majority of civil society participants are members of global policy networks and that they draw heavily upon existing epistemic communities is quite encouraging. These policy networks could be the basis upon which more robust, distributed collaboration structures could be built. We will explore these possibilities in the future research described in the penultimate section.

RECONCILING THEORY AND OBSERVATION IN GLOBAL GOVERNANCE

Based on this analysis, what follows are some initial thoughts about the relevance of the existing theoretical model. First, the frontstage/backstage elements of the model continue to be of critical importance. There appears to be an important distinction on the part of policy actors in their formal public pronouncements and their private backstage behavior. Based on Goffman (1959) and subsequent work in this area, that is what we would expect to find. This backstage behavior is seen as providing a critical venue or space, upon which successful frontstage or "onstage" behavior is based. More importantly, this means that the nice and tidy presentation of the WSIS goals and process, as well as its theoretical intentions, meets a very messy reality as the process actually unfolds on the ground.

In addition, there seems to be an emerging recognition that an appropriate strategy might be to include civil society representatives within government delegations. This would allow civil society delegates to attend governmental meetings and "report" back to the overall civil society plenary about the debates, discussions, positions, and alternatives. One CSP member who produced an excellent account of the Paris intersessional meeting suggested that this had been done with great success on one of the western European delegations.

Further, this study supports the overall assertion of the model that international conferences matter to the global governance of cyber infrastructure. These conferences play an important role in facilitating the convergence of expectations among actors that is required for regime formation to occur. In this case, the multiple WSIS preparatory processes, while contentious to the end, were able to keep most of the relevant participants in this multistakeholder process on board and the final *WSIS Declaration of Principles* combined with the final *WSIS Action Plan* provide a framework for "governing" the information society between the December 2003 Geneva Summit and the November 2005 Tunis Summit.

Another aspect of these final documents in relation to the theoretical model for the study, is the clear importance of preparing for and actively participating in the preparatory processes. As such, issues such as the inability for Prepcom 3 to reach consensus on these draft principles and action plan, and the subsequent decision to hold a resumed "Prepcom 3a" presented a significant challenge to civil society participation in the process.

Another implication for our theoretical model is in the context of epistemic communities. Significant levels of knowledge and information resources are shared on these various mailing lists. However, these resources are not being collected and organized for later use. Further, because the archive is in plain text, it does not save the attachments, and does not hypertext the links, making it cumbersome to go back and capture those valuable knowledge resources. These conclusions and others continue to guide us in our future research, described in the following section.

LIMITATIONS

We have developed a research design that is most appropriate to the phenomena under examination. Also, we have triangulated our findings by bringing together qualitative and quantitative approaches. However, all social science research has limitations. While our survey is well designed and was pilot tested internationally, and across the sectors relevant to the study (government, private sector, civil society), it is still limited to those participants in the WSIS process, and more specifically, to those WSIS participants that provided their e-mail address to the secretariat in registering for the summit. To address this limitation, we have compared the study sample both to the sampling frame and to the population of all registered WSIS preparatory delegates on key demographic variables (i.e., gender, region, organizational type), and found that only organizational type was significantly different, with a slight overrepresentation of civil society participants. In order to account for this difference, we have developed normalized weights for the study to slightly reduce the impact of civil society participants in the study sample. We have also analyzed the study sample for any potential nonresponse bias, or time series bias, and found none to be significant.

Nonetheless, the lack of a random sample decreases the ability to generalize these findings beyond the WSIS participants. Also, upon further reflection, some of the measures, could have been strengthened, and employed greater triangulation. However, given the numerous precautions that we have taken, we feel comfortable generalizing to the population of WSIS delegates, but are uncomfortable making strong generalizations to the entire population of elite ICT policy actors in general. Also, we have taken great pains to recognize our own potential biases and to keep them out of the analysis. While we have been participant observers, we have refrained from becoming overly involved in any of the actual policy discussions and have avoided the numerous factional and ideological battles that have emerged (with the exception of becoming embroiled in a fairly strong ideological debate over the relative merits and demerits of free and open source software through our plan to use commercially available collaboration technology). Finally, the qualitative aspects of this study could be subject to other interpretations. Our member-checking and other verification strategies should moderate these limitations.

CHAPTER 6

Global Alliance for ICT and Development: What Went Right, and Wrong?

INTRODUCTION

As we discussed in Chap. 5, many analysts see the UN WSIS as a major success for multistakeholder global governance. Even with the tremendous challenges we outlined in that chapter, WSIS served as a catalyst for stimulating a number of transnational advocacy networks, some of which are still active (especially in Internet governance, which we will review in Chap. 7). However, we also see that several major issues were unresolved at the end of WSIS, namely Internet governance and a range of issues related to the use of the Internet and ICTs for international development. These unresolved issues led in part to the creation of two new innovative multistakeholder global governance mechanisms at the end of WSIS: (1) the IGF; and (2) GAID. If one reflects upon the arguments discussed in Chaps. 3 and 4, these two initiatives almost perfectly align with the debate we framed as a battle between a GII that was aligned with the international regime principles of a GIS or one aligned with the principles of GEC.

Both of these multistakeholder initiatives were given five-year mandates. However, these two new multistakeholder initiatives had very different structures, and radically different trajectories. After its initial evaluation, the IGF was renewed for another five years, and on 16 December 2015 the UN General Assembly in the WSIS +10 review renewed the IGF for

© The Author(s) 2017
D.L. Cogburn, *Transnational Advocacy Networks in the Information Society*, Information Technology and Global Governance,
DOI 10.1057/978-1-137-48361-4_6

another ten years. We will review the IGF in the next chapter. In contrast, the GAID was closed after its initial five-year period. Perhaps the most successful element to come out of the GAID was the launch of the Global Initiative for Inclusive Information and Communication Technologies (G3ICT). In this chapter we explore what went right for the GAID, and what went horribly wrong.

BACKGROUND AND POTENTIAL OF A GLOBAL ALLIANCE FOR ICT

On 8 February 2005, as a preparatory document for the second phase of WSIS we released a concept paper proposing the creation of a Global Alliance for ICT. The idea of the concept paper was to stimulate a debate about the need to establish a mechanism to bring the public to Internet policy development as an effective successor to the United Nations Information and Communication Technologies (UNICT) Task Force. The UNICT Task Force was a remarkable innovation in developing a broad dialog over the international policy issues surrounding ICTs and the evolution of the information society. Formed in 2003, the Task Force was able to bring together representatives of governments, nongovernmental and civil society organizations, corporations, and unaffiliated experts to engage in a broad dialog intended to "provide overall leadership to the United Nations role in helping to formulate strategies for the development of ICTs and putting those technologies at the service of development and, on the basis of consultations with all stakeholders and Member States, forging a strategic partnership between the United Nations system, private industry and financing trusts and foundations, donors, governments and other relevant stakeholders in accordance with relevant United Nations resolutions" (Plan of Action, UNICT Task Force).

Initially, the Task Force was scheduled for sunset in 2004, but with the incredible demands of the United Nations–sponsored WSIS, its mandate was extended through 2005.

However, given the groundbreaking structure of the Task Force and its concomitant work program, we saw it as appropriate to stimulate a debate about what institutional form should embody this important mandate after WSIS concluded.

The growth and use of the Internet and World Wide Web has illustrated both the need for and the possibilities of global collaboration among relevant stakeholders. In an increasing number of domains, ranging from scientific associations to political campaigns through community-based organizations, the sharing of information over the Internet and other forms of computer-mediated communication has improved the ability for people and organizations to collaborate quickly and mobilize support for their participation in policy processes, including WSIS (Cogburn 2003b; Cogburn 2005a; Cogburn 2006b).

Taking advantage of the experiences of the ICT Task Force and merging them with even more innovative efforts at developing broader collaboration, the Internet can be used to bring Internet governance more effectively to the public and the public more effectively to ICT governance. This paper discusses alternative and innovative means to do this.

Background: The Role of Information in Global Policy Formulation

The role of knowledge and information in governance at the international level has changed as a result of the Internet. The flow of information has been essential to the creation of global agreements since the beginning of the United Nations. Since international organizations, whether public or nongovernmental, are not sovereign, decision-making is different than is the case at the national level. International agreements can only be reached by consensus. Consensus means that all parties accept a decision because of its overall value, even when they may have reservations about elements of the agreement.

Consensus is possible because the parties to it share information and can be sure that the results are known and that their interests have been communicated. In earlier times, consensus was made possible by bringing the parties together physically in negotiating sessions. While these could be preceded by exchanges of information in the form of documents, expert groups and in-person consultations, the processes were not particularly open, particularly to the public, but even to specialized government officials. This lack of openness may not have been crucial when the decisions to be reached either did not need public involvement or if the states that were negotiating the agreements could guarantee public support.

Most of the issues of international concern in the twenty-first century are not amendable to restricted processes of decision. In most economic and social fields, consensus requires participation by civil society, since many of the aspects are not within the control of governments or the implementation of decisions requires the "consent of the governed" or by the private sector when investments or technology are produced there. This applies to issues ranging from the environment, human rights, education and migration policy, crime and trade. While the international system is still based on nation-states, and as a result governments must formally reach international agreements, but the consensus must involve other participants as well.

The basis of power at the international level is legitimacy. To be legitimate, policy decisions have to be considered by those affected by them to be lawful and to have been arrived at by lawful procedures. If they are not so considered, the decisions simply will not be implemented successfully.

A key element to achieving legitimacy for international agreements is to ensure that they are arrived at through procedures that are considered to be open, transparent and permitting full participation. This, in turn, requires a free and effective flow of information. Nowhere is this more obvious than in the areas connected with information and communications technology, both because this is about information and because the use of information is not something that is easily controlled by states.

METHODS OF MOBILIZING INFORMATION FOR INTERNATIONAL POLICY-MAKING

Over the past 60 years, the United Nations has evolved a process for mobilizing information in the context of policy making. The dozens of international conferences on economic and social issues, especially those dealing with the environment and the advancement of women, have used similar means to engage both governments and civil society in their preparatory processes as well as in the conferences themselves. An examination of these indicates both the advantages and limitations of the current methods for engaging stakeholders in policy dialog.

Traditional Method

Most United Nations conferences and other policy negotiation forums have used a set of methods for engaging civil society. They have been based on a combination of print media and face-to-face communication.

Print media communication included reports prepared by the Secretariat, in-session documentation and public information. In addition, nongovernmental organizations (NGOs) often provided coverage of the processes as well as seeking to make written inputs into the processes. The coverage of environmental negotiations by the International Institute for Sustainable Development has been notable for this.

In many ways, the traditional system is based on NGOs that have been accorded official status by the Economic and Social Council or by the conferences themselves. Based on that, NGOs with status could participate in meetings as observers and, if they were of a sufficient status, could speak and present documents to intergovernmental bodies and meetings. The role of official NGOs dates back to the United Nations Charter when this was seen as the most acceptable means of engaging non-state actors in deliberations.

The limitations of this method were that the documents were not always easy to access and organizations had to be physically present at all stages of negotiation to be able to make an input—usually very indirect, via government delegations or through the Secretariat—into the process. The number of people who could be involved personally was highly limited. While this was true for all regions, it was particularly true for persons and groups from developing countries who lacked the resources to attend the various meetings, especially the crucial preparatory meetings.

Modern Method

The advent of the Internet has permitted the addition of communication techniques that have permitted a much wider dissemination of information. Documents are now distributed by the United Nations over the Internet to those who want them through publicly accessible websites. NGOs maintain their own websites, often linking into the official sites, and coverage of negotiations is usually posted online. Plenary sessions of meetings are often video streamed so that anyone with an Internet connection can see them.

In addition, some organizations establish list-serves that permit a form of asynchronous communication among different membership groups. There have been some "virtual expert group meetings" that have been tried as a way to engage more persons at lower costs.

The UNICT Task Force has provided a good example of how these techniques can be used, with its online forums, exchange of information, and use of techniques to broadcast meetings.

While the modern methods have increased the availability of information to those who want to receive it, and have helped allow non-state actors like various NGO caucuses to formulate common positions, they have still been mostly passive. To be able to use the information to participate in policy discussions, parties still have had to be physically present at meetings. Even the process of developing positions over distance has been cumbersome, involving as it does asynchronous and individual communication.

What has been missing is the ability to communicate synchronously in real time and to participate directly in policy discussions. The technologies to do this exist, as will be seen, but the structure to apply them is still lacking.

More Modern Method

The missing element is the capacity to collaborate over the Internet. While corporations and academic institutions are increasingly using collaborative techniques, ranging from teleconferencing to video conferencing over the Internet (which is considerably less expensive than traditional videoconferencing) through the use of text chats to implement programs.

The difficulty in the past has been that these techniques have been expensive or not widely available to users. In the last several years, software developers using the World Wide Web have created collaborative methods that permit synchronous communication as well as other Internet forums. These can now be applied to specific functions at the international level.

The World Federation of United Nations Associations (WFUNA), working with Syracuse University, is engaged in one such experiment. They are building a "policy collaboratory" to enhance the participation of their WSIS Task Force in the various preparatory processes of the Tunis phase of the summit.

The concept of a collaboratory, which is drawn from the extensive use in the physical sciences, is based on the strategic use of information and communications technologies within a defined social context to enable groups of people who are geographically distributed to work effectively on knowledge-oriented projects. This approach allows use of the Internet as the underlying infrastructure to bring together different individuals and groups working on common themes using ICTs. A number of social scientists have been exploring the expansion and application of this concept to other human domains, such as HIV/AIDs research, and even to global policy processes (Olson *et al.* 2002; Cogburn 2003b, 2006).

Concept of a Global Alliance

The concept of a collaboratory could be built into another emerging concept, that of the global alliance. This is a new approach to mobilizing support. It consists of finding a structured way to bring together a wide range of geographically dispersed stakeholders. There are an increasing number of examples. For this chapter we have examined several existing alliances, which include the following:

1. The Global AIDS Alliance
2. The Global Alliance for Diversifying the Science and Engineering Workforce
3. The Global Alliance for TB Drug Development
4. The Global Alliance for Workers and Communities

To see how these alliances work we looked at five factors: who is involved in the alliance, by what method are they involved, what are their main activities, how do they make an input into the policy process, and how are the alliances financed.

Some Conclusions About Existing Alliances

The four alliances are different in composition and theme, but share certain commonalities. All were set up to provide a method of bringing together diverse parties interested in an issue who might not be able to meet in person. All have included both national-level organizations and international organizations, including in several cases, organizations of the United Nations system. All have made an effort to involve individuals and groups from developing countries.

All have had Internet-based information exchange. These include online publications, bibliographies, newsletters and, in some cases, videos from conferences.

The activities are varied, but involve an effort to engage the member-organizations and through them those organizations' members. The alliance serves the function of selecting important information. All of the alliances have a secretariat.

All of the alliances seek to influence public policy making at the national level and several seek to do so at the international level. Interested donors finance most of the alliances, while some provide funding through membership fees.

Why It Would Be Relevant to ICT

The area of ICT is particularly amenable to a global alliance approach. Like the examples, ICT involves multiple stakeholders, some governmental, some nongovernmental, some from the private sector, some from the not-for-profit sector, some national and some international. The involvement of persons and organizations from developing countries is particularly important, given both the nature of the subject matter and the political context of the World Summit for an Information Society and its likely follow-up.

The alliance concept, which involves membership based on self-selection, seems particularly applicable to ICT and the connections with the Internet are inherent in the subject.

An alliance, which is based on voluntary participation and the exchange of information, raises fewer issues of precedent than does an arrangement built around a formal institution like a Task Force. As a result, the coverage of issues and the involvement of interested parties could be greater than has been possible with more traditional methods. But how would such an alliance would work?

A Global Alliance for ICT and Development

If a global alliance were to be used as a way of building on and extending the work of the UNICT Task Force it would have to ensure a free flow of information, provide for systematic input into the policy process, be reasonably inexpensive to access (taking into consideration the differential levels of access of its members and the public), and be cross-platform compatible (thus facilitating the widest possible degree of participation in the alliance). The principled development of the socio-technical infrastructure of a policy collaboratory could help to facilitate these objectives.

Any successful collaboratory development would not take place in a vacuum, but would build on the existing processes and mechanisms for communication already in use by the Task Force, such as making documents available, updating web pages frequently to allow interested parties to be current, and the use of listserves and online forums could easily be transferred to an alliance model.

An effort would be required, however, to make the alliance a truly interactive policy collaboratory. This would mean that many of the alliance activities could begin to take advantage of synchronous communication and collaboration practices. As has been shown in previous work, this collaboratory approach should focus on three areas: (1) people-to-people, (2) people-to-resources, and (3) people-to-facilities (Olson *et al.* 2002;

Cogburn 2003, 2006). This systematic approach could integrate roles now being played by various expert groups, and include seminars and colloquia. The purpose would be to use these methods to explore issues and reach tentative policy conclusions that could be used by governments in their negotiation processes.

It would also permit a structured exchange of experience about monitoring progress in any programs or plans of action that would emerge from WSIS and other intergovernmental processes.

Because an alliance would be focused on issues and a form of pre-consensus on how they should be treated in international discussions, this mode would allow, on a noncommitment basis, governments and international organizations to interact with civil society.

An alliance could be built around a combination of self-standing issue conferences, which could be both in person and online or online alone, or conferences that were organized in the context of intergovernmental discussions of ICT issues. The purpose would be both to inform the members of the alliance, and to provide a channel for organized feedback into the process. They would also permit collaboratory discussions among different groups, with a view to developing partnerships and cooperation, especially among developing country members.

Setting up such an alliance would need investment in support infrastructure (both substantive and technical). While an alliance would not need the same amount of resources as a formal organization, it would need staff and facilities. Members themselves could provide some of the resources, but the experience of other alliances suggests that a central secretariat would be essential.

Because the Economic and Social Council has provided the mandate for the ICT Task Force, it would not be unreasonable for it to endorse an alliance. The alliance could also be considered as part of the follow-up to WSIS, and one that has minimal financial implications for the international organizations concerned.

For the alliance to function over a longer term, it would need to find a secure method of finance. Options for this exist, based on experience of other alliances, ranging from finding funding from donors through the levying of membership fees. If the latter option were to be chosen, consideration would have to be given to membership fees set on an ability-to-pay basis. A Global Alliance for ICT could be an effective and fitting successor to the UNICT Task Force.

ESTABLISHING THE UN GLOBAL ALLIANCE
FOR ICT AND DEVELOPMENT

On 17 April 2006, United Nations Secretary-General Kofi Annan approved the launch of the GAID. In the press release announcing the creation of the GAID, the Secretary-General stated that "as stressed by the 2005...World Summit on the Information Society (WSIS), information and communication technology must be effectively integrated into development activities if the internationally agreed development goals, including the Millennium Development Goals, are to be achieved within the agreed time frame" (UN http://www. un.org/press/en/2006/dev2572.doc.htm). It is worth quoting the Secretary-General at length in his overview of the mission and structure of GAID.

> The mission of the Global Alliance for ICT and Development will be to facilitate and promote such integration by providing a platform for an open, inclusive, multistakeholder cross-sectoral policy dialogue on the role of information and communication technology in development. It will thus contribute to linking the outcomes of the World Summit on the Information Society with the broader United Nations development agenda. The Alliance will organize thematic events addressing core issues related to the role of information and communication technology in economic development and eradication of poverty, employment and enterprise in pro-poor growth scenarios, with particular focus on health, education, gender, youth, disabled and disadvantaged segments of society. Groups of participants would coalesce around specific topics of mutual interest put forward for discussion. In building on existing initiatives and institutions and promoting synergy among them, the Alliance will make extensive use of the latest web-based collaborative technologies, thus minimizing the need for physical meetings. The Global Alliance will function primarily as a decentralized network, open to participation for all stakeholders, including Governments, business, civil society and international organizations. The Alliance will aim significantly to expand the circle of participants in policy and partnership debate beyond the traditional set of stakeholders, by actively engaging constituencies that currently are not adequately involved, particularly non-governmental participants from developing countries, media, academia, youth and women's groups. The Alliance will hold its inaugural meeting on 19 June in Kuala Lumpur. (UN http:// www.un.org/press/en/2006/dev2572.doc.htm)

The secretariat for GAID was housed in UNDESA under the leadership of Sarbuland Khan, Executive Coordinator of the Secretariat of the Global Alliance for ICT and Development and the Alliance was chaired by Craig Barrett, Chairman of the Board, Intel Corporation. Together, they put into place four governing bodies for GAID: (1) Steering Committee; (2) Strategy Council; (3) Group of High-Level Advisors; and (4) Network of Champions. They also put into place Communities of Expertise, Regional Networks, and Stakeholder Networks. In addition to all this organizational structure, the GAID was responsible for organizing "one annual thematic Global Forum," as a rule, in April–May so that the results of discussions could be presented at the annual substantive session of ECOSOC (GAID 2007). With strategic guidance and vision provided by the Strategy Council, and executive direction and priority setting coming from the Steering Committee, a Group of High-Level Advisors was created to provide policy and expert advice to the Strategy Council and the Steering Committee.

Overall there was the Global Alliance itself, and various international organizations, private sector, and civil society organizations identified as members, such as UNESCO, the ISOC and, Intel. A Steering Committee advised the Executive Coordinator. The highest multistakeholder body of GAID was the Strategy Council, which consisted of 74 multistakeholder members (30 representing governments, 15 private sector, 17 civil society, and 12 international organizations). Members of the GAID Strategy Council were appointed on behalf of the United Nations Secretary-General, with those governments and international organizations on the Global Alliance identifying who would be their actual representatives. The functions of the Strategy Council were as follows:

1. Provides overall strategic guidance and vision to the Alliance, in particular by identifying priorities and themes to be addressed;
2. Contributes to the development of an action-oriented policy platform that promotes the scalability, replicability and sustainability of the activities of the Alliance by providing stakeholder inputs through a consultative process;
3. Undertakes and promotes awareness-raising and advocacy campaigns for ICT for development and for the Global Alliance, with the support of GAID Secretariat;

4. Helps disseminate the results of policy dialog and think tank functions of the Alliance to policymakers, practitioners and to wider stakeholder constituencies, with a view to capacity building and strengthening feedback between policies, planning, and program implementation;
5. Contributes to the formulation of advice to the Secretary-General and to the UN system on issues related to ICT for development;
6. Promotes multistakeholder partnerships and initiatives with innovative networking and information-sharing approaches, with a view to improving coordination and enhancing impact;
7. Promotes fundraising for GAIDinitiatives with innovative networking a, and events; and
8. Reviews the annual report on the activities of the Alliance and the financial report from the Secretariat. (GAID, Terms of Reference for Strategy Council)

The GAID Steering Committee consisted of 12 members, all designated on behalf of the Secretary-General for a one-year renewable term. Steering Committee members served in their personal capacity.

Functions of the GAID Steering Committee were as follows:

1. Provides executive direction to the work of the Alliance and its Secretariat via approval of the business plan for the Alliance on a regular basis;
2. Defines the medium and long-term priorities of the Alliance in consultation with the Strategy Council and all relevant stakeholders;
3. Endorses the establishment and mandates of thematic Communities of Expertise to carry out well-defined, specific tasks, within one or more focus areas of the Alliance;
4. Reviews periodic progress reports from the Communities of Expertise;
5. Endorses the establishment of stakeholder networks, Regional Networks and Regional Centers of Excellence;
6. Reviews periodic progress reports from the Regional Networks and Regional Centers of Excellence;
7. Endorses recommendations of the secretariat as regards partnerships, sponsorship of events, and so on;
8. Spearheads activities to raise funds and in-kind contributions by members, partners, and other organizations;

9. Identifies and transmits relevant cutting-edge and emerging issues and inputs on ICT for development, including those contributed by the Strategy Council, High-level Advisors, and members of the Champions Network, to the Secretary-General;
10. Exercises a leadership role in high-level advocacy and policy advice in the field of ICT for development and for the Global Alliance; and
11. Liaises, with the assistance of the Secretariat, with other global bodies working in the field of ICT for Development.

The High-Level Advisors group was composed of "distinguished practitioners, policy-makers and experts recognized in their respective fields who are able and willing to contribute to and support the mission and objectives of the Global Alliance. Advisors serve in their personal capacity. High-Level Advisors are designated by the Executive Coordinator in consultation with the Chairman of GAID, for a two-year renewable term" (GAID, 2007). Functions of the Group of High-Level Advisors include the following:

1. Bring to the attention of the Alliance relevant developments in theory and/or practice in the field of ICT for development;
2. Provide to the Strategy Council and Steering Committee policy and expert advice on areas within the remit of the Global Alliance based upon their research and/or practical experience, including through reports, papers, presentations, and participation in virtual and face-to-face dialog sponsored by the Global Alliance;
3. Respond to explicit requests for information and input originating with the Strategy Council and/or Steering Committee;
4. Contribute, in the format best suited to their individual areas of expertise, time and other resources to the activities of the Communities of Expertise, Regional Networks and/or Stakeholders Groups of their interest.

Finally, the Network of Champions was composed of "practitioners, as well as experts and activists in ICT4D, including at the grassroots and community levels, who demonstrated commitment to and engagement in ICT4D work and who commit themselves to champion and support the mission and objectives of the Global Alliance through their personal efforts and through networks in which they participate" (GAID, 2007). The functions of the Network of Champions include the following:

1. Facilitates the diffusion of knowledge and experience in innovative uses of ICT for the attainment of development goals and of relevant GAID's activities and initiatives by bringing these to bear on the day-to-day involvement of the Network's participants in ICT4D.

2. Promotes the implementation of the recommendations/outcomes of the Alliance as well as the lessons learned and best practices identified in GAID's work, as applicable, through their activities in the field and in expert forums at all levels in order to achieve a more coordinated and effective approach to implementing ICT- for-development activities;

3. Fosters formation of partnerships by linking willing parties (within and outside of GAID) with complementary skills and resources in the priority areas adopted by the Strategy Council and encouraging their collaboration, including by (a) identifying opportunities to coordinate or streamline cooperation among actors and existing initiatives and (b) matching unmet development needs with innovative solutions;

4. Provides "bottom-up" flow of information on implementation of GAID activities on the ground to the Steering Committee and the Strategy Council, with particular focus on lessons learned, obstacles and challenges identified, and proposals and initiatives for enhancing the impact of the Alliance;

5. Responds to specific requests for information and input originating with the Strategy Council and/or Steering Committee.

Innovative Elements in the Global Alliance for ICT and Development

The mission, structure, and establishment of GAID were admirable. It was clear throughout the WSIS processes that development issues were of key importance to many in the global civil society community, and were paramount for developing countries. Although this structure is extremely complex (and there was no fixed budget to support it), there is an enormous amount right with the way GAID was established. Drawing from the announcement above, we will highlight some of the key elements:

(1) *Promoting an open and inclusive multistakeholder policy dialog on the role of ICT in development*: This element of GAID was exactly what was required in this area coming out of WSIS. Also, the fact

that GAID was being established under private sector leadership (the initial GAID chair was Craig Barrett, CEO of Intel)—which was a concern of many civil society WSIS participants—actually held a great deal of promise. Barrett and his colleagues planned to actively recruit private sector participants into this important development space.

(2) *Linking GAID with the broader UN development agenda, including the Millennium Development Goals (MDGs) and the outcomes of WSIS*: The international development community was already aligning itself toward the ambitious goal of achieving the MDGs. Aligning the GAID with these initiatives should accelerate the importance of the Alliance and enabled much broader participation from international organizations and other development actors, especially those interested in achieving the WSIS outcomes.

(3) *Focus on events related to and of interest to excluded voices*: From the beginning, the Alliance had a focus on convening events related to marginalized and excluded voices in the global development process (especially persons with disabilities, gender, and youth).

(4) *Explicit plans for structuring GAID as a virtual organization*: There is an explicit focus on exploiting web-based collaborative technologies to minimize the need for physical meetings.

(5) *Explicitly multistakeholder*: GAID was structured as a decentralized network, open to participation from all stakeholders, including governments, business, civil society, and international organizations (as we discuss below, this turned out to be both a blessing and a curse).

(6) *Expanding participation of marginalized and excluded voices in events and policy discussions*: GAID aimed to significantly expand the circle of participants in policy and partnership debate beyond the traditional set of stakeholders, by actively engaging constituencies that currently are not adequately involved, particularly nongovernmental participants from developing countries, media, academia, youth, and women's groups. The purpose of this active involvement was to ensure that those voices were heard in the development of policy and strategy for utilizing ICTs for development. This sentiment would be heralded loudly by the global disability community later in 2006, when it participated in the adoption of the United Nations convention on the Rights of Persons with Disabilities (CRPD), as both a human rights

and development instrument, under the banner of "nothing about us, without us"—developed by Disabled Persons International (DPI), one of the leading global grassroots disability networks.

(7) Finally, GAID scheduled its first meeting to be held in Kuala Lumpur, Malaysia, putting a keen focus on developing countries.

In his message to the Steering Committee of the Global Alliance for ICT and Development on 27 September 2006 at the United Nations Headquarters in New York, United Nations Secretary-General Kofi Anan highlighted the importance of the GAID to achieving global development objectives, and the inclusion of marginalized voices, and is worth quoting at length:

> We must translate the vision of a truly GIS into reality. Toward this end, as you know, I have convened the Internet Governance Forum, which will focus on what needs to be done to ensure greater participation of all stakeholders in matters of public policy that may arise in the management of the Internet. Another important direction of work towards an open and prosperous information society is, of course, the use of ICT as a tool for advancing development. The ICT Task Force has also helped in this effort. When I called on Silicon Valley to devote more of its energies to meeting the needs of the poor, the Task Force helped the industry respond quickly and creatively. One of the Task Force's successful spin-offs, the Global e-Schools and Communities Initiative, continues to create new opportunities for learning and development. Now, the new Global Alliance for ICT and Development will build on these achievements. The Alliance's design draws on lessons learned from the ICT Task Force, the World Summit on the Information Society and other multistakeholder processes. But while the Task Force was limited in size, with fixed membership, the Alliance will be bigger and, most important, will have the flexibility to encourage additional organizations and individuals to participate. The idea is to develop a decentralized "network of networks" on a global scale, so that the Alliance can draw in the relevant stakeholders, particularly as new issues emerge. (GAID, 2007)

It was clear that the Global Alliance was designed to build on the success of the more narrow and limited UNICT Task Force, but to open it up to broader participation. The inaugural Meeting of the GAID was hosted by the Government of Malaysia, and included addresses by Prime Minister Badawi, and Minister of Science, Technology and

Innovation, Dr. Jamaluddin. The meeting also included opening statements by Mark Malloch Brown, Deputy Secretary-General of the United Nations and Leonel Fernandez, President of the Dominican Republic. It even organized the World Summit Award, as a flagship initiative of UNDESA and its GAID. http://www.youthaward.org/partners/ united-nations-global-alliance-ict-and-development-un-gaid.

The Global Alliance held its second meeting in Silicon Valley in February 2007. This GAID meeting was seen as historic, not only because of its follow-up to the successful inaugural meeting in Kuala Lumpur, but because it was seen as the first time the United Nations had held a major meeting in San Francisco, since its founding there on 24 October 1945 as representatives of 50 countries gathered at the United nations Conference on International Organization and drew up the United Nations Charter (http://www.un.org/en/sections/history/history-united-nations/). Just before this meeting, on 2 July 2007, what has become the most successful outcome of the Global Alliance—the Global Initiative for Inclusive Information and Communication Technologies (G3ICT)—was held in New York City under the leadership of the BDT of the ITU and the Boston-based Wireless Internet Institute. The launch of G3ICT, called a "Flagship Advocacy Initiative" of GAID, was timed to coincide with the signing ceremony of the UN Convention on the Rights of Persons with Disabilities. However, contrary to the espoused spirit of GAID, this was held as an "invitation-only" event.

PROBLEMS AND CHALLENGES IN THE GLOBAL ALLIANCE FOR ICT AND DEVELOPMENT

However, while many of these issues held so much promise for this new multistakeholder organization, many of them also represented a challenge. Because GAID was a complicated, multitiered, voluntary structure, with its members geographically distributed around the world, and no real annual meeting structure, some of these structural elements may have led to its downfall (the structure of IGF was quite different as we will see in Chap. 7). Specifically, the openness and somewhat informal nature of the GAID, with the plan that groups of participants would coalesce around specific topics of mutual interest put forward for discussion may not have been a sufficient organizing principle to sustain the network. Furthermore, it appears the GAID had no internal budget. It was asserted that "Alliance activities will be funded by voluntary contributions, both financial and in-kind (such as providing networking support, hosting meetings, contributing to logistical or staff support, co-producing publications, etc.)" (GAID 2007).

In contrast to the complex structure of GAID, the IGF had only a MAG, which was appointed by the UN Secretary-General in the same way the Strategy Council, Steering Committee, and High-Level Advisors were appointed to GAID. The MAG was/is responsible for organizing the content of the annual Internet Governance Forum, by sorting through proposals that come through Dynamic Coalitions (DC), which are multistakeholder and approved by the MAG. This is a much simpler structure, and is perhaps one of the leading reasons the IGF was more successful than was GAID.

In 2009, Craig Barrett was replaced as chair of the Global Alliance by Abu-Ghazaleh, CEO of Talal Abu-Ghazaleh Organization, who had served as GAID Co-Chair for three years under Barrett. Sha Zukang, Undersecretary-General of the United Nations Department of Economic and Social Affairs (UNDESA) appointed Abu-Ghazaleh to this new role. While Abu-Ghazaleh was a well-respected businessman in the Arab region, and known widely within the United Nations system, he did not command the recognition of his predecessor. Nor did Abu-Ghazaleh have the connections to Silicon Valley that Intel and Craig Barrett did, and was not able to mobilize their continued interest in GAID. In 2010, the Internet Governance Forum was renewed, but the GAID had a soft sunset.

Some of these problems with GAID were anticipated in advance. Following the in-principle approval by the UN Secretary-General in July 2004 for a potential "Global Alliance on Information and Communication Technology," an evaluation was produced in December 2004. This evaluation focused "primarily on an assessment of demand, vision, value add and *modus operandi* for the potential Alliance" (unpublished background document, 2004, p. 1). The evaluation saw "[a]s a baseline, the Alliance is expected to be open, neutral, and multistakeholder in nature defining a common catalytic language on global ICT issues, with a light and flexible structure of operation" (unpublished, 2004, p. 1). This evaluation argued that "[d]ue to a narrow window of opportunity it will require rapid outreach to a wide diversity of stakeholders to generate early and effective buy-in" (unpublished, 2004). It also suggests options for "founding partners, initial sponsors, and future members; outreach and consultation processes; financing mechanisms; a draft charter and business plan; product differentiation from previous and existing entitles; and articulation of its role and relationship *vis-à-vis* the

UN System, the Millennium Summit +5, and WSIS and their respective follow-up" (unpublished, 2004, p. 1). Some of these recommendations were followed, and others were not. However, there are numerous elements of this document that were prescient in predicting the failure of the GAID.

To begin with, the evaluation recommended a "light and flexible structure of operation." However, what emerged in the development of the GAID was an enormous, complicated bureaucratic networked organization, without sufficient resources to support such a structure. Perhaps this structure emerged out of a desire to have sufficient outreach to the various and diverse communities to try to achieve the "buy-in" discussed by this document. Like this book, this report saw 2005 as a watershed year for a convergence of activity related to ICT and development. The report highlights the launch of a variety of public–private sector initiatives, including the GIIC, the GBDe , the Global Knowledge Partnership (GKP), the World Economic Forum (WEF), the ICC, and the World Bank (Development Gateway Foundation). This report identified the membership and action plans of these various initiatives as being "duplicative and overlapping" (Unpublished, 2004, p. 1). The year 2005 reaped the benefits of three converging developments: (1) the recognition by both developed and developing country governments that there was a need for "concerted global action on ICT and ICT4D"; (2) private sector recognition of the same need; and (3) a similar recognition by multistakeholder coalitions and transnational advocacy networks. After the completion of WSIS Tunis in November 2005, there is an expected decade of global ICT and ICT4D activities with the WSIS follow-up and the Millennium Summit +5, and activity related to the implementation of the Millennium Development Goals (MDGs).

This evaluation document saw a clear set of pros and cons with the launch of a new ICT-focused Alliance. "On the pro side, the MS+5 and WSIS and the ensuing 2005–2015 time frame is compelling, and the need for a new cross-sectoral multistakeholder approach can be argued strongly as the global ICT sector matures into a development enabler and development imperative. On the con side, there is the perennial risk of failure through private sector skepticism of multilateral effectiveness; donor and government confusion on the role of the private sector; entanglement in an uncertain MS+5 and WSIS process; and a radically altered geopolitical landscape" (unpublished, 2004, p. 2).

Two other key elements which were recommended in this initial evaluation report were not followed, and are likely to have reduced the longevity of GAID. The first area is the degree to which the substantive issues of the GAID were seen as being best handled within the GAID. The evaluation report argued that "[t]aking an international development goal/ MDG-focused approach would ensure that the Alliance contributes to the global efforts to facilitate development. Streams of work could include e-strategy development and their integration into national development strategies; policy and regulatory reform; multistakeholder partnerships; pro-poor business models; connectivity, capacity-building and content; funding mechanisms; participation in ICT policy and government mechanisms." This wide range of work streams clearly has overlap with those emerging within the Internet Governance Forum, with each of these areas being found increasingly in IGF workshops and plenary sessions.

The second key element was the recommendation that "[t]he Alliance should wherever possible use collaborative means of digital communication to the greatest extent possible in order to make inputs and outputs truly interactive" (unpublished, 2004). While GAID made some attempts at using these collaboration technologies, they were always on the periphery. GAID leadership seemed more comfortable with organizing traditional United Nations meetings, which focus primarily on face-to-face interaction. It was also recommended in this unpublished evaluation that they should have a "distinctly arm's length relationship to the UN-system" (unpublished, 2004, p. 3). It continued to recommend that "[a] stand-alone body...based on cross-sectoral multistakeholder participation with its own funding (diversified membership fees) and a mandate for bringing partners together for informal consultations with decision-making made in existing fora" (unpublished, 2004, p. 3). It continued by saying it should "build on existing initiatives and not re-invent them" (unpublished, 2004, p. 4).

When discussing the "value add" of the new Alliance, the evaluation makes the strongest case possible for why it should exist (and be successful):

By looking beyond simply embracing the "business environment" to new business models for development the Alliance would make the case for shareholder support for new and innovative investments, and constituted as the first cross-sectoral and multistakeholder initiative of its kind, with a clear focus on the achievement of the MDGs toward 2015. Because an Alliance would be focused on issues and a pre-consensus on how they should be treated in international discussions, this model would allow on a non-commitment basis, governments and international organizations to interact with civil society. It will be an effective vehicle to bring together powerful and clearly motivated ICT4D players and might help to overcome a sense of summit and task force fatigue. It would also permit a structured exchange of experience about monitoring progress in programmes and plans of action that emerge from MS+5 and WSIS and other intergovernmental processes. (unpublished, 2004, p. 3)

Many of these elements were realized in the GAID. However, the second half of these recommendations—listed under "Product Differentiation"—were not followed at all.

How will the Alliance be differentiated from previous and existing initiatives? Attracting private sector, civil society and non-ICT participants for medium-/long-term involvement will be accomplished through buy-in to its status of pre-eminent legitimacy. This will require it to be fully open; fully representative; fully transparent; fully empowered; fully funded; fully relevant; as the nexus between ICT and the MDGs for scaling and replication; as the crucible for global concerted and coordinated initiatives and interventions from 2005–2015; as the forum for permanent reflection on global ICT and ICT4D issues; as embracing Science, Technology, Innovation and Development; as the follow-up mechanism for MS+5 WSIS; fully agile; fully influential; fully catalytic; and fully results oriented etc., etc., etc. In short, the Alliance will live or die via product differentiation. (Unpublished, 2004, p. 3)

Almost none of these things occurred, and as predicted the GAID died as a result. GAID was never fully funded; it never had open processes to participate; never included any remote-participation options for meetings; it created staggeringly complex governance structures, and was always underfunded, with no fixed budget from the United Nations. It was envisioned that the Alliance would be "self-sustaining on the basis of members' willingness and ability to contribute to common objectives. Associations that would like to support a nominee for executive board positions may additionally be asked to cover the costs of their nominee's participation" (unpublished, 2004, p. 5). This approach to funding, along with a very small secretariat was envisioned to "assure a sustained, reliable flow of resources without jeopardizing openness and inclusiveness" (unpublished, 2004, p. 5). Unfortunately for GAID, this never happened. Coupled with the shift from a highly recognized chairman, Craig Barrett, of a global corporation such as Intel, to a less recognized regional business leader in Abu Ghazaleh, the fate of GAID was sealed.

Finally, in some ways, with the IGF taking on more and more issues related to ICT4D, the *raison d'être* of the GAID was essentially integrated into the IGF. One example of this integration is found in the leading initiative coming out of GAID, the G3ICT, which has for several years now, become a very active participant in the IGF (especially the IGF Dynamic Coalition on Accessibility and Disability). Further, with both initiatives being supported by UNDESA and many of the same multistakeholder actors participating in both, pressure to close GAID was intense.

Conclusions: GAID and the GII/GIS versus GII/GEC Debate

This chapter has attempted to present a case study of the short-lived UN Global Alliance for ICT and Development (GAID). It has tried to highlight the tremendous potential of the GAID, and to illuminate the geopolitical space within which it was launched. The Global Alliance had tremendous potential, and was definitely an exciting and important outcome of the second WSIS. So why did it fail? Above, I have pointed to several plausible reasons for this failure: its sprawling bureaucracy, lack of attention to openness and transparency, and infrequent to nonexistent use of the collaborative ICT that were seen and proposed as so central to its existence, inability to mobilize transnational advocacy networks to participate actively, transition to a less recognized regional business leader, and the increasing encroachment of ICT4D issues into the substantive agenda of the Internet Governance Forum. There are also other reasons, such as lack of sustained connection between the GAID and relevant epistemic communities in the ICT4D academic space.

All of these reasons make sense, and are likely to have caused the death of GAID. However, there is another issue that perhaps underlies several of these. The GAID was launched with a much more progressive philosophical agenda; one more in line with the GII/GIS agenda and including some elements back to the NWICO agenda. It is possible that over time, many of the global private sector participants on which the GAID was based and relied so heavily in its *raison d'être* simply decided to withhold their funding and support for this initiative and instead to support the Internet Governance Forum. By starving the GAID of resources, they were perhaps able to shift many if not all of the critical issues and debates that were to be handled by the GAID, into the much more functional IGF. In Chap. 7, we will explore the creation, evolution, and successes of the Internet Governance Forum, especially in its ability to mobilize and integrate transnational advocacy networks into its structures. However, we will also pick up this argument of the better alignment of the IGF with the GII/GEC international regime principles.

CHAPTER 7

Internet Governance Forum: What Went Right?

INTRODUCTION

In Chap. 6, we discussed the GAID, one of the two new, innovative multistakeholder organizations to emerge out of the end of the WSIS processes. In this chapter, we discuss the other one, the IGF. Here, we present a case study of the history and evolution of the IGF. Through several very clever maneuvers, the UN created the IGF as a multistakeholder vehicle to carry the debates about Global Internet Governance that were left unresolved at the conclusion of the second phase of WSIS in Tunisia, in 2005. It was granted an initial five-year mandate, and, unlike its sister organization GAID, after this initial review, it was renewed for another five years. More importantly, at the recent United Nations General Assembly meeting in December 2015 as part of the WSIS+10 review, the IGF mandate was extended for another ten years. Just from these extensions, we can see the obvious "success" of the IGF, especially relative to GAID. However, this chapter will explore this question in more detail, and attempt to uncover the underlying factors contributing to the perceived success and effectiveness of the IGF. This chapter will also continue our discussion from Chap. 5, and highlight the extended role played by the IGF in fostering transnational advocacy networks.

© The Author(s) 2017   201
D.L. Cogburn, *Transnational Advocacy Networks in the Information Society*, Information Technology and Global Governance,
DOI 10.1057/978-1-137-48361-4_7

When comparing IGF to GAID, we see the former as offering a "new hope" for transnational civil society advocacy, and point to several factors that have enabled this to happen.

BACKGROUND

When the United Nations was founded in 1945, the opening words of the UN Charter were "We The Peoples of the United Nations...." Although this central international organization has been at the center of the Westphalian state system since its inception, it has continuously wrestled with the thorny problem of how to involve the actual persons in whose name the organization is formed in its policy processes. There have been a wide variety of attempts to address this problem. One example is the World Federation of United Nations Associations (WFUNA), formed in 1946 in the Grand Duchy of Luxembourg. Twenty-two United Nations Associations (UNAs) came together on 2 August 1946 to form WFUNA the year after the UN Charter was proclaimed Hüfner (2009). Another major step forward occurred with the United Nations Conference on Environment and Development (UNCED), more popularly known as the "Rio Summit" or the "Earth Summit." Approximately 2400 nongovernmental organization (NGO) representatives were accredited to the Earth Summit, with another 17,000 participating in the parallel Global Forum. The Earth Summit adopted Agenda 21, a nonbinding action plan, which included in Section III a focus on how the UN could strengthen the participation of numerous non-state and other excluded actors in its processes. This approach has become known as the "Major Groups" framework, and creates special opportunities for nine major groups: (1) women; (2) children and youth; (3) indigenous peoples; (4) nongovernmental organizations; (5) local authorities; (6) workers and trade unions; (7) business and industry; (8) scientific and technological community; and (9) farmers UN (1992). This Major Groups framework, or some variation of it, became the de facto approach taken by numerous United Nations conferences, meetings, and events, especially those related to the environment and sustainable development. While the Major Groups framework was seen as a step forward, it left out several groups—perhaps most importantly the more than 1 billion persons in the world living with some form of disability WHO/World Bank, 2011. Persons with Disabilities were also left out of the subsequent Millennium Development Goals (MDGs), but would be addressed in the CRPD and even later in the Sustainable Development Goals (SDGs) designed to help realize the 2030 Sustainable Development Agenda.

In 2001, the UN General Assembly adopted the WSIS resolution, designed to help facilitate the convening of the WSIS. The WSIS resolution was explicitly multistakeholder, and created an opportunity for business and civil society to participate directly in the summit on a relatively coequal basis. The WSIS processes generated a large number of global civil society mechanisms to facilitate involvement in the diverse substantive issue areas related to the information society.

With increased pressure on more civil society involvement in these global governance processes, the Cardoso report came out in 2004, and was an attempt to restructure how civil society organizations could engage with the UN structures.

With the end of the WSIS in 2005, two new global multistakeholder bodies were created, and were designed to advance the agenda coming out of the summit. These two multistakeholder bodies were the UN GAID and the IGF. Both the GAID and IGF were given five-year mandates, and were explicitly multistakeholder in nature.

More recently, the Third World Conference on Disaster Risk Reduction (3WCDRR) held in Sendai, Japan, adopted a modified approach to the use of the Major Groups framework.

In 2005, the second phase of the historic WSIS concluded in Tunis. The WSIS processes generated numerous global governance innovations, including formal multistakeholder participation in UN conferences and two new multistakeholder institutions, the IGF and the GAID. IGF and GAID were both given five-year mandates, but GAID has subsequently been abolished while IGF will celebrate its tenth anniversary in November 2015 and in all likelihood will be renewed again. One reason for the success of IGF is the active involvement of transnational civil society advocacy networks that have fueled this experiment in multistakeholder global governance.

WGIG: MULTISTAKEHOLDER PRECURSOR TO THE IGF

In Chap. 5, we highlighted the important role played by WSIS for the development of the GIS in general, and Internet governance in particular. WSIS was characterized as a major site of contestation for the principles, norms, and values of the emerging regime for GII. In some ways, this debate can be seen most clearly by the two baskets of issues that were seen as unresolved at the end of the first phase of WSIS. These issues are generally seen as (1) development issues and (2) Internet governance.

At the close of WSIS Geneva, the summit called on the United Nations Secretary-General to establish a multistakeholder Working Group on Internet Governance (WGIG). WGIG was tasked with identifying a working definition of Internet governance and asked to try to help clarify the policy issues and debates that were outstanding in the WSIS.

In the period between WSIS Geneva and WSIS Tunis, the WGIG met frequently, and produced a series of very interesting background reports and proposals. In the definition they returned to, the WSIS Tunis process became enshrined in the WSIS Outcome Documents and the focus of "Enhanced Cooperation" between the participants in Internet governance. In its final report, which was used as an input in the second phase of WSIS, the WGIG proposed the creation of the IGF:

> The WGIG identified a vacuum within the context of existing structures, since there is no global multi-stakeholder forum to address Internet-related public policy issues. It came to the conclusion that there would be merit in creating such a space for dialogue among all stakeholders. This space could address these issues, as well as emerging issues, that are cross-cutting and multidimensional and that either affect more than one institution, are not dealt with by any institution or are not addressed in a coordinated manner. (WGIG 2005, p. 10)

Also the Government of Argentina made a strong statement in support of the creation of the IGF in a very eloquent statement worth quoting at length:

> We recognize the efforts deployed by the initiators of the Internet, and the need to guarantee a stable and secure operation of this efficient tool for humanity. We are also convinced that there is a need for an evolutionary process towards a new transparent, democratic, and multilateral framework, with the participation of government, private sector, civil society and international organizations. We support the evolution and internationalization of the Internet governance system, based on the Geneva Principles through existing and future mechanisms, institutions and fora.
>
> It is our conviction that all stakeholders—governments, the private sector, civil society and other interested parties—should actively participate in Internet governance in a coordinated and balanced manner, commensurate with their respective roles and responsibilities.

We recall that the main responsibility of all stakeholders is awareness raising, capacity building and to propose solutions to accelerate availability and affordability of Internet in developing world.

In order to strengthen the global multistakeholder interaction and cooperation on public policy issues and developmental aspects relating to Internet governance we propose a forum.

This forum should not replace existing mechanisms or institutions but should build on the existing structures on Internet governance, should contribute to the sustainability, stability and robustness of the Internet by addressing appropriately public policy issues that are not otherwise being adequately addressed (referred to in para...) excluding any involvement in the day-to-day operation of the Internet. It should be constituted as a neutral, non-duplicative and non-binding process to facilitate the exchange of information and best practices and to identify issues and make known its findings, to enhance awareness and build consensus and engagement. Recognizing the rapid development of technology and institutions, we propose that the forum mechanism periodically be reviewed to determine the need for its continuation. (Argentina 2005)

With this strong support, IGF was created at the close of WSIS Tunis, with its mandate described in paragraph 72 of the *Tunis Agenda for the Information Society*:

"We ask the UN Secretary-General, in an open and inclusive process, to convene, by the second quarter of 2006, a meeting of the new forum for multistakeholder policy dialogue—called the Internet Governance Forum (IGF). The mandate of the Forum is to:

a. Discuss public policy issues related to key elements of Internet governance in order to foster the sustainability, robustness, security, stability, and development of the Internet;

b. Facilitate discourse between bodies dealing with different cross-cutting international public policies regarding the Internet and discuss issues that do not fall within the scope of any existing body;

c. Interface with appropriate intergovernmental organizations and other institutions on matters under their purview;

d. Facilitate the exchange of information and best practices, and in this regard make full use of the expertise of the academic, scientific, and technical communities;

    e. Advise all stakeholders in proposing ways and means to accelerate the availability and affordability of the Internet in the developing world;

    f. Strengthen and enhance the engagement of stakeholders in existing and/or future Internet governance mechanisms, particularly those from developing countries;

    g. Identify emerging issues, bring them to the attention of the relevant bodies and the general public, and, where appropriate, make recommendations;

    h. Contribute to capacity building for Internet governance in developing countries, drawing fully on local sources of knowledge and expertise;

    i. Promote and assess, on an ongoing basis, the embodiment of WSIS principles in Internet governance processes;

    j. Discuss, *inter alia*, issues relating to critical Internet resources; and

    k. Help to find solutions to the issues arising from the use and misuse of the Internet, of particular concern to everyday users."

Publish Its Proceedings

While the second phase of WSIS was able to handle the contentious issues of Internet governance better than the first phase, at the end of the deliberations it still produced a new innovative multistakeholder body to provide an ongoing space for these issues. On 27 April 2006, the United Nations General Assembly adopted resolution 60/252 on the WSIS, which included the invitation to the Secretary-General "in an open and inclusive process, to convene a new forum for multi-stakeholder policy dialogue called the Internet Governance Forum" (UNGA, 2006, A/RES/60/252).

THE INTERNET GOVERNANCE FORUM

Unlike the Global Alliance for ICT and Development discussed in Chap. 6, the IGF has a very simple structure. In February 2006, the United Nations Secretary-General established what is now known as the MAG, whose members are appointed by the Secretary-General after extensive consultation. The first chair of the MAG was Indian economist Nitin Desai, who had served as UN Undersecretary-General for Economic and Social Affairs from 1992 to 2003 and also as the Secretary-General's Special Advisor for Internet governance.

Supporting the MAG is a small secretariat based in the United Nations Office in Geneva, led by an Executive Coordinator. Markus Kummer, the seasoned Swiss diplomat who also coordinated the WGIG was appointed as the first IGF Executive Coordinator (a position now held de facto, though not de jure by Chengetai Masango, IGF Program and Technology Manager). These two bodies (MAG and Secretariat) make up the governance structure of the IGF, with substantive proposals to the annual forum coming to the MAG through a collection of Dynamic Coalitions. These Dynamic Coalitions are "informal, issue-specific groups comprising members from various stakeholder communities" (IGF n.d.). According to the IGF website, in order to establish a Dynamic Coalition, a statement following a meeting of the interested parties should include the following elements:

1. The need for the dynamic coalition,
2. An action plan,
3. A mailing list,
4. The contact person(s), and
5. A list of representatives from at least three stakeholder groups.

Once established, coalitions must follow three basic principles of inclusiveness and transparency for carrying out their work: open membership, open mailing lists, and open archives. (IGF, n.d.). The IGF has established a Dynamic Coalition Coordination Group (DCCG) which meets monthly. All Dynamic Coalitions are asked to appoint representatives to the DCCG, and all DCCG meetings are open and all DC members are invited to attend.

At present there are 16 active Dynamic Coalitions. Ten additional Dynamic Coalitions have been listed as inactive. The range of policy issues covered by the Dynamic Coalitions is impressive, going from accessibility and disability to blockchain technologies. Table 7.1 presents these by their stated subject matter.

The IGF is by definition a non–decision-making, multistakeholder body. Statement #77 of the WSIS Tunis Agenda notes that "[t]he IGF would have no oversight function and would not replace existing arrangements, mechanisms, institutions or organizations, but would involve them and take advantage of their expertise. It would be constituted as a neutral,

Table 7.1   Active and inactive dynamic coalition in the IGF

Active	Inactive
Accessibility and disability	Framework of principles for the Internet
Accountability	Online collaboration
Blockchain technologies	A2K@IGF (access to knowledge)
Child online safety	Access and connectivity for remote, rural and dispersed communities
Community connectivity	Privacy
Core Internet values	Stop spam alliance
Freedom of expression and freedom of the media on the Internet	Open standards
Gender and Internet governance	*Diversité Linguistique*
Innovative approaches to connecting the unconnected	Global localization platform
Internet and climate change	Social media and legal issues
Internet rights and principles	
Network neutrality	
Platform responsibility	
Public access in libraries	
Internet of things	
Youth coalition on Internet governance	

non-duplicative and non-binding process. It would have no involvement in day-to-day or technical operation of the Internet."

For the first time, the IGF allowed members of civil society from around the world to come together with members of the private sector, and with members of the government at the international, national, regional, and even local levels to frame together as well as to debate and discuss issues related to Internet governance. Its inaugural meeting was held in Athens, Greece, in 2006. Subsequent meetings were in Rio de Janeiro, Brazil; Hyderabad, India; and in November 2009, Sharm-el-Sheikh, Egypt.

But the IGF does not limit itself to only annual meetings. Borrowing from international organization operations and shaped by its United Nations environment, the IGF has an annual cycle of regular consultations and advisory board meetings in preparation for each annual meeting as well as ongoing virtual opportunities for posting responses and participating online. (See the IGF website at www.intgovforum.org for links to these functions.) It also has spawned 'dynamic coalitions' (each focusing on specific themes) and multistakeholder workshops as well as national and regional IGFs.

There are a number of ongoing efforts to begin the evaluation process. The IGF itself has solicited comments, posted comments as they are received, and is preparing a summary document of these responses to be presented at the Egypt meeting. (It asks a series of seven questions posted on its website.) Other efforts include a study done by students of Professor John Mathiason of Syracuse University also posted at the IGF website; a survey (using survey monkey) conducted by DiploFoundation, and a survey done by the ISOC (see the 13 May 2009 IGF Geneva Consultation posted on the IGF website).

This paper contributes to this discussion building on concepts from knowledge transfer theory, public administration theory, and organizational sociology. It uses the notion of a knowledge transfer episode (KTE) (see Levinson 2009) and examines several KTEs from the IGF annual cycles.

As Levinson (2009) notes, it is important to evaluate the IGF as a "whole network," an innovation linking groups from disparate sectors, cultures, geographies, and organizations including those in developed as well as developing nations. A "whole" network refers to a holistic review of a networked institution such as the IGF (Provan et al. 2007). Thus, we provide here a conceptual framework for evaluating the IGF as a "whole network," using the argument by Provan et al. (2007, p. 29, 23) that "networks have been widely recognized by both scholar and practitioners as an important form of multi-organizational governance...(and evaluating the effectiveness of such networks requires looking for) the attainment of positive network level outcomes that could not normally be achieved by individual organizational participants acting independently."

Further, we include a measure of the construction of collaboration as an element in examining network effectiveness with particular reference to the IGF. We ask whether the IGF plays a role in the construction of collaboration. (Earlier we have written about collaboration in a range of contexts including virtual cross-national teams. See, for example, Cogburn and Levinson (2008). Our work here builds on these findings and explores how collaboration is constructed at the IGF.)

Thus, this chapter contributes to the evaluation discussion through research that goes beyond one individual or one organization's response or point of view. Rather, it reports on effectiveness elements including the presence of common constructions, as they emerge over time in this multistakeholder organization. The longitudinal dimension we call for here provides added richness to the evaluation and complements the more personal, individual responses and surveys reported on the IGF website.

THE IGF AS A "WHOLE" NETWORK[1]

Examining the effectiveness of the IGF as a whole network requires best a longitudinal and dynamic focus. It is important to track changes over the IGF's four-year life cycle beginning with the preparations for its inaugural meeting in Athens, Greece and ending with the preparations for its fourth annual meeting in Sharm-el-Sheikh, Egypt in November 2009.

It is also useful to view the IGF as a whole network that is also a new political opportunity structure. In studying the outcome of a cross-national, regional institution, NAFTA, Kay (2005) vividly illustrates how a new networked structure, the NAFTA, catalyzed and brought together previously disparate nation-state rooted and focused labor unions. This possible ability to link previously unconnected organizations and/or individuals and cultures adds another element to be considered in an evaluation of a whole network.

EVALUATING WHOLE NETWORK EFFECTIVENESS: AN OVERVIEW

Based on a detailed analysis of prior studies of network effectiveness, this chapter is organized in the following three sections: the structure of the whole network, the form of the network, and the processes of the network including what Levinson (2009) terms co-processes such as those involved in the construction of collaboration and its outcomes.

Network Structure

Here there are at least six elements to be considered. These range from the size of the network to the degree of its embeddedness, each element possessing implications for evaluating effectiveness.

A simple measure of network structure is the size of the network. How many nodes does the network involve? In the case of the IGF, we can count the number of participating organizations at its Annual Meetings (and related events) and give an overall answer as to the size of the network with regard to the annual meeting. We can also count the number of organizations participating virtually. In sum, it is a large size network, crossing organizational, country, and occupational boundaries. The IGF links previously unconnected organizations in ways analogous to the introduction of NAFTA.

Another common measure of network structure is the degree of its embeddedness. Embeddedness (Granovetter 1985) refers to the degree to which an organization is interlinked or connected with other organizations, often at different levels. Rundle (2005) points out that there are over 18 different institutions including ICANN that deal with Internet governance. The IGF's embeddedness and informal interconnections with these institutions has increased over time. For example, there are sessions at the IGF related to ICANN and vice versa. There also have been some possible turf-related issues with at least one of these institutions, the ITU. This degree of overall embeddedness, even with some dissensus with one networked institution, also indicates possible access to resources including knowledge resources. This data points to the early embeddedness of the IGF, with linkages of varying degrees to Internet governance-related institutions in the Internet governance policy space. Turning to government organizations, private sector organization, and civil society organizations reveals a pattern of increasing interconnections and information flow whether at consultations, annual meetings, or online.

Two related measures are the stability of the network and its degree of institutionalization or regularization/routinization. The IGF has maintained its cycle of annual meeting, preparatory meetings/consultations, and advisory board meetings. It is, however, undergoing mandatory review as it approaches its fifth year of operations. An easy way to determine the degree of institutionalization is to look at several dimensions related to the institutionalization process (Levinson 2006). One dimension is the presence of analogies. Here we argue that the multistakeholderism inherent in the IGF reflects multistakeholderism in other global governance-related domains such as the environment or trade. The use of this term is growing in other governance areas as well, such as multistakeholderism in local community projects. A second dimension is the presence of replications. Here, again, there is clear and striking data from the IGF. During the last year, the number of country-level or regional IGFs has grown dramatically, with the most recent being the inaugural IGF/USA held in October 2009 in Washington, DC.

The governance structure of a network (Kenis and Provan 2009) also relates to its effectiveness. There are three main types of network governance structures: shared governance, lead organization, and network administrative organization (NAO), each with its own implications for effectiveness, depending upon the type of network and its tasks/goals.

In the case of the IGF, the governance structure follows the NAO model with a small administrative secretariat. While there has been discussion at various consultations regarding having a larger or better-funded secretariat, feedback from most IGF participants indicates that they are satisfied with the current structure.

Related to the governance structure, is the nature of the network leadership. It, too, makes a difference for effectiveness of the "whole" network. Nitin Desai, the current Chair of the IGF and Chair since its inception, honed his network-focused leadership skills in other United Nations-related settings including environmental governance issues. Stakeholders consistently express respect for his work as well as that of the small secretariat. China, at the 13 May 2009 consultation, expressed its respect for the secretariat even as it disagreed with other stakeholder calls for a continuation of the IGF.

Network Form

The elements of a network's form relate closely to its structure. From its participatory strength to its degree of goal consensus, these elements connect with other studies of assessment of network effectiveness.

There are two separate measures of participation strength in the network: depth of participation and width of participation. Klijn et al. (2008) measure participation depth with a focus on citizen involvement. Depth relates to more intense involvement such as the movement from informing and consulting to coproducing. They ask us to look at who sets the agenda, who brings the ideas in, and who makes the final decision to help measure participation depth. At the IGF, the presence of the cycle of consultations and the input of ideas from the consultations to the advisory group (the MAG) indicates that there is a high degree of participatory depth, although it is the MAG that makes the decisions regarding the IGF operations and its meeting agenda.

Width (small to medium to wide) refers to a variety of outcomes and depth to a greater satisfaction with outcomes. With regard to width, it is important in the case of the IGF to examine to what extent there are diverse participants, especially from developing nations. Here we would place the participatory strength at medium, since the IGF has yet to figure out how best to involve those from the least developed nations.

At the same time, it is one of those rare networks related to Internet governance where participants from civil society, government organizations ranging from nation-state to regional and even local, private sector organizations, and international organizations are interlinked on a relatively equal basis and in dialog. These cross-sector linkages, of course, are also cross-cultural and cross-national, adding to the participatory strength. The overall number of cultures involved is large and diverse ranging from African nations, China, Cuba, European Union, and Russia on to the Pacific islands and to the USA.

Finally, while the consultations reveal a range of satisfaction with outcomes of discussions, some but not all participants have expressed a desire to have the IGF be a decision-making body. The depth measure also seems to be at the medium level.

Three other elements relate here to network effectiveness: trust, reputation, and influence. While trustworthiness does appear in the literature to be connected with effective networks, there is a longitudinal aspect as well as a network administration aspect that is relevant to this study. Early in the life cycle of the IGF, there probably was little cross-sector and even cross-cultural trust. Over time, and as we would argue, through the process of engagement in cross-stakeholder dialog, trust among participants, for the most part, has grown. (We base this assessment on informal conversations with participants, as well as on content analysis of consultations.) With regard to the network administration aspect, Kenis and Provan (2009) point out that when there is an NAO, as there is at the IGF, there does not have to be high levels of trust among all participants. (The highest levels of trust are required when there is a situation of shared governance.)

Similar patterns occur with regard to reputation and influence. The reputation of the IGF has grown since its inception; new participants from a range of organizations have participated with each IGF cycle. This may, in part, relate to the location of a host country. However, there is also an increase in the participation from the private sector in different parts of the world. Influence relates here to the presence or absence of influence of the network as a whole.

Again, a longitudinal view is necessary to assess this element. At the IGF's inception, there was great uncertainty and even skepticism as to whether the IGF would work as a multistakeholder body. There were no such models in the Internet governance arena, although there were some related models in environmental governance. Over time, ideas generated at the IGF appear to have influence in other related arenas such as ICANN and the ITU.

A final element related to network form and effectiveness is goal consensus. While content analyses of IGF consultations and summary papers indicate an absence of complete consensus on many points, there does appear to be moderate consensus, even regarding the continuation of the IGF itself. Literature on network effectiveness notes that there need not be perfect goal consensus; rather an effective network as a whole can exhibit moderate consensus (Kenis and Provan 2009).

Network Processes and Co-processes

Beginning with the construction of collaboration (including the acceptance of others' views) and on to the flow of ideas (and their impacts), this cluster of elements constitutes a key component in evaluating network effectiveness.

Writing that effective collaboration "leverages differences among participants to produce innovative, synergistic solutions" and "balances divergent stakeholder concerns," Hardy, Lawrence and Grant (2005, p. 58) provide a baseline for discussing whole network effectiveness and especially the IGF. Naturally, such processes involve communication and negotiation over time. They also include the possible presence of coproduction processes.

Levinson (2009) defines coproduction as the joint work of stakeholders related to policy discussions and outcomes. Viewing specifically coproduction processes, Murphy (2004) highlights being socially present, setting forth individual perspectives and recognizing others' perspectives, cocreating shared perspectives, crafting shared goals and purposes, and producing shared documents.

There are, indeed, four factors that facilitate such processes: conditions at the initiation stage (such as trust, conflict, and social capital); the ground rules for such collaborative processes; the leadership including mediation and facilitation expertise, and cross-cultural communication skills. Ansell and Gash (2008) point out that trust and interdependence can emerge over time.

The nature of the IGF itself and its very definition provide a platform for collaboration possibilities. Bringing together unlike participants to discuss and share ideas fosters awareness of others' views, forges information flow channels that might not have existed previously, and, over time, can facilitate knowledge transfer. We can measure this in many ways. One example is to examine the number of ideas generated; another is the variety of ideas; a third is the creation of new structures to accelerate cross-organizational knowledge flow such as the IGF dynamic coalitions and the IGF workshops, each of which must be, by definition, multistakeholder in nature. The IGF, then, is an effective network in ensuring awareness (but not necessarily agreement) of other views and in transferring ideas and knowledge. It is also, over time, a locus for generating and shaping new ideas, some of which "stick" and others of which are discarded. (See, for example, Levinson and Smith 2008 where one KTE, the case of the speed dialogs, provides evidence of idea generation and idea transfer that does not take hold or "stick.")

Another measure is the presence of common constructions of the network as a whole. The dynamic coalitions that emerged from dialog from the first meeting of the IGF in Athens are an example of a common construction as are the agendas and formats coproduced for each Annual Meeting.

One understudied network process that is vital for evaluating the IGF is the presence or absence of interorganizational learning. Faster than intraorganizational learning, Holmqvist (2004) points out that it is less burdened by prior experience and current practice. There is a short-term form of interorganizational learning that is also useful in this evaluation: bricolage. Bricolage involves the "remixing reconstructing and reusing of separate artifacts, actions, ideas, signs, symbols and styles in order to create new insight or meanings" (Deuze 2006). It usually stems from surprises as opposed to anticipating problems in advance—it is a form of just-in-time learning. Simply put, it uses what a network has on hand to solve problems or to take advantage of new opportunities.

Cleaver (2002) who studies organizations and change in the field of resource management in Tanzania points out that institutions are formed through bricolage. He highlights the networks of social relations in which these institutions are embedded. The creation of the IGF itself certainly reflects bricolage processes amidst the WSIS backdrop of controversy and uncertainty regarding internet governance.

Looking at the past four years of the IGF and its networked processes reveals KTE episodes capturing bricolage. Even the creation of the dynamic coalitions provides evidence of bricolage. While the term dynamic coalition does date back to United Nations sponsored meetings related to environmental governance (Levinson 2006), the actual forms that the IGF-related dynamic coalitions have taken reflect processes of such improvisational and interorganizational learning.

Improved community capacity is another dimension related to network effectiveness and co-processes. Here one can look at the IGF and its discussions over the past four years and ask the question of what community and what capacity. If it is the question of developing nations' capacity for Internet governance (central to the founding concept of the IGF), then there appears to be improved community capacity for some nations and regions with regard to Internet policy issues and policy-making, especially with regard to civil society. Yet this is only a partial answer; there is, as noted earlier, still a gap with regard to the least developed nations and civil society from such settings. Related to this measure is a question regarding the possible presence of new ways of behaving and managing. While there is much anecdotal evidence regarding the new patterns of interacting among stakeholders at the IGF, it may be too early to judge.

Finally, how satisfied are the organizations involved in the IGF? Here the survey posted by the IGF with an online summary provides the best channel for answers. Most but not all (see the earlier comments from China) of the participants are satisfied with the IGF, although almost all respondents have suggestions for improvements. This dimension is sensitive to political realities and philosophies. There is a possible mismatch between the idea of a multistakeholder dialog entity and political systems that do not encourage unfettered dialog.

CONCLUSION

This chapter evaluates the IGF both as a whole network and as a locus for constructing collaboration and related co-processes. We have shown how it provides the foundation for crafting collaborations through its formulas and its implementation of both dynamic coalitions and workshops. The chapter also adopts a longitudinal view, recognizing change over the four-year life cycle of this institutional innovation. The IGF, as a whole, has achieved outcomes that could not have been achieved by individual organizations or by an individual sector itself. Providing an evaluation framework for a whole network such as the IGF, it examines each of the 16 elements in order to provide a formative evaluation of a multistakeholder, networked organization such as the IGF and contribute to the dialog at the fourth annual meeting in Egypt and beyond. As noted earlier, it may be too early to evaluate all elements; however, this work supplies a foundation for both a multidimensional and holistic approach to the Internet Governance Forum as a four-year-old networked, institutional innovation.

NOTE

1. This section draws upon the organizational structure and insights from Levinson and Cogburn 2011a and 2011b, with many thanks to my colleague and collaborator Nanette Levinson.

CHAPTER 8

The Civil Society Internet Governance Caucus as Transnational Advocacy Network

INTRODUCTION

While the IGF has enabled a great deal of transnational civil society involvement in its processes, both in the MAG and via their participation and leadership in the various Dynamic Coalitions relevant to their interests, perhaps the best example of transnational advocacy networks within the IGF comes from the Civil Society Internet Governance Caucus (IGC). The IGC was founded in March 2003, early in the WSIS processes and was first discussed in Chap. 5. The purpose of this section of the chapter is to better understand the evolution, structure, policy preferences of the Internet Governance Caucus (IGC), and its impact on the processes of global Internet governance.

As we discussed in Chap. 5, there were a number of top-down and bottom-up structures that formed within the WSIS processes to facilitate civil society participation. Some of these structures included the (in)famous Civil Society Bureau (CSB), the CSP, which was an e-mail mailing list, and a host of Thematic Caucuses and Working Groups.

One of these Thematic Caucuses was the Civil Society Internet Governance Caucus (IGC). The IGC is primarily organized around an e-mail listserv (governance@lists.cpsr.org), the archives of which may be found at: http://lists.cpsr.org/lists/info/governance, hosted by the Computer

© The Author(s) 2017   217
D.L. Cogburn, *Transnational Advocacy Networks in the Information Society*, Information Technology and Global Governance,
DOI 10.1057/978-1-137-48361-4_8

Professionals for Social Responsibility (CPSR). It has 464 subscribers (which includes a number of people, of whom about ten are registered with more than one e-mail address). The IGC was formed out of the preparatory processes for the UN WSIS—more about that below—and while it does have limited opportunities per year when some of its members can meet face to face (normally —two to three times per year), there has never been a time when the majority of "members" were collocated. This e-mail-based organizational structure mimics the larger civil society organized for WSIS and is reported on in Cogburn (2005a).

Members of the IGC are individuals acting in their own personal capacity, who come together voluntarily (many of them do belong to the same organizations, such as the APC, the IGP, Information Technology for Change (IT4Change), and the CRIS Campaign. More about the impact of these organizations is discussed below. There is no salary or funding associated with being a member, participant, or leader in the Internet Governance Caucus (at least directly). While a constitution was eventually developed, the original organizational structure was very loose, and the two "co-coordinator" structure remained in place.

Conceptual Framework

The concept of Transnational Advocacy Networks (TANs) was given life with the seminal work of Keck and Sikkink (1998). TANs are defined as "networks of activists, distinguishable largely by the centrality of principled ideas or values in motivating their formation" (Kick and Sikkink 1998). These TANS are expected to have a collection of participants working internationally on policy issue(s) who have (1) shared values; (2) a common discourse; (3) a dense exchange of information; and (4) seek to influence policy (Keck and Sikkink 1998).

In addition, Keck and Sikkink (1998) suggest three components of the composition of a Transnational Advocacy Network:

(1) *Networked organizational form*: "mnizational eck and Sikkink (1998) suggest three components of the composition of a Transnational Advocacy Network";

(2) *Advocacy-based*: "these networks are organized to promote causes, principled ideas, and norms, and they often involve individuals advocating policy changes that cannot be easily linked to a rationalist understanding of their anizational"

(3) *Transnational in scope*: Not limited to any one country, but fluid between domestic and international realms, "luid between domestic and international realms, incipled ideas, and norms, and they often involve individuals advo

And they continue by arguing a TAN can include any combination of the following types of actors, with heavy emphasis on the first category:

(1) International and domestic nongovernmental research and advocacy organizations;
(2) Local social movements;
(3) Foundations;
(4) The media;
(5) Churches, trade unions, consumer organizations, and intellectuals;
(6) Parts of regional and international intergovernmental organizations; and
(7) Parts of the executive and/or parliamentary branches of government (adapted from Keck and Sikkink 1998, p. 9).

While a lot has been written subsequently about how this concept works, this basic, seminal definition is still helpful in specifying how we understand a TAN.

Research Questions

This section asks three grand tour questions: (1) What is the evolution and structure of the IGC? (2) To what degree does the IGC reflect the model of a Transnational Advocacy Network (TAN)? (3) What are the key policy preferences of the IGC and how have they changed over time? Each of these broad questions has one or more specific, operationalized research questions. The complete structure of the research questions for this study are provided below:
RQ1: What is the evolution and structure of the IGC?

- RQ1.1 How was the IGC created?
- RQ1.2 What key organizations and people comprise the IGC as represented by a named-entities analysis?
- RQ1.3 What types of actors comprise the IGC?
- RQ1.4 What regions comprise the IGC?

- RQ1.5 Which IGC members have been most *active* in the IGC as represented by their frequency of posting on the mailing list?
- RQ1.6 Which IGC members have been most *influential* in the IGC as represented by the frequency of responses on the mailing list?
- RQ1.7 How has the membership, participation, and structure of the IGC changed over time?
- RQ2: To what degree does the IGC reflect the model of a Transnational Advocacy Network (TAN)?
- RQ2.1 Does the IGC have *shared values?*
- RQ2.2 Does the IGC have a *common discourse?*
- RQ2.3 To what degree does the IGC have a *dense exchange of information?*
- RQ2.4 To what degree does the IGC *seek to influence policy?*
- RQ2.5 Are there any clear linkages between the IGC and an epistemic community?
- RQ3: What are the key policy preferences of the IGC and how have they changed over time?
- RQ3.1 What are the most frequently occurring words in the IGC and have they changed over time?
- RQ3.2 What are the most frequently occurring phrases in the IGC and have they changed over time?
- RQ3.3 What key topics are extracted from the IGC?
- RQ3.4 What have been the key accomplishments of the IGC?
- RQ3.5 What has been the tone and sentiment of the IGC?

Methodology: CRISP–DM

This chapter will focus on a computationally text analysis of substantial data on the IGC. It will use the Provalis ProSuite for data analysis, specifically QDA Miner 4.0 and WordStat 7.1. In order to try to standardize the approach to text mining, many data scientists use the Cross-Industry Standard Process for Data Mining (CRISP–DM) for text mining. This is a rigorous but flexible methodology with six stages, which are (1) purpose; (2) data availability; (3) data preparation; (4) model development; (5) results; and (6) deployment (recommendations). The methodology allows for substantial iteration, and lessons learned at any stage of the project can trigger iteration and going back through each of the stages.

Data Availability

Data for this study come from the public e-mail archives of the IGC, as well as its website and participant observation of the network at international meetings. The original email archive was located at CPSR. However, the listserv was transferred to another website. Public website data can be scraped using a variety of parsing, scraping, and scripting tools. In this instance, I used the tool SiteSucker (http://sitesucker.com). Sitesucker allows the user to set certain parameters and limitations in terms of the data downloaded from the site.

Data Preparation

E-mail data are extremely rich in metadata and content. However, it does require some preparation and cleaning. In this case, my primary data cleaning technique was to develop an exclusion list/dictionary. An exclusion list was created to exclude the most common words. To the default exclusion list, we added numerous words related to boiler plate information related to the listserv. We also applied a transformation to ignore duplicate paragraphs.

In addition, we have used the automatic import feature to add several key variables to the data set, including FROM; TO; CC; SUBJECT; DATE; TIME; and IP address (from which we calculated geolocation information—latitude and longitude). Each document has been given a YEAR and DATE variable, to enable us to explore longitudinal changes in the data.

Model Development

This study takes a multiphase, mixed-methods approach to model development. In the first phase, it focuses on inductive approaches, and in the second phase moves to deductive approaches to answer the specific research questions. The inductive approach starts with a basic descriptive analysis of the keywords frequency by case analysis and phrase frequency by case analysis. Phrase frequency analysis will extract—two- to five-word phrases. We will also assess the degree to which these analyses change over time and in relation to key external events in Internet governance. Also in this phase, we will use a topic extraction engine, to identify the key top-ics within the data set, as represented by the collection of words that are closely clustered together and the interpreted topics/themes they appear to represent. These approaches will enable us to answer RQ1.1; RQ2.

The second phase will take a deductive approach and will build a series of categorization models designed to answer the remaining research questions. One categorization model will be based on the conceptual approaches to TANs. Additional categorization models will be built iteratively, based upon the findings of the inductive phase of the study, including the keyword and phrase frequency by case analysis and the named entity extraction models. We will then apply these categorization models to the data set to see the degree to which those concepts are rep-resented in the data. These approaches will enable us to answer RQ2.1, RQ2.2, and RQ2.3.

BRIEF HISTORY OF THE INTERNET GOVERNANCE CAUCUS

In the WSIS, civil society organizations were encouraged to participate energized by the UN General Assembly resolution mandating the creation of the conference, and the relatively coequal role of civil society and busi-ness with governments.

Through a series of top-down and bottom-up processes, the global civil society participants in WSIS created a number of structures to participate in the WSIS processes (Cogburn 2005; Klein 2005). Fourteen Thematic Caucuses and Working Groups were founded as well as two (Cross-cutting) Multistakeholder Caucuses, and six Regional Caucuses.

For Internet governance, this structure was initially called the ICT Global Governance Caucus, and was founded by Y.J. Park and Wolfgang Kleinwachter. The caucus was eventually renamed as the Civil Society Internet Governance Caucus (IGC).

At the end of WSIS Geneva (2003), the Summit adopted the *WSIS Declaration of Principles* and the *WSIS Plan of Action*. These two documents set the tone and structure of the WSIS processes in the Tunis phase of the Summit (2005). At the conclusion of WSIS Tunis, a *Tunis Agenda* was adopted, which included a particular focus on "enhanced cooperation" in Internet governance.

It seems clear that the earliest record of the Internet Governance Caucus was early in the preparatory processes for the first phase of WSIS. At that point, it was called the ICT Governance Caucus. Figure 8.1 below illustrates the positioning of the IGC within the various other WSIS CS Thematic Caucuses and Working Groups.

The specific background to the earliest formation of the IGC is still a bit sketchy. However, it seems that the earliest progenitor of the kernel of the IGC was Y.J. Park of Korea. According to Wolfgang Kleinwachter, Park made [a] "relevant statement" about Internet Governance issues at the Western Asia Preparatory Conference for WSIS, from 4 to 6 February 2003 (http://www.escwa.un.org/). The Final Declaration of the Beirut conference suggested under the heading of "Ensuring Governance of Internet and ICT Resources" that "the issue of Internet security is critical for the region. National and regional efforts should be coordinated, taking into consideration the importance of secure infrastructure and data flow in concordance with international standards and guidelines" (Beirut Declaration, p. 4). Further, under the heading of "Securing National Domain Names," the Beirut Declaration says:

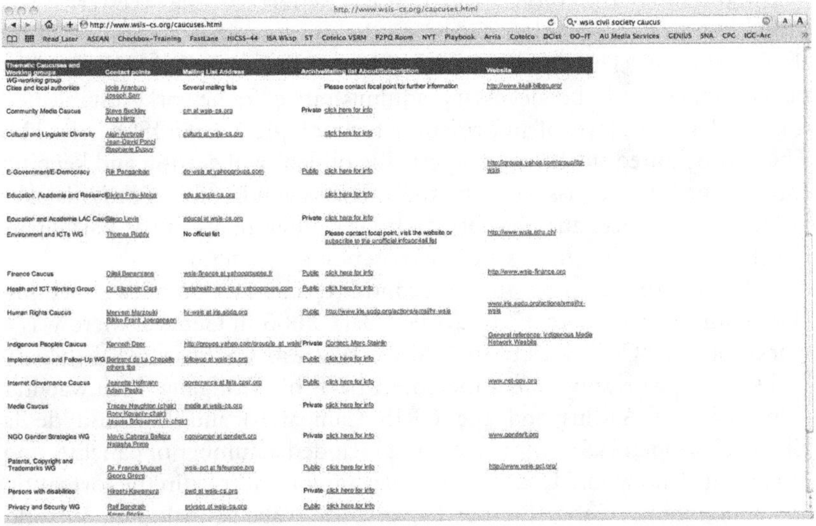

Fig. 8.1 The Internet Governance Caucus within the WSIS CS structures

The responsibility for root directories and domain names should rest with a suitable international organization and should take multilingualism into consideration. Countries' top-level domains and Internet Protocol (IP) address assignment should be the sovereign right of countries. The sovereignty of each nation should be protected and respected. Internet governance should be multilateral, democratic and transparent and should take into account the needs of the public and private sectors as well as those of the civil society. (Beirut Declaration, p. 4)

Internet governance was also mentioned in the Beirut Declaration under the heading of "Reforming Legal, Regulatory and Policy Matters," where it states that "the existence of a supportive and predictable legal framework is an important prerequisite for enhancing trust in ICTs and e-business…other areas involving legal issues relevant to electronic transactions include:… Internet governance" (Beirut Declaration, p. 3).

These developments seem to be the earliest recorded introduction of Internet governance issues into the WSIS processes. And they seem to have been introduced by Y.J. Park, who would go on to become the first co-coordinator of the Internet Governance Caucus (called the ICT Governance Caucus) along with Wolfgang Kleinwachter.

Interestingly, the Official ECOSOC Report of the Western Asia Preparatory Meeting only referred to the more limited statement under the heading of "The Development of Laws," the idea that "[l]aws must be developed and the necessary administrative frameworks established for good governance of information technologies" (ECOSOC, P. 11). This more limited statement suggests the difficulty of getting and keeping Internet governance issues onto the official agenda of this "multistake-holder" conference, and the relative power differentials of the participating stakeholders, but that is a discussion point for later.

Following this meeting, in the second Preparatory Committee meeting (Prepcom 2), held from 17 to 28 February 2003 in Geneva, there was a workshop on "Civil Society in WSIS" (WSIS in CS Flyer, 21 February 2003). This workshop was moderated by Prof. Wolfgang Kleinwachter (University of Aarhus and the CRIS Campaign) and Bertrand de la Chappelle (Open WSIS Initiative), and included a number of panelists and discussants who would later go on to play important roles in the formation and functioning of the Internet Governance Caucus, including Vittorio Bertola (ISOC Italy and ICANN's At Large Advisory Committee); Hans Klein (Georgia Tech, CPSR, and later IGP principal investigator); Amadeu Abril, ICANN Director, Andrei Korotkow (Vice Minister, Russian Ministry of Telecommunications and Member of ICANN Governmental Advisory Committee); Philipp Grabensee (ICANN GNSO Names Council); Robert Guerra (CPSR); Izumi Zizu (Glocom Tokyo); Jean-Gabriel Mastrangelo (UNESCO), and Nick Moraitis (Youth Caucus). The workshop was organized by ICANN and the Open WSIS Initiative.

According to Kleinwachter, "after the workshop we moved to the ILO rerstaurant [sic] where we discussed the need to establish an institutionalized platform which we called "CS Internet Governance Caucus" (IGC)". However, my observation notes have the original name as the "CS ICT Governance Caucus (IGC)." Kleinwachter continues: "Originally, Internet Governance was not a main issue in the WSIS. First priority for WSIS was bridging the digital divide, however the ITU was very interested to bring the Internet Governance (IG) debate under the WSIS umbrella as a counterplatform to ICANN, which was established in 1988 as an alternative to ITU efforts to get the control over the DNS and the A Root Server" (Kleinwachter, 1 August 2010).

In March 2003, the e-mail listserv of the Internet Governance Caucus was established, and hosted by the CPSR. CPSR is a global alliance of computer scientists, headquartered in San Francisco, California, that promotes the responsible use of computer technology. It was incorporated in 1983 (based on earlier discussions begun in 1981). Several well-known organizations were given an initial boost by CPSR, including Privaterra, the Public Sphere Project, EPIC—the Electronic Privacy Information Center, and the Twenty-first Century Project. Several CPSR board members and leaders were key to CPSR involvement in the IGC, including William Drake, Hans Klein, and Robert Guerra.

The first e-mail of the IGC listserv was sent by Y.J. Park on 1 April 2003, and was entitled "Terms of Reference." The text is reproduced below, and it highlights numerous issues and themes that have continued throughout the lifespan of the IGC:

Dear all,
 As of today, Internet Governance Caucus has 20 or so people
 on the list who have shown their interests in joining this group as members. No news or update from any
 volunteered members yet since last February, let me start the ball rolling. This is the first draft proposal for ToR of this caucus for discussion and I want to invite your comments on this.
 Thank you,
 YJ

Here, we see the person who would become the first coordinator exerting leadership among a growing group of Internet governance experts trying to get the nascent network off the ground. This message includes organizational elements (a terms of reference, indication of interest of "membership" numbering about 20, references to the "caucus"), and requests for volunteers, and open invitations to "comment" on a draft text. The short draft Terms of Reference for the IGC included six sections: (1) background; (2) scope; (3) deliverables of IGC; (4) membership of IGC; (5) mailing list; and (6) open for comments.

This message was followed two days later by a clarifying response, trying to limit the scope of the caucus:

> >*No news or update from any volunteered members yet since last*
> >*February, let me start the ball rolling. This is the first draft proposal*
> >*for ToR of this caucus for discussion and I want to invite your*
> >*comments on this.*
>
> Perhaps we should decide whether we only want to cope with legal and participatory structure (as per 2.1 and mostly 2.3) or also with actual policy issues (such as 2.2).
>
> If we want to do both, then we should be aware that there is a wide range of policy issues beyond the introduction of multilingual domain names, including the introduction of new top-level domain names, the dispute resolution problems (including trademark protection versus non-commercial usage protection), ENUM (which brings potentially huge privacy concerns) and so on.
>
> I'm not sure whether it makes any sense to deal with all the policy issues inside this caucus (by the way, I'd not duplicate the discussions we're already having in ICANN) but, if we want to talk about policy, we should perhaps include a more generic list of issues in the reference, and then have a mechanism to choose the ones we want to address (including any new ones that might arise in the next months and we cannot foresee now).
>
> --
>
> vb. [Vittorio Bertola]

In these earliest emails, we see an encapsulation of the *zeitgeist* of the IGC that had been expressed in the February 2003 meetings in Geneva and raising a number of important Internet governance issues, some of which continue to command attention in the IGC today.

The first two coordinators of the caucus up until December 2003 were Y.J. Park (Korea) and Wolfgang Kleinwachter (Germany). The emergence of the IGC should also be seen within the context of the other organic civil society structures emerging to contest with the top-down bureaucratic structures being imposed on civil society during this period (see Cogburn 2005).

STRUCTURE AND GOVERNANCE OF THE IGC

The IGC was formed out of the preparatory processes for the UN WSIS—more about that below—and while it does have limited opportunities per year when some of its members can meet face to face (normally two to three times per year), there has never been a time when the majority of "members" were collocated. Although this is a global voluntary organization with no funding, the IGC has remained relatively stable. It has a website (currently located at: http://igcaucus.org). It holds annual elections, and has been able to put in place processes to nominate key civil society participants in critical international policy processes, including civil society participation in the Commission on Science and Technology for Development (CSTD), the NetMundial High-Level Multistakeholder Committee, and many others.

Members of the IGC are individuals acting in their own personal capacity, who come together voluntarily (many of them do belong to the same organizations, such as the APC, the IGP, Information Technology for Change (IT4Change), and the CRIS Campaign (more about the impact of these organizations below). There is no salary or funding associated with being a member, participant, or leader in the Internet Governance Caucus (at least directly).

While a constitution was eventually developed, the original organizational structure was very loose, and the two "co-coordinator" structure remains in place.

Our third research question asks how the IGC works. Here we want to focus on its institutional structures, especially its structures for decision-making, leadership, and governance.

FROM INFORMAL TO FORMAL: THE IGC LISTSERV

As described above, the IGC started from two interrelated components: substantive and process-oriented. Both will continue to be important aspects of the IGC. The substantive component emerged from Y.J. Park (Korea) working at the Western Asia Regional Preparatory Meeting to get substantive IG issues on the agenda and into the formal Beirut Declaration. The second process-oriented component comes from Wolfgang Kleinwachter (Germany) and Bertrand de la Chapelle (France) moderating a workshop on modalities for Civil Society involvement in WSIS, and an informal "backstage" dinner in the ILO restaurant to discuss organizational structures for getting Internet governance issues into the organically emerging civil society structures for WSIS.

The IGC is primarily organized around an e-mail listserv (governance@lists.cpsr.org), the archives of which may be found at: http://lists.cpsr.org/lists/info/governance, hosted by the CPSR. Given the geographically distributed nature of the emerging Internet Governance Caucus, the e-mail listserv made sense and became the key integrating mechanism for the network.

The listserv has 464 subscribers (which includes a number of people, about ten that are registered with more than one e-mail address). This e-mail-based organizational structure mimics the larger civil society organized for WSIS and reported on in Cogburn 2005.

Over the 13 years of its existence, this mailing list has been used to address a wide range of policy and organizational issues for both the WSIS processes and subsequently those of the Internet Governance Forum, and even other related processes such as NETmundial. It currently has over 28,000 messages.

IGC RELATIONSHIP TO BROADER CIVIL SOCIETY PLENARY

Concomitant to the establishment of the IGF was the question of how to integrate its work into the emerging structures of the broader WSIS civil society. Cogburn (2005) identified two competing loci of power that were emerging within the WSIS Civil Society. The "top-down" structure was the Civil Society Bureau (CSB). The CSB was imposed on civil society by a bureaucratic UN structure struggling to come to grips with how to handle the participation of such a large, diverse, heterogeneous grouping as civil society in this new "multistakeholder" process. The CSB consisted of handpicked "representatives" of civil society, who would come to serve as the official interface between civil society and the governmental bureaucracy.

In contradistinction to this top-down CSB were the organic "bottom-up" structures emerging within civil society. The emerging leadership of civil society pointed to the CSP, the listserv for the civil society members participating in WSIS, as the highest and most legitimate authority representing civil society. This CSP list was owned by Karen Banks (APC) and Adam Peak (Glocom Tokyo). Following CSP in the informal WSIS CS hierarchy was the "Content & Themes" (C&T) Working Group. C&T was designed to have representatives from all of the various CS thematic and regional groups, and was responsible for crafting official civil society input into the WSIS policy processes. C&T included a number of listservs to support its structures, including (1) general list; (2) coordination list; (3) drafting team; (4) speakers' nomination committee; and (5) a translation team. The following e-mail is an example of the tension that would quickly emerge between the CSB and the CSP/C&T:

Hello all,
The following info from the WSIS secretariat is forwarded from the bureau list. FYI. The bureau list was finally created as of yesterday, April 16.
How about planning one or two Internet Governance-related roundtables during the upcoming summit?
Best,
YJ

----

6. Summit Events

The basic guidelines for organizing a special event at the Summit have been finalized by the WSIS Executive Secretariat and the Secretariat of the host country. They will be posted on the www.geneva2003.org website in the next days
(we will make an announcement as soon as available).

As proposals will start coming in, the CS Bureau will be requested to examine them and make recommendations on their relevance to the Summit Events Steering Committee. The latter is composed of the Secretariat of the host country (Switzerland), the Canton of Geneva and the WSIS Executive Secretariat

You will understand that the number of proposals will exceed the available space and resources available at the Summit site. The Summit Events Steering Committee may consider grouping or reshaping events in order to accommodate a maximum of requests. Therefore, the advice of the CS Bureau will be very important.

The Internet Governance Caucus was a participant in all of these structures, and used them to try to inject its emerging policy perspectives into the WSIS processes.

IGC ELECTIONS

As the IGC gained traction, it continued to try to formalize its organizational structures. The original co-coordinators of the IGC were replaced in 2003 by Jeanette Hofmann (Germany) and Adam Peake (Tokyo), and other co-coordinators have included Ian Peter (Australia) and Parminder Singh (India), Vittoria Bertola (Italy) and Avri Doria (US). The tradition of two co-coordinators has continued, with the exception that they now have staggered terms to ensure continuity and institutional memory within the caucus. The current co-coordinators are Jeremy Malcolm (Australia/Malaysia) and Ginger Paque (US/Venezuela).

These annual elections became an onerous task, and in 2008, the IGC leadership turned to the author and his research center for assistance. We began to help the IGC conduct elections for its coordinators, and successfully led two successive elections for its co-coordinator, as well as a major vote on amending its charter in 2009 and its nomination process for recommended MAG members also in 2009 (with an average participation in all these processes close to 100 members).

IGC CHARTER AND AMENDMENTS

At the conclusion of WSIS in 2005 in Tunisia, it was clear that Internet governance issues were going to continue to be a contentious global issue (along with the development issues that were also left unresolved). Two new global institutions emerged to address these issues, the UN GAID to deal with the "development" issues left unresolved by WSIS and the IGF to deal with the unresolved issues of Internet governance. Both institutions were given five-year mandates, and both have continued to operate within the issue area(s) of their assigned space.

In order to respond to this new global environment, the IGC made a decision to evolve beyond its WSIS roots, to serve as the vehicle for organizing civil society involvement in the newly emerging Internet Governance Forum. In order to serve in this capacity, its organizational structures had to evolve and become more complex. The charter was one of the first places to start.

The IGC Charter was first approved on 14 October 2006, following a two-week voting period. This new charter was substantially longer than the original one drafted in 2003. It now had 20 sections, including (1) Vision; (2) Mission; (3) Objectives and Tasks; (4) Membership; (5)

Organizational Roles; (6) Coordinators; (7) Duties of Coordinators; (8) Selection of Coordinators; (9) Recall of Coordinators; (10) Replacement of a Coordinator; (11) Appeals Team; (12) Duties of the Appeals Team; (13) Working methods; (14) Posting Rules for the IGC; (15) Suspension of Posting Rights; (16) Recommendations and Requests for Suspending Posting Rights; (17) Decisions; (18) Ad Hoc Subgroups; (19) Voting Process; and (20) Amendments to the Charter. This revised charter suggests that the organizational structure of the IGC was evolving to cope with the complexities being required of the network to participate in global IG processes. One additional dimension was the development of a website/content management system for the IGC (http://igcaucus.org).

One of the most contentious institutional issues the IGF has faced, has been the amendment of its charter to deal with what are called "trolls." Trolls, generally, are people who register for open e-mail listservs, and use them to disrupt discussion and sow chaos and discord among the list. The IGC has attracted a number of these purported trolls, and has had a very difficult time dealing with them. The challenge was how to define—within this very loose transnational network—a sufficient consensus to remove someone from the list.

IGC's Relationship with Broader IGF

Finally, the IGC has established a tight integration with the Internet Governance Forum. Many of its earliest leaders have become key figures in the leadership structures of the IGF, especially, Avri Doria (who is a consulting member of the IGF secretariat), Adam Peak, Jeanette Hoffman, Y.J. Park, and Wolfgang Kleinwachter, all of whom have served on the IGF MAG, its informal governing body, and several other IGF participants, such as Milton Mueller, Robert Guerra, Bertrand de la Chapelle, have participated every year in proposing workshops and panels which make up the substance of the IGF. Further, many of the IGF members have helped to create new Dynamic Coalitions—key multistakeholder vehicles within the IGF designed to advance arguments and an understanding of key policy issues.

When we look at the IGC participation in the Dynamic Coalition process, another measure is the degree to which there is discussion on the IGF mailing list about the dynamic coalitions. In the aggregate, there have been substantial mentions of the currently active Dynamic Coalitions or their key topics and themes ($n = 12,603$) and also of the inactive Dynamic Coalitions or their current key topics and themes ($n = 10,535$). When we look deeper, we find that of the current IGF Dynamic Coalitions, the discussion on the IGC list shows a great deal of interest, if not involvement, in the currently active Dynamic Coalitions. For example, Network Neutrality has been one of the most talked about topics within the IGC (n = 3559), followed by Accountability (2712), Freedom of Expression (2250), Gender (1253) and Accessibility and Disability (1163). Figure 8.x presents an overview of these key policy preferences within active IGF Dynamic Coalitions.

However, within inactive IGF Dynamic Coalitions, the IGC members are also active, including Privacy (4330), Online Collaboration (4013), and Linguistic Diversity (1494).

Types of Actors in the IGC

The IGC has no "headquarters" and no official office space anywhere. It has no budget, and no physical location whatsoever (unless you count the physical location of the server which maintains the listserv). The participants on the list come from, and reside in countries all around the world, in nearly every region and continent. Africa, Latin America, Asia, Australia, Europe, and North America all feature prominently. Many of these individuals are living and working in countries and regions different from where they were born. Collectively, the transnational criteria seem to be met by the IGC as well. There has been some debate within the IGC about the appropriateness of including persons from government and/or the private sector on the listserv. In general, the debates have settled on civil society members only (although this is not enforced).

Regional Distribution of the IGC

Although there is substantial participation in the IGC from the Global North, there is also considerable participation from the Global South and from developing countries in particular. This developing country participation includes those in leadership positions.

Active Members of the IGC

When looking at the current data for overall message postings on the listserv, the top poster is Paarminder (n = 1384, 4.9 %), followed by Michael Gurstein (n = 1037, 3.6 %), followed closely by Salanieta (n = 1014, 3.6 %) and McTim (n = 978, 3.4 %). Although the frequency of posting is just one empirical measure of activity on the list, activity does not necessarily equate to influence. While some well-known and highly influential IGC members also figure toward the top, such as Jeremy Malcolm (n = 640, 2.3 %) and Milton Mueller (n = 586, 2.1 %), other influential members are farther down in the frequency list, such as Anriette Esterhuysen (n = 287, 1.0 %) and Jeanette Hofmann (n = 261, 0.9 %). Again, this current analysis has to be taken with some skepticism, because several participants post with multiple e-mail addresses, which need to be aggregated to get a complete picture. Nonetheless, this current snapshot provides interesting insights.

Influential Actors in the IGC

When using the "phrase-finder" tools, we find other interesting observations, such as identifying when the full name at the bottom was included in the text of the e-mail. We can identify the top names in the email listserv, which are highlighted below: Jeremy Malcom (n = 4424), Ian Peter (n = 3672), Michael Gurstein (n = 2.956), Ginger Paque (n = 2.661), Roland Perry (n = 2265), Avri Doria (n = 2181), Izumi Aizu (n = 2084), and Milton Mueller (n = 2014).

In addition to the phrase-finder to look for names, we can cross-check this by looking for named entitles. Here we can find single names that may have been dropped out with the parameters of the phrase-finder, and other influential organizations. Here we find some of the same persons as listed above, with some new additions, including influential names such as Parminder (n = 4298) and Wolfgang (n = 3108) who were missing from the first list. The top ten single names include Sala/Salanieta (n = 6527), Jeremy (n = 5464), Ginger (n = 4816), Peter (n = 4562), Parminder (n = 4298), Ian (n = 3776), Wolfgang (n = 3108), Avri (n = 3049), Izumi, n = 3035), Milton (n = 2868), Norbert (n = 2657), McTim (n = 2577), and Bill (n = 2424).

GIGANET AS EPISTEMIC COMMUNITY

Finally, many of the academics associated with the IGC (and overall with the IGF), including Peng Hwa Ang, Wolfgang Kleinwachter, Milton Mueller, Nanette Levinson, Jeanette Hoffmann, Laura DeNardis, William Drake, Hans Klein, Derrick Cogburn (the author), Y.J. Park, and John Laprise, have led the creation of the GigaNet http://giga-net.org/). GigaNet is a global association of scholars studying Internet governance, and was founded in June 2006 as a pre-conference to the ICA Annual Meeting held in Dresden, Germany. The pre-conference was organized primarily by Professors Wolfgang Kleinwachter and Peng Hwa Ang, who wanted to see an academic follow-up to the WGIG, and saw that there was no "natural home for Internet Governance research and education" (GigaNet Listserv, 18 April 2016). Peng Hwa was serving in the leadership of ICA, and Kleinwachter was serving as president of the Communication Law and Policy (CLAP) section of the International Association for Media and Communication Research (IAMCR). Together with sponsorship from UNESCO secured by Kleinwachter, ICA, IAMCR and UNESCO cosponsored the inaugural gathering as an ICA pre-conference meeting in Rathen, Germany cochaired by Kleinwachter and Peng Hwa. The meeting was attended by "[a]bout 40 academics from 20 countries and some leading universities (including Oxford, Stanford, Harvard, LSE)" (GigaNet Listserv, 18 April 2016). The meeting concluded with the agreement to create a new network for Internet governance researchers called the GIGANET, and the idea of a Summer School on Internet Governance (SSIG). The first GigaNet meeting was held later that year on the day before the first IGF held in Athens, Greece (and the first SSIG a year later in July 2007 in Meissen). Every subsequent year has seen the IGF host the GigaNet Annual Symposium on the eve of the opening of the Forum. Although that "zero" day has now become crowded with events, GigaNet was the first to take this coveted slot. In addition to this Annual Symposium, GigaNet has held several midyear workshops, and following its roots, its leadership has worked diligently to integrate GigaNet members and Internet governance research into mainstream academic associations, including ICA, IAMCR, the International Studies Association (ISA), American Political Science Association (APSA), Association of Internet Researchers (AoIR), and many others.

There is a substantial, though not perfect, overlap between GigaNet members and the Internet Governance Caucus. Most of the early leadership of GigaNet were also active in the earliest days of WSIS, and many of those were active in the founding of the IGC, especially Kleinwachter and Park, who founded the IGC and served as its first two co-coordinators.

This overlap in membership has been mutually beneficial, and enabled IGC members to draw upon the expertise, theoretical and empirical research, organizational skills, and contacts of GigaNet members as they engage in policy development and make substantive contributions to the IGF, and its various Dynamic Coalitions (as we will see below). However, this relationship has also been beneficial to GigaNet members. They have been able to draw upon their participation in the IGF to have one foot in the advocacy/activist world and another in the respected academic world. While some people feel this relationship is too close, and compromises some GigaNet researchers who blur this boundary fairly regularly, others see true synergy as GigaNet operates as a de facto "epistemic community" for the Internet Governance Caucus.

EVOLUTION OF THE IGC

Between the Geneva WSIS and the Tunis WSIS, Internet governance issues took on an even greater urgency. It was clear that there would not be a consensus on the Internet governance issues. In an effort to address this issue, between the two conferences, a Working Group on Internet Governance (WGIG) was convened, and was staffed by many key members of the IGC. After WSIS, the IGC went through a major transformation. The successful multistakeholder nature of WSIS gave birth to two new global multistakeholder bodies, one to address the outstanding issues of Internet Governance (the UN Internet Governance Forum—IGF) and another to address all the other outstanding issues (Global Alliance on ICT and Development—GAID). Both the IGF and GAID were given initial five-year mandates. While the GAID eventually died an unceremonious death, the IGF mandate was renewed for another five years, and recently at the historic WSIS+10 review meeting at the UN General Assembly, the IGF's life was extended for another ten years.

The establishment of the IGF on the heels of the conclusion of WSIS breathed new life into the IGC, and it gained increasing membership and other WSIS civil society activists saw the IGF as the next and best forum for their global civil society activism.

IS THE IGC A TRANSNATIONAL ADVOCACY NETWORK?

In order to be classified as a Transnational Advocacy Network (TAN) according to a very strict definition, the IGC would have to meet three criteria. In this section, we review the data to assess the degree to which the IGC meets these criteria.

Does the IGC Have Shared Values?

The top 20 issues discussed on the listserv suggest a fairly coherent set of values within the IGC. For example, following civil society, which is by far the most frequently used phrase (n = 19,061) as might be expected for a civil society network, the most frequently occurring phrases include Human Rights (n = 8353), Multistakeholder (n = 4097), Remote Participation (n = 3690); Public Interest (n = 3594); Enhanced Cooperation (n = 3319); Public Policy (n = 3146); Private Sector (n = 3105); Developing Countries (n = 2647); and Information Society (n = 2563). With the exception of the phrase Private Sector, these phrases are all suggestive of a broad, progressive approach to the information society that is open, inclusive, and supportive of human rights and developing countries.

Does the IGC Have a Common Discourse?

In addition to the names, the named entity extraction can also identify important organizations, which are a key part of the shared discourse of the IGC. Here we see IGF (n = 44,865), IGC (n = 39,384), ICANN (n = 19,305), MAG (n = 13,882), IG (n = 8541), WSIS (n = 8499), CS (n = 7754), ITU (n = 7335), CSTD (n = 6103), and Rights (n = 45453).

To What Degree Does IGC Have a Dense Exchange of Information?

Various types of information are exchanged on the IGC website. There are policy-specific types of information, references, links, documents, conference announcements and registration information, grant and fellowship opportunities, new book announcements, and registration information. Partially in jest, we note that "Information" is listed 4222 times on the listserv, and the most frequently mentioned companies are: Google (n = 5209) and Facebook 2271, and the most frequently mentioned countries are China (n = 2203) and the USA (n = 2199).

To What Degree Does the IGC Seek to Influence Policy?

The second big characteristic of a TAN is that it be advocacy based. This criterion means that the network will "plead the causes of others or defend a cause or proposition." TANS are "organized to promote causes, principled ideas, and norms" (Keck and Sikkink 1998, pp. 8–9). In this case, the

IGC has consistently advocated for a range of policy ideas and attempted to influence the discussions, both at WSIS and its outcome documents and the subsequent Internet Governance Forum. These policy issues have ranged from development issues, human rights, access issues, and participation (including remote participation) in IGF processes, composition of the MAG of the IGF, and several others (discussed below in more detail). In many cases, the "consensus" position of the IGC goes beyond where individual members are comfortable, and as such even touches on the secondary criteria described by Keck and Sikkink as when "individuals advocating policy changes that cannot be easily linked to a rationalist understanding of their "interests"."

Epistemic Communities and the IGC

There appears to be several "epistemic communities" operating within the IGC. Two of these are particularly influential, namely the IGP (full disclosure: I am a principal and member of the scientific committee of the IGP) and the GigaNet. A large number of academics are individual members of the IGC, and many of these individual members are also members of a scholarly network called GigaNet (again, full disclosure: I am one of the founders of GigaNet and served on its inaugural steering committee, and have served as Vice-Chair of GigaNet). As an example, GigaNet is mentioned a total of 507 times within the IGC email listserv archive, including substantial evidence of collaboration and resource-sharing between the two organizations. (On a side note, GAID is actually mentioned even more frequently (n = 628) on the listserv.)

Another organization that serves as an informal epistemic community for the IGC is the APC. Although not strictly an academic association or network, APC produces a tremendous amount of very influential, policy-relevant research. Their publications are used not only by IGC members in their advocacy work, but throughout the IGF process.

Leaders in all three organizations have been appointed to very senior roles in various global governance processes representing civil society and academia.

WHAT ARE IGC POLICY PREFERENCES?

Our fourth research question asks what the policy objectives of the IGC are. One should first understand that the IGC represents a highly diverse and sometimes contentious grouping of global civil society activists.

Nonetheless, there is a great deal of policy coherence to the IGC objectives, which are very much in line with the principles and values of the GII/GIS as discussed in Chap. 4. For example, when reviewing the archive of the IGC listserv, the phrase Internet Freedom appears 1814 times. A categorization model of progressive policy preferences would definitely be reflected very strongly within the IGC discussions.

For this section, we will focus on using our content analysis tools to explore the subset of IGC data from 2008 to 2010. However, before we begin that process, we will look at a submission by the IGC to the potential themes to be taken up at the Vilnius IGF (IGF 5). The three themes are recommended by the IGC:

1. Network Neutrality
2. A Development Agenda for Internet Governance
3. Internet Rights and Principles

This is a consistent, but narrower grouping of recommendations than that submitted for the Hyderabad meeting, two years earlier (IGF 3). There the IGC submitted the following:

1. Enhanced Cooperation
2. Network Neutrality
3. A Development Agenda for Internet Governance
4. Transparency and Inclusive Participation in Internet Governance

Frequently Occurring Words

We start exploring the IGC Policy Preferences by looking at the most frequently occurring words in the data set.

When we explore the IGC data set of 14,034 messages using word frequency and case occurrences, we can begin to see a series of interesting themes springing forth from the data. However, please remember, this is an exploratory technique, and these descriptions should be carefully evaluated.

For example, ICANN appears 21,388 times and in 27 % of the messages in the data set; MAG appears 11,255 times and in 15 % of the messages. You can also see the names of those members of the IGC that are the most active (meaning, either they are posting themselves, people are responding to their messages, or people are talking about them). The first name we saw appearing in the data set is Parminder, followed by Ian. This makes sense because Parminder and Ian served as co-coordinators during the bulk of the time covered by this data set. The next most frequently occurring names are Ginger and Jeremy. Again, this makes sense because Ginger and Jeremy also served as the IGC co-coordinators, who succeeded Ian and Parminder. However, after these four recent co-coordinators, we see other "active" members popping up. Jeanette (who is also a former co-coordinator from the early years of the IGC); Drake (11.2 %), Wolfgang (10.8 %), Mueller (12.1 %), and Guerstein (7.2 %), all very active and influential members of the caucus).

When looking at the data set organized by case occurrence, we see that the word "Rights" has occurred in 28 % of all messages; "development" has occurred in 24 % of all messages; "participation" has occurred in 23.4 % of all messages. These findings are in harmony with the key policy issues the IGC finally decided to recommend for the upcoming Vilnius IGF meeting.

Frequently Occurring Phrases

Our next step in understanding the IGC policy processes is to look at the most frequently occurring phrases, and also examine how they have changed over time.

When looking at key themes that emerge from the phrase-finder, we find: "civil society" (n = 9328; 26.1 %), "human rights" (n = 6191; 11.0 %), "Tunis Agenda" (n = 2455; 8.0 %), "remote participation" (n = 1957; 5.4 %), "private sector" (n = 1888; 7.7 %), "net neutrality" (n = 1817; 5.4 %), "IGF secretariat" (n = 1810; 6.5 %), "Internet rights" (n = 1294; 3.9 %), "developing countries" (n = 1254; 3.9 %), "WSIS principles" (n = 1242; 3.4 %), "stakeholder groups" (n = 1232; 5.8 %), "Internet users" (n = 1190; 4.6 %), "Asia Pacific" (n = 1100; 7.3 %), "Development Agenda" (n = 1052; 3.5 %), "Freedom of Expression" (n = 1034; 4.5 %), "Global Governance" (n = 1016; 4.2 %), and "Internet rights and principles" (n = 866; 2.9 %). Figure 8.2 below illustrates the results of the phrase finder analysis.

Key Accomplishments

There has been a great deal of activity on the IGC website, but what have been the accomplishments of all this activity. Clearly there have been IGC recommendations and appointments of civil society participation in a number of key global processes. However, even from its inception, the

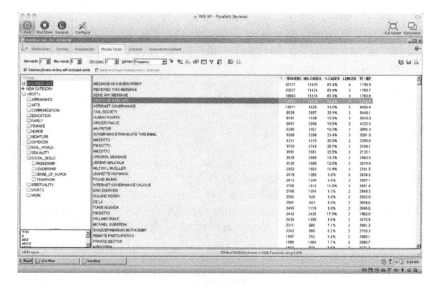

Fig. 8.2 Sample of the results of the "phrase-finder" analysis in Wordstat

IGC has been able to produce policy statements, speakers, and interventions in a wide variety of international policy processes. Most of these statements, speakers and interventions have been seen as credible and respected policy components.

Finally, our last research question asks what factors facilitate and/or inhibit the IGC from achieving its policy objectives. Here, we aim to highlight the institutional factors that allow the IGC to make an impact on the multistakeholder processes of global governance for the Internet, as well as illuminating its limitations.

IGC AND THE IGF MAG

To begin with, we will look at the environment in which IGC is operating currently, and the expectations that fall on its institutional shoulders. First, one of the biggest responsibilities of the IGC is to organize a process to select a recommended slate of civil society actors for consideration by the United Nations Secretary-General to be appointed to the MAG, known as the MAG. The MAG is the de facto governing body of the Internet Governance Forum, and augments the limited capabilities of the official secretariat. Achieving a balance of gender, region, seniority, and other factors has been seen as of critical importance. For each year of the MAG's existence, the IGC has been able to lead a process to submit a slate of names for consideration by the IGF secretariat to submit for consideration to the UN Secretary-General. The IGC has also had substantial success at getting many of those candidates appointed to the MAG. (One interesting side note: there are other civil society actors who have managed to get appointed to the MAG without going through the IGC nominating processes, which may indicate a less than perfect representation of civil society by the IGC.)

IGC and IGF Workshops

The IGC has also been able to work to encourage the submission of workshop proposals for the annual IGF, and to identify speakers to occupy seats available for civil society on IGF plenary panels and other workshops.

IGC and IGF Policy Positions/Statements

Since 2008, the IGC has used its transnational network to develop 14 key contributions and statements. These include the following in reverse chronological order:

1. Renewal/Restructuring of the Multistakeholder Advisory Group
2. Main Session Themes for IGF, Hyderabad
3. Format IGF, Hyderabad
4. Review of IGF
5. Rights as a Theme for IGF
6. IGF Role
7. IGF Review Process
8. The Way Forward (Internet Rights and Principles as a Major Theme for IGF 4)
9. April 2009 Statement in Response to Program Paper
10. June 2009 Statement Re ICANN Joint Project Agreement
11. July 2009 Statement Re IGF Review (Questionnaire)
12. Submission of the IGC on Themes for the Vilnius Meeting of the IGF
13. Submission of the IGC in Taking Stock of the Sharm-el-Sheikh Meeting of the IGF
14. An Open Letter from the Internet Governance Caucus to the United Nations Secretary-General, Ban Ki-Moon

Given the degree of contentiousness on the IGC list, even among the "legitimate" members, and not to mention the addition of the "trolls," it is pretty remarkable that this loosely organized, unfunded, transnational advocacy network has been able to produce such a steady stream of inputs into a fairly arcane and complicated global policy process as the IGF.

LIMITATIONS OF THE IGC

The limitations of the IGC really focus on three areas: (1) its lack of financial resources; (2) its inability to use more advanced technologies to facilitate remote or distributed participation; and (3) organizational structures that make it difficult to remove members from its ranks, and particularly from its listserv (which is the primary vehicle it uses for coordination).

Tone and Sentiment of IGC Discussions

Finally, we want to understand the overall nature of the tone and sentiment on the IGC listserv.

DISCUSSION

This study has helped to accomplish a number of important goals. We have been able to better understand the history of an important transnational civil society network. Does this network qualify as a Transnational Advocacy Network in terms of the seminal definition promulgated by Keck and Sikkink (1998)?

We have also been able to highlight the problems of the IGC. While its stability has been remarkable, there have been so many contested issues within the IGC that numerous factions have emerged, and spun off from the IGC (e.g., BestBits). These organizations are "encroaching" on the space of the IGC.

From this exploratory study, we have learned a great deal about the Internet Governance Caucus. We see it as a Transnational Advocacy Network that in spite of its shortcomings, has been a surprisingly robust and effective mechanism for facilitating transnational civil society participation in global Internet governance processes. The paper also points to a number of issues that the IGC might want to consider as it moves forward into the next phase of the Internet Governance Forum, which has been just reauthorized for another five-year mandate.

In our analysis of the IGC, we see that a very small number of individuals and organizations played a key role in creating the network, and creating a mechanism that facilitates a diverse group of civil society actors from around the world to come together to participate in a new form of global multistakeholder participation in global governance. It has relied almost solely on its e-mail listserv to organize its work, and the later addition of the Drupal-based content management system helped strengthen the network. The network leaders also recognized the need for additional technologies to assist with organizational features such as voting. The current co-coordinators of the IGC have put in place some tools to facilitate these voting processes and "consensus calls."

Interestingly, the IGC has used very few, if any, synchronous collaboration tools. This is in part because the IGC falls under the grip of the rest of the WSIS civil society structures, which have given in to the dogmatic philosophical principles of the Free/Libre Open Source Software (FLOSS) advocates. These approaches "prevent" the WSIS civil society structures from being able to use software that is commercial and proprietary. As such, many of the more powerful synchronous collaboration tools, that might enable the IGC to meet, discuss, debate, and prepare for participation in IGF and other meetings are not employed. These synchronous collaboration tools could provide a major boost to the ability for the IGC to continue to grow and become a more powerful force for bringing civil society ideas into the multistakeholder processes of global Internet governance.

In addition, we have been able to demonstrate a methodological innovation. While the author of this paper has been actively involved in nearly all of these activities since the early 1990s, and the participant observation and subject matter expertise is certainly helpful, this technique shows what type of analysis can be done on large-scale, text-based data sets that are available to the public, and that can be accessed and analyzed for relatively little cost. While this analysis used the Provalis ProSuite of tools as the primary software for analysis, most if not all of this analysis could be performed using the open-source data analysis language R within RStudio, and a variety of packages to extend the functionality, such as Rtm.

PART 4

Snowden and Implications for Multistakeholder Global Governance of an Information Society

CHAPTER 9

Relinquishing the Root: Snowden, NETmundial, and the IANA Transition

INTRODUCTION

WSIS and the post-WSIS institutions—GAID and more importantly the IGF—relieved a lot of pressure on ICANN for fundamental reform in the international regime to govern the Internet. ICANN continued to function, and was responsible for the IANA functions that were still overseen by the MoA with the NTIA. Overall, a high degree of stability and predictability returned to Internet governance. Then, on 5 June 2013, information started to trickle out about US surveillance of the Internet, and the complicity of many well-known ICT companies, including huge social media giants and other Internet companies. These "Snowden revelations," named after former NSA analyst-turned-whistle-blower Edward Snowden, landed like a bombshell into the Internet governance landscape, reigniting regime contestation and calls for the USA to relinquish its long-held special role in the key governance functions of the Internet. This chapter explores the Snowden revelations, which led to the NETmundial conference in Brazil, and subsequently, to the USA agreeing to what I call "relinquish the root" as a homage to the famous book by Milton Mueller (2002). Specifically, these events led to the USA agreeing to transition one of the key Internet governance processes—maintenance of the IANA functions—to a new global, multistakeholder body, developed by the global community. This chapter will not be a complete history of the Snowden revelations, but

© The Author(s) 2017   247
D.L. Cogburn, *Transnational Advocacy Networks in the Information Society*, Information Technology and Global Governance,
DOI 10.1057/978-1-137-48361-4_9

it will highlight the extent of the leaks and the impact it had on global Internet governance.

SNOWDEN

On 5 June 2013, *The Guardian* newspaper revealed that it was in possession of leaked classified documents from the NSA, one of the most secretive components of the US intelligence community. In this initial release of documents, there was evidence that Verizon had been required to hand over the metadata (data about the data) from millions of phone calls in the USA. While many analysts and observers suspected this was happening, this was clear evidence. At this point, the source of the leaked documents was not revealed, only that there were many more documents available.

Following these initial revelations, on 6 June a specific NSA program— called PRISM— was exposed. This release of documents indicated that the NSA had direct access to servers of numerous US technology companies. June 8 led to the disclosure of another specific NSA program, this one called Boundless Inforalmost, which indicated that the NSA had captured three billion pieces of intelligence on US citizens. These revelations were stunning, but they were only the tip of the proverbial iceberg. On 9 June 2013, the source of the documents was confirmed, along with the identity of the informant. Edward Snowden, a former NSA contractor, stationed in Hawaii, had surreptitiously captured a treasure trove of NSA documents directly from their servers to which he had access. It was not possible to deny the authenticity of the documents, and Snowden immediately went into deeper hiding. The revelations continued.

On 14 June the leaked documents revealed that the USA spies on Hong Kong and Chinese citizens, and hacks into Internet backbones. On 16 June the documents revealed that both the USA and the UK monitor communications of foreign diplomats.

More Internet companies were in the crosshairs on 19 June, with the revelation of another specific NSA program, this one entitled Project Chess, where it was shown that the NSA practices surveillance of Skype. On 27 June, Project Evil Olive/Stellar Wind was revealed in the Snowden documents, detailing the practice of NSA harvesting of online user metadata. This was followed immediately on 28 June with *The Guardian* asserting that the NSA monitors one billion mobile phone calls. On 29 June, the leaked documents revealed that the USA monitors the EU,

UN, and foreign embassies in New York, DC, and Brussels. On 30 June the documents revealed that the NSA spies on ordinary German citizens. On 6 July, Project Fairview was revealed, which indicated that the NSA was monitoring Brazilian citizens through telecommunications. Project Upstream was revealed on 10 July exposing the NSA program collecting data transmitted through fiber-optic cables. Finally, on 1 September, it was revealed that the NSA had spied on the Brazilian and Mexican presidents.

While many in the USA and around the world were stunned and shocked by the extent of these revelations, none were perhaps more vocal than Brazilian president Dilma Rousseff. She used her speech to the United Nations General Assembly on 23 September 2013 to accuse the USA of having violated international law. She called for a global meeting on the future of Internet governance, and offered to host such a meeting.

The Eighth Internet Governance Forum, held in Bali, Indonesia, from 22 to 25 October 2013, was dominated by these issues, but was nonetheless surprisingly civil and productive. Some, including US Ambassador David Gross, called the Bali IGF one of the best ever.

However, shortly after Bali, on 27 November 2013, the EC called the US practices a breach of international trust and urged action to "restore trust" in EU–US data flows. Even with all this pressure, it was still surprising to most when on 14 March 2014, the USA, through the National Telecommunications and Information Administration announced the intent to transition the global coordination of the core Internet governance activities of: (1) managing the DNS root zone; (2) allocation of IP address spaces, including those made to Regional Internet Registries; and (3) protocol registry responsibilities, all three known collectively as the IANA functions to a "multistakeholder body." NTIA did list four principles that had to be adhered to in a transition proposal that it required to have broad community support:

(1) Support and enhance the multistakeholder model;
(2) Maintain the security, stability, and resiliency of the Internet DNS;
(3) Meet the needs and expectations of the global customers and partners of the IANA services; and,
(4) Maintain the openness of the Internet (NTIA 2014).

This NTIA challenge to the global community came only one month before the manifestation of the challenge presented by President Dilma Rousseff materialized in the historic NETmundial conference.

NETMUNDIAL: PLOTTING THE FUTURE OF GLOBAL INTERNET GOVERNANCE

The Montevideo Statement

After the release of the Snowden revelations, President Rousseff and the EC were not the only two institutions working to prompt a change in the global governance of the Internet. On 7 October 2013, shortly after President Rousseff's thundering speech at the UN General Assembly, the leaders of the majority of organizations in the world responsible for the actual technical management of the Internet infrastructure released a statement from their landmark meeting in Montevideo, Uruguay. The participants included the Regional Internet Registries (RIRs)— AFRINIC, American Registry for Internet Numbers (ARIN), Asia-Pacific Network Information Center (APNIC), Latin America and Caribbean Internet Addresses Registry (LACNIC), Réseaux IP Européens Network Coordination Centre (RIPE NCC), the Internet Architecture Board (IAB), the ICANN, IETF, ISOC, and the World Wide Web Consortium (W3C).

Without mentioning the Snowden revelations directly, these leaders declared the need to further evolve the mechanism for Internet governance, in a way that can "address emerging issues faced by stakeholders in the Internet" (Montevideo Statement, ICANN, 2013). The short statement made four critical points:

- They reinforced the importance of globally coherent Internet operations, and warned against Internet fragmentation at a national level. They expressed strong concern over the undermining of the trust and confidence of Internet users globally due to recent revelations of pervasive monitoring and surveillance.
- They identified the need for ongoing effort to address Internet governance challenges, and agreed to catalyze community-wide efforts toward the evolution of global multistakeholder Internet cooperation.

- They called for accelerating the globalization of ICANN and IANA functions, toward an environment in which all stakeholders, including all government, participate on an equal footing.

Here we see a warning against Internet fragmentation, urging the acceleration of the IANA transition and expressing a strong expression of concern about actions that are "undermining the trust and confidence of Internet users globally due to recent revelations of pervasive monitoring and surveillance" (Montevideo Statement, ICANN, 2013).

The gravitas of this announcement delivered by the technical leadership of the Internet governance ecosystem, coupled with the emotional plea by President Rousseff and the European Union, laid the groundwork for the productive period around the world leading up to the NETmundial conference. From 23 to 24 April 2014, the Brazilian government hosted NETmundial: A Global Multistakeholder Meeting on the Future of Internet Governance.

Preparing for NETMundial

The Brazilian Government authorized 1Net and CGI.br to take a lead in organizing this historic conference. A rather elaborate multistakeholder structure was created to convene and oversee this conference. Three key committees were appointed: (1) a High-Level Multistakeholder Committee, comprised of 27 members, including 12 countries, 12 multistakeholder community representatives (three from each community), and 3 from International Organizations (full disclosure: the author was appointed to and served on this High-Level Multistakeholder Committee (HLMC) for NETmundial), responsible for fostering political involvement and the international community; (2) an Executive Multistakeholder Committee, comprised of 17 members, eight from Brazil (appointed by CGI.br) and nine from the global multistakeholder community, responsible for actually organizing the event; and (3) a Logistics and Organizational Committee, responsible for all logistical aspects of the event. Each of these committees was filled with nominees from various relevant multistakeholder communities. There was also a Council of Governmental Advisors, open to all governments that desired to participate in the meeting, and a chair to oversee the process.

The idea for the NETmundial organizers was to create a structure that could serve as a model process for a multistakeholder Internet governance process; one that did not privilege certain actors—namely governments—over others.

In order to speak at the conference, all participants, including governments, had to line up behind one of the four microphones, in the line for their respective stakeholder: (1) Governments/International Organizations; (2) Technical Community/Academia; (3) Civil Society; and (4) Private Sector.

Another unique aspect of NETmundial, at least a major differentiator from IGF, was the plan to have an outcome document, the *NETmundial Statement*. You may remember from our discussion in Chap. 7, that IGF specifically had no outcome document. While IGF is sometimes criticized for this feature, in theory it helps to alleviate some of the negotiation and posturing that tends to accompany other international conferences. The IGF is much more about knowledge and networks than it is about specific policy outcomes.

However, under the circumstances of the Snowden revelations, the NETmundial organizers knew they needed a different type of conference. The plan was to end the conference with a consensus, but nonbinding, *NETmundial Statement* on the future principles and values for Internet governance and a roadmap for the evolution of the Internet governance ecosystem. But, in keeping with the spirit of the conference, the organizers wanted to enable anyone from anywhere in the world to be able to contribute to the process of drafting this statement, whether or not they were planning to be present in São Paulo.

To accomplish this goal, they set up what they called a "Multistakeholder Contribution System." During the period leading up to the conference, the organizers solicited submission from groups and individuals from around the world, and were pleased with the results. A total of 188 contributions were submitted through the Multistakeholder Contribution System, from 46 different countries. As many as 147 individuals and 136 organizations contributed to the process. There was roughly equal interest in both categories of submission: 65 submissions focused on the request for principles and 69 focused on the roadmap (54 submissions were combined). However, most of the submissions came from only five countries, with the USA (31), Brazil (16), UK (7), India (7) and Switzerland (6) accounting for 45 % of all submissions (for more detail, see: http://netmundial.br/wp-content/uploads/2014/05/Content-Contribution-Summary_1703_final.pdf). The conference organizers produced a summary of these submissions, and used them to produce the first draft of the NETmundial Statement, which was the basis for the negotiations during the conference.

NETmundial Outcome Document

As we have discussed earlier in multiple chapters, most United Nations and other International Conferences that have outcome documents, focus very heavily on the preparatory period to negotiate the text of the outcome document. These conference outcome documents are rarely if ever drafted at the actual conference, and are almost never negotiated at the conference. The details of these documents are subjected to the give-and-take of conference diplomacy, as different actors use the process to secure concessions that are most important and relevant to their interests. While this may make sense from a logistical perspective, it does "feel" a little odd. The participants at the conference or summit, do not actually negotiate the outcome of the summit.

The NETmundial organizers attempted to change this by actually trying to negotiate the text at the conference. They did of course start with the draft document coming out of the pre-conference phase, but the final text was still being negotiated at the conference. And, even with all the goodwill of the organizers, they were confronted with one of the challenges of trying to negotiate such a text in real time—the logistics. How do you do it, and how do you try to make this process as fair and transparent as possible?

Ultimately, the organizers resorted to using the HLMC as a vehicle for discussing the various final drafts, and trying to hold the meetings in rooms that were as accessible as possible to the registered NETmundial participants. After a great deal of controversy, the NETmundial statement was finally finished and put to the floor for an open vote/or rather acclamation. With the exception of the delegation from Russia, there was unanimous support for the final statement.

The final NETmundial Statement, included the two elements: (1) Internet governance principles; and (2) Roadmap for the Internet governance ecosystem. The principles section covered a series of key international policy issues that were important and familiar to the participants, including: human rights and shared values; protection of intermediaries; culture and linguistic diversity; unified and fragmented space; security, stability and resilience of the Internet; open and distributed architecture; enabling environment for sustainable innovation and creativity; Internet governance process principles, and open standards. The section on the roadmap included sections on institutional improvement, and a way forward beyond NETmundial.

For most participants and observers, NETmundial was seen as a major success. Even though it was being held in the aftermath of the highly contentious Snowden revelations, and the subsequent Montevideo Statement, the Brazilian government was able to convene a major international multistakeholder Internet governance conference that helped to identify a new set of principles and norms for Internet governance. People "felt" good about participating in the conference, and were energized upon leaving. It was palpable.

However, one problem with the NETmundial conference was that it was a one-off event, not linked to anything going forward, with no international organization at the core. Most supporters of the IGF felt that even with some of its operational advances in convening a multistakeholder conference, NETmundial was a poor substitute for an IGF. The best one could hope for was to "bring the NETmundial" into the IGF, which has happened over the years, through a series of workshops and panels at IGF exploring the impact of NETmundial. One such panel was convened at the Istanbul IGF, during the GigaNet Annual Symposium.

Antecedents to the Outcome Document

Given that the NETmundial Statement was lauded as such a triumph of the multistakeholder submission process, it begs the question of how influential were different stakeholders and participants in that submission process on the text of the final statement. It is likely that some contributions, or categories of contributions, were more influential than others, and some ideas made their way into the final document more completely than did others. In order to explore this question, we developed a study to ask four related research questions:

1. What were the dominant themes found across all stakeholder submissions?
2. What concepts and themes were similar and different between various stakeholder communities?
3. What concepts and themes were similar and different between regions?
4. What submissions were most influential in determining the final text of the NETmundial outcome document?

In order to pursue this brief study, we started by coding all the submissions with two variables: (1) Stakeholder (government, international organization, private sector, civil society, technical, academia, regional IGF, ICANN, Aggregate; and (2) Region (USA, Latin America, western Europe, eastern Europe; Africa, Middle East, Australia/New Zealand, and Multiple. International Organizations were identified in the region where they were headquartered.

As Fig. 9.1 indicates, governments submitted more submissions than any other stakeholder to the NETmundial submission process. However, civil society was not far behind. The private sector, academia, and technical organizations lagged fairly far behind in terms of number of submissions.

Also, while the "multiple" region variable appears to have made the most submissions, western Europe and the USA dominated the submissions, followed by Latin America. Figure 9.2 illustrates the demographics of these submissions. Using a phrase frequency by case analysis, the dominant themes we find in our analysis correspond roughly with those contained in the final NETmundial statement. Figure 9.3 illustrates this distribution, focusing on human rights, civil society, information society, root zone, freedom of expression, and digital economy.

However, when we look at a heat map of cross-tabulated concepts, we see certain concepts favored more heavily by civil society and others by government submissions, with civil society focusing more on access, freedom, and rights while governments focused more on ICANN and multistakeholder.

Through a similarity index, we can also see how similar the government and private sector submissions are, and how civil society and international organization submissions are the next most similar. Next in line stands

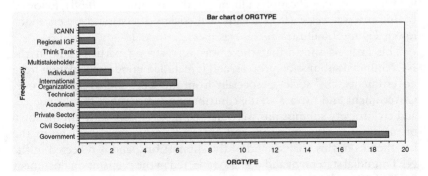

Fig. 9.1 Multistakeholder Submissions to NETmundial Outcome Document

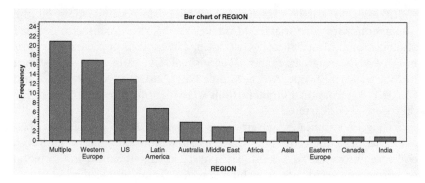

Fig. 9.2   Regional Distribution of NETmundial Submissions

academia, all alone, followed by the technical community submissions. Figure 9.4 highlights these findings, which will become even more important when we get to our final question.

When looking at our regional similarity index in Fig. 9.5, we see the USA standing alone, followed by western Europe. However, what is absolutely fascinating about this analysis is how far away the submissions by eastern Europe are. When we remember that the Russian delegation ended up not embracing the final NETmundial statement, and instead submitting their own final statement, sort of like a dissenting or minority opinion, this makes sense (http://netmundial.br/wp-content/uploads/2014/05/Russian-representatives-statement_2404.pdf).

Finally, when we use a classification model to try to assess the relative influence of different stakeholders on the final outcome document, there is a very strong classification influence from governments (0.58), followed by the private sector (0.22), with civil society (0.16) and others much lower. Figure 9.6 illustrates this classification model.

This analysis shows that there was very strong participation in the NETmundial submission process, and it included good participation from governments, civil society, especially from the USA and western Europe. Government and private sector contributions were most closely aligned, and civil society submissions were aligned most closely with international organizations. Human rights and Internet governance was one of the key themes of this analysis and of the submissions, and is reflected in the NETmundial statement and was also reflected in the preparation document for IGF 2014. Interestingly, even in the wake of the Snowden revelations,

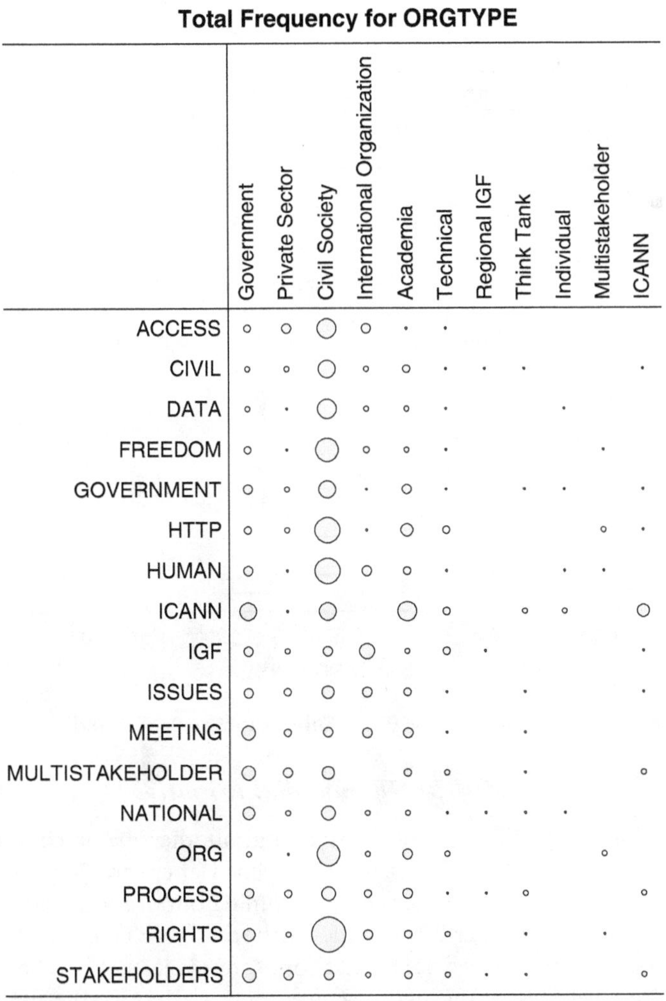

Total Frequency for ORGTYPE

	Government	Private Sector	Civil Society	International Organization	Academia	Technical	Regional IGF	Think Tank	Individual	Multistakeholder	ICANN
ACCESS	○	○	◯	○	·	·					
CIVIL	○	○	◯	○	○	·	·	·			·
DATA	○	·	◯	○	○	·			·		
FREEDOM	○	·	◯	○	○	·				·	
GOVERNMENT	○	○	◯	·	○	·		·	·		·
HTTP	○	○	◯	·	○	○				○	·
HUMAN	○	·	◯	○	○	·			·	·	
ICANN	◯	·	◯		◯	○		○	○		◯
IGF	○	○	○	◯	○	○	·				·
ISSUES	○	○	○	○	○	·		·			·
MEETING	◯	○	○	○	○	·		·			
MULTISTAKEHOLDER	◯	○	○		○	○		·			○
NATIONAL	◯	○	○	○	○	·	·	·	·		
ORG	○	·	◯	○	○	○				○	
PROCESS	◯	○	◯	○	○	·	·	○			○
RIGHTS	◯	○	◯	○	○	○		·	·		
STAKEHOLDERS	◯	○	○	○	○	○	·	·			○

Fig. 9.3 Distribution of Themes within NETmundial Submissions

surveillance did not show up as a key theme across all submissions, and was only found in a very limited number of documents ($n = 15$), with the majority of those coming from civil society (5), followed by governments (3) and academia (2).

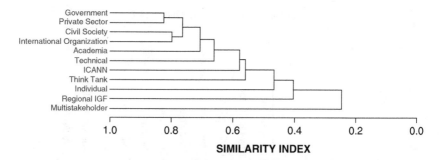

Fig. 9.4   Similarity of Multistakeholder Submissions to NETmundial

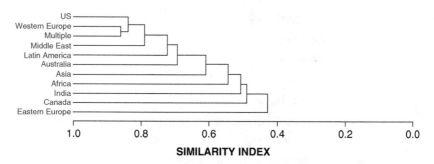

Fig. 9.5   Similarity Index for Regional Submissions to NETmundial

NMI: The NETmundial Initiative

The findings of this study notwithstanding, another major challenge to the legacy of NETmundial was what happened afterwards. Much of the goodwill and "multistakeholder energy" coming out of São Paulo was met with news on 6 November 2014 of the creation of a NETmundial Initiative (NMI) (see: https://www.netmundial.org/press-release-1). Take a quick look at the websites of the two organizations, and notice the immediate differences. (NETmundial: http://netmundial.br; and the NETmundial Initiative: https://www.netmundial.org) Whereas the former conference was organized by the government of Brazil, one of the leading countries of the global South, and a member of the informal BRICS alliance, the latter NMI was organized by the World Economic Forum (WEF).

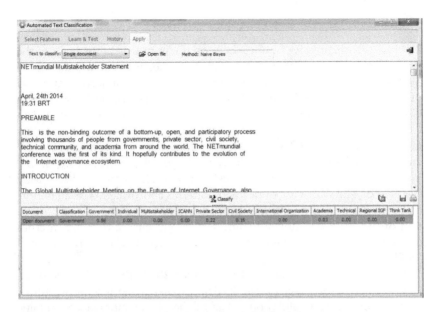

Fig. 9.6 Classification Model of NETmundial Submissions

While some of these issues have since been ironed out, and it boasts an impressive and diverse Coordination Council (https://www.netmundial.org/council), the NMI has been met with a growing number of civil society and academics, along with business and governments, treating it with tremendous skepticism (for example, see https://www.publicknowledge.org/news-blog/blogs/world-economic-forums-netmundial-initiative; https://www.internetsociety.org/news/internet-society-statement-netmundial-initiative; and also https://www.eff.org/deeplinks/2014/08/internet-governance-and-netmundial-initiative--flawed-attempt-turning-words-action) Rossini and others argued that the NMI had essentially "hijacked" the true NETmundial and was proceeding along a trajectory that was very suspicious. The processes of organizing the initial NMI meetings seemed more focused on co-optation of participants, rather than the transparency and openness that came out of the NETmundial Brazil event.

IANA Transition

To close this chapter, we want to focus on the transition at the heart of the emergence of a new Internet governance regime, and one not many people thought possible. On 9 June 2016, the NTIA announced its approval of the plan developed by the IANA Stewardship Transition Coordination Group (ICG) to transition the combined IANA functions described in Chap. 4 to a new global multistakeholder body (https://www.ntia.doc. gov/press-release/2016/iana-stewardship-transition-proposal-meets-criteria-complete-privatization). This was huge news, and each step in the long march toward these final stages of this development has been justly celebrated. The NTIA announcement said this approval "marks an important milestone in the U.S. Government's effort to complete the transition of the Internet's domain name system and ensure that the Internet remains a platform for innovation economic growth, and free speech" (NTIA 2016).

Following NETmundial, on 1 September 2014, the IANA Transition Coordinating Group met for the first time. This group felt the weight of its enormous responsibilities on behalf of the global Internet community. The ICG consisted of 30 individuals, who represented 13 different stakeholder communities, by whom they were elected (https://www.ianacg. org/coordination-group/icg-members/). Unlike for WSIS, IGF, or even NETmundial, these communities were very carefully defined, to represent the incredibly diverse public policy and technical interests within the global Internet community. These communities, which will play a big part in the oversight of the IANA functions under the new regime, including the following communities (the corresponding number of seats on the ICG).

ALAC—At-Large Advisory Committee (2)
ASO—Address Supporting Organization (1)
ccNSO—Country Code Name Supporting Organization (4)
GAC—Governmental Advisory Council (5)
GNSO—Generic Names Supporting Organization (3)
gTLD Registries—Global/Generic Top-Level Domain Registries (2)
ICC/BASIS—Business Action for Support of the Information Society (1)
IAB—Internet Architecture Board (2)
IETF—Internet Engineering Task Force (2)
ISOC—Internet Society (2)
NRO—Number Resource Organization (2)
RSSAC—Root Server System Advisory Committee (2)
SSAC—Security and Stability Advisory Committee (2)

ICANN Board Liaison (1)

IANA Staff Liaison Expert (1)

Each of these communities had its own process to elect its representatives, and each had its own process for involvement in the ICG. However, one of the overarching elements of the process was a commitment to transparency and openness. The need for trust in the process from so many diverse stakeholders around the world demanded such openness. They have made available an invaluable set of resources about this historic process, including all documents, call and meeting archives (including agendas, audio recordings in all six UN languages), chat transcripts, proposals, correspondence, a public drop box, and background on all ICG members. Full analysis of this treasure trove is beyond the scope of this book. However, we look forward to fully exploiting these resources in the future.

Nonetheless, even in the scorching spotlight of public scrutiny and the sense of historic responsibility, this committee was able to produce a consensus plan that met the stated requirements of NTIA, in order for them to relinquish oversight of the IANA functions.

Then, almost a year later at the 55th meeting of the ICANN, from 5 to 10 March 2016 in Marrakech, Morocco, the report and proposal of the IANA Transition Coordination Group were accepted.

The full proposal is 210 pages long, but to summarize very briefly, what the ICG proposes, and what has now been accepted by NTIA, is the following:

1. A new Post-Transition IANA (PTI) will be formed as a new, separate, legal entity. This PTI will be an affiliate/subsidiary of ICANN, and will become the IANA Functions Operator for names, in contract with ICANN.
2. Oversight and monitoring of the PTI will be performed by a Customer Standing Committee (CSC), focusing on contractual requirements and service level expectations.
3. A multistakeholder IANA Function Review process will be established to conduct performance reviews.
4. For numbers, ICANN will continue to serve as the IANA Functions Operator and will be under contract to the five RIRs to perform those functions.
5. There will be a Service Level Agreement (SLA) between the RIRs and the IANA Numbering Services Operator.

6. To advise the RIRs on the IANA Functions Operator's performance, a review Committee (RC) will be established, with community representatives from each region.
7. For the protocol parameters, ICANN will continue to serve as the IANA registries operator, as it has in the past, and will continue to rely on the oversight provided by the IETF, ICANN, and the IAB.

These elements, and the various community processes engaged in to reach them, have met the criteria established by NTIA to relinquish the root.

CHAPTER 10

Toward a Model of Transnational Advocacy Networks as Multistakeholder Global Governance: Conclusions and Future Research

INTRODUCTION

This chapter closes the book with a discussion of what we have learned about multistakeholder participation in global governance for the Information society broadly, and for the Internet in particular. We argue that the IGF represents a new form of international institution, which through its unique nature as a nonbinding multistakeholder forum for Internet Governance has contributed to the "convergence of expectations" predicted by international regime theory as the foundation for an emergent global governance mechanism. It discusses the critical role of Transnational Advocacy Networks (TANs) as a model for multistakeholder partnerships, especially what they mean for power dynamics in conference diplomacy. The chapter explores the factors that enabled some transnational networks to persist and thrive, while others failed, and sees linkages with epistemic communities and the use of ICTs as critical to network effectiveness. We conclude the chapter by making specific recommendations for civil society and the United Nations to harness the potential of TANs as a model for multistakeholder global governance, especially through the use of what we call "Policy Collaboratories," and lay out an agenda for future research.

© The Author(s) 2017
D.L. Cogburn, *Transnational Advocacy Networks in the Information Society*, Information Technology and Global Governance,
DOI 10.1057/978-1-137-48361-4_10

Multistakeholder Participation in Global Governance

At the beginning of this book, we started with the UN Charter and its reference to "We the Peoples of the United Nations...." It is to this statement that we will return in the closing of this book. Finding ways for ordinary citizens and other non-state actors to be able to participate in the discussions and decision-making processes about issues that affect their daily lives remains a goal. It may be an elusive goal, but it is a goal nonetheless. This "multistakeholderism" as some call it, somewhat derisively, is not a quasi-religious tenet. For those who appreciate multistakeholder global governance, we see challenges, yes, but we also see a more open, transparent, and democratic process, involving the consent of the governed. We see the expertise of civil society, the knowledge networks, and linkages with epistemic communities; we see longevity and institutional memory as government actors change on the stage every 36–48 months.

This multistakeholder global governance is appropriate to consider for all domains, and the findings in this book are relevant for a range of issues, including environment, sustainable development, finance, city and urban development, disaster risk reduction, and even perhaps international security. However, we have shown that these approaches are particularly relevant for a focus on the information society, where ICTs are being put into the service of such a diverse range of human needs and, as we say, will forever change how we live, work, and play.

We think these processes are especially relevant for Internet governance. For many people, the Internet, the World Wide Web, and all the content we access over fixed and mobile networks are visible manifestations of the information society. Of course, we understand clearly that there are highly technical and specialized areas of Internet governance. I am sure some of the chapters and discussions in this book have left many readers with glazed eyes. However, that technical component should not be wielded as a sword or barrier to exclude participants. As they learn about these processes, these new entrants into the process should not be allowed to disrupt or impede progress. However, through legitimate peripheral participation (LPP), first discussed by Lave and Wenger (1991), the participants should be able to meaningfully observe the processes, and slowly build themselves up to be able to make a contribution to the process. And it is this potential contribution that makes multistakeholder participation so important and so exciting. It is the "wisdom of the crowds," the valuable insights and diversity that these participants bring to the table. In our work, this also means ensuring the process is open for the more than one billion people in the world who are living with some form of disability (WHO/World Bank 2011).

TRANSNATIONAL ADVOCACY NETWORKS AND MULTISTAKEHOLDER GLOBAL GOVERNANCE

This book has been about harnessing the potential of civil society participation in multistakeholder global governance through transnational advocacy networks. As we mentioned in Chaps. 1 and 2, quite a lot has been written about TANs, and other concepts about the new transnational activism, and global civil society. This book seeks to contribute to that dialog, but it does so from the perspective of the participants. While there are interesting theoretical elements about this work, there is a decidedly practical aspect as well. What can we learn from the decades covered in this book about how to support the work of transnational activists, working in networks, formally and informally, to try to participate in critically important discussions and decision-making processes that are critical to their own existence?

What roles do these networks play? We have shown how these networks are able to integrate newcomers into a highly complex, and for many intimidating, global environment. These networks of persistent actors are able to aggregate people of similar interests, and like minds, to work together toward common goals. The WSIS brought together so many people. For some of these participants, WSIS was their very first time on the international stage, watching these dizzying preparatory processes, with all their procedures, terms, acronyms, and culture. Participating in a transnational advocacy network made that process much easier for some. For others WSIS was not a new process for them, it was but the latest stage in a decades-, or even centuries-old struggle. For some of the women's groups advocating for gender equality, to indigenous voices, and even persons with disabilities, organizing within the WSIS processes of Content & Themes, the Civil Society Bureau and Plenary, was exciting, at times frustrating, but these structures allowed the veterans of international structure for human rights, and communication rights to expand their power and influence as they embraced this larger tent of a GIS.

WSIS allowed so many diverse civil society networks to emerge, but only a few have persisted. Why? We have seen in our analysis here that one of the primary transnational advocacy networks to emerge out of the WSIS processes and continues to have a tremendous influence within its policy domain is the Civil Society Internet Governance Caucus (IGC). Starting way back in March 2003, the IGC has had over a decade of sustained engagement in issues related to Internet governance. There are a number of reasons we have explored which have led to this resilience. There are some of the internal structures of the IGC that have facilitated its longevity. Its charter, and regular elections are two important elements. The IGC has had a long succession of Co-Coordinators (Co-Cos), and this turnover has been healthy for the IGC. The fact that the IGC was able to transition out of WSIS and immediately into the IGF certainly helped. And the fact that the IGF had its initial five-year mandate extended to ten years, and has now been extended for another ten years bodes well for the IGC. The IGC was also able to take on new voices, coming out of the WSIS, who had not necessarily seen themselves as players in Internet governance, but who saw in the IGC and Internet Governance a vehicle for effectively raising issues about human rights, freedom of expression, and a whole host of other issues. Concomitantly, the ineffectiveness and ultimate demise of the post-WSIS counterpart, the UN Global Alliance for ICT and Development (GAID) also contributed to this longevity. In addition, the linkages and overlapping membership with the GigaNet, have allowed this academic organization to serve as a de facto epistemic community for the IGC. Scholars working within GigaNet produce research and analysis that serves the interests of activists working on specific issues within IGC. And, as the IGF structures continued to evolve, and with the creation of the Dynamic Coalitions, IGC activists were able to populate those DCs, and use their GigaNet alliances to produce substantive policy recommendations, workshops, and other relevant events.

Unfortunately, the IGC is not without its problems. We discussed some of these in Chap. 8 and others we have left off the pages of this volume. In my analysis of the IGC, I do not "blame" anyone for its shortcomings; although there are many challenging personalities within the IGC. This transnational advocacy network is being asked to do an almost impossible task—bringing together the most heterogeneous stakeholder in the WSIS and post-WSIS processes, with the most diverse policy perspectives—all while having no budget, and no large, well-financed global apparatus or

50 years of intergovernmental precedent to fall back on. So, my analysis is that the IGC has actually done a fantastic job, under these circumstances. It has done such a good job, that even people who have been badly scathed by some of its members, and have endured some of its worst offences, have continued to participate in the IGC.

One of the biggest problems with the IGC is that it has made poor use of the technology in which its members profess expertise. As we discussed in Chap. 8, its primary technology is an e-mail listserv. Its web portal, developed later, has certainly been helpful, but has certainly not been used to its full potential. And, the IGC even today, makes almost no use of synchronous ICTs or other collaboration tools. This overreliance on asynchronous tools allow some personalities to become more "outsized" in this environment than they are in person, or than they might be with the use of other technologies. These shortcomings have led to a slow, steady, and now increasing erosion of membership out of the IGC and into some of the newer, more hospitable civil society spaces, such as the BestBits Coalition (http://bestbits.net/). Its website says: "The network is called 'Best Bits' because it does not aim to present a single solution for ratification by the assembled groups, but rather to offer an open space where each group can present and advocate for the initiatives that they believe offer the best positive agenda for advancing broadly shared civil society interests in Internet governance." Also, since the Best Bits Coalition emerged out of the IGF Dynamic Coalition on Online Collaboration, Best Bits has made much better use of collaboration tools and technologies. This use of ICTs, as well as linkages with active knowledge-producing and scientific communities are the two key elements of the long-term sustainability and success of transnational advocacy networks working in multistakeholder global governance.

THE UNIQUENESS OF THE IGF AND THE TRAGEDY OF THE GAID

The venue also matters. Where the transnational advocacy networks focus their attention also plays a critical role in the success or failure of the network. The IGC has been "lucky" in a sense that since WSIS, it has been able to focus its attention on the IGF. We have highlighted in Chaps. 6 and 7 the differences between the GAID and the IGF, and what the former got wrong that the latter got right. While being a multistakeholder organization, GAID privileged one stakeholder—the private sector—over all others. Calling it a "pay to play" organization, and requiring it to be led by a CEO business leader harmed its credibility. While the aims were admirable—to get the private sector more energized about engaging in the development activities that could benefit from ICTs—the delivery was problematic. The incredibly complicated and bureaucratic structure created for GAID, saddled it with lethargy, when it claimed to be quick and nimble. And with no sustained budget to support this bloated structure, it failed. In addition, it used very little ICT in the delivery and structure of its organization, even though as we illustrated in Chap. 6 that the use of collaboration technologies and other ICTs was in its mandate.

In contrast, the IGF developed a very simple structure, a MAG for oversight, and multistakeholder Dynamic Coalitions to develop content. This, coupled with its clear annual forum, which was open and transparent (not invitation-only), and included almost from the beginning, remote participation options, made IGF a clear winner out of the two siblings. Further, the decisions that IGF would not be a "decision-making" body and would not have any outcome document meant IGF participants could focus on content and substantive discussion. From an international regime theory perspective, IGF is much more aligned to produce a "convergence of expectations in a given area[s] of international affairs" than some conferences. While imperfect, and now facing its own venue "competition" from the World Economic Forum's NETmundial Initiative (NMI), and a variety other initiatives, the resilience and value of the IGF was confirmed in December 2015, when the United Nations General Assembly in its WSIS +10 review agreed to extend its mandate for another ten years. Another testament to the triumph of IGF over GAID is that the leading and most successful initiative to come out of GAID, namely the Global Initiative for Inclusive Information and Communication Technologies (G3ICT), is now an active participant in the IGF.

PARTNERS OR PAWNS?

So, to return to our original question, are civil society actors participating in these multistakeholder global governance processes, partners or pawns? The clear answer is both. There is value in having the legitimacy of a rich, and diverse, civil society participation. Just look at how the NMI was so widely criticized upon its launch for "hijacking" the true Brazilian NETmundial conference, and for violating the principles and spirit of NETmundial, while trying to claim its mantle, has now incorporated many of these critics. It has a rich and diverse (regional, gender, racial, and ethnic) multistakeholder coordinating body, with very well-respected civil society participants. While I do find this turn of events interesting, it does help to make my point. The participation of these respected civil society actors does legitimize the process— hence they are serving as pawns—but that does not mean they cannot affect change from that position. Hence they are partners. However, the NMI is only one example, this analysis has to take us through each of the ever-increasing multistakeholder processes for Internet governance, the Information Society, and other related areas. Transnational civil society is stretched pretty thin, as it tries to participate in the Commission on Sustainable Development (UNCSD), the CSTD, OECD meetings, Sustainable Development 2030 meetings, including the HLPF, Habitat III, ICANN, ISOC, IGF, Global Commission on Internet Governance, NMI, WEF, and on, and on, and on. Further, we argue that the proliferation of these conferences and meetings, puts even more pressure on civil society that are located in what I have called Global Nodal Cities (such as New York, Geneva, Paris, Vienna, and Washington, DC). So many "multistakeholder" meetings are held in these cities every week that the demands on the time of activists in these cities are enormous. This reality leads us to resurrect a concept we first started exploring and experimenting with during the WSIS processes, what we called a "Policy Collaboratory."

TRANSNATIONAL ADVOCACY NETWORKS AND GLOBAL GOVERNANCE

Building Accessible Cyber Infrastructure in the Global Disability Community

To address these challenges, before turning to our recommendations and future research, we will end this book with a brief overview of a broad approach we are taking to enhance the engagement of civil society broadly speaking, and the disability community specifically in global governance processes.

The global community is facing a historic moment for inclusive social and economic development. Fueled by technological advances and sociopolitical changes at the United Nations, there is an important confluence of several global development and human rights initiatives, including the CRPD, the 2030 Agenda for Sustainable Development (SDGs); UN Habitat III (H3) and the emerging New Urban Agenda, and the WSIS +10. All of these initiatives could assist persons with disabilities that make up approximately 15 % of every country's population (WHO 2011).

These initiatives also present opportunities for persons with disabilities to become more involved in the deliberations, decision-making, follow-up, implementation, and monitoring processes of these major global initiatives and the "global governance" processes they represent.

Take, for example, the Ninth Conference of States Parties (COSP) to the CRPD, held from 13 to 15 June 2016 at United Nations Headquarters in New York City. The theme for COSP 9 is "Implementing the 2030 development agenda for all persons with disabilities: Leaving no one behind." Similarly, the theme for the inaugural 2016 HLPF for the SDGs held from 11 to 20 July 2016 is "Ensuring that No One is Left Behind." The overall theme for Habit III, scheduled for Quito, Ecuador, from 17 to 20 October is the New Urban Agenda. Finally, the focus of the WSIS+10 Outcome Document is the use of the Internet and ICTs to support the implementation of the new Sustainable Development Agenda.

This convergence of initiatives presents an opportunity to advance the goals of more than one billion persons with disabilities around the world for a more inclusive global community that supports their social, political, and economic rights. However, as previous research has shown, there exist numerous challenges to enhancing the active and effective participation of persons with disabilities in global governance processes.

Collaboratories and Transnational Civil Society

In the mid-1980s, scientists working with the US NSF solidified the conception of an important institutional innovation, the scientific collaboratory. A "collaboratory" blends the words "collaborate" and "laboratory" and seeks to use ICTs to create an environment where

US scientists who were geographically distributed could collaborate as if they were in the same physical space (Wulf 1989). The popularity of this collaboratory approach quickly spread beyond the NSF to include NIH, NASA and other federal agencies (Finholt and Olsen 1997). In 2003, NSF commissioned a blue-ribbon panel to revisit the idea of a collaboratory and to explore how the concept could be further extended to other scientists, including social and behavioral scientists as well as humanities scholars. This newer, broader conception of the collaboratory is known as "cyber infrastructure," and is designed to help collaborative infrastructure to become more widespread and available to fuel scientific discoveries and socioeconomic development in a wide range of fields (Atkins et al. 2003).

The purpose of this study is to better understand the socio-technical infrastructure that might enhance the participation of persons with disabilities and the global disability community in the multiple and complex national, regional, and international processes of global governance; and to develop a prototype Disability-Inclusive Development (DID) Policy Collaboratory accessible to persons with disabilities. This study focuses on the UN network on Disability Inclusion and Accessible Urban Development (DIAUD), as they attempt to participate in the processes for the UN conference on Housing and Sustainable Urban Development (Habitat III). The study is enabling us to gain a deeper understanding of the potential of accessible cyber infrastructure to enable persons with disabilities, the global disability community, and broader constituencies to participate in global governance processes.

This project aims to use the accumulated wisdom, best practices, and lessons learned from our decades-long work building virtual organizations and global virtual teams, and accessible cyber infrastructure and cyber learning environments to address as many of these challenges as possible and to enhance the participation of persons with disabilities and the global disability community in each of these important initiatives.

The project has three major phases between 1 June 2016 and 31 May 2017. *Phase One* focuses on the rapid prototyping and development of the DID Policy Collaboratory, with the goal of serving as a platform to support various networks within the global disability community to engage more effectively in global governance processes. While the DID Collaboratory is designed to support multiple networks, this phase of the study is focusing on supporting the *Global Multistakeholder Network on* DIAUD. DIAUD network members were appointed by the United Nations Department of Economic and Social Affairs (UNDESA), specifically the Secretariat for the CRPD and the Division of Social Policy and Development (DSPD). DIAUD is focused on developing and integrating disability-inclusive development contributions into the New Urban Agenda (NUA) and outcome document for the United Nations Conference on Housing and Sustainable Urban Development (Habitat III), held in Quito, Ecuador, 17–20 October 2016. Through the use of the DID Policy Collaboratory, DIAUD was able to increase the number of references in the NUA to persons with disabilities from 6 in the May 0-Draft, to 15 in the final adopted version.

We developed and administered a web-based baseline survey (O^1) of all DIAUD network participants ($N = 55$), with a planned follow-up survey (O^2) after Habitat III in October. The survey has 85 total items, divided into six sections: (1) Demographic Information; (2) Participation in UN Conferences; (3) Participation in non-UN conferences; (4) Collaboration within the DIAUD Network; (5) Experience with ICTs; and (6) Trust and Social Capital. We have also administered the baseline survey to a control group of the global disability community. We will also include them in the follow-up data collection. Our response rate to the survey was close to 50 % ($n = 20$).

After the baseline data collection, we began building the prototype cyber infrastructure for the DID Collaboratory (disabilityinclusivedevelopment.net) and introduced the DIAUD network to its mechanisms.

While the specific components of the cyber infrastructure are dynamic and can be changed, based on usage patterns and feedback from the network, it currently includes the following broad categories of social and technical resources: (1) *People-to-People*, such as photo directories of members and CRM services; (2) *People-to-Resources*, such as background resources, paper archives, and document repositories; and (3) *People-to-Facilities*, such as synchronous accessible audio-video web conferencing and application sharing.

In *Phase Two*, the project broadens participation in the DID Collaboratory to support other networks and working groups engaged in related global governance initiatives described above. Formative evaluation will facilitate iterative development of the socio-technical infrastructure of the collaboratory.

Phase Three of the project focuses on summative evaluation and potential recommendations for further institutionalization of this collaboratory approach.

RECOMMENDATIONS

Where does one end up after reading this book? For the scholars and theorists only, I will make some recommendations in the final closing section for future research. And there are plenty. However, for those scholar-practitioners, international organizations, and transnational advocates, there are additional recommendations.

RECOMMENDATIONS

Multistakeholder Governance of the Information Society

It is possible to envision a world that has a new intentional regime to govern global cyberspace; one that attempts to balance the corporate and national security interests of governments, with the social and economic development goals of the rest of the world. In some ways, it may be possible to make this process even easier because of the rich foundation and multiple years of experimentation that has occurred in this space of privatized and globalized multistakeholder governance for the Internet. NETmundial added to the urgency of this call, because that was exactly the scope the meeting intended to address, creating new principles for the multistakeholder global governance of the Internet.

In response to the Snowden revelations, many leaders in the international community reacted strongly to the concrete evidence of the extent of US surveillance of the Internet. Perhaps none was stronger than Brazilian President Dilma Rousseff. Her charge during her speech at the United Nations General Assembly meeting set off a barrage of developments in the Internet governance landscape. NETmundial was an historic opportunity to address these issues, but it appears that that momentum has been usurped by an initiative led by the World Economic Forum, which is aligned with a different set of global principles.

Policy Collaboratories to Enable
Transnational Advocacy Networks

First, a significant effort should be made on the part of conference organizers to ensure that multiple mechanisms of virtual participation are made available to all aspects of the conference preparatory processes and to the conference itself. These "virtual" mechanisms must go beyond additional mailing lists and websites with information. These virtual mechanisms should embrace the principles described above to support geographically distributed collaborative knowledge work and learning. These CMC tools should be highly interactive, rich media, and include voice, video, whiteboards, slides, websites, and other digital media. They should include a focus on enhancing the connections between three aspects of distributed policy collaboration, which are: (1) people-to-people communication; (2) people-to-resources, and other forms of organically organized digital repositories; and (3) people-to-facilities, meaning synchronous access to the physical spaces of these preparatory meetings.

Second, in order to be more inclusionary and to harness the vision and potential contributions of a diverse group of participants, a significant effort should be invested in human capacity building around the technical issues involved in the conference. Building the capacity for delegations around the world to understand many of the complex thematic issues that are emerging—such as global Internet governance—and to assess how these issues impact them, and to develop policy positions on them will be critical. Further, training among the civil society participants about how to engage in multistakeholder conference diplomacy, ways to engage productively with governments, and with private sector delegates would be invaluable. Here again, embracing the many lessons learned about how to build human capacity in a geographically distributed manner is crucial to the success of these capacity-building efforts (Cogburn and Levinson 2003).

Finally, the transnational advocacy networks should engage in the difficult work of dealing with the questions of representation, legitimacy, and structures within their organizations and networks. This difficult work includes developing the mechanisms for involving remote and diverse participation, including persons with disabilities, creating structures that are as open and transparent as possible, taking steps to eliminate the cliquishness and secrecy (perceived or otherwise), developing coherent and consistent mechanisms for integrating and involving new people into the process, and evolving clear steps for decision-making.

Unfortunately, there are very limited resources available to civil society, and even fewer global institutional mechanisms. Those institutional mechanisms that are there continue to fight and contest within the sector for primacy space, and to protect their positions as "representatives" of the world's civil society. Governments do not have to deal with many of these issues. The United Nations identifies who are the member-states, and each of those states has its own sovereignty and political processes—for better or worse—for determining whom its representatives will be at such summits. The private sector, while still mostly representing the larger multinational corporations and not small, medium, and micro-sized organizations, and in many cases not any private sector from the developing world, has the institutions and resources to organize its participation. It is the civil society that is most vulnerable in this process, and it is their diverse voices, which matter tremendously— even at a distance—to the success of the communication information and communication society that are in danger of being silenced.

Finally, this section ends with a series of recommendations to promote the principles, values, norms, decision-making procedures, and enforcement mechanisms of a new international regime to govern the global Internet.

Regime Principles for Global Multistakeholder Internet Governance

Principles
Based on this analysis, the primary principles for Internet governance should be to facilitate stability of the Internet, stimulate demand, and continue to make Internet governance institutions more responsive to the needs and perspectives of the diverse group of global stakeholders now involved in these processes. That may mean that there should be closer integration of the results from regional and national IGFs. Because far more people will find it cost effective to attend these national and regional meetings, their input should be stronger.

Norms
The norm of multistakeholder participation is one of the critical values, and it should be preserved. There should be no diminution of the norm of multistakeholder participation, and in fact, the role of non-state actors should continue to be enhanced. Non-state actors should not be limited to short bursts of presentation slots (five minutes) while governments can take the floor repeatedly.

Values
Most of the Internet governance institutions have gone a long way toward facilitating remote participation over the last 15 years. Both ICANN and IGF enable fairly robust options for remote participation, not only

through viewing a streaming video and audio feed, but also through web conferencing options. So receiving information from these meetings has become quite good, and mostly limited by one's stamina. However, the information flows and remote participation need to go both ways. It should become easier, and more commonplace, for remote participants to deliver presentations, lead discussions, comment freely, and generally be supported as much as possible. There should be little or no "privileging" of those face-to-face participants.

Decision-making Procedures

The decision-making procedures within Internet governance processes should remain multistakeholder decision-making. It appears to me that one example that could be a model is the decision-making procedures within the IGF MAG. While they operate under Chatham House Rules, and it is impossible to know how the decision-making processes actually work without being in the room, the MAG has produced eight IGF meetings, that for the most part are substantive, and seen as valuable (at least for the thousands of participants that attend).

Enforcement Mechanisms

One of the longstanding problems with international regime theory and Internet governance in particular is enforcement. How are decisions of the governance mechanisms enforced? The strongest aspect of the current regime are the decisions that come from ICANN, and the voluntary implementation of the technical standards that come out of the IETF, W3C and other technical standardization bodies. The weakest aspect of the current regime, and this is largely by design, is the IGF. While IGF can and does play an important role in facilitating a convergence of principles, norms, and values it has no enforcement power.

SIGNIFICANCE

This is an important research program in a number of ways. It contributes to the literature on global governance, regime theory, and provides empirical evidence in support of one of the major debates within the international studies literature on the relative importance of power versus knowledge in influencing regime emergence. This research program also contributes to a growing stream of literature exploring the emergence of transnational networks of civil society actors and particularly their use of ICTs.

From a practical perspective, this research program provides important strategic recommendations for ways to strengthen the development and growth of transnational policy-actor networks involved in global ICT policy, and ways to use new networked organizational forms—such as a policy collaboratory—to enhance their linkages with epistemic communities. Through this work, these international networks of scholars and scientists will be in a much better position to connect with their counterparts in the developing world. Lessons learned in this project will also be relevant for other areas of global governance such as trade, energy, and environmental policy. Also, the potential savings to the world community of finding better ways to use ICTs to organize these global policy processes is tremendous, especially for a conference organized around ICTs, spending over $12 million to organize the preparatory processes, which could be greatly strengthened by the use of such policy collaboratories.

We have linked this entire research project to my Global Graduate Seminar on Globalization and the Information Society: Information, Communication and Development. For close to a decade, this *Globalization Seminar* involved global virtual teams of students from up to six universities (three from South Africa and three from the USA) in a "Beyond Being There" experience (Hollan and Stornetta 1992) of distance-independent learning. Using highly interactive, rich-media web conferencing and collaboration tools, these global virtual teams engage in complex problem-solving of information and communication policy and strategy tasks (Cogburn and Levinson 2003; Cogburn et al. 2002; Cogburn and Zhang 2004).

Finally, from a policy perspective, this research program may help policymakers to make better decisions internationally. This assertion is grounded primarily in the argument that by strengthening the policy actor/epistemic community linkages, we will help to facilitate the development of more data-driven policy. Further, by enhancing the role of civil society and developing countries, we are strengthening the human-centered and socioeconomic development approaches to the information society; both of which will have a tremendous impact on the continued growth and development of cyber infrastructure.

FUTURE RESEARCH

This study generates nearly as many questions as it answers, which is a "good thing" from a researcher's perspective. There are a number next steps suggested by this study. The potential data sets to inform this study are legion, and we plan to take these techniques to engage in a broader analysis of data from those sites. We plan to augment the text analysis with interviews of subject matter experts.Some of my recommendations for follow-up to this study include the following (some of which my research lab will be pursuing, and others which we will not):

1. Develop better measures for the key concepts, such as epistemic community and membership in a policy network;
2. Develop the structural equation model that was hinted at in this paper but not utilized.
3. As Edwards (2001) has noted, one of the limitations of the epistemic communities literature is that there is no clear sense of how new entrants become members of an epistemic community. Following Edwards (2001) it might be possible to use concepts of Situated Learning and Legitimate Peripheral Participation (Lave and Wenger 1991) to better understand both the epistemic communities that exist around the WSIS processes, as well as how to integrate newcomers into the complex WSIS policy formulation processes.

The grounded theory developed from the analysis contributes to answering the research questions presented above, and will also help us to write a detailed ethnography of civil society and developing country involvement in the WSIS process, from the perspectives of the various participants. We will also prepare mini case studies on specific delegations participating in the process (e.g., South Africa, APC, WFUNA, and CRIS). We will use member-checking to help validate our findings. By presenting the summary results to the delegates with whom we are working in the study, we will be able to gauge our accuracy in reflecting the WSIS and post-WSIS processes from their own perspectives.

According to the note on basic structures for civil society at WSIS, the first principle for the sector is that "there must be multiple avenues and means for participation, and that all civil society entities can select the nature, level and extent of participation according to their needs and interests" (Ó Siochrú et al. 2003). This was a very prescient statement;

however, forces within civil society limited those choices with a stringent focus on open source software orthodoxy. During the second phase of WSIS, we engage in a strategic intervention called the *ICT Policy Collaboratory* (*i*PC). The *i*PC is one component of a larger project called *"From Pawns to Partners."*

What are "Pawns"? Pawns are chess pieces. They are accorded the lowest value and position on the board. While they are able to achieve some victories, it is very difficult or impossible to win a match with just pawns. In the opening stages of a match, they are positioned for the best strategic advantage, but they have very little impact on the process; they are "expendable." The goal of the multistakeholder process should be to build genuine engagements with the transnational civil society and developing countries, not as pawns, but as partners.

REFERENCES

Abbate, J. (2000). *Inventing the internet*. Cambridge, MA: MIT Press.
Abbate, J. (2012). L'histoire de l'Internet au prisme des STS. *Le temps des médias, 1*(18), 170–180.
Acharya, A. (2013, October). *The competing and convergent logics of global governance*. Paper presented at the Why Govern? Conference, American University, Washington, DC.
Aday, S., & Livingston, S. (2008). Taking the state out of state—Media relations theory: How transnational advocacy networks are changing the press—State dynamic. *Media, War & Conflict, 1*, 99–107.
Aday, S., & Livingston, S. (2009). NGOs as intelligence agencies: The empowerment of transnational advocacy networks and the media by commercial remote sensing in the case of the Iranian nuclear program. *Geoforum, 40*, 514–522.
Administration, N. T. a. I. (2016). Update on the IANA transition.
Adler, E. (1992). The emergence of cooperation: National epistemic communities and the international evolution of the idea of nuclear arms control. *International Organization, 46*(1), 101–145.
Adler, N. J. (1997). *International dimensions of organizational behavior* (4th ed.). Cincinnati: South-Western.
Adler, E., & Haas, P. M. (1992). Epistemic communities, world order, and the creation of a reflective research program. *International Organization, 46*, 367–390.
African Development Bank. (1995). *African development report*. Abidjan: ADB.
African Development Bank. (1998). *African development report*. Abidjan: ADB.
African Development Bank. (1999). *African development report*. Abidjan: ADB.

© The Author(s) 2017 281
D.L. Cogburn, *Transnational Advocacy Networks in the Information Society*, Information Technology and Global Governance,
DOI 10.1057/978-1-137-48361-4

Aigrain, P. (2011, September). *Another narrative.* Paper presented at the PARADISO Conference, Brussels.

Ailon, G. (2008). Mirror, mirror on the wall: Culture's consequences in a value test of its own design. *Academy of Management Review, 33*(4), 885–904.

Akrich, M. (1998). Les utilisateurs, acteurs de l'innovation. *Education permanente, 134,* 79–90.

Albergotti, R. (2014, May 2). Google, Microsoft, Apple to notify users about subpoenas in privacy nod. *The Wall Street Journal.* http://online.wsj.com/news/articles/SB10001424052702304677904579538320088504240

Alvarez, R. M., Sherman, R. P., & VanBeselaere, C. (2003). Subject acquisition for web-based surveys. *Political Analysis, 11*(1), 23–43.

Amant, K. S. (2002). When cultures and computer collide: Rethinking computer-mediated communication according to international and intercultural communication expectations. *Journal of Business and Technical Communication, 16*(2), 196–214.

Anciaux, A. (1995, February 22). Les résultats inattendus (effets sérendips) du RMI et du Minimex. *Journée d'étude sur l'insertion,* Conseil Général, Département du Nord, Conseil départemental d'insertion.

Anderson, N. (2012, August 29). Government admits defeat, gives back seized Rojadirecta domains. *Ars Technica.* http://arstechnica.com/tech-policy/2012/08/government-goes-0-2-admits-defeat-in-rojadirecta-domain-forfeit-case/

Anderson, J., & Rainie, L. (2014, March). *Digital life in 2025.* Washington, DC: Pew Research Center. http://www.pewinternet.org/files/2014/03/PIP_Report_Future_of_the_Internet_Predictions_031114.pdf

Ansell, C., & Gash, A. (2008). Collaborative governance in theory and practice. *Journal of Public Administration Research and Theory, 18*(4), 543–571.

Appiah, K. A., & Sassen, S. (1999). *Globalization and its discontents: Essays on the new mobility of people and money.* New York: New Press.

Apple, Inc. (2014). Government information requests. Cupertino: Apple, Inc. http://www.apple.com/privacy/government-information-requests/

Appleton, S., & Teal, F. (1998). Human capital and economic development. Economic research paper 39. The African Development Bank. http://afdb.org/news/publication/

Arnbak, A., & Goldberg, S. (2014, July). *Loopholes for circumventing the constitution: Warrantless bulk surveillance on Americans by collecting network traffic abroad.* Paper presented at Privacy Enhancing Technologies Symposium (HOTPETS'14), Amsterdam.

Arnold, M. A., Darmon, E., Dejean, S., & Pénard, T. (2014). *Graduated response policy and the behavior of digital pirates: Evidence from the French three-strike (Hadopi) law.* Newark: University of Delaware Department of Economics http://ssrn.com/abstract=2380522.

Aronson, J., & Cowhey, P. (1988). *When countries talk: International trade in telecommunications services.* Cambridge, MA: Ballanger.

Assange, J. (2014). *When Google met WikiLeaks*. New York: OR Books.

Association for Progressive Communications/Campaign for Communication Rights in the Information Society. (2003). *Involving civil society in ICT policy: The world summit on the information society*. Johannesburg: STE Publishers.

Atkins, D. E., Droegemeier, K. K., Feldman, S. I., Garcia-Molina, H., Klein, M. L., Messerschmitt, D. G., et al. (2003). *Revolutionizing science and engineering through cyberinfrastructure: Report of the blue-ribbon advisory panel on cyberinfrastructure*. Washington, DC: National Science Foundation.

Atton, C. (2005). *An alternative internet*. Edinburgh: Edinburgh University Press.

Avant, D. D., Finnemore, M., & Sell, S. K. (Eds.). (2010). *Who governs the globe?* (Vol. 114). Cambridge, UK: Cambridge University Press.

Axelrod, R. M. (1984). *The evolution of cooperation*. New York: Basic Books.

Axelrod, R. (1985). *The evolution of cooperation*. New York: Basic Books.

Babe, R. E. (Ed.). (1994). *Information and communication in economics* (Vol. 32). Boston: Springer Science & Business Media.

Baker, A. (2013, May 27). The YouTube war. *Time Magazine*. http://content.time.com/time/magazine/article/0,9171,2143557,00.html

Balkin, J. M. (2004). Digital speech and democratic culture: A theory of freedom of expression for the information society. *New York University Law Review, 79*, 1.

Balkin, J. M. (2014). Old school-new school speech regulation. *Harvard Law Review, 127*, 1.

Ball, J. (2013, June 8). NSA's Prism surveillance program: How it works and what it can do. *The Guardian*. Retrieved from http://www.theguardian.com/world/2013/jun/08/nsa-prism-server-collection-facebook-google

Bamogo, D., et al. (1996, October). *The Impact of new communication and information technologies in developing countries: A case study of Burkina Faso*. Paper presented at the international workshop on Information Technology for Development UNU/INTECH, Maastricht.

Bang, H., & Esmark, A. (2009). Good governance in network society: Reconfiguring the political from politics to policy. *Administrative Theory & Praxis, 31*, 7–37.

Bantam Books. (1963). Inc. v. Sullivan, 372 US 58, Justia.

Barker, J. (2004). Grossly excessive penalties in the battle against illegal file-sharing: The troubling effects of aggregating minimum statutory damages for copyright infringement. *Texas Law Review, 83*, 525.

Barnes, N., & Reilly, K. (2007). *Conceptualizations of transnational networks: A selective literature review*. Paper presented at the International Studies Association 48th Annual Convention, Chicago.

Barnett, M., & Finnemore, M. (2005). The power of liberal international organizations. In M. Barnett & R. Duvall (Eds.), *Power in global governance*. New York: Cambridge University Press.

Baumgartner, T., & Pahl-Wostl, C. (2013). UN-Water and its role in global water governance. *Ecology and Society, 18*(3), 3.

Bell, D. (1976). *The coming of post-industrial society: A venture in social forecasting.* New York: Basic Books.

Bell, M. (2011, August 12). BART San Francisco cut cell services to avert protest. *The Washington Post.* Retrieved from http://www.washingtonpost.com/blogs/worldviews/post/bart-san-francisco-cut-cell-services-to-avert-protest/2011/08/12/gIQAfLCgBJ_blog.html

Bendrath, R. (2009, February). *Global technology trends and national regulation: Explaining variation in the governance of deep packet inspection.* Paper presented at the International Studies Association Annual Convention, New York. Retrieved from http://userpage.fu-berlin.de/~bendrath/Paper_Ralf-Bendrath_DPI_v1-5.pdf

Beniger, J. (2009). *The control revolution: Technological and economic origins of the information society.* Cambridge, MA: Harvard University Press.

Benkler, Y. (1999). Free as the air to common use: First Amendment constraints on the enclosure of the public domain. *New York University Law Review, 74*(2), 414–426.

Benkler, Y. (2006). *The wealth of networks: How social production transforms markets and freedom.* New Haven: Yale University Press.

Benkler, Y. (2011a). A free irresponsible press: WikiLeaks and the battle over the soul of the networked fourth estate. *Harvard Civil Rights-Civil Liberties Law Review, 46*, 311.

Benkler, Y. (2011b). WikiLeaks and the PROTECT-IP Act: A new public-private threat to the internet commons. *Daedalus, 140*(4), 154–164.

Benkler, Y., Roberts, H., Faris, R., Solow-Niederman, A., & Etling, B. (2013, July 25). Social mobilization and the networked public sphere: Mapping the SOPA-PIPA debate. *Berkman Center Research Publication* (16). Retrieved from http://cyber.law.harvard.edu/node/8416

Bennett, C., & Raab, C. D. (2003). *The governance of privacy: Policy instruments in global perspective.* Cambridge, MA: MIT Press.

Bernauer, T., Böhmelt, T., & Koubi, V. (2013). Is there a democracy–civil society paradox in global environmental governance? *Global Environmental Politics, 13*(1), 88–107.

Berners-Lee, T. (2010, December). Long live the Web: A call for continued open standards and neutrality. *Scientific American.*

Betsill, M., & Bulkeley, H. (2004). Transnational networks and global environmental governance, the cities for climate protection program. *International Studies Quarterly, 48*(2), 471–493.

Bhalla, A. S. (Ed.). (1992). *Small and medium enterprises: Technology policies and options.* London: Intermediate Technology Publications.

Bhata, A. (1999). *The status of Ethiopian local content development: An overview of Ethiopian websites.* UNECA.

Bianco, A. (2010, November 26). OnSmash, RapGodfathers websites seized by authorities. *MTV RapFix*. http://rapfix.mtv.com/2010/11/26/onsmash-rapgodfathers-websites-seized-by-authorities/

Blanck, P., Hill, E., Siegel, C. D., & Waterstone, M. (2004). *Disability civil rights law and policy*. St. Paul: Thomson/West Publishers.

Blum, S. C. (2008). What really is at stake with the FISA Amendments Act of 2008 and ideas for future surveillance reform. *BU Pub. Int. LJ, 18*, 269.

Bobbitt, P. (2002). *The shield of Achilles: War, peace, and the course of history* (Vol. 960). New York: Knopf.

Bockman, J., & Eyal, G. (2002). Eastern Europe as a laboratory for economic knowledge: The transnational roots of neoliberalism. *American Journal of Sociology, 108*, 310–352.

Böhmelt, T., Koubi, V., & Bernauer, T. (2014). Civil society participation in global governance: Insights from climate politics. *European Journal of Political Research, 53*(1), 18–36.

Boorstin, E. S. (2004). *Music sales in the age of file sharing*. Unpublished doctoral dissertation, Princeton University, Princeton.

Borking, J. J., & Raab, C. (2001). Laws, PETs and other technologies for privacy protection. *Journal of Information, Law and Technology, 1*, 1–14.

Bort, J. (2013, September 11). Marissa Mayer: 'It's treason' for Yahoo to disobey the NSA. *Business Insider*. Retrieved from http://www.businessinsider.com/marissa-mayer-its-treason-to-ignore-the-nsa-2013-9#ixzz3ACFMhyyU

Bortzmeyer, S. (n.d.). RFC 2826: IAB technical comment on the unique DNS root. *Mon Blog*. http://www.bortzmeyer.org/2826.html

Borzel, T. A., & Risse, T. (2005). Public-private partnerships: Effective and legitimate tools of international governance? In E. Grande & L. W. Pauly (Eds.), *Complex sovereignty: On the reconstitution of political authority in the twenty-first century*. Toronto: University of Toronto Press.

Bosker, B. (2011, February 2). Rojadirecta.org one of several sites SEIZED by U.S. authorities. *The Huffington Post*. Retrieved from http://www.huffingtonpost.com/2011/02/02/rojadirecta-org-seized_n_817458.html

Boudon, R. (1991). *La place du désordre: Critique des théories du changement social* (pp. 184–190). Paris: Presses Universitaires de France.

Bourcier, D. (2011). La sérendipité du droit. In D. Bourcier & P. Van Andel (Eds.), *La sérendipité, le hasard heureux* (pp. 173–183). Paris: Hermann.

Bowker, G. C., & Star, S. L. (2000). *Sorting things out: Classification and its consequences*. Cambridge, MA: MIT Press.

Bowker, G. C., Baker, K., Millerand, F., & Ribes, D. (2010). Toward information infrastructure studies: Ways of knowing in a networked environment. In J. Hunsinger, L. Klastrup, & M. Allen (Eds.), *International handbook of Internet research*. New York: Springer.

Braman, S. (2004). *The emergent global information policy regime*. Springer.

Braman, S. (2006). *Change of state: Information, policy, and power.* Cambridge, MA: MIT Press.

Braman, S. (2010). Internet policy. In M. Consalvo & C. Ess (Eds.), *The handbook of internet studies* (pp. 137–167). Malden: Wiley.

Braman, S. (2011, May). *Designing for instability: Internet architecture and constant change.* Paper presented at Media in Transition 7 (MIT7) unstable platforms: The promise and peril of transition. Cambridge, MA.

Braman, S. (2012a). Internationalization of the Internet by design: The first decade. *Global Media and Communication, 8*(1), 27–45.

Braman, S. (2012b). Privacy by design: Networked computing, 1969–1979. *New Media & Society, 14*(5), 798–814.

Breitmeier, H., Young, O. R., & Zürn, M. (2006). *Analyzing international environmental regimes. From case study to database.* Cambridge, MA: MIT Press.

Breindl, Y. (2009). *Internet use by transnational advocacy networks: A case study of the "no software patents" campaign.* Paper presented at the proceedings of the *WebSci'09: Society On-Line,* Athens.

Bricklin, D. (2001). The cornucopia of the commons. In A. Oram (Ed.), *Peer-to-peer: Harnessing the power of disruptive technologies* (pp. 59–63). Sebastopol: O'Reilly.

Bronznan, N. C. (2014, October 20). When U.S. companies help the NSA. *ProPublica.* Retrieved from http://www.propublica.org/podcast/item/podcast-when-u.s.-companies-help-the-nsa/

Brophy, P. (1999). Through the net to freedom: Information, the internet and human rights. *Journal of Information Science, 25,* 351–364.

Brousseau, E., & Marzouki, M. (2012). Old issues, new framings, uncertain implications. In E. Brousseau, M. Marzouki, & C. Méadel (Eds.), *Governance, regulation and powers on the internet* (pp. 368–397). Cambridge: Cambridge University Press.

Brousseau, E., Marzouki, M., & Méadel, C. (Eds.). (2012). *Governance, regulation, and powers on the internet.* Cambridge, UK: Cambridge University Press.

Brown, M. M. (1998, October 1). Speech at the Virtual Commonwealth Dialogue Session, Multimedia Asia 1998 conference [quoted in R. Sani (1998) 'Of opportunities and Challenges', *New Straits Times,* Kuala Lumpur.

Bygrave, L. A., & Bing, J. (Eds.). (2009). *Internet governance: Infrastructure and institutions.* Oxford: Oxford University Press.

Callaghy, T., & Ravenhill, J. (Eds.). (1993). *Hemmed in: Responses to Africa's economic decline.* New York: Columbia University Press.

Carbonnier, J. (1988). *Flexible droit: Pour une sociologie du droit sans rigueur.* Paris: Librairie générale de droit et de jurisprudence (LGDJ).

Cardoso, F. E. (2004). *We the peoples: Civil society, the United Nations and global governance.* Report of the Panel of Eminent Persons on United Nations-Civil Society Relations. *UN document UN A/58, 817.*

Carpenter, C. (2007). Setting the advocacy agenda: Theorizing issue emergence and nonemergence in transnational advocacy networks. *International Studies Quarterly, 51*, 99–120.

Carte, T. A., Chidambaram, L., & Becker, A. (2006). Emergent leadership in self-managed virtual teams. *Group Decision and Negotiation, 15*(4), 323–343.

Castells, M. (1996, second edition, 2009). *The rise of the network society, the information age: Economy, society and culture* (Vol. I). Malden/Oxford: Blackwell. ISBN 978-0-631-22140-1.

Castells, M. (1998). *The end of millennium* (Vol. 3). Cambridge, MA: Blackwell.

Castells, M. (1998, second edition, 2010). *End of Millennium, The information age: Economy, society and culture* (Vol. III). Malden/Oxford: Blackwell.

Castells, A. L. (2004). *Friction: An ethnography of global connection.* Princeton: Princeton University Press.

Castells, M. (1942, 2012). *Networks of outrage and hope: Social movements in the internet age.* Malden/Cambridge: Polity Press.

Castells, M. (2007). Communication, power and counter-power in the network society. *International Journal of Communication, 1*(1), 238–266.

Castells, M. (2009). *Communication power.* Oxford: Oxford University Press.

Castro, D. (2013). *How much will PRISM cost the U.S. cloud computing industry?* Washington, DC: The Information Technology & Innovation Foundation.

Cavoukian, A. (2006). *The 7 foundational principles: Implementation and mapping of fair information practices.* Toronto: Information and Privacy Commissioner of Ontario Retrieved from https://www.privacyassociation. org/media/presentations/11Summit/RealitiesHO1.pdf.

Cavoukian, A. (2010). Privacy by design: The definitive workshop. A foreword by Ann Cavoukian, Ph. D. *Identity in the Information Society, 3*(2), 247–251.

Cavoukian, A. (2012). *Privacy by design: Report of the Information & Privacy Commissioner of Ontario, Canada.* Toronto: Information and Privacy Commissioner of Ontario.

Celik, A. P. (Ed.). (2007). *Foundations of the Global Alliance for ICT and Development* (Vol. 1). New York: United Nations Publications.

Cerf, V. G., & Kahn, R. E. (1974). A protocol for packet network interconnection. *IEEE Transactions on Communication Technology, COM-22*(V 5), 627–641.

Center for Democracy & Technology. (2009). *Analysis of S. 773, Cybersecurity Act of 2009. Center for Democracy & Technology.* Washington, DC: Center for Democracy & Technology Retrieved from: https://www.cdt.org/security/20090511_rocksnowe_analysis.pdf.

Center for Democracy & Technology. (2010). *Analysis of S. 773, Cybersecurity Act of 2009.* Washington, DC: Center for Democracy & Technology Retrieved from https://www.cdt.org/security/20090511_rocksnowe_analysis.pdf.

Center for Democracy & Technology. (2011, November 15). *Growing chorus of opposition to 'Stop Online Piracy Act'.* Washington, DC: Center for Democracy & Technology.

Center for International and Strategic Affairs. (1983). *International regimes*. Ithaca: Cornell University Press.

Chadwick, A., & Howard, P. N. (Eds.). (2010). *Routledge handbook of Internet politics*. London: Taylor & Francis.

Chan, S. (2008). Cross-cultural civility in global civil society: Transnational cooperation in Chinese NGOs. *Global Networks, 8*, 232–252.

Chander, A., & Le, U. P. (2014, April). Breaking the Web: Data localization vs. the global Internet. *UC Davis Legal Studies Research Paper Series 378*.

Checkel, J. (2001). Why comply? Social learning and European identity change. *International Organization, 55*(3), 553–588.

Chengetai, M. (2008). The Internet Governance Forum: Its development, function and future. In W. Benedek, V. Bauer, & M. Kettemann (Eds.), *Internet governance and the information society: Global perspectives and European dimensions* (pp. 63–77). Utrecht: Eleven International Publishing.

Cheniti, T. (2009). *Global Internet governance in practice: Mundane encounters and multiple enactments*. Unpublished doctoral dissertation, University of Oxford, Oxford.

Cieply, M. (2010, June 30). 9 domain names seized in fight against Internet theft. Media Decoder. *The New York Times*. Retrieved from http://mediadecoder.blogs.nytimes.com/2010/06/30/in-anti-theft-effort-officials-seize-9-domain-names

Cisco, I. (2012). *Cisco visual networking index: Forecast and methodology, 2011–2016*. CISCO White paper, 2011–2016.

Civil Contingencies Act. (2004). London: The Parliament of the United Kingdom. Retrieved from http://www.legislation.gov.uk/ukpga/2004/36/contents

Civil Society Internet Governance Caucus. (n.d.). IGC governance mailing list. *Individual posting*.

Claburn, T. (2011, February 18). ICE Confirms Inadvertent Web Site Seizures. *InformationWeek*. Retrieved from http://www.informationweek.com/news/security/vulnerabilities/229218959

Clark, A. M., Friedman, E. J., & Hochstetler, K. (1998). The sovereign limits of global civil society: A comparison of NGO participation in UN world conferences on the environment, human rights, and women. *World Politics, 51*(1), 1–35.

Clark, D. (1998). Powerline communications: Finally ready for prime time? *IEEE Internet Computing, 2*(1), 10–11.

Cleaver, F. (2002). Reinventing institutions: Bricolage and the social embeddedness of natural resource management. *European Journal of Development Research, 14*(2), 11.

CNN. (2010, June 20). *Transcript: State of the Union with Candy Crowley*. Interviews with Senators Lieberman, Murkowski, Feinstein and Lugar. Retrieved from http://transcripts.cnn.com/TRANSCRIPTS/1006/20/sotu.01.html

Cocotas, A. (2013, May 8). The Facebook advertising ecosystem explained. *Business Insider*. Retrieved from http://www.businessinsider.com.au/explaining-facebooks-ad-products-2013-5

Cogburn, D. L. (1996). Bold proposals endorsed by information society conference. I-Ways.

Cogburn, D. L. (1998a). Globilization and state autonomy in the information age: Telecommunications sector restructuring in South Africa. *Journal of International Affairs, 51*(2), 583–604.

Cogburn, D. L. (1998b). *Global electronic commerce in Africa?: Contribution towards a way forward—A concept paper in support of the African Information Society Initiative.* Geneva: International Telecommunication Union.

Cogburn, D. L. (2000). Globalization and human capacity in the knowledge economy: Understanding geographically distributed collaborative learning between developed and developing countries. In *Globalization and lifelong learning: Critical perspectives.* Mahwah: Lawrence Erlbaum Associates.

Cogburn, D. L. (2001). *Global governance in cyberspace (or did e-commerce kill the net?).* Paper presented at the 2001 Annual Meeting of the International Studies Association, Chicago.

Cogburn, D. L., Zhang, L., & Khothule, M. (2002). *Going global, locally: The socio-technical influences on performance in distributed collaborative learning teams,* ACM international conference proceedings series.

Cogburn, D. L. (2003a). Governing global information and communications policy: Emergent regime formation and the impact on Africa. *Telecommunications Policy, 27,* 135–153.

Cogburn, D. L. (2003b). HCI in the so-called developing world: What's in it for everyone. *Interactions, 10*(2), 80–87.

Cogburn, D. L., & Zhang, L. (2004). Still going global, locally: The impact of team mode in a distributed collaborative learning environment (Revised, extended, and updated version of 2003 paper). *IADIS International Journal on WWW/Internet, 1*(2).

Cogburn, D. L. (2004a). Elite decision-making and epistemic communities: Implications for global information policy. In S. Braman (Ed.), *The emergent global information policy regime.* Houndsmills: Palgrave Macmillan.

Cogburn, D. L. (2004b). Global internet governance: Building human capacity through geographically distributed policy collaboratories. In *Internet governance* (pp. 299–305). Geneva: International Telecommunication Union.

Cogburn, D. L. (2004c). Diversity matters, even at a distance: Evaluating the impact of computer mediated communication on civil society participation in the World Summit on Information Society. *Information Technology and International Development, 1*(4), 15–40.

Cogburn, D. L. (2005a). Diversity matters, even at a distance: Evaluating the impact of computer-mediated communication on Civil Society participation in the World Summit on the Information Society. *Information Technology and International Development, 1*(4), 15–40.

Cogburn, D. L. (2005b). Global idea networks: The Impact of transnational policy-actor networks and epistemic communities on perceived policy power in the World Summit on the Information Society. *International Studies*, 1–55.

Cogburn, D. L. (2005c, September). *Global internet governance: Who's winning, who's losing, and who cares?* Paper prepared for delivery at the 2005 Annual Meeting of the American Political Science Association, Washington, DC.

Cogburn, D. L. (2005d). Partners or pawns? The impact of elite decision-making and epistemic communities in global information policy on developing countries and transnational civil society. *Knowledge, Technology & Policy, 18*(2), 52–82 American Political Science Association, Washington, DC.

Cogburn, D. L. (2006a). Emergent regime formation for the information society and the impact on Africa. In A. D'Costa (Ed.), *The new economy in development*. New York: Palgrave.

Cogburn, D. L. (2006b). Inclusive Internet governance: Enhancing multistakeholder participation through geographically distributed policy collaboratories. In J. Kurbalija & V. Katrandjiev (Eds.), *Global multistakeholder diplomacy*. Malta/Geneva: DiploFoundation.

Cogburn, D. L. (2008). Enabling effective multistakeholder participation in global Internet governance through accessible cyberinfrastructure. In A. Chadwick & P. N. Howard (Eds.), *The handbook of Internet politics*. London: Routledge.

Cogburn, D. L. (2010, September). *Using computer assisted content analysis to explore multistakeholder participation in the UN Internet Governance Forum*. Presentation at the American Political Science Association, Washington, DC.

Cogburn, D. L. (2013). *Ways of the Wicked (WCIT): Understanding the relationship between transnational NGO policy preferences and global conference outcomes through the analysis of large-scale textual data*. Presentation at the American Political Science Association Annual Meeting, Chicago.

Cogburn, D. L. (2016). *Accessibility in global governance: The (in)visibility of persons with disabilities*. Washington, DC: Institute on Disability and Public Policy.

Cogburn, D. L. (Forthcoming). Globalization and human capacity in the knowledge economy: Understanding geographically distributed collaborative learning between developed and developing countries. In D. Mulenga (Ed.), *Globalization and lifelong learning: Critical perspectives*. Mahwah: Lawrence Erlbaum Associates.

Cogburn, D. L., & Addom, B. K. (2006, March 22). *In whose name?: A multimodal exploration of transnational deliberative democratic practices in multistakeholder global information policy formulation processes*. Paper presented at the Annual Meeting of the International Studies Association, San Diego.

Cogburn, D. L., & Foss, C. P. (1996, May 14). Information and communications for development: Nationalism, regionalism, and globalism in building the global information society: GIIC report on the Global Information Society and Development Forum, Midrand.

Cogburn, D. L., & Hafkin, N. J. (Eds.). (1997). *Meeting the challenges of building national information and communications infrastructure in Africa with public and private sector cooperation.* Washington, DC: CSIS and the United Nations Economic Commission for Africa.

Cogburn, D. L., & Kurup, D. R. (2006, April 13). Tech U: The world is our campus. *Network Computing,* pp. 57–63.

Cogburn, D. L., & Levinson, N. S. (2003a). U.S.–Africa virtual collaboration in globalization studies: Success factors for complex, cross-national learning teams. *International Studies Perspectives,* 4(1), 34–51. doi:10.1111/1528-3577.04103.

Cogburn, D. L., & Levinson, N. (2008). Teaching globalization, globally: A 7-year case study of South Africa—U.S. virtual teams. *Information Technologies and International Development,* 4(3), 75–88.

Cogburn, D. L., Zhang, L., & Khothule, M. (2002). Going global, locally: The socio-technical influences on performance in distributed collaborative learning teams. *ACM International Conference Proceedings Series,* pp 52–64.

Cogburn, D. L., Mueller, M., McKnight, L., Klein, H., & Mathiason, J. (2005a). The US role in global internet governance. *IEEE Communications Magazine,* 43(12), 12–14.

Cogburn, D. L., Johnsen, J. F., & Bhattacharyya, S. (2008a). Distributed deliberative citizens: Exploring the impact of cyberinfrastructure on transnational civil society participation in global ICT policy processes. *International Journal of Media & Cultural Politics,* 4(1), 27–49.

Cogburn, D. L., Pagé, C. M., & Yang, S.-U. (2008b). Perceived policy power at the World Summit on the Information Society: How epistemic communities and global policy networks matter. Paper presented at the NCA, San Diego.

Cogburn, D. L., Zakaria, N., Padovano, S., & Clincy, A. (2012). *Understanding transnational NGO (TANGO) decision-making and participation in global governance processes using computational analysis of large-scale textual data.* Presentation for the Annual Meeting of the American Political Science Association, New Orleans.

Cohen, J. E. (1995). A right to read anonymously: A closer look at copyright management in cyberspace. *Connecticut Law Review, 28,* 981.

Coldewey, D. (2010, November 29). Peter Sunde seconds the idea of an alternative root DNS. *TechCrunch.* Retrieved from http://techcrunch.com/2010/11/29/peter-sunde-seconds-the-idea-of-an-alternative-root-dns/

Collins, S. (2011, February 17). *Statement on Introduction of Cyber Security and Internet Freedom Act of 2011.* United States Senate: Washington DC. Retrieved from http://politechbot.com/docs/collins.cybersecurity.bill.floor.021711.txt

Comitê Gestor da Internet no Brasil (CGI.br). (n.d.). *About the CGI.br.* São Paulo: CGI.br.

Communications Act of 2003 [U.K.]. London: The Parliament of the United Kingdom. Retrieved from http://www.legislation.gov.uk/ukpga/2003/21/contents

Connors, M. (1997). *The race to the intelligent state: Charting the global information economy into the 21st century*. Oxford: Capstone.

Cooper, D. (2014). Brazil enacts 'Marco Civil' Internet civil rights bill. *Inside Privacy*. Retrieved from http://www.insideprivacy.com/international/brazil-enacts-marco-civil-internet-civil-rights-bill/

Coppel, J. (2000). E-Commerce: Impacts and Policy Challenges. Retrieved from

Council of Europe. (CoE). (2003, June 24). *Political message from the Committee of Ministers to the World Summit on the Information Society (WSIS.)* Council of Europe, Strasbourg.

Council of Europe. (CoE). (2004, December 15). Specific terms of reference of the Multidisciplinary Ad-Hoc Committee of Experts on the Information Society (CAHSI). Council of Europe, Strasbourg. Retrieved from https://wcd.coe.int/ViewDoc.jsp?id=803697

Council of Europe. (CoE). (2005, May 13). Declaration of the Committee of Ministers on human rights and the rule of law in the Information Society. Council of Europe, Strasbourg. Retrieved from https://wcd.coe.int/ViewDoc.jsp?id=849061

Council of Europe. (CoE). (2012, March 15). Internet governance: Council of Europe Strategy 2012–2015. CoE Committee of Ministers. Strasbourg. http://www.coe.int/t/dghl/cooperation/economiccrime/cybercrime/Documents/Internet%20Governance%20Strategy/Internet%20Governance%20Strategy%202012%20-%202015.pdf

Council of Europe. (CoE). (n.d.a). Integrated project "Making democratic institutions work" (2002–2004). Council of Europe, Strasbourg. Retrieved from http://www.coe.int/t/dgap/democracy/activities/previous%20projects/default_EN.asp

Council of Europe. (CoE). (n.d.b). Good governance in the information society. *Council of Europe*. Strasbourg. Retrieved from http://www.coe.int/t/dgap/democracy/Activities/GGIS/Default_en.asp

Council of Europe. (CoE). (n.d.c). Public participation in Internet governance. Council of Europe. Strasbourg. Retrieved from http://www.coe.int/t/dgap/democracy/Activities/GGIS/Public_participation_internet_governance/Default_en.asp

Country profile: China. (n.d.). *OpenNet Initiative*. Ottawa: Citizen Lab at the Munk School of Global Affairs, University of Toronto/The Berkman Center for Internet & Society at Harvard University/The SecDev Group.

Cowhey, P. F. (1990). The international telecommunications regime: The political roots of regimes for high technology. *International organization, 44*(02), 169–199.

Cowhey, P. F. (1990). The international telecommunications regime: The political roots of regimes for high technology. *International Organization, 45,* 169–199.

Cowhey, P. F. (1993). Domestic institutions and the credibility of international commitment: Japan and the United States. *International organization, 47*(02), 299–326.

Cowie, J. (2011, November). Could it happen in your country? *Dyn Research [Company Website]*. Retrieved from http://research.dyn.com/2012/11/could-it-happen-in-your-countr/

Cox, K. (Ed.). (1997). *Spaces of globalization: Reasserting the power of the local*. New York: The Guilford Press.

Crawford, S. (1983). The origin and development of a concept: The information society. *Bulletin of the Medical Library Association, 71*(4), 380–385.

Creech, H., & Willard, T. (2001). *Strategic intentions: Managing knowledge networks for sustainable development*. Winnipeg: International Institute for Sustainable Development.

Crocker, S., Dagon, D., Kaminsky, D., McPherson, D. D., & Vixie, P. (2011). Security and other technical concerns raised by the DNS filtering requirements in the PROTECT IP Bill [White paper]. *Domain Incite*. Retrieved from http://domainincite.com/docs/PROTECT-IP-Technical-Whitepaper-Final.pdf

Cybersecurity Act of 2010. S.773. 111th Congress (2009–2010). Retrieved from https://www.congress.gov/bill/111th-congress/senate-bill/773

Cybersecurity and Internet Freedom Act of 2011. S.413. 112th Congress (2011–2012). Retrieved from http://thomas.loc.gov/cgi-bin/bdquery/z?d112:SN00413

D'Onfro, J. (2014, October 8). Google chairman Eric Schmidt: Government surveillance is going to 'end up breaking the Internet.' *Business Insider*. http://www.businessinsider.com/eric-schmidt-government-surveillance-will-end-up-breaking-the-internet-2014-10

Daft, R. L., & Lengel, R. H. (1986). Organizational information requirements, media richness and structural design. *Management Science, 32*(5), 554–571.

Danaher, B., Smith, M., Telang, R., & Chen, S. (2012). The effect of graduated response anti-piracy laws on music sales: Evidence from an event study in France. *The Journal of Industrial Economics, 62*(3), 541–553.

Dann, G. E., & Haddow, N. (2008). Just doing business or doing just business: Google, Microsoft, Yahoo! and the business of censoring China's Internet. *Journal of Business Ethics, 79*(3), 219–234.

de Carbonnel, A. (2014). Putin plays cat and mouse with Russian online critics. *Reuters*. Retrieved from http://www.reuters.com/article/2014/09/04/russia-internet-idUSL6N0PY2GA20140904.

Dehghan, S. K. (2012, January 5). Iran clamps down on internet use. *The Guardian*. Retrieved from http://www.theguardian.com/world/2012/jan/05/iran-clamps-down-internet-use

Deibert, R. J. (1998). Altered worlds: Social forces in the hypermedia environment. In C. J. Alexander & L. A. Pal (Eds.), *Digital democracy: Policy and politics in the wired world* (pp. 23–43). Toronto: Oxford University Press.

Deibert, R. J. (2000). International plug'n play? Citizen activism, the internet, and global public policy. *International Studies Perspectives, 1*(3), 255–272.

Deibert, R. J. (2013). *Black code: Inside the battle for cyberspace.* Toronto: McClelland & Stewart.

Deibert, R., Palfrey, J., Rohozinski, R., & Zittrain, J. (2010). *Access controlled: The shaping of power, rights, and rule in cyberspace.* Cambridge, MA: MIT Press.

Dejean S., Pénard T., & Suire, R. (2010). Une première évaluation des effets de la loi Hadopi sur les pratiques des Internautes français. Rennes: Université de Rennes. Laboratoire M@rsouin. Retrieved from http://www.marsouin.org/ IMG/pdf/NoteHadopix.pdf

DeNardis, L. (2009). *Protocol politics: The globalization of Internet governance.* Cambridge, MA: MIT Press.

DeNardis, L. (2010, September). The privatization of Internet governance. Yale Information Society Project Working Paper Draft. Paper presented at Fifth Annual GigaNet Symposium, Vilnius. Retrieved from: http://api.ning.com/ files/8q30Xud1XrmD6Sd5rOiSolcw3agdQi5NNoWZrQGmOIpKc0fdqfKN 0Ax5Z8ZypNexdCwBicqDKcADrRU5hs4ZQjBy0RPTgBmK/ DENARDISThePrivitizationofInternetGovernance.pdf

DeNardis, L. (2012). Hidden levers of Internet control: An infrastructure-based theory of Internet governance. *Journal of Information, Communication & Society, 15*(5), 720–738.

DeNardis, L. (2013). The emerging field of Internet governance. In W. Dutton (Ed.), *Oxford handbook of internet studies.* Oxford: Oxford University Press.

DeNardis, L. (2014). *The global war for Internet governance.* New Haven: Yale University Press.

DeNardis, D., & Raymond, M. (2013, November 14). Thinking clearly about multistakeholder Internet governance. *Mark, thinking clearly about multistakeholder Internet governance.*

Denson, G. R. (2011, November 11). Courbet's *Origin of the world* still too scandalous for media-savvy *Facebook! The Huffington Post.* Retrieved from http:// www.huffingtonpost.com/g-roger-denson/courbets-1866-the-origin-_b_ 1087604.html

Department of Homeland Security (U.S.). (2013). What is critical infrastructure?. Washington, DC. http://www.dhs.gov/what-critical-infrastructure.

Department of Transportation (U.S.). (2011, January 3). Federal motor vehicle safety standard; Engine control module speed limiter device, 76 *Federal Register, 78.*

Deuze, M. (2006). Participation, remediation, bricolage: Considering principal components of a digital culture. *The Information Society, 22*(2), 63–75.

Dimitrov, R. S. (2003). Knowledge, power, and interests in environmental regime formation. *International Studies Quarterly, 47*(1), 123–150.

Dobusch, L., & Schussler, E. (2014). Copyright reform and business model innovation: Regulatory propaganda at German music industry conferences. *Technological Forecasting and Social Change, 83*, 24–39.

Dosi, G. (1984). *Technical change and industrial transformation.* London: Macmillan.

Dou, D., Li, J., Qin, H., Kim, S., & Zhong, S. (2007). Understanding and utilizing the hierarchy of abnormal BGP events. *Proceedings of the Seventh Siam International Conference on Data Mining* (pp. 467–472). doi:10.1.1.116.7352.

Drake, W. (1988). WATTC-88: Restructuring the international telecommunication regulations. *Telecommunications Policy, 12,* 217–233.

Drake, W. (1989). The CCITT: Time for reform. In *Reforming the global network: The 1989 ITU plenipotentiary conference* (pp. 28–43). London: International Institute of Communications.

Drake, W. J. (1994). Asymmetric deregulation and the transformation of the international telecommunications regime. In E. M. Noam & G. Pogorel (Eds.), *Asymmetric deregulation: The dynamics of telecommunications Policies in Europe and the United States* (pp. 137–203). Norwood: Ablex Pub. Co.

Drake, W. J. (2000). The rise and decline of the international telecommunication regime. In C. T. Marsden (Ed.), *Regulating the global information society* (pp. 124–177). London: Routledge.

Drake, W., & Kalypso, N. (1992). Ideas, interests and institutionalization: 'Trade in services' and the Uruguay round. In P. Haas (Ed.), Knowledge, power and international policy coordination [Special issue]. *International Organization, 45,* 37–100.

Drezner, D. W. (2004). The global governance of the Internet: Bringing the state back in. *Political Science Quarterly, 119*(3), 477–498.

Drizin, M. J. (2003, August). The more things change, the more things stay the same... *Stakeholder Power: Monthly Insights on Building Business Loyalty.* http://www.stakeholderpower.com/story.cfm?article_id=551

Drucker, P. F. (1970). *Technology management and society.* London: Heinemann.

Dunn, D. H. (Ed.). (1996). *Diplomacy at the highest level: The evolution of international summitry.* New York: Macmillan Press.

Economist Intelligence Unit (EIU). (2011, March 1). Democracy index 2011. *Democracy under stress.* Retrieved from http://www.eiu.com/public/topical_report.aspx?campaignid=DemocracyIndex2011

Edwards, K. (2001a). *Epistemic communities, situated learning and open source software development.* Epistemic cultures and the practice of interdisciplinarity, Trondheim.

Eger, J. (1996, June 4–6). Asia in the global information economy: The rise of region states, the role of telecommunications. Paper presented at the *International conference on 'Satellite and Cable Television in Chinese and Asian regions',* Taipei.

Elkin-Koren, N. (2006). Making technology visible: Liability of Internet service providers for peer-to-peer traffic. *New York University Journal of Legislation & Public Policy, 9*(15), 15–76.

Ellis, J., Arnone, M., Levinson, N., & Cogburn, D. L. (2014, January). Evaluating the role of face-to-face residencies in cross-national, accessible cyberlearning. In *2014 47th Hawaii International Conference on System Sciences* (pp. 62–71). IEEE.

Epstein, D. (2013). The making of information governance institutions. *Journal of Information Technology, 28*(2), 137–149.

Essers, L. (2010). Facebook sued over app center data sharing in Germany. *PCWorld*. Retrieved from http://www.pcworld.com/article/2018981/facebook-sued-over-app-center-data-sharing-in-germany.html

European Commission. (2012, January 25). General data protection regulation. Brussels.

European Digital Rights. (EDRi). (2007). EDRi campaign on CoE recommendation failing to uphold freedom of expression. EDRi. Brussels. Retrieved from https://edri.org/coerec200711/

Evans, P. (2000). Counter-hegemonic globalization: Transnational networks as political tools for fighting marginalization. *Contemporary Sociology, 29*(1), 230–241.

Evans, P. (2000a). Fighting marginalization with transnational networks: Counter-hegemonic globalization. *Contemporary Sociology, 29*(1), 230–241. Retrieved from http://www.jstor.org/stable/2654947

Evans, P. (2000b). Fighting marginalization with transnational networks: Counter-hegemonic globalization. *Contemporary Sociology, 29*(1), 230–241. Retrieved from http://www.jstor.org/stable/2654947

Executive Office of the President of the U.S. (2009a). *Cyberspace policy review. Assuring a trusted and resilient information and communications infrastructure*. Washington, DC. Retrieved from https://www.whitehouse.gov/assets/documents/Cyberspace_Policy_Review_final.pdf

Executive Office of the President of the U.S. (2009b, May 29). Remarks by the president on securing our nation's cyber infrastructure. Office of the Press Secretary, Executive Office of the President. Washington, DC. Retrieved from http://www.whitehouse.gov/the_press_office/Remarks-by-the-President-on-Securing-Our-Nations-Cyber-Infrastructure.

Ezell, S., Atkinson, R., & Wein, M. (2013, September 25). Localization barriers to trade: Threat to the global innovation economy. Washington, DC: Information Technology and Innovation Foundation.

Farrell, H. (2003). Constructing the international foundations of e-commerce— The EU-US Safe Harbor Arrangement. *International Organization, 57*(2), 277–306.

Farrell, N. (2009, September 3). Australia's internet goes down for an hour. *The Inquirer*, London. Retrieved from http://www.theinquirer.net/inquirer/news/1532262/australia-internet-goes-hour

Fayette, A. (2010, June 24). U.S. "kill switch": The ripple effect. OpenNet Initiative. Retrieved from https://opennet.net/blog/2010/06/us-kill-switch-the-ripple-effect

Feiock, R. C. (2013). The institutional collective action framework. *Policy Studies Journal, 41*(3), 397–425.

Fernback, J., & Papacharissi, Z. (2007). Online privacy as legal safeguard: The relationship among consumer, online portal, and privacy policies. *New Media & Society, 9*(5), 715–734.

Finholt, T. (2002a). Collaboratories: Science over the internet. In *AAAS science and technology policy yearbook* (339–344). Washington, DC: American Association for the Advancement of Science.

Finholt, T. (2002b). Collaboratories. *Annual Review of Information Science and Technology American Society for Information Science, 36,* 74–107.

Finholt, T. A., & Olson, G. M. (1997). From laboratories to collaboratories: A new organizational form for scientific collaboration. *Psychological Science, 8,* 28–36.

Fischer, L. R., & Schaffer, K. B. (1993). Older volunteers: Enlisting the talent.

Fisk, N. W. (2009). *Understanding online piracy: The truth about illegal file sharing.* Santa Barbara: Praeger Publishers.

Flichy, P. (2007). *The internet imaginaire.* Cambridge, MA: MIT Press.

Florida, R., & Kenney, M. (1991). Transplanted organizations: The transfer of Japanese industrial organization to the US. *American Sociological Review, 56,* 381–398.

Flyverbom, M. (2011). *The power of networks: Organizing the global politics of the internet.* Cheltenham: Edward Elgar Publishing.

Fontanella-Khan, J. (2014, April 10). Microsoft cloud system wins EU privacy regulators' approval. *The Financial Times.* Retrieved from: http://www.ft.com/cms/s/0/aeeb7350-c0a1-11e3-a74d-00144feabdc0.html#axzz3a90kX99O.

Forge, S. (1995). *The consequences of current telecommunications trends for the competitiveness of developing countries.* Washington, DC: World Bank.

Foucault, M. (1973). *The order of things: An archeology of the human sciences.* New York: Vintage.

Franklin, M. I. (2013). *Digital dilemmas: Power, resistance, and the Internet.* Oxford: Oxford University Press.

Freeman, C. (1982). *The economics of industrial innovation.* London: Pinter.

Freeman, C. (1994a). The diffusion of information and communication technology in the world economy in the 1990's. In R. Mansell (Ed.), *The management of information and communication technologies: Emerging patterns of control* (pp. 8–41). London: Aslib.

Freeman, C. (1996). The factory of the future and the productivity paradox. In W. Dutton (Ed.), *Information and communication technologies* (pp. 123–141). Oxford: Oxford University Press.

Freiden, R. (1996). *International telecommunications handbook.* Boston: Artech House.

Fricker, R., & Schonlau, M. (2002). Advantages and disadvantages of Internet research surveys: Evidence from the literature. *Field Methods, 14*(4), 347–367 http://www.schonlau.net/publication/02fieldmethods.pdf.

Friedman, E. J. (2005). The reality of virtual reality: The internet and gender equality advocacy in Latin America. *Latin American Politics and Society, 47,* 1–34.

Fuchs, C. (2010). Web 2.0, prosumption, and surveillance. *Surveillance & Society, 8*(3), 288–309.

Fuchs, C. (2012). The political economy of privacy on Facebook. *Television & New Media, 13*(2), 139–159.

Fuller, M. (Ed.). (2008). *Software studies: A lexicon.* Cambridge, MA: MIT Press.

GAID. (2007). *Progress report 2006: Global alliance for information and communication technologies and development.* GAID.

Gallagher, S. (2014, September 6). When NSA and FBI call for surveillance takeout, these companies deliver. *Ars Technica.* Retrieved from http://arstechnica.com/tech-policy/2014/09/when-nsa-and-fbi-call-for-surveillance-takeout-these-companies-deliver/

Geere, D. (2010, December 10). Peter Sunde starts peer-to-peer DNS system. *Wired Magazine.* Retrieved from http://www.wired.co.uk/news/archive/2010-12/02/peter-sunde-p2p-dns

Geist, M. A. (2001). Is there a there there? Toward greater certainty for Internet jurisdiction. *Berkeley Technology Law Journal, 16,* 1345.

Gellman, B. (2014, August 15). U.S. firm helped the spyware industry build a potent digital weapon for sale overseas. *The Washington Post.* http://www.washingtonpost.com/world/national-security/spyware-tools-allow-buyers-to-slip-malicious-code-into-youtube-videos-microsoft-pages/2014/08/15/31c5696c-249c-11e4-8593-da634b334390_story.html

Gelman, L. H. (2000, January 1). *Talking politics: The role of conference diplomacy and non-state actors in the global regime process.* Doctoral dissertation. Retrieved from ProQuest. (Paper AAI9989593).

Gersick, C. J. (1988). Time and transition in work teams: Toward a new model of group development. *Academy of Management journal, 31*(1), 9–41.

Giacomello, G. (2005). *National governments and control of the Internet: A digital challenge.* London: Routledge.

Giliker, P. (2010). *Vicarious liability in tort: A comparative perspective* (Vol. 69). Cambridge, UK: Cambridge University Press.

Gillespie, T. (2014). The relevance of algorithms. In T. Gillespie, P. Boczkowski, & K. Foot (Eds.), *Media technologies.* Cambridge, MA: MIT Press.

Gilson, J. (2011). Transnational advocacy: New spaces, new voices. *Alternatives: Global, Local, Political, 36*(4), 288–306.

Gilson, J. (2013). Communicating practice in transnational advocacy: Examples from Southeast Asia. *Globalizations, 10*(4), 571–585.

Ginsburg, J. C. (2002). From having copies to experiencing works: The development of an access right in US copyright law. *Journal of the Copyright Society of the USA, 50,* 113.

Glanz, J., & Markoff, J. (2011, June 12). U.S. underwrites Internet detour around censors. *The New York Times*. Retrieved from http://www.nytimes.com/2011/06/12/world/12internet.html

Global Advisory Committee. (n.d.). GAC observers. The Internet Corporation for Assigned Names and Numbers (ICANN).

Global Contract Foundation. (2003, September 14–26). *Does input lead to impact?: How governments treated civil society proposals in drafting the 21 September 2003 Draft Declaration*. Distributed at the Third WSIS Preparatory Committee Meeting, Geneva.

Goffman, E. (1959). *The presentation of self in everyday life*. New York: Doubleday.

Goldman, E. (2012, July 18). Celebrating (?) the six-month anniversary of SOPA's demise. *Forbes.com*. Retrieved from http://www.forbes.com/sites/ericgoldman/2012/07/18/celebrating-the-six-month-anniversary-of-sopas-demise/

Goldsmith, J., & Wu, T. (2006). *Who controls the Internet? Illusions of a borderless world*. Oxford: Oxford University Press.

Google, Inc. (2014). *Google transparency report*. Menlo Park. Retrieved from http://www.google.com/transparencyreport/userdatarequests/countries/

Google, Inc. (n.d.). *Google ideas*. Menlo Park. Retrieved from http://www.google.com/ideas/about/

Gourevitch, P. (1978). The second image reversed: The international sources of domestic politics. *International Organization, 32*(4), 881–912. doi: 10.1017/S002081830003201X.

Gourevitch, P. (1978a). The international system and regime formation. *Comparative Politics, 10*, 419–438.

Gourevitch, P. (1978b). The second image reversed: The international sources of domestic politics. *International Organization, 32*, 881–911.

Gourevitch, P. (1986). *Politics in hard times: Comparative responses to international economic crisis*. New York: Cornell University.

Granovetter, M. (1985). Economic action and social structure: The problem of embeddedness. *American journal of sociology, 91*, 481–510.

Greenwald, G. (2013). NSA Prism program taps in to user data of Apple, Google and others. *The Guardian*. Retrieved from http://www.theguardian.com/world/2013/jun/06/us-tech-giants-nsa-data

Greenwald, G. (2014). *No place to hide: Edward Snowden, the NSA, and the US surveillance state*. New York: Metropolitan Books.

Greenwald, G., MacAskill, E., Poitras, L., Ackerman, S., & Rushe, D. (2013, July 12). Microsoft handed the NSA access to encrypted messages. *The Guardian*. Retrieved from http://www.theguardian.com/world/2013/jul/11/microsoft-nsa-collaboration-user-data

Groenewald, M., & Lehlokoe, D. (1991). Towards an electronic commerce policy for South Africa. Proceedings of the INET'99, Annual Meeting of the Internet Society. http://www.isoc.org/inet99/1g/1g_4.htm

Gupta, D. (2008). Nationalism across borders: Transnational nationalist advocacy in the European Union. *Comparative European Politics, 6*, 61–80.

Gupta, J., & Pahl-Wostl, C. (2013). Editorial on global water governance. *Ecology and Society, 18*(4), 54.

Guthrie, D. (2005). Information technology and state capacity in China. In R. Latham & S. Sassen (Eds.), *Digital formations: IT and new architectures in the global realm*. Princeton: Princeton University Press.

Haas, E. B. (1980). Why collaborate? Issue linkage and international regimes. *World Politics, 32*, 367–368.

Haas, E. B. (1990). *When knowledge is power: Three models of change in international organizations*. Berkeley: University of California Press.

Haas, P. M. (1992). Introduction: Epistemic communities and international policy coordination. *International organization, 46*, 1–35.

Haas, E. B., Williams, M. P. T., & Babai, D. (1977). *Scientists and world order: The uses of technical knowledge in international organizations*. Berkeley: University of California Press.

Hall, E. T. (1976). *Beyond culture*. Garden City: Anchor Books/Doubleday.

Halzack, S. (2012, January 20). PIPA/SOPA debate: Where do the GOP candidates stand? *The Washington Post*. Retrieved from http://www.washingtonpost.com/business/economy/pipasopa-debate-where-do-the-gop-candidates-stand/2012/01/20/gIQAQ0egDQ_story.html

Hamelink, C. J. (1986, August 25–30). *Information technology and the Third World*. Paper presented at the 15th Conference of the International Association for Mass Communication Research, New Delhi.

Hampson, R. (2013, June 11). Is Snowden a traitor or a public servant? *USA Today*. Retrieved from http://www.usatoday.com/story/news/nation/2013/06/10/snowden-leaks-nsa-privacy-terrorist/2408803/

Handel, M., & Herbsleb, J. D. (2002, November). What is *chat doing in the workplace?* In Proceedings of the 2002 ACM conference on Computer supported cooperative work, 1–10. ACM.

Hanegraaff, M. (2015). Transnational advocacy over time: Business and NGO mobilization at UN climate summits. *Global Environmental Politics, 15*(1), 82–104.

Hanna, N. (1991). The information technology revolution and economic development. *World Bank Discussion Papers*, No. 120, Washington, DC: World Bank.

Hanna, N., et al. (1996). The East Asian miracle and information technology. *World Bank Discussion Papers*, No. 326, Washington, DC: World Bank.

Hanseth, O., Aanestad, M., & Berg, M. (2004). Guest editors' introduction: Actor-network theory and information systems. What's so special? *Information Technology & People, 17*, 116–123.

Hardings, N. (2011, March 8). Could the UK government shut down the web? *The Independent*. Retrieved from http://www.independent.co.uk/life-style/

gadgets-and-tech/features/could-the-uk-government-shut-down-the-web-2235116.html

Hardy, C., Lawrence, T. B., & Grant, D. (2005). Discourse and collaboration: The role of conversations and collective identity. *Academy of Management Review, 30*(1), 58–77.

Harris, J. (1998). Globalization and the technological transformation of capitalism. *Race & Class, 40*(2/3), 21–34.

Hasenclever, A., Mayer, P., & Rittberger, V. (2000). *Is distributive justice a necessary condition for a high level of regime robustness?* Retrieved from http://www.uni-tuebingen.de/uni/spi/taps/tap36.htm

Haufler, V. (2001). *A public role for the private sector: Industry self-regulation in a global economy.* Washington, DC: Carnegie Endowment for International Peace.

Haute Autorité pour la Diffusion des œuvres et la Protection des droits d'auteur sur Internet. (HADOPI). (2011, May 18). *Hadopi, biens culturels et usages d'internet: pratiques et perceptions des internautes français. 2ème vague barométrique,* Paris. Retrieved from http://www.hadopi.fr/actualites/agenda/hadopi-biens-culturels-et-usages-d-internet-pratiques-et-perceptions

Haute Autorité pour la Diffusion des œuvres et la Protection des droits d'auteur sur Internet. (HADOPI). (2012). *HADOPI, 1 an ½ après son Lancement.* Paris. Retrieved from http://www.HADOPI.fr/sites/default/files/page/pdf/note17.pdf

Haywood, T. (1995). *Info-rich, Info-poor: Access and exchange in the Global Information Society.* London: Bowker-Saur.

Heeks, R. (1999). Information and communication technologies, poverty and development. *Working Paper* No. 5, IDPM, Manchester.

Heide, T. (2000). Copyright in the EU and US: What access-right. *Journal of the Copyright Society of the USA, 48,* 363.

Heinke, R., & Rafter, H. (1994, July). Rough justice in cyberspace: Liability on the electronic frontier, *Computer Law.*

Helberger, N., Huygen, A., & Van Eijk, N. (2009, February). Ups and downs: Economic and cultural effects of file sharing on music, film and games. *Culture and Science, Economic Affairs and Justice,* 2012-33.

Henry, L., Mohan, G., & Yanacopulos, H. (2004). Networks as transnational agents of development. *Third World Quarterly, 25,* 839–855.

Hertzman, C. P., Meagher, N., & McGrail, K. M. (2013). Privacy by design at population data BC: A case study describing the technical, administrative, and physical controls for privacy-sensitive secondary use of personal information for research in the public interest. *Journal of the American Medical Informatics Association, 20*(1), 25–28.

Herweijer, M., & Winter, H. B. (1995). Evaluation of legislation: Change or improvement? In W. J. M. Kickert & F. A. van Vught (Eds.), *Public policy & administration sciences in the Netherlands.* London: Prentice Hall.

Hildreth, P., Kimble, C., & Wright, P. (1998). *Computer mediated communications and international communities of practice.* Paper presented at the Proceedings of Ethicomp '98, Rotterdam.

Hill, J. F. (2014, May). *The growth of data localization post-Snowden: Analysis and recommendations for US policymakers and business leaders.* Paper presented at Conference on the Future of Cyber Governance of The Hague Institute for Global Justice, The Hague.

Hiller, J. (2002). *Internet law & policy.* Upper Saddle River: Prentice Hall.

Hirsch, D. D. (2014). In search of the Holy Grail: Achieving global privacy rules through sector-based codes of conduct. *Ohio State Law Journal, 74,* 1029.

Hodge, J., & Miller, J. (1996, October). Information technology in South Africa. Paper presented at the international workshop on Information Technology for Development, UNU/INTECH, Maastricht.

Hoepman, J. (2014). Privacy design strategies. In N. Cuppens-Boulahia, F. Cuppens, S. Jajodia, A. Abou El Kalam, & T. Sans (Eds.), *ICT systems security and privacy protection* (pp. 446–459). Berlin: Springer.

Hofstede, G. (1980). *Culture's consequences: International differences in work related values.* Beverly Hills: Sage.

Hofstede, G. (2001). *Culture's consequences: Comparing values, behaviors, institutions, and organizations across nations* (2nd ed.). Thousand Oaks: Sage.

Hofstede, G. (2002). Dimensions do not exist: A reply to Brendan McSweeney. *Human Relations, 55*(11), 1355–1361.

Hofstede, G. (2005). *Cultures and organizations: Software of the mind,* 2nd, revised, illustrated ed. New York: McGraw-Hill.

Hofstede, G., & Bond, M. H. (1988). The confucius connection: From cultural roots to economic growth. *Organizational Dynamics, 16*(4), 4–21.

Hollan, J., & Stornetta, S. (1992). *Beyond being there.* Paper presented at the proceedings of the SIGCHI conference on human factors in computing systems.

Holmqvist, M. (2004). Experiential learning processes of exploitation and exploration within and between organizations: An empirical study of product development. *Organization science, 15*(1), 70–81.

Holton, J. A. (2001). Building trust and collaboration in a virtual team. *Team Performance Management, 7*(3/4), 36–47.

Horvitz, R. (2013). *Geo-database management of white space vs. open spectrum.* Amsterdam: Open Spectrum Foundation.

Horwitz, R. B. (1991). *The irony of regulatory reform: The deregulation of American telecommunications.* New York: Oxford University Press on Demand.

Hosein, G. (2010). No hiding place. *Index on Censorship, 39*(1), 58–68.

Howard, P. N., & Hussain, M. M. (2013). *Democracy's fourth wave?: Digital media and the Arab Spring (Oxford studies in digital politics).* New York: Oxford University Press.

Howard, P., Agarwal, S., & Hussain, M. (2011). The dictators' digital dilemma: When do states disconnect their digital networks? *Issues in technology innovation* (Vol. 13). Washington, DC: Brookings Institution.

Hu, X. (2013, July 5). *Internet universality*. Presentation prepared for the Annenberg-Oxford Media Policy Summer Institute, Oxford. Retrieved from http://www.global.asc.upenn.edu/fileLibrary/PDFs/xianhong.pdf

Hüfner, K. (2009). WFUNA–World federation of United Nations associations. In *A concise encyclopedia of the United Nations* (pp. 856–856). Brill.

Hudson, A. (2001). NGOs' transnational advocacy networks: From 'legitimacy' to 'political responsibility'? *Global Networks: A Journal of Transnational Affairs, 1*(4), 331.

Hyunjin, K., & McAllister, M. P. (2011). Selling you and your clicks: Examining the audience commodification of Google. *TripleC (Cognition, Communication, Co-Operation): Open Access Journal for a Global Sustainable Information Society, 9*(2), 141–153.

ICANN alternative: Peter Sunde unveils the P2P DNS project. (2015, March 10). Aerosvit Cargo [Company website]. Retrieved from http://www.aerosvitcargo.com/icann-alternative-peter-sunde-unveils-the-p2p-dns-project/

Institute for Prospective Technological Studies. (2013, April). Digital Music Consumption on the Internet: Evidence from Clickstream Data. European Commission's Joint Research Center. Brussels. Retrieved from http://www.scribd.com/doc/131005609/JRC79605

International Bank of Reconstruction and Development. (1994). *Adjustment in Africa: Reforms, results and the road ahead*. Oxford: OUP.

International Federation of the Phonographic Industry (IFPI). (2012). Digital Music Report. Retrieved from http://www.ifpi.org/content/library/DMR2012.pdf

International Telecommunication Union. (1998). Resolution 73 of the Plenipotentiary Conference of the International Telecommunication Union. Minneapolis: ITU. Retrieved from http://www.itu.int/council/wsis/R73.html

Internet Architecture Board. (2000, May). IAB Technical Comment on the Unique DNS Root. *RFC Editor*. Retrieved from http://www.rfc-editor.org/rfc/rfc2826.txt

Internet Assigned Numbers Authority. (IANA). (n.d.). Root files. IANA. Los Angeles.

Internet brings new thinking and shopping. (1999, May 11). *The Daily Nation*. Nairobi.

Internet Corporation for Assigned Names and Numbers. (ICANN). (2014, July 29). *Motion to Quash Writ of Attachment*. Washington, DC: U.S. District Court for the District of Columbia. Retrieved from https://www.icann.org/en/system/files/files/ben-haim-motion-to-quash-writs-1-29jul14-en.pdf

Internet Governance Forum (IGF). (2009, May 13). Open consultations. Available from http://www.intgovforum.org/cms/index.php/component/content/article/71-transcripts-/410-transcript-of-the-13-may-open-consultations-

Internet Governance Forum (IGF). (n.d.). About the MAG. Secretariat of the Internet Governance Forum (IGF). Geneva.

Internet growth statistics. (n.d.). *Internet World Stats* [Website]. Retrieved from http://www.internetworldstats.com/emarketing.htm

Irving, L., Klegar-Levy, K., Everette, D. W., Reynolds, T., & Lader, W. (1999). *Falling through the net: Defining the digital divide*. A Report on the Telecommunications and Information Technology Gap in America. Washington, DC: National Telecommunications and Information Administration, US Department of Commerce.

Israel, E., & Alonso, S. (2014, October 2). Brazil's anti-spying Internet push could backfire, industry says. *Reuters*. http://uk.reuters.com/article/2013/10/02/us-brazil-internet-idUKBRE9910F120131002

ITT. (1997). 'The global information economy: The way ahead'. Report of the Australian Information Industries taskforce (ITT). Canberra: Australia Government's Department of Industry, Science and Tourism.

ITU. (1984). Remarks prepared for delivery by Mr. Al Gore, US Vice President. Found on the Internet at: http://www.itu.int/dms_pub/itu-s/oth/02/01/S02010000414E05PDFE.PDF

ITU. (1998). *World telecommunications development report*. Geneva: International Telecommunications Union.

Jarvenpaa, S. L., & Leidner, D. E. (1999). Communication and trust in global virtual teams. *Organization Science, 10*, 791–815.

Jaszi, P. A. (1996). Caught in the net of copyright. *Oregon Law Review, 75*, 299.

Jenkins, R. (2001). *Corporate codes of conduct: Self-regulation in a global economy*. Geneva: United Nations Research Institute for Social Development.

Jensen, M. (2002). The African Internet: A status report. Retrieved from http://demiurge.wn.apc.org/africa/projects.htm

Johnson, M. (2011, February 10). The "Internet kill switch" debate: Knocking over entire web systems. *The Economist*. Retrieved from http://www.economist.com/blogs/multimedia/2011/02/internet_kill_switch_debate

Joinson, A. N. (2001). Self-disclosure in computer-mediated communication: The role of self-awareness and visual anonymity. *European Journal of Social Psychology, 31*(2), 177–192.

Jordan, L., & Van Tuijl, P. (2000). Political responsibility in transnational NGO advocacy. *World Development, 28*, 2051–2065.

Kahler, M. (Ed.). (2009). *Networked politics: Agency, power, and governance*. Ithaca: Cornell University Press.

Kahler, M., & Lake, D. A. (Eds.). (2003). *Governance in a global economy: Political authority in transition*. Princeton: Princeton University Press.

Kahn, J. (2005, September 8). Yahoo helped Chinese to prosecute journalist. *The New York Times*. Retrieved from http://www.nytimes.com/2005/09/07/business/worldbusiness/07iht-yahoo.html?_r=1&

Kaufmann, J. (1968). *Conference diplomacy: An introductory analysis*. New York/Leiden: A. W. Sijthoff.

Kaufmann, J. (1988). *Conference diplomacy: An introductory analysis* (Vol. 62). Dordrecht: Martinus Nijhoff Publishers.

Kaufmann, J. (1989). *Effective negotiation: Case studies in conference diplomacy.* Norwell/Dordrecht: M. Nijhoff.

Kay, T. (2005). Labor transnationalism and global governance: The impact of NAFTA on transnational labor relationships in North America. *American Journal of Sociology, 111*(3), 715–756.

Keck, M. E., & Sikkink, K. (1955, 1998). *Activists beyond borders: Advocacy networks in international politics.* Ithaca: Cornell University Press.

Keck, M. E., & Sikkink, K. (1998). *Activists beyond borders: Advocacy networks in international politics.* Ithaca: Cornell University Press. www.jstor.org/stable/10.7591/j.ctt5hh13f

Keck, M. E., & Sikkink, K. (1998a). *Activists beyond borders advocacy networks in international politics.* Ithaca: Cornell University Press.

Keck, M. E., & Sikkink, K. (1998b). *Activists beyond borders advocacy networks in international politics.* Ithaca: Cornell University Press.

Keck, M. E., & Sikkink, K. (1998c). *Activists beyond borders advocacy networks in international politics.* Ithaca: Cornell University Press.

Keck, M. E., & Sikkink, K. (1998d). *Activists beyond borders advocacy networks in international politics.* Ithaca: Cornell University Press.

Keck, M. E., & Sikkink, K. (1999). Transnational advocacy networks in international and regional politics. *International Social Science Journal, 51,* 89–101.

Keck, M. E., & Sikkink, K. (2014). *Activists beyond borders: Advocacy networks in international politics.* Ithaca: Cornell University Press.

Kelly, K. (1999). *New rules for the new economy-10 ways the network economy is changing everything.* London: Fourth Estate Limited.

Kenis, P., & Provan, K. G. (2009). Towards an exogenous theory of public network performance. *Public Administration, 87*(3), 440–456.

Kenney, R., & Florida, M. (1993). *Beyond mass production: The Japanese system and its transfer to the United States.* New York: Oxford University Press.

Keohane, R. O., & Nye, J. S. (1977). *Power and interdependence: World politics in transition.* Boston: Little, Brown.

Keohane, R. (1984). *After hegemony.* Princeton: Princeton University Press.

Keohane, R., & Nye, J. (1989). *Power and interdependence.* New York: Harper Collins.

Keohane, R. O., & Nye Jr., J. S. (1998). Power and interdependence in the information age. *Foreign Affairs, 77*(5), 81–94.

Keohane, R. O., & Victor, D. G. (2011). The regime complex for climate change. *Perspectives on Politics, 9*(1), 7–23.

Khagram, S., Riker, J. V., & Sikkink, K. (2002). *Restructuring world politics: Transnational social movements, networks, and norms* (Vol. 14). Minneapolis: University of Minnesota Press.

Khondker, H. H. (2011). Role of the new media in the Arab Spring. *Globalizations, 8*(5), 675–679.

Kidman, A., & Allen, D. (2012, February 23). Telstra lost the Internet, not sure why. *Gizmodo Australia*. Retrieved from http://www.gizmodo.com.au/2012/02/telstra-lost-the-internet-not-sure-why/

Kiesler, S., & Sproull, L. (1992). Group decision making and communication technology. *Organizational Behavior and Human Decision Processes, 52*(1), 96–123.

Kim, L. (1999, June 10). *National innovation systems in developing countries: Lessons from the Korean experience.* Paper presented at UNU/INTECH, Maastricht.

Kim, W. C., & Mauborgne, R. (1999). Strategy, value innovation, and the knowledge economy. *Sloan Management Review, 40*, 41–54.

Kingdon, J. (1984). *Agendas, alternatives and public choices.* Boston: Little, Brown.

Kingdon, J. W. (1995). *Agendas, alternatives, and public policies.* New York: Addison-Wesley Longman.

Kingdon, J. W. (2002). *Agendas, alternatives, and public policies.* New York: Longman.

Kingdon, J. W. (2003). *Agendas, alternatives, and public policies.* New York: Longman Pub Group.

Kirschenbaum, M. (2003, August 29). Virtuality and VRML: Software studies after Manovich. *Electronic Book Review.* Retrieved from http://www.electronicbookreview.com/thread/technocapitalism/morememory

Kittleson, M. (1995). An assessment of the response rate via the postal service and e-mail. *Health Values., 18*(2), 27–29.

Klein, H. (2005). Understanding WSIS: An institutional analysis of the UN world summit on the information society. *Information Technologies and International Development, 1*(3–4), 3–13.

Klijn, E. H., Edelenbos, J., Kort, M., & van Twist, M. (2008). Facing management choices: An analysis of managerial choices in 18 complex environmental public—Private partnership projects. *International Review of Administrative Sciences, 74*(2), 251–282.

Kling, R. (1996). Synergies and competition between life in cyberspace and face-to-face communities. *Social Science Computer Review, 14*(1), 50–54.

Konkel, F. (2014, July 11). How the CIA partnered with Amazon and changed intelligence. *Defense One.* Retrieved from http://www.defenseone.com/technology/2014/07/how-cia-partnered-amazon-and-changed-intelligence/88555/

Kopel, K. (2013). Operation seizing our sites: How the federal government is taking domain names without prior notice. *Berkeley Technology Law Journal, 28*, 859.

Kramer, A. E. (2013, July 14). N.S.A. Leaks revive push in Russia to control net. *The New York Times.* http://www.nytimes.com/2013/07/15/business/global/nsa-leaks-stir-plans-in-russia-to-control-net.html

Krasner, S. D., (1942). World Peace Foundation, & University of California, Los Angeles. Center for International and Strategic Affairs. (1983). *International regimes* Ithaca: Cornell University Press.

Krasner, S. D. (Ed.). (1983a). *International regimes*. Ithaca: Cornell University Press.

Krasner, S. D. (Ed.). (1983a). *International regimes*. Ithaca: Cornell University Press.

Krasner, S. D. (1983b). Structural causes and regime consequences: Regimes as intervening variables. In S. D. Krasner (Ed.), *International regimes*. Ithaca: Cornell University Press.

Krasner, S. D. (1991). Global communications and national power: Life on the Pareto frontier. *World Politics, 43*(03), 336–366.

Kraut, R. E., Lewis, S. H., & Swezey, L. W. (1982). Listener responsiveness and the coordination of conversation. *Journal of personality and social psychology, 43*(4), 718.

Kravets, D. (2012, March 6). Uncle Sam: If it ends in .com, it's .seizable. *Wired*. Retrieved from http://www.wired.com/2012/03/feds-seize-foreign-sites/

Krippendorff, K. (2004). *Content analysis: An introduction to its methodology*. Thousand Oaks: Sage.

Kulesza, J. (2012). *International internet law*. New York: Routledge.

La Rovere, R. (1996). Information technology diffusion in small and medium sized enterprises: Elements for policy definition. *Information Technology for Development, 1*(4), 169–181.

La Rue, F. (2011, May 16). *Special Rapporteur on the promotion and protection of the right to freedom of opinion and expression* (U.N. Doc. A/HRC/17/27). United Nations General Assembly, Human Rights Council. New York. Retrieved from http://www2.ohchr.org/english/bodies/hrcouncil/docs/17session/A.HRC.17.27_en.pdf

La Rue, F. (2013, April 17). *Special Rapporteur on the promotion and protection of the right to freedom of opinion and expression* (U.N. Doc. A/HRC/23/40) United Nations General Assembly, Human Rights Council. New York. Retrieved from http://www.ohchr.org/Documents/HRBodies/HRCouncil/RegularSession/Session23/A.HRC.23.40_EN.pdf

Lang, S. (2009). Gendering European publics? Transnational women's advocacy networks in the European Union. In *Media agoras: Democracy, diversity and communication* (pp. 198–219). London: Routledge.

Lasta, N. A. (2013). Facebook integrated with atlas for big data analytics and more relevant ads. *Social Barrel*. Retrieved from: http://socialbarrel.com/facebook-integrated-with-atlas-for-big-data-analytics-and-more-relevant-ads/51217/

Latour, B. (1987). *Science in action: How to follow scientists and engineers through society*. Cambridge, MA: Harvard University Press.

Latour, B. (1996). On actor-network theory. *Soziale Welt, 47*, 369–381.

Latour, B. (2005). *Reassembling the social: An introduction to actor-network-theory*. Oxford: Oxford University Press.

Latour, B. (2008). A cautious Prometheus? A few steps toward a philosophy of design (with special attention to Peter Sloterdijk). In F. Hackne, J. Glynne, & V. Minto (Eds.), *Proceedings of the 2008 annual international conference of the Design History Society*. Boca Raton: Universal Publishers.

Lave, J., & Wenger, E. (1991). *Situated learning—Legitimate peripheral participation*. Cambridge, UK/New York: Cambridge University Press.

Law, J. (2009). Actor network theory and material semiotics. In *The new Blackwell companion to social theory* (pp. 141–158). Chichester/Malden: Wiley.

Law, J., & Hassard, J. (1999). *Actor network theory and after*. Malden: Wiley.

Lea, M., & Spears, R. (1991). Computer-mediated communication, deindividuation and group decision-making. *International Journal of Man-Machine Studies, 34*(2), 283–301.

Lee, O. (2002). Cultural differences in e-mail use of virtual teams: A critical social theory perspective. *Cyberpsychology & Behavior, 5*(3), 227–232.

Lee, T. B. (2011, December 8). ICE admits year-long seizure of music blog was a mistake. *Ars Technica*. Retrieved from http://arstechnica.com/tech-policy/2011/12/ice-admits-months-long-seizure-of-music-blog-was-a-mistake/

Lee, T. B. (2012, May 4). Waiting on the RIAA, feds held seized Dajaz1 domain for months. *Ars Technica*. Retrieved from http://arstechnica.com/tech-policy/2012/05/waiting-on-the-riaa-feds-held-seized-dajaz1-domain-for-months/

Lee, J. A., Liu, C. Y., & Li, W. (2013). Searching for Internet freedom in China: A case study on Google's China experience. *Cardozo Arts & Entertainment Law Journal, 31*(2), 405–434.

Leggatt, H. (2009, September 17). Microsoft launches behavioral targeting for mobile ads. *BizReports*. Retrieved from http://www.bizreport.com/2009/09/microsoft_launches_behavioral_targeting_for_mobile_ads.html

Leiner, B. M., Cerf, V. G., Clark, D. D., Kahn, R. E., Kleinrock, L., Lynch, D. C., et al. (2009). A brief history of the Internet. *ACM SIGCOMM Computer Communication Review, 39*(5), 22–31.

LeMay, R. (2011, February 3). No internet "kill switch" for Australia, says Conroy. *Delimiter*. Retrieved from http://delimiter.com.au/2011/02/03/no-internet-kill-switch-for-australia-says-conroy/

Lemay-Hébert, N., & Mathieu, X. (2014). The OECD's discourse on fragile states: Expertise and the normalization of knowledge production. *Third World Quarterly, 35*(2), 232–251.

Leong, N. (2007). The transnational advocacy network: Framing state-NGO relations in the anti-large dam campaign. *Networks, 9*, 103–128.

Lessig, L. (1999). *Code: And other laws of cyberspace*. New York: Basic Books.

Lessig, L. (2004). *Free culture: How big media uses technology and the law to lock down culture and control creativity*. New York: The Penguin Press.

Lev-Aretz, Y. (2013). Copyright lawmaking and public choice: From legislative battles to private ordering. *Harvard Journal of Law & Technology, 27*(1), 203.

Levy, M. A., Young, O. R., & Zürn, M. (1995). The study of international regimes. *European journal of international relations, 1*(3), 267–330.

Levinson, N. (2006). *Powering Internet governance: Ideas, institution, and change*. American Political Science Association.

Levinson, N. S. (2009). *NGOs in global Internet governance: Co-creation processes, collective learning, and network effectiveness.* In APSA 2009 Toronto Meeting Paper.

Levinson, N. (2010). Co-creating processes in global governance: The case of the Internet Governance Forum. *Fifth Annual Global Internet Governance Academic Network Conference,* Vilnius.

Levinson, N. S. (2012a). *Constructing global governance in an Internet era: Culture, co-processes and non-state actors.* Paper presented at the International Studies Association Annual Meeting, San Diego.

Levinson, N. S. (2012b). *Ecologies of representation: Knowledge, networks, & innovation in Internet governance.* Paper presented at the American Political Science Association Annual Meeting, Washington, DC.

Levinson, N., & Cogburn, D. L. (2011). *Globalizing multistakeholder governance: A mixed methods case study of the first five years of the UN internet governance forum.* Paper presented at the 52st annual convention of the international studies association, Montreal, Canada.

Levinson, N. S., & Cogburn, D. L. (2011a, February). *Globalizing multistakeholder governance: A mixed methods case study of the first five fears of the UN Internet Governance Forum.* Presentation at the Annual Convention of the International Studies Association, Montreal.

Levinson, N. S., & Cogburn, D. L. (2011b, July). *Improvising Internet governance: Emerging trends in the Internet Governance Forum.* Paper presented at the International Association for Media & Communication Research Annual Meeting, Istanbul.

Levinson, N. S., & Marzouki, M. (2014, June). *IOs and the transforming global Internet policy Architectures.* Paper presented at the 5th ECPR Standing Group on Regulatory Governance Biennial Conference, Barcelona.

Levinson, N. S., & Smith, H. (2008). *The Internet governance ecosystem: Assessing multistakeholderism and change.* American Political Science Association 2008 Annual Meeting, Boston.

Liebelson, D. (2013, November 26). The government's secret plan to shut off cellphones and the Internet, explained. *Mother Jones.* Retrieved from http://www.motherjones.com/politics/2013/11/internet-phone-kill-switch-explained

Lim Fat, D. (1998, July 7). *Information technology and development, experiences from Mauritius.* Paper presented at the World Bank Pacific Island Knowledge Assessment Stakeholders workshops, Fiji.

Lipschutz, R. (1996). *Global civil society and global governance: The politics of nature from place to planet.* Albany: State University of New York Press.

Litman, J. (1994). The exclusive right to read. *Cardozo Arts and Entertainment Law Journal, 13,* 29.

Litman, J. (2001). *Digital copyright.* Amherst: Prometheus Books.

Livingston, S., & Klinkforth, K. (2014). Narrative power shifts: Exploring the role of ICTs and informational politics in transnational advocacy. *International Journal of Technology, Knowledge and Society, 6*(5), 43–63.

Local social ad spending set to surge. (2012, May 21). *eMarketer*. Retrieved from http://www.emarketer.com/Article/Local-Social-Ad-Spending-Set-Surge/1009061

Lohr, S. (2014, June 10). Microsoft protests order to disclose email stored abroad. *The New York Times*. Retrieved from http://www.nytimes.com/2014/06/11/technology/microsoft-protests-order-for-email-stored-abroad.html

Lovan, W. R., Murray, M., & Shaffer, R. (2004). *Participatory governance: Planning, conflict mediation and public decision-making in civil society.* Burlington: Ashgate Publishing Ltd.

Lynn, S. (2002, February 24). *President's report: ICANN—The case for reform.* The Internet Corporation for Assigned Names and Numbers (ICANN). Marina del Ray. Retrieved from http://archive.icann.org/en/general/lynn-reform-proposal-24feb02.htm

Maass, P., & Poitras, L. (2014, October 10). Core secrets: NSA saboteurs in China and Germany. *The Intercept*. https://firstlook.org/theintercept/2014/10/10/core-secrets

MacAskill, E. (2010, December 1). WikiLeaks website pulled by Amazon after US political pressure. *The Guardian*. Retrieved from http://www.guardian.co.uk/media/2010/dec/01/wikileaks-website-cables-servers-amazon

MacAskill, E. (2013). NSA paid millions to cover Prism compliance costs for tech companies. *The Guardian*. Retrieved from http://www.theguardian.com/world/2013/aug/23/nsa-prism-costs-tech-companies-paid

MacBride, S. (1980). *The MacBride Commission Report: Many Voices, One World.* Paris: UNESCO. http://www2.hawaii.edu/~rvincent/mcbcon1.htm

Machlup, F. (1962). *The production and distribution of knowledge.* New Jersey: Princeton University Press.

MacKinnon, R. (2010). Google rules. *Index on Censorship, 39*(1), 32–45.

MacKinnon, R. (2012). *Consent of the networked: The world-wide struggle for Internet freedom.* New York: Basic Books.

Maclay, C. M. (2010). Protecting privacy and expression online: Can the global network initiative embrace the character of the Net? In J. P. R. Deibert, R. Rohozinski, & J. Zittrain (Eds.), *Access controlled: The shaping of power, rights, and rules in cyberspace* (pp. 87–108). Cambridge, MA: MIT Press.

MacLean, D., Souter, D., Deane, J., & Lilley, S. (2002b). *Louder voices: Strengthening developing country participation in international ICT decision-making.* London: Commonwealth Telecommunications Organization.

MacLean, D. (2003). The quest for inclusive governance of global ICTs: Lessons from the ITU in the limits of national sovereignty. *Information Technology and International Development, 1*(1), 1–18.

MacLean, D., Souter, D., Deane, J., & Lilley, S. (2002). *Louder voices: Strengthening developing country participation in international ICT decision-making.* London: Commonwealth Telecommunications Organization.

MacLean, D., Souter, D., Deane, J., & Lilley, S. *Louder voices: Strengthening developing country participation in international ICT decision-making.* London: The Commonwealth Telecommunications Organization and The Panos Institute (London).

Maier, K. (1998). *Into the house of the ancestors: Inside the new Africa.* Toronto: John Williamson.

Malcolm, J. (2008). *Multi-stakeholder governance and the Internet Governance Forum.* Wembley: Terminus Press.

Mann, A. (2009). Spaces for talk: Information and Communication Technologies (ICTs) and genuine dialogue in an international advocacy movement. *Asian Social Science, 4,* 3–13.

Manning, R. (1985, July 26). Software industry's on the trail of video 'Robin Hoods.' *The Chicago Tribune.*

Manovich, L. (2001). *The language of new media.* Cambridge, MA: MIT Press.

Mansell, R., & Tremblay, G. (2013, February). *Renewing the knowledge societies vision: Towards knowledge societies for peace and sustainable development.* Report presented at the UNESCO WSIS+10 Conference, Paris.

Mansell, R., & Wehn, U. (1998a). *Knowledge societies: Information technology for sustainable development.* Oxford: Oxford University Press.

Manson, H. (1998). There is a will, but is there a way? *Computer World, 32*(26), 6–7.

Mansell, R. a. U. W. (1998). Knowledge societies: Information technology for sustainable development.

Mantelero, A. (2013). The EU proposal for a general data protection regulation and the roots of the 'right to be forgotten'. *Computer Law & Security Review, 29*(3), 229–235.

Manuel, T. (2000). *Concluding remarks by the Chairman, Hon. Trevor Manuel, Governor of the Fund and Bank for South Africa, at the Closing Joint Session.* Prague, 2000 Annual Meetings of the International Monetary Fund and World Bank Group. http://www.imf.org/external/am/2000/speeches/pr68e.pdf

Marino, M. C. (2006, December 4). Critical code studies. *Electronic Book Review.* Retrieved from http://www.electronicbookreview.com/thread/electropoetics/codology

Markle Foundation. (2002). *A roadmap: Gobal policymaking for information and communications technologies: Enabling meaningful participation by developing-nation stakeholders.* New York: Markle Foundation.

Marlin-Bennett, R. (2001, February 4). *ICANN and the global digital divide.* Paper presented at the Annual Meeting of the International Studies Association, Chicago.

Marsden, C. (2011, March 8). The Internet kill-switch: UK law. *Internet Law Sussex*. Retrieved from http://internetsussex.blogspot.com/2011/03/internet-kill-switch-uk-law.html

Martin, X., Mitchell, W., & Swaminathan, A. (1994). Beyond mass production: The Japanese system and its transfer to the United States. *Academy of Management. The Academy of Management Review, 19*(3), 600.

Marx, K. (2014). *The communist manifesto*. New York: International Publishers Co.

Masnick, M. (2011, December 8). Feds falsely censor popular blog for over a year, deny due process, hide all details.... *Techdirt*. Retrieved from http://www.techdirt.com/articles/20111208/08225217010/breaking-news-feds-falsely-censor-popular-blog-over-year-deny-all-due-process-hide-all-details.shtml

Massaro, T. M. (1990). Equality and freedom of expression: The hate speech dilemma. *William & Mary Law Review, 32*, 211.

Masuda, Y. (1980). *The information society as post-industrial society*. Washington, DC: World Futures Society.

Mathiason, J. (2004). A framework convention: An institutional option for Internet governance. Internet Governance Project, Syracuse.

Mathiason, J. (2008). *Internet governance: The new frontier of global institutions*. New York: Routledge.

Mayer-Schönberger, V., & Hurley, D. (2000). Globalization of communication. In J. Nye (Ed.), *Governance in a globalizing world* (pp. 135–154). Washington, DC: Brookings Institution Press.

Mayton, W. T. (1984). Seditious libel and the lost guarantee of a freedom of expression. *Columbia Law Review, 84*, 91–142.

McCroskey, J. C., & Richmond, V. P. (1990). Willingness to communicate: Differing cultural perspectives. *Southern Journal of Communication, 56*(1), 72–77.

McCarthy, M. T. (2002). USA Patriot Act. *Harvard Journal on Legislation, 39*, 435–521.

McCombs, M. E., & Shaw, D. L. (1972). The agenda-setting function of mass media. *Public opinion quarterly, 36*(2), 176–187.

McLaughlin, A. (2010, July 22). A major milestone for Internet security. *The White House Blog*. Washington, DC: Executive Office of the President of the United States. Retrieved from http://www.whitehouse.gov/blog/2010/07/22/a-major-milestone-internet-security

Medows, D. B. (2012). The sound of silence: The legality of the American 'Kill Switch Bill'. *Case Western Reserve Journal of Law, Technology & the Internet, 4*, 59.

Meinrath, S. D., Losey, J. W., & Pickard, V. W. (2011). Digital feudalism: Enclosures and erasures from digital rights management to the digital divide. In M. Zelkowitz (Ed.), *Advances in computers (Vol. 81): The Internet and mobile technology* (pp. 237–287). Amsterdam: Elsevier.

Mell, P. (2002). Big Brother at the door: Balancing national security with privacy under the USA PATRIOT Act. *Denver University Law Review, 80*, 375.

Meltzer, J. (2014). *Supporting the Internet as a platform for international trade.* Washington, DC: The Brookings Institution.

Merton, R. K. (1936). The unanticipated consequences of purposive social action. *American Sociological Review, 1*(6), 894–904.

Michelson, E. S. (2006). Clicking toward development: Understanding the role of ICTs for civil society. *Guest Editor 2 Technology within Society, 415*, 53.

Miller, C. C. (2012, September 13). As violence spreads in Arab world, Google blocks access to inflammatory video. *New York Times*, September 17, 2012. Retrieved from http://www.nytimes.com/2012/09/14/technology/google-blocks-inflammatory-video-in-egypt-and-libya.html

Miller, C. C. (2014, March 21). Revelations by Snowden damage U.S. tech industry. *The New York Times.* Retrieved from http://www.nytimes.com/2014/03/22/business/fallout-from-snowden-hurting-bottom-line-of-tech-companies.html

Miller, J., & Mitter, S. (1998, November 24). *International software trade: A 3-phase model for capability building in developing countries.* Paper presented at the workshop on 'Challenges and Opportunities for Globally Distributed work: The Case of Software in Developing Countries', UNU/INTECH, Maastricht.

Mimoso, M. (2014). Justice dept. eases gag order on FISA, national security letter reporting. *Threatpost.* Retrieved from http://threatpost.com/justice-dept-eases-gag-order-on-fisa-national-security-letter-reporting/103903

Minar, N., & Hedlund, M. (2001). A network of peers—Peer-to-peer models through the history of the Internet. In A. Oram (Ed.), *Peer-to-peer: Harnessing the power of disruptive technologies* (pp. 9–20). Sebastopol: O'Reilly.

Mitchell, J. C. (1973). *Networks, norms and institutions.* The Hague: Mouton.

Mitrou, L., & Karyda, M. (2012, June). *EU's data protection reform and the right to be forgotten—A legal response to a technological challenge?* Paper presented at the 5th International Conference of Information Law and Ethics, Corfu.

Monberg, J. (2005). Science and technology studies: Approaches to Internet research. *The Information Society, 21*(4), 281–284.

Mora, A. (2014, March 8). Actualizado: Los Andes en Emergencia y Tachira sin Internet: Estado Alma de la Lucha democratica de Venezuela. *Apuntes de una Periodista, por Angélica Mora.* Retrieved from http://angelicamorabeals.blogspot.com/2014/03/en-venezuela-estado-tachira-sin-internet.html

Mueller, M. (2002). *Ruling the root: Internet governance and the taming of cyberspace.* Cambridge, MA: MIT press.

Mueller, M. L. (2004). *Ruling the root: Internet governance and the taming of cyberspace.* Cambridge, MA: MIT Press.

Mueller, M. L. (2010). *Networks and states: The global politics of Internet governance.* Cambridge, MA: MIT Press.

Mueller, M., Kuerbis, B., & Page, C. (2007a). Democratizing global communication? Global civil society and the campaign for communication rights in the information society. *Journal of Communication, 1,* 267–296.

Mueller, M., Mathiason, J., & Klein, H. (2007b). The Internet and global governance: Principles and norms for a new regime. *Global Governance, 3*(2), 237–254.

Murphy, E. (2004). Recognising and promoting collaboration in an online asynchronous discussion. *British Journal of Educational Technology, 35*(4), 421–431.

Musiani, F. (2013a, October 31). *Network architecture as Internet governance.* Paris: ADAM. Retrieved from http://adam.hypotheses.org/1852

Musiani, F. (2013b, May). *A decentralized domain name system? User-controlled infrastructure as alternative Internet governance.* Paper presented at 8th Media in Transition (MiT8) conference, Cambridge, MA.

Musiani, F. (2015). *Nains sans géants. Architecture décentralisée et services Internet.* Paris: Presses des Mines.

Nagel, C., & Staeheli, L. (2010). ICT and geographies of British Arab and Arab American activism. *Global Networks, 10,* 262–281.

Nakamura, K. H., Addis, C. L., & Lum, T. (2010). *US initiatives to promote global Internet freedom: Issues, policy, and technology.* Washington, DC: Congressional Research Service.

Nakashima, E. (2010, February 4). Google to enlist NSA to help it ward off cyberattacks. *The Washington Post.* Retrieved from http://www.washingtonpost.com/wp-dyn/content/article/2010/02/03/AR2010020304057.html

National Intelligence Council. (2012). *Global trends 2030: Alternative worlds.* Washington, DC: Office of the Director of National Intelligence.

National Research Council (US), & Committee on a National Collaboratory, & Establishing the User-Developer Partnership. (1993). *National collaboratories: Applying information technology for scientific research.* Washington, DC: National Academy Press.

Nations, U. (2003). World summit on the information society. New York. A/RES/57/238

National Telecommunications and Information Administration. (1998). *Statement of Policy on the management of Internet names and addresses.* Washington, DC: U.S. Department of Commerce.

National Telecommunications and Information Administration. (1999). *Falling through the net: Defining the digital divide.* Washington, DC: U.S. Department of Commerce, National Telecommunications and Information Administration.

Negroponte, N. (1998, January). The third shall be first. *Wired.*

Nelson, P. (2002). New agendas and new patterns of international NGO political action. *Voluntas: International Journal of Voluntary and Nonprofit Organizations, 13,* 377–392.

Nelson, R. R., & Wright, G. (1992). The rise and fall of American technological leadership: The post-war era in historical perspective. *Journal of Economic Literature, 30*(4), 1931–1964.

NETMundial. (2014, April 23). *Working Session 1.* Transcript from NETMundial: Global multistakeholder meeting on the future of Internet governance, Sao Paulo.

Netanel, N. W. (1999). Recent developments in copyright law. *Texas Intellectual Property Journal, 7,* 331.

Neuendorf, K. A. (2002). *The content analysis guidebook.* Thousand Oaks: Sage.

New York investigators seize 10 websites that illegally streamed copyrighted sporting and pay-per-view events. (2011, February 2). U.S. Customs and Immigration Enforcement. Washington, DC. Retrieved from http://www.ice. gov/news/releases/new-york-investigators-seize-10-websites-illegally-streamed-copyrighted-sporting-and

Nimmer, D. (2002). Appreciating legislative history: The sweet and sour spots of the DMCA's commentary. *Cardozo Law Review, 23,* 909.

Nimmo, K. (2009, March 23). Rockefeller: Internet is 'number one national hazard.' *InfoWars.com.* Retrieved from http://www.infowars.com/rockefeller-internet-is-number-one-national-hazard/

Nixon, R. (2014, April 25). U.S. says it built digital programs abroad with an eye to politics. *The New-York Times.* Retrieved from http://www.nytimes. com/2014/04/26/world/us-ran-social-media-programs-in-afghanistan-and-pakistan.html?_r=3

N. T. I. A. (2014). NTIA announces intent to transition key internet domain name functions [press release]. Retrieved from https://www.ntia.doc.gov/ press-release/2014/ntia-announces-intent-transition-key-internet-domain-name-functions

Nucifora, A. (2002, October 18). Web research: Is it fantasy or reality? *The Business Journal.* http://milwaukee.bizjournals.com/milwaukee/stories/2002/10/21/smallb5.html

O'Brien, D. (2014). *Venezuela's Internet crackdown escalates into regional blackout.* Washington, DC: Electronic Frontier Foundation.

O'Brien, R., Goetz, A. M., Scholte, J. A., & Williams, M. (2000). *Contesting global governance: Multilateral economic institutions and global social movements.* Cambridge: Cambridge University Press.

Ó Siochrú, S. (2004, June–July). Will the real WSIS please stand-up? The historic encounter of the 'Information Society' and the 'Communication Society' Paper for: '*Gazette—The International Journal for Communication Studies*' 66(3/4).

Ó Siochrú, S., Kleinwaechter, W., & Bloem, R. (2003). Civil Society at the WSIS: Basic Structures. http://www.wsis-cs.org/cs-overview.html

OECD. (1995a). *National policy frameworks for information infrastructures.* Report of the Working Party on 'Telecommunications and Information Service Policies', Directorate for Science, Technology and Industry; Committee for Information, Computer and Communications Policy. OECD, Paris.

OECD. (1995b). *Technology, productivity and job creation Vol. I and II: The OECD job strategy.* Paris: OECD.

OECD. (1996). *The knowledge-based economy.* Paris: OECD.

OECD. (1997). *Towards a global information society.* Paris: OECD.

OECD. (1998). *The economic and social impacts of electronic commerce: Preliminary findings and research agenda.* Directorate for Science, Technology and Industry, Committee for Information, Computer and Communications Policy. Paris: OECD.

Office of Science and Technology Policy. (n.d.). PCAST members. Executive Office of the President of the U.S. Washington, DC. Retrieved from https://www.whitehouse.gov/administration/eop/ostp/pcast/about/members

Olaniran, B. A. (1994). Group performance in computer-mediated and face-to-face communication media. *Management Communication Quarterly, 7*(3), 256–281.

Olaniran, B. A. (2001). The effects of computer-mediated communication on transculturalism. In *Transcultural realities* (pp. 83–105). Thousand Oaks: Sage.

Olson, G. M., & Olson, J. S. (2000). Distance matters. *Human-Computer Interaction, 15,* 139–179.

Olson, G. M., Atkins, D. E., Clauer, R., Finholt, T. A., Jahanian, F., Killeen, T. L., et al. (1998). The Upper Atmospheric Research Collaboratory. *Interactions, 5,* 48–55.

Olson, G. M., Finholt, T. A., & Teasley, S. D. (2000). Behavioral aspects of collaboratories. In S. H. Koslow & M. F. Huerta (Eds.), *Electronic collaboration in science* (pp. 1–14). Mahwah: Lawrence Erlbaum Associates.

Olson, G. M., Teasley, S., Bietz, M. J., & Cogburn, D. L. (2002). *Collaboratories to support distributed science: The example of international HIV/AIDS research.* Paper presented at the proceedings of the 2002 annual research conference of the South African institute of computer scientists and information technologists on enablement through technology, New York.

Opderbeck, D. W. (2011). Cybersecurity and executive power. *Washington University Law Review, 89,* 795.

Opderbeck, D. W. (2012). Does the Communications Act of 1934 contain a hidden Internet kill wwitch? *Federal Communications Law Journal, 65,* 1.

OpenNet Initiative. (2013). OpenNet Initiative.

Orsini, A. (2013). Multi-forum non-state actors: Navigating the regime complexes for forestry and genetic resources. *Global Environmental Politics, 13*(3), 34–55.

Orsini, A., & Compagnon, D. (2013). From logics to procedures: Arguing within international environmental negotiations. *Critical Policy Studies, 7*(3), 273–291.

Orsini, A., Morin, J. F., & Young, O. (2013). Regime complexes: A buzz, a boom, or a boost for global governance? *Global Governance, 19,* 27–39.

Padovani, C., & Pavan, E. (2008). Information networks, Internet governance and innovation in world politics. In F. Amoretti (Ed.), *Electronic constitution: Social, cultural and political implications* (Electronic ed., pp. 154–173). Hershey: Information Science Reference.

Palfrey, J. (2008). The public and the private at the United States border with cyberspace. *Mississippi Law Journal, 78*, 241–294.

Palfrey, J. G., & Gasser, U. (2012). *Interop: The promise and perils of highly interconnected systems*. New York: Basic Books.

Pallas, C. L., & Uhlin, A. (2014). Civil society influence on international organizations: Theorizing the state channel. *Journal of Civil Society, 10*(2), 184–203.

Panopoulou, E., Tambouris, E., & Tarabanis, K. (2009). eParticipation initiatives: How is Europe progressing. *European Journal of ePractice, 7*, 1–12.

Papacharissi, Z. (2010). *A private sphere: Democracy in a digital age*. Cambridge, UK: Polity Press.

Pavan, E. (2012). *Frames and connections in the governance of global communications: A network study of the Internet governance forum*. Lanham: Lexington Books.

Pekerti, A. A., & Thomas, D. C. (2003). Communication in intercultural interaction: An empirical investigation of idiocentric and sociocentric communication styles. *Journal of Cross-Cultural Psychology, 34*(2), 139–154.

Pelkola, D. (2012). A framework for managing privacy-enhancing technology. *Software, IEEE, 29*(3), 45–49.

Perez, C. (1983). Structural change and the assimilation of new technologies in the social and economic system. *Futures., 15*, 357–375.

Peterson, T. (2013). How Facebook's partner categories level the playing field. *ADWEEK*. http://www.adweek.com/news/technology/how-facebooks-partner-categories-level-playing-field-good-148536

Peukert, C., Claussen, J., & Kretschmer, T. (2013). Piracy and movie revenues: Evidence from Megaupload: A tale of the long tail? Available at SSRN 2176246.

Pfanner, E. (2012, December 22). Italian appeals court acquits 3 Google executives in privacy case. *The New York Times*. Retrieved from http://www.nytimes.com/2012/12/22/business/global/italian-appeals-court-acquits-3-google-executives-in-privacy-case.html

Pleming, S. (2009, June 16). U.S. State Department speaks to Twitter over Iran. *Reuters*. Retrieved from http://www.reuters.com/article/2009/06/16/us-iran-election-twitter-usa-idUSWBT01137420090616

Poort, J., & Rutten, P. (2010). Legal, economic and cultural aspects of file sharing. *Communications & Strategies, 1*(77), 35–54.

Porat, M. V. (1977). *The information economy: Definition and measurement*. Report for Office of Telecommunications, US Department of Commerce.

Powell, A., Piccoli, G., & Ives, B. (2004). Virtual teams: A review of current literature and directions for future research. *ACM Sigmis Database, 35*(1), 6–36.

President's Council of Advisors on Science and Technology. (2013, November). Report to the President: Immediate opportunities for strengthening the nation's cybersecurity. Executive Office of the President, Washington, DC.

President's Review Group on Intelligence and Communications Technologies. (2013, December 12). Liberty and security in a changing world: *Report and*

318   REFERENCES

recommendations of the president's review group on intelligence and communications technologies. Executive Office of the President of the U.S., Washington, DC. Retrieved from http://www.whitehouse.gov/sites/default/files/docs/2013-12-12_rg_final_report.pdf

Price, R. M. R. M. (2003). Transnational civil society and advocacy in world politics. *World Politics, 55,* 579–606.

Prioritizing Resources and Organization for Intellectual Property Act of 2008, 18 U.S.C. §2323.

Protecting Cyberspace as a National Asset Act of 2010. S.3480. 111th Congress (2009). Retrieved from http://thomas.loc.gov/cgi-bin/bdquery/z?d111:SN03480

Provan, K. G., Fish, A., & Sydow, J. (2007). Interorganizational networks at the network level: A review of the empirical literature on whole networks. *Journal of Management, 33*(3), 479–516.

Quah, D. (1998). *The invisible hand and the weightless economy.* Paper presented at London School of Economics for the MacArthur Foundation.

Raboy, M., & Landry, N. (2006). *Civil society, communication, and global governance: Issues from the World Summit on the Information Society.* New York: Peter Lang Publishing.

Raboy, M., Landry, N., & Shtern, J. (2010). *Digital solidarities, communication policy and multi-stakeholder global governance: The legacy of the World Summit on the Information Society.* New York: Peter Lang Publishing.

Radcliffe, S. A. (2001). Development, the state, and transnational political connections: State and subject formations in Latin America. *Global Networks, 1,* 19–36.

Raphael, J. R. (2009, March 11). Google's behavioral ad targeting: How to reclaim control. *PCWorld.* Retrieved from http://www.pcworld.com/article/161096/google_behavioral_ad_targeting_reclaim_control.html

Raustiala, K., & Victor, D. G. (2004). The regime complex for plant genetic resources. *International Organization, 58*(02), 277–309.

Reaching for the kill switch: The costs and practicalities of switching off the Internet in Egypt and elsewhere. (2011, February 10). *The Economist.* Retrieved from http://www.economist.com/node/18112043

Records of the General Conference. (2009, October). 35th Session. UNESCO, Paris. Retrieved from http://www.unesco.org/education/institutes/35cresolutions.pdf

Records of the General Conference. (2011). 36th Session. UNESCO, Paris. Retrieved from http://unesdoc.unesco.org/images/0021/002150/215084e.pdf

Records of the General Conference. (2013, November). 37th Session. UNESCO, Paris. Retrieved from http://unesdoc.unesco.org/images/0022/002261/226162e.pdf

Recchia, S. P. (2002). International environmental treaty engagement in 19 democracies. *Policy studies journal, 30*(4), 470–494.

Reich, R. (1992). *The work of nations: Preparing ourselves for 21st century capitalism*. New York: Vintage Books.

Rejeski, D. (2003, December). Making policy in a Moore's Law world. *Ubiquity, 4*(42).

Ribes, D., & Lee, C. (2010). Sociotechnical studies of cyberinfrastructure and e-research: Current themes and future trajectories. *Computer Supported Cooperative Work, 9*(3-4), 231–244.

Richards, J. (2012). *A guide to national security: Threats, responses and strategies*. Oxford: Oxford University Press.

Richardson, D. (1995, March). *Community electronic networks: Sharing Lessons learned in Canada with our African colleagues*. Paper presented at the international conference on 'Africa faces the Superhighway', Tunis.

Rioux, M., & Fontaine-Skronski, K. (2014, July). *Conceptualizing institutional changes in a world of great transformations: From the old telecommunications regime to the new global Internet governance*. Paper presented at the World Congress of Political Science, Montreal.

Rischard, J.-F. (2002). Global issues networks: Desperate times deserve innovative measures. *The Washington Quarterly, 26*, 17–33.

Rittberger, V., & Mayer, P. (1993). *Regime theory and international relations*. New York: Oxford University Press.

Rittberger, V. (1995). With the assistance of Peter Mayer. *Regime Theory and International Relations*.

Roberts, P. (2014, January 27). If this is cyberwar, where are all the cyberweapons? *MIT Technology Review*. http://www.technologyreview.com/news/523931/if-this-is-cyberwar-where-are-all-the-cyberweapons/

Rocco, E. (1998). *Trust breaks down in electronic contexts but can be repaired by some initial face-to-face contact*. Paper presented at the proceedings of the SIGCHI conference on human factors in computing systems, New York.

Rodrigues, M. G. M. (2016). The prospects for transnational advocacy across the IBSA bloc–a view from Brazil. *Third World Quarterly, 37*(4), 703–720.

Rogerson, K. (2004). Talking past each other: International organization Internet policy in the developing world. *International Politics, 41*(2), 176–195.

Rojas, Jose I. (1998). *Liability of service providers, content providers and end-users on the Internet*, 507 PLI/PAT. 1009.

Romer, P. M. (1987). Crazy explanations for the productivity slowdown. In S. Fisher (Ed.), *NBER macroeconomics annual* (pp. 163–202). Cambridge, MA: MIT Press.

Rostow, W. (1953). *The process of economic growth*. Oxford: Clarendon Press.

Roussel, N., & Gueddana, S. (2007). *Beyond beyond being there: Towards multi-scale communication systems*. Paper presented at the Proceedings of the 15th international conference on Multimedia.

Rubinstein, I. S. (2011). Regulating privacy by design. *Berkeley Technology Law Journal, 26*, 1409.

Ruggiero, S. (2012). Killing the internet to keep America alive: The myths and realities of the internet kill switch. *SMU Science & Technology Law Review, 15,* 241.

Rundle, M. C. (2005). Beyond Internet governance: The emerging international framework for governing the networked world. *Berkman Center Research Publication,* (2005-16).

Russell, A. (2012, October 7). Histories of networking vs. the history of the Internet. Paper presented at the SIGCIS Workshop, Copenhagen.

Sachs, J. (1999). *Helping the world's poorest.* Retrieved from http://www.cid.harvard.edu/cidinthenews/articles/sf9108.html

Sage, G. H. (1999). Justice do it. *Sociology of Sport Journal, 16,* 206–235.

Samuelson, P. (1999). Intellectual property and the digital economy: Why the anti-circumvention regulations need to be revised. *Berkeley Technology Law Journal, 14,* 519.

Samuelson, P., & Wheatland, T. (2009). Statutory damages in copyright law: A remedy in need of reform. *William and Mary Law Review, 51,* 439.

Sass, Erik. (2014, November 13). Social media spending will double by 2018, thanks to mobile, programmatic. *The Social Graf: MediaPost.* Retrieved from http://www.mediapost.com/publications/article/238176/social-spend-will-double-by-2018-thanks-to-mobile.html

Sassen, S. (2004). Local actors in global politics. *Current Sociology, 52,* 649–670.

Sassen, S. (2006). *Territory, authority, rights: From medieval to global assemblages.* Princeton: Princeton University Press.

Saudi Arabia threatens to block Skype, WhatsApp and Viber. (2013, March 25). *Al Arabiya.* Retrieved from:http://english.alarabiya.net/en/business/technology/2013/03/25/-Saudi-Arabia-threatens-to-block-Skype-WhatsApp-Viber.html

Schaar, P. (2010). Privacy by design. *Identity in the Information Society, 3*(2), 267–274.

Schafer, V. (2015). Part of a whole: RENATER, a 20-year old network within the Internet. *Technology and Culture, 50*(2), 217–235.

Schäferhoff, M., Campe, S., & Kaan, C. (2009). Transnational public-private partnerships in international relations: Making sense of concepts, research frameworks, and results. *International Studies Review, 11*(3), 451–474.

Schattschneider, E. (1964). The semisovereign people. New York: Holt, Rinehart and Winston, 1960.

Schechter, M. G. (2001). *United nations-sponsored world summits: Focus on impact and follow-up.* New York: United Nations University Press.

Schechter, M. G. (2005). *United nations global conferences.* London: Routledge.

Schemeil, Y. (2012). Global governance: Evolution and innovation in international relations. In E. Brousseau, M. Marzouki, & C. Meadel (Eds.), *Governance, regulation and powers on the Internet* (pp. 186–208). Cambridge, UK: Cambridge University Press.

Schemeil, Y. (2013). Bringing international organization in: Global institutions as adaptive hybrids. *Organization Studies, 34*(2), 219–252.

Schemeil, Y., & Eberwein, W. D. (2014, July). *Coalesce or collapse: Further exploration into international organizations' cooperative behavior.* Paper presented at the IPSA World Congress, Montreal.

Scherer, M. (2013, June 24). The informers: Why a new generation of hacktivists is driven to spill the U.S government's secrets. *Time Magazine.* Retrieved from http://content.time.com/time/magazine/article/0,9171,2145506,00.html

Schiffres, M. (1985). The shadowy world of computer 'hackers.' *U.S. News & World Report.*

Schiller, H. I. (1971). Mass communications and American empire.

Schmidt, H. (2011, May 12). The administration unveils its cybersecurity legislative proposal [Blog entry]. *The White House Blog.* Executive Office of the President. Washington, DC. Retrieved from http://www.whitehouse.gov/blog/2011/05/12/administration-unveils-its-cybersecurity-legislative-proposal

Schollmeier, R. (2002). A definition of peer-to-peer networking for the classification of peer-to-peer architectures and applications. In *Proceedings of the first International Conference on Peer-to-Peer Computing* (pp. 27–29). New York: Institute of Electrical and Electronics Engineers (IEEE).

Scholte, J. (2001). Civil Society and Democracy in Global Governance. *Warwick University: Centre for the Study of Globalisation and Regionalisation.* CSGR Working Paper No. 65/01.

Scholte, J. A. (2012). A more inclusive global governance? The IMF and civil society in Africa. *Global Governance: A Review of Multilateralism and International Organizations, 18*(2), 185–206.

Schonfeld, E. (2010, July 6). TV Shack flouts the feds by moving video piracy site to offshore domain. *TechCrunch.* http://techcrunch.com/2010/07/06/tv-shack-piracy

Schramm, W. (1964). *Mass media and national development: The role of information in the developing countries* (Vol. 25). Stanford: Stanford University Press.

Schroeder, M. B. (2014). Executive leadership in the study of international organization: A framework for analysis. *International Studies Review, 16*(3), 339–361.

Schubert, S., & Gupta, J. (2013). Comparing global coordination mechanisms on energy, environment, and water. *Ecology and Society, 18*(2), 22.

Schumpeter, J. A. (1939). *Business cycles: A theoretical, historical and structural analysis.* New York: McGraw-Hill.

Sell, S. K. (1998). *Power and ideas: North-South politics of intellectual property and antitrust.* Albany: SUNY Press.

Seltzer, W. (2010). Free speech unmoored in copyright's safe harbor: Chilling effects of the DMCA on the First Amendment. Retrieved from http://works.bepress.com/wendy_seltzer/3/

Setlock, L. D., Fussell, S. R., & Neuwirth, C. (2004). Taking it out of context: Collaborating within and across cultures in face-to-face settings and via instant messaging. In *Proceedings of the 2004 ACM conference on computer supported cooperative work* (pp. 604–613). New York: ACM.

Shachaf, P. (2008). Cultural diversity and information and communication technology impacts on global virtual teams: An exploratory study. *Information & Management, 45*(2), 131–142.

Shane, P. M. (2012). Cybersecurity: Toward a meaningful policy framework. *Texas Law Reivew.*

Shapiro, C., & Varian, H. R. (1999). *Information rules: A strategic guide to the network economy.* Boston: Harvard Business Press.

Sharpe, A. (2011, January 30).Internet blackout—It couldn't happen here, could it? *CRITique.* London, England: Charles Russell LLP. Retrieved from https://charlesrussell.wordpress.com/tag/civil-contingencies-act-2004/

Shawki, N. (2010). Political opportunity structures and the outcomes of transnational campaigns: A comparison of two transnational advocacy networks. *Peace & Change, 35,* 381–411.

Shiffman, J. (2003). Generating political will for safe motherhood in indonesia. *Social Science & Medicine, 56*(6), 1197–1207. doi:10.1016/S0277-9536(02)00119-3.

Shutting down the Internet: Thou shalt not kill. (2013, April 13). *The Economist.* Retrieved from http://www.economist.com/news/special-report/21574633-turning-entire-internet-nuclear-option-best-not-exercised-thou-shalt-not-kill

Sia, C. L., Tan, B. C., & Wei, K. K. (2002). Group polarization and computer-mediated communication: Effects of communication cues, social presence, and anonymity. *Information Systems Research, 13*(1), 70–90.

Singel, R. (2012, August 29). Oops! Copyright cops return seized RojaDirecta domain names—19 months later. *Wired.* Retrieved from http://www.wired.com/2012/08/domain-names-returned/

Singhal, A. (2012, August 10). An update to our search algorithms. *Inside Search.* Mountain View: Google Inc. Retrieved from http://insidesearch.blogspot.com/2012/08/an-update-to-our-search-algorithms.html

Sisario, B. (2010a, December 13). Piracy fight shuts down music blogs. *The New York Times.* http://www.nytimes.com/2010/12/14/business/media/14music.html

Sisario, B. (2010b, December 19). Music web sites dispute legality of their closing. *The New York Times.* Retrieved from http://www.nytimes.com/2010/12/20/business/media/20music.html?_r=0

Slaughter, A.-M. (2001). The accountability of government networks. *Indiana Journal of Global Legal Studies, 8*(2), 347–367.

Smith, J., Chatfield, C., & Pagnucco, R. (1997). *Transnational social movements and global politics: Solidarity beyond the state.* Syracuse: Syracuse University Press.

Smythe, E., & Smith, P. J. (2006). Legitimacy, transparency, and information technology: The world trade organization in an era of contentious trade politics. *Sustainable Development, 12*, 31–53.

Soete, L. (1986). Technological innovation and long waves: An inquiry into the nature and wealth of Christopher Freeman's thinking. In R. M. Macleod (Ed.), *Technology and the human prospect: Essays in honour of Christopher Freeman.* London: Pinter.

Soete, L., & Turner, R. (1984). Technology diffusion and the rate of technical change. *The Economic Journal, 94*, 612–623.

Soete, L. L., & Weel, B. J. (1999). *Schumpeter and the knowledge-based economy: On technology and competition policy.* Maastricht: MERIT, Maastricht Economic Research Institute on Innovation and Technology.

Soghoian, C. (2010). Caught in the cloud: Privacy, encryption, and government back doors in the web 2.0 era. *Journal on Telecommunications & High Technology Law, 8*, 359.

Soghoian, C. (2011). *The law enforcement surveillance reporting gap.* Bloomington: Center for Applied Cybersecurity Research, Indiana University.

Solove, D. J. (2007). *The future of reputation: Gossip, rumor, and privacy on the Internet.* New Haven: Yale University Press.

Solove, D. J. (2008). *Understanding privacy.* Cambridge, MA: Harvard University Press.

Solove, D. J. (2011). *Nothing to hide: The false tradeoff between privacy and security.* New Haven: Yale University Press.

Soma, J. T., Smith, P. J., & Sprague, R. D. (1985). Legal analysis of electronic bulletin board activities. *New England Law Review, 7*, 571.

Soros, G. (1998). *The crisis of global capitalism: Open society endangered.* New York: PublicAffairs.

Soros, G. (2002b). *George soros on globalization* (1st ed.). New York: Public Affairs.

Soroka, S. N. (2003). Media, public opinion, and foreign policy. *Harvard International Journal of Press/Politics, 8*, 27–48.

Soros, G. (2000). *Open society: Reforming global capitalism* (1st ed.). New York: PublicAffairs.

Soros, G. (2002a). *George Soros on globalization* (Vol. 1st). New York: PublicAffairs.

Souter, D. (2010). *Towards inclusive knowledge societies. A review of UNESCO's action in implementing the WSIS outcomes.* Paris: UNESCO.

South African Department of Communications. (2000). *Green paper on electronic commerce for South Africa.* Pretoria: South African Department of Communications.

Soyez, D. (2000). Anchored locally–linked globally. Transnational social movement organizations in a (seemingly) borderless world. *GeoJournal, 52*, 7–16.

Spar, D. (1999). Lost in (cyber)space: The private rules of online commerce. In C. Culter, T. Porter, & V. Haufler, (Eds.), *Private authority and international affairs* (Ch. 47). Albany: SUNY Press. (Spar refined this view in her 2001 book, *Ruling the waves* [New York: Harcourt Brace, 2001]).

Sports Streaming/Torrent Links Site Victorious in Court. (2010, May 10). *Torrentfreak.* Retrieved from http://torrentfreak.com/sports-streaming-torrent-links-site-victorious-in-court-100510/

Sproull, L. S., Kiesler, S., & Zubrow, D. (1984). Encountering an alien culture. *Journal of Social Issues, 40*(3), 31–48.

Sproull, L. (1986). Using electronic mail for data collection in organizational research. *Academy of Management Journal, 29*(1), 159–169.

Star, S. L. (1999). The ethnography of infrastructure. *American Behavioral Scientist, 43*(3), 377–391.

Star, S. L., & Bowker, G. C. (2002). How to infrastructure. In L. A. Lievrouw (Ed.), *Handbook of new media* (pp. 151–162). London: Sage.

Star, S. L., & Ruhleder, K. (1994). Steps towards an ecology of infrastructure: Complex problems in design and access for large-scale collaborative systems. In *Proceedings of the conference on computer supported cooperative work* (pp. 253–264). New York: ACM Press.

Strange, S. (1982). Cave! hic dragones: a critique of regime analysis. *International organization, 36*(02), 479–496.

Statement for the Record. (2011, May 23). Hearing before the U.S. Senate Homeland Security and Governmental Affairs Committee. U.S. Senate, 131th Congress 1. (Testimony of Reitinger, P., Butler, R., Schwartz, A., & Chipman, J.) Retrieved from http://www.justice.gov/ola/testimony/112-1/05-23-11-odag-chipman-testimony-re-protecting-cyberspace---assessing-the-white-house-proposal.pdf

Stefancic, J., & Delgado, R. (1992). A Shifting balance: Freedom of expression and hate-speech restriction. *Iowa Law Review, 78,* 737.

Steffek, J., & Ferretti, M. P. (2009). Accountability or "good decisions"? The competing goals of civil society participation in international governance. *Global Society, 23,* 37–57.

Stein, L. (2009). Social movement web use in theory and practice: A content analysis of US movement websites. *New Media & Society, 11,* 749–771.

Stiglitz, J. E. (1985). Information and economic analysis: A perspective. *Economic Journal., 95,* 412–456.

Stone, D. (2002). Introduction: Global knowledge and advocacy networks. *Global Networks, 2,* 1–12.

Stop Online Privacy Act. HR 3261. 112th Congress (2011–2012). Retrieved from http://thomas.loc.gov/cgi-bin/query/z?c112:H.R.3261

Studies on file sharing. (n.d.). *La Quadrature du Net Wiki.* Retrieved from https://wiki.laquadrature.net/Studies_on_file_sharing

Sudweeks, F., & Simoff, S. J. (2005, January). Leading conversations: Communication behaviours of emergent leaders in virtual teams. In *Proceedings of the 38th Annual Hawaii International Conference on System Sciences* (pp. 108a–108a). IEEE.

Talero, E., & Gaudette, P. (1995). Harnessing information for development: A proposal for a World Bank Group vision and strategy. *Information Technology for Development, 6*(3), 145–188.

Tallberg, J., Sommerer, T., Squatrito, T., & Jönsson, C. (2013). *The opening up of international organizations: Transnational access in global governance.* Cambridge, UK: Cambridge University Press.

Tarrow, S. (2001). Transnational politics: Contention and institutions in international politics. *Annual Review of Political Science, 4,* 1–20.

Tarrow, S. G. (2005). *The new transnational activism.* New York: Cambridge University Press.

Teal, F. (1999). *Why can Mauritius export manufacturers and Ghana not?* Working paper no. 10. Centre for the study of African Economies, Institute of Economics and Statistics, University of Oxford.

Tehranian, J. (2007). Infringement nation: Copyright reform and the law/norm gap. *Utah Law Review,* 537.

Ten Heuvelhof, E. F., & de Bruijn, J. A. (1995). Governing: Structure and process-contingent interventions. In W. J. M. Kickert & F. A. Vaught (Eds.), *Public policy and administration sciences in the Netherlands* (pp. 163–176). London: Prentice Hall.

The Pirate Bay Co-Founder Starting A P2P Based DNS To Take On ICANN. (2010, December 1). *Digitizor* [Website]. Retrieved from http://digitizor.com/2010/12/01/the-pirate-bay-co-founder-starting-a-p2p-based-dns-to-take-on-icann/

Thompson, K. (2012). Not like an Egyptian: Cybersecurity and the Internet kill switch debate. *Texas Law Review, 90*(2), 465–495.

Ting-Toomey, S. (1999). *Communicating across cultures.* New York: Guilford Press.

Toffler, A. (1970). *Future shock.* In Book Club (Ed.). New York: Random House.

Torzillo, J., & Scott, L. (2010, June 22). Designing with E-Stop switches. *Machine Design.* Retrieved from http://machinedesign.com/archive/designing-e-stop-switches

Triandis, H. (1988). Collectivism and individualism: A reconceptualization of a basic concept in cross-cultural social psychology. In G. K. Verma & C. Bagley (Eds.), *Cross cultural studies of personality, attitudes, and cognition* (pp. 60–65). London: Macmillan.

Trompenaars, F., & Hampden-Turner, C. M. (2000). *Building cross-cultural competence: How to create wealth from conflicting values.* New Haven: Yale University Press.

Tufekci, Z., & Wilson, C. (2012). Social media and the decision to participate in political protest: Observations from Tahrir Square. *Journal of Communication, 62*(2), 363–379.

Twitter, Inc. (2014). Twitter privacy policy. San Francisco, CA. Retrieved from https://twitter.com/privacy

Twitter sues US government over spying. (2014, October 7). *BBC News*. Retrieved from http://www.bbc.com/news/technology-29528665

UK riots: Text of David Cameron's address to Commons. (2011). *The Telegraph*. Retrieved from http://www.telegraph.co.uk/news/uknews/crime/8695272/UK-riots-text-of-David-Camerons-address-to-Commons.html

UN. (1992). *Agenda 21. United Nations Conference on Environment and Development (UNCED), Rio de Janeiro, Brazil.* New York: United Nations.

UN General Assembly. (2002). *Resolution 56/183 World Summit on the Information Society.*

UNDP. (1999). *Human development report 1999.* Oxford: Oxford University Press.

UNESCAP. (1999). *Economic and Social Survey of Asia and the Pacific.*

Uniting and Strengthening America by Providing Appropriate Tools Required to Intercept and Obstruct Terrorism (USA Patriot Act) Act, H. R. 3162, 107th Cong. (2001).

US 'launched Flame cyber attack on Sarkozy's office'. (2012, November 21). *BBC News*. Retrieved from http://www.bbc.com/news/world-europe-20429704

U.S. Senate. (2010b). Committee Reports. 111th Congress (2009). Senate Report 111–368. Washington, DC: The Library of Congress. Retrieved from http://thomas.loc.gov/cgi-bin/cpquery/R?cp111:FLD010:@1(sr368)

U.S. Senate. (2011). *Protecting cyberspace: Assessing the White House proposal—Senate hearing 112–221.* Washington, DC: U.S. Government Printing Office Retrieved from http://www.gpo.gov/fdsys/pkg/CHRG-112shrg67638/html/CHRG-112shrg67638.htm.

U.S. Senate Committee on Homeland Security and Governmental Affairs. (2011, May 23). *Protecting cyberspace: Assessing the White House proposal.* Washington, DC: Government Printing Office. Retrieved from http://www.gpo.gov/fdsys/pkg/CHRG-112shrg67638/html/CHRG-112shrg67638.htm

U. W. H. O. (2011). World report on disability. Retrieved from http://www.refworld.org/docid/50854a322.html. Accessed 20 Nov 2016.

Vaidhyanathan, S. (2001). *Copyrights and copywrongs: The rise of intellectual property and how it threatens creativity.* New York: University Press.

Vaidhyanathan, S. (2012). *The Googlization of everything: (And why we should worry).* Oakland: University of California Press.

van Andel, P., & Bourcier, D. (2012). *De la sérendipité, dans la science, la technique, l'art et le droit.* Paris: Hermann.

van Beijnum, I. (2011, January 30). How Egypt did (and your government could) shut down the Internet. *Ars Technica*. Retrieved from http://arstechnica.com/tech-policy/2011/01/how-egypt-or-how-your-government-could-shut-down-the-internet/

van Eeten, M. (2009, November 14). *Where is the governance in Internet governance?* Paper presented at GigaNet Annual Symposium, Sharm-el-Sheikh.

van Schewick, B. (2010). *Internet architecture and innovation.* Cambridge, MA: MIT Press.

Verhulst, S. (2003). *Internet: A stronger voice for the South.* Paper presented at the Annual Meeting of the International Communication Association, San Diego.

von Arx, K. G., & Hagen, G. R. (2002). Sovereign domains: A declaration of independence of ccTLDs from foreign control. *Richmond Journal of Law and Technology, 9,* 4–8.

Vyorst, D. (2013, November 7). Bali and beyond: An internet governance forum debrief. *Internet Society.* Washington, DC. http://www.isoc-dc.org/2013/11/bali-and-beyond-an-internet-governance-forum-debrief/

Wakefield & Cushman. (2013). *Data centre risk index 2013.* London: Cushman & Wakefield LLP.

Walpole, H. (1754). Three princes of Serendip. *Folk tale.*

Walsh, J. P., Kucker, S., Maloney, N. G., & Gabbay, S. (2000). Connecting minds: Computer-mediated communication and scientific work. *Journal of the American Society for Information Science, 51*(14), 1295–1305.

Walther, J. B., Loh, T., & Granka, L. (2005). Let me count the ways the interchange of verbal and nonverbal cues in computer-mediated and face-to-face affinity. *Journal of language and social psychology, 24*(1), 36–65.

Wang, L. (2003). Protecting BGP routes to top-level DNS servers. *IEEE Transactions on Parallel and Distributed Systems, 14,* 851–860.

Wangwe, S. (1996). The information revolution and economic and social exclusion in developing countries: A case study of Tanzania. In *International workshop on Information Technology for Development.* Maastricht: UNU/INTECH.

Wapner, P. (1997). Governance in global civil society. In O. R. Young (Ed.), *Global governance: Drawing insights from the environmental experience.* Cambridge, MA: MIT Press.

Wasserman, T. (2012, August 1). Email takes up 28 % of workers' time. Mashable. Retrieved from http://mashable.com/2012/08/01/email-workers-time/

Watson, P. J. (2010, June 21). Lieberman: China can shut down the Internet, why can't we? *Infowars* [Website]. Retrieved from http://www.infowars.com/lieberman-china-can-shut-down-the-internet-why-cant-we/

Watson, P. J. (2013, June 19). Russian cyberspace head calls for Internet kill switch. *Infowars* [Website]. Retrieved from http://www.infowars.com/russian-cyberspace-head-calls-for-internet-kill-switch/

Weber, R. P. (1990). Basic content analysis (No. 49), Sage.

Weber, R. H. (2009). *Shaping Internet governance: Regulatory challenges.* New York: Springer.

Weber, R. H. (2011). The right to be forgotten: More than a Pandora's box? *Journal of Intellectual Property, Information Technology and e-Commerce Law*, 2, 120–130.

Weilemann, P. R. (2000). The summit meeting: The role and agenda of diplomacy at its highest level. *NIRA Review*, 7(2), 16–20.

Weiss, T. G., Carayannis, T., & Jolly, R. (2009). The 'third' United Nations. *Global Governance: A Review of Multilateralism and International Organizations*, 15(1), 123–142.

WHO. (2011). *World report on disability*. Mealta: World Health Organization. Retrieved from http://www.who.int/disabilities/world_report/2011/en/

Whyte, W. F. (Ed.). (1991). *Participatory action research*. Newbury Park: Sage.

Wiest, D., & Smith, J. (2007). Explaining participation in regional transnational social movement organizations. *International Journal of Comparative Sociology*, 48, 137.

Williams, C. (2011, November 1). Cameron told not to shut down Internet. *The Telegraph*. Retrieved from http://www.telegraph.co.uk/technology/news/8862335/Cameron-told-not-to-shut-down-internet.html

Wilson, P. (1999). African opportunities in the transition to a knowledge economy. *Africa Development Review*, 10(1), 36–49.

Winder, D. (2011). Could the British Government switch off our Internet? *PC Pro*. Retrieved from http://www.pcpro.co.uk/features/365407/could-the-british-government-switch-off-our-internet

Working Group on Internet Governance (WGIG). (2005, June). *Report of the Working Group on Internet Governance*. Château de Bossey, Switzerland.

Working Group on Internet Governance, *Report of the Working Group on Internet Governance*. (2005). Found on the Internet at: http://www.wgig.org/docs/WGIGREPORT.pdf

World Health Organization (WHO). (2013). *World report on disability*. Geneva; 2011.

World Summit on the Information Society, Civil Society. (2003a, November). Overview of the Civil Society Elements and How to Get Involved. Retrieved from http://www.wsis-cs.org/cs-overview.html

World Summit on the Information Society (WSIS). (2003a, December 12). Plan of Action. WSIS. (WSIS-03/GENEVA/DOC/5-E).

World Summit on the Information Society (WSIS). (2003b, December 13). Declaration of Principles. WSIS. (WSIS-03/GENEVA/DOC/4-E).

World Summit on the Information Society (WSIS). (2005a, November 18). Tunis commitment. (WSIS. WSIS-05/TUNIS/DOC/7-E).

World Summit on the Information Society (WSIS). (2005b, November 18). Tunis agenda for the information society. WSIS. (WSIS-05/TUNIS/DOC/6 (Rev. 1)-E).

World Summit on the Information Society (WSIS). (2006a). Basic information: About WSIS. Retrieved from http://www.itu.int/wsis/basic/about.html

World Summit on the Information Society (WSIS). (2006b, October 5). The different actors in the information society. WSIS. http://www.itu.int/wsis/basic/actors.html

World Summit on the Information Society (WSIS). (2007, July 2). The multi-stakeholder participation in WSIS and its written and unwritten rules, WSIS.

World Trade Organization (WTO). (1997, April). South Africa, Schedule of Specific Commitments. Geneva, Committee on Trade in Services.

Wralstad Ulmschneider, G., & Lutz, J. M. (2014). USA Patriot Act. In *The encyclopedia of criminology and criminal justice*. Hoboken: Blackwell Publishing Ltd.

Wulf, W. A. (1989, March 17–18). The national collaboratory—A white paper. Appendix A in *Towards a National Collaboratory*. The unpublished report of an invitational workshop held at the Rockefeller University.

Yanacopulos, H. (2005). The strategies that bind: NGO coalitions and their influence. *Global Networks, 5*, 93–110.

Yen, A. C. (2001). A personal injury law perspective on copyright law in an Internet age. *Hastings Law Journal, 52*, 929.

Yoo, Y., & Alavi, M. (2004). Emergent leadership in virtual teams: What do emergent leaders do? *Information and Organization, 14*(1), 27–58.

Young, O. R. (1985). The age of the Arctic. *Foreign Policy, 61*, 160–179.

Yuan Wang, K., & Clegg, S. (2002). Trust and decision making: Are managers different in the People's Republic of China and in Australia? *Cross Cultural Management: An International Journal, 9*(1), 30–45.

Zacher, M. W., & Sutton, B. A. (1996). *Governing global networks: International regimes for transportation and communications* (Vol. 44). Cambridge/New York: Cambridge University Press.

Zakaria N., & Cogburn, D. L. (2006, June). *Webs of culture: Applying high and low-context theory to understand decision-making behaviors in transnational NGO networks involved in WSIS*. Paper presented at the 2006 Annual Meeting of the International Communication Association, Dresden.

Zakaria, N., & Cogburn, D. L., (2007, May). *Are we really different or simply unique? Understanding online intercultural communication behaviors during globally distributed collaboration*. Paper presented at the 2007 Annual Meeting of the International Communication Association, San Francisco.

Zakaria, N., & Cogburn, D. L. (2008). Webs of culture: Applying intercultural communication theory to understand distributed decision-making processes. *International Business Research, 1*(3), 115–123.

Zakaria, N., & Cogburn, D. L. (2010). Context-dependent vs. content-dependent: An exploration of the cultural behavioural patterns of online intercultural communication using e-mail. *International Journal of Business and Systems Research, 4*(3), 330–347.

Zelli, F., & van Asselt, H. (2013). The institutional fragmentation of global environmental governance: Causes, consequences, and responses. *Global Environmental Politics, 13*(3), 1–13.

Zhang, Y., Luo, J., & Hu, H. (Eds.). (2006). *Wireless mesh networking: Architectures, protocols and standards.* Boca Raton: Auerbach Publications.

Ziewitz, M., & Pentzold, C. (2014). In search of Internet governance: Performing order in digitally networked environments. *New Media & Society, 16*(2), 306–322.

Zimmer, M. (2010). Privacy protection in the next digital decade: 'Trading up' or a 'race to the bottom'? In B. Szoka & A. Marcus (Eds.), *The next digital decade: Essays on the future of the Internet.* Washington, DC: TechFreedom.

Zittrain, J. (2008). *The future of the Internet—And how to stop it.* New Haven: Yale University Press.

Zittrain, J., & Edelman, B. (2003). Internet filtering in China. *Internet Computing, IEEE, 7*(2), 70–77.

Zmijewski, E. (2008). Attention: Iran is not disconnected! [Blog entry]. Manchester: Dyn Research. Retrieved from http://www.renesys.com/2008/02/attention-iran-is-not-disconne-1/

INDEX

A

access, 81. *See also under* Internet connection

accessibility, 120, 198, 207, 208, 232

Advanced Research Projects Agency (ARPA), 94, 113

Advanced Research Projects Agency Network (ARPANET), 94–5

African Information Society Initiative (AISI), 9, 14, 63, 64, 114, 119

agenda setting, 35

Agreement on Basic Telecommunications (ABT), 9, 67, 109

Alexander, Fiona, 12

American University, 106, 107

Anarchy Problematique, 24–8, 53, 76

Association for Progressive Communication (APC), 6, 9, 120, 132, 169, 218, 227, 229, 237, 278

B

Bangemann Commission Report, 114

Barrett, Craig, 18, 187, 191, 194, 197

blockchain technologies, 207, 208

Brazil, Russia, India, China, and South Africa (BRICS), 67

Brussels Principles, 72, 73, 111

Buenos Aires Action Plan (BAAP), 72

Business Action to Support the Information Society (BASIS), 104, 113, 142

C

Cerf, Vint, 10, 18, 93, 95, 96

Civil Society Bureau (CSB), 18, 119, 143–6, 153, 171, 217, 228

Civil Society Internet Governance Caucus/ICT Governance Caucus (IGC), 14, 104, 119, 120, 217–43

Civil Society Plenary (CSP), 18, 119, 142, 147, 148, 168, 174, 217, 228, 229

© The Author(s) 2017

D.L. Cogburn, *Transnational Advocacy Networks in the Information Society*, Information Technology and Global Governance, DOI 10.1057/978-1-137-48361-4